A Double-Edged Sword

A Double-Edged Sword

*Jehanne d'Arc and Claims to
Divine Sanction in Acts of War*

BRENDA E. NOVACK

☙PICKWICK *Publications* · Eugene, Oregon

A DOUBLE-EDGED SWORD
Jehanne d'Arc and Claims to Divine Sanction in Acts of War

Copyright © 2014 Brenda E. Novack. All rights reserved. Except for brief quotations in critical publications or reviews, no part of this book may be reproduced in any manner without prior written permission from the publisher. Write: Permissions, Wipf and Stock Publishers, 199 W. 8th Ave., Suite 3, Eugene, OR 97401.

Pickwick Publications
An Imprint of Wipf and Stock Publishers
199 W. 8th Ave., Suite 3
Eugene, OR 97401
www.wipfandstock.com

ISBN 13: 978-1-62564-238-7

Cataloging-in-Publication data:

Novack, Brenda E.

A double-edged sword : Jehanne d'Arc and claims to divine sanction in acts of war / Brenda E. Novack.

xvi + 358 p. ; 23 cm. Includes bibliographical references and index.

ISBN 13: 978-1-62564-238-7

1. Joan, of Arc, Saint, 1412–1431. 2. War—Religious aspects—Christianity. 3. War—Moral and ethical aspects. 4. Just war doctrine. 5. Hitler, Adolf, 1889–1945. 6. Bonhoeffer, Dietrich, 1906–45. I. Title.

BT736.2 N591 2014

Manufactured in the U.S.A.

Excerpts from "Anthem," "Joan of Arc," "The Captain," and "If it Be Your Will" excerpted from *Stranger Music: Selected Poems and Songs* by Leonard Cohen. Copyright © 1993 Leonard Cohen. Reprinted by permission of McClelland & Stewart. Excerpt from "Who Am I?" by Dietrich Bonhoeffer reprinted with the permission of Scribner Publishing Group from LETTERS AND PAPERS FROM PRISON, REVISED, ENLARGED ED. by Dietrich Bonhoeffer, translated from the German by R. H. Fuller, Frank Clark, et al. Copyright © 1953, 1967, 1971 by SCM Press Ltd., and also by permission of SCM Press, London. All rights reserved. Biblical quotations are from the New Revised Standard Version Bible, copyright © 1989, Division of Christian Education of the National Council of the Churches of Christ in the United States of America.

To my parents

Contents

Acknowledgments ix
Introduction xi

Part One: Jehanne d'Arc

1. Jehanne d'Arc: Her Mission in Context 3
   Approaching Jehanne 3
   Jehanne's Mission in Historical Context 5

2. The Theology of Jehanne d'Arc: Practical, Prophetic Mysticism 35
   Practical Mysticism 39
   The Prophetic as Mystical Calling 53
   Answering the Call: Operative Elements of Practical, Prophetic Mysticism 77
   The Cost of Practical, Prophetic Mysticism 101

Part Two: Righteous Warfare and Its Applicability

3. Righteous Warfare and Human Agency 113
   Secular-Theological Considerations Regarding Human Agency 113
   Just War Theory 147
   Daughter of God: Constructing a Model of Righteous Warfare and Human Agency 157

4. Applying the Model 165
   Case Study One—Adolf Hitler et al. 167
   Case Study Two—Dietrich Bonhoeffer 228
   Reflection on the Case Studies and Model 302

Conclusion 305

Appendix: Model of Righteous Warfare and Human Agency 311

Bibliography 317

Index 329

Acknowledgments

SINCERE APPRECIATION TO THE family of Dr. Owen Sheehy-Skeffington and the French Department of Trinity College Dublin for financial support which enabled me to conduct research in France in relation to this work. Special thanks to Dr. Linda Hogan of Trinity College Dublin for reading the manuscript with care during the various stages of its development and providing valuable guidance and support. Thanks also to Dr. Andrew Pierce of Trinity College Dublin for insights with respect to the focus and shaping of the material in the early stages. Gratitude to Dr. Olivier Bouzy of the Centre Jeanne d'Arc in Orléans for extensive commentary on the manuscript, and to Rev. Dr. Martin Rumscheidt for his attentive reading of the manuscript and helpful commentary. I thank my parents for enduring my pursuit of this endeavor which took me great distances from them during their late, vulnerable years. Humble gratitude to Jehanne d'Arc and Dietrich Bonhoeffer for their inspiration, immeasurable courage, and selfless service to peace, justice, and love.

Introduction

ALTHOUGH IMPLICIT AND OVERT claims to divinely sanctioned warfare have operated throughout history, influencing public perception, opinion, and allegiance with respect to violent conflict, frequently, such claims are not openly acknowledged or critically assessed. In this work, I devise a method of addressing claims to divinely sanctioned violence, particularly in the context of war and through the lens of fifteenth-century warrior-saint and French nationalist, Jehanne d'Arc. There is no way to determine whether or not divinely sanctioned violence exists, and I do not undertake to establish whether or not it does. However, claims to divinely sanctioned violence *do* exist and are potentially powerful and destructive, particularly when overlooked or underestimated as this renders them insidious. I propose that the most effective and least dangerous way of responding to such claims is to evaluate them against a compelling claim to divinely sanctioned violence—an arguably rare phenomenon—since it is necessary to discern what divinely sanctioned violence *might* look like if it *does* exist, and a compelling claim can function as a model.

It is because she is compelling that I have chosen Jehanne as my model, and also because she is challenging, she provides one of the clearest articulations of a claim to divinely sanctioned violence, and there are abundant primary materials documenting her case. She is compelling by virtue of the positive qualities that informed her participation in warfare, because of her extraordinary achievements, and because of her reluctant martyrdom. She is challenging because the notion of divinely sanctioned violence is disturbing and yet Jehanne presents a compelling claim. I do not seek to prove the legitimacy of Jehanne's claim, or any claim to divinely sanctioned violence, but to distinguish between more and less compelling claims. Because it is compelling, Jehanne's claim is viewed as instructive in evaluating other claims of this nature. I therefore seek to apprehend what apparently constituted divine revelation, sanction, and servantship in her case. Investigating Jehanne's life and death, I construct a theoretical model representative of divine prophetic calling, divinely sanctioned righteous warfare, and divinely sanctioned human agency and test its practical applicability and usefulness via two case studies. Testing the model using historical cases in order to determine whether or not it functions effectively is ethically imperative if it is to be advanced as a tool for evaluating present and future claims to divinely sanctioned violence. This work thereby addresses a need, not only to identify and bring claims of divinely sanctioned violence to the forefront, but to develop a strategy for thoughtfully examining them.

Declaring that she was instructed directly by messengers of God to do so, Jehanne, between the ages of seventeen and eighteen, rallied and led the French army in multiple battles against the united English and Burgundian forces during the Hundred Years' War.[1] Her purpose was to drive the English from France, to relieve the French people of their suffering under foreign occupation, and to restore French kingship and nationhood. She was condemned to death by fire at age nineteen by her enemies, maintaining that she acted as a willing agent of God. Jehanne fought for peace, justice, and equilibrium, demonstrating a preference for peace over war and exerting minimal appropriate force while displaying compassion for all and uncompromised respect for the value of human life. Although the model based on her example corresponds in some respects to the just war tradition, it sets a higher standard, demands a more comprehensive level of conformity, addresses claims to divine sanction specifically, and incorporates the essential element of righteousness, establishing a high threshold for what is considered a compelling claim to divinely sanctioned violence.

While the term "just war" suggests that a particular war might be just in itself, Jehanne's example does not support this notion but suggests that particular forms of engagement in warfare or particular acts of violence might be considered acceptable, necessary, just, and righteous in certain circumstances. To entertain the possibility of a particular war containing aspects of divine sanction is not to place the entire war within a framework of divine sanction, nor is it to incite war or to glorify any act of war, even one that might be considered divinely sanctioned. In fact, Jehanne's

---

1. The Burgundians were French allies of the English against the Armagnacs or French royalist party.

example supports the notion that all war and all acts of human-on-human violence are intrinsically evil, whether or not participation in them is considered divinely sanctioned or otherwise justifiable; thus, a divinely sanctioned act might at once be considered contextually righteous and inherently evil. Jehanne's example does not suggest divine approval of war itself, but that particular acts of war—certain manners of participation in pre-existent war—might reasonably be construed as divinely sanctioned. Her message confirms restoration of peace and justice as an acceptable end of defensive war, it encourages restraint in the use of violence, and it promotes basic respect and compassion as necessary means by which all acts of force ought to be carried out.

As the title of this work suggests, any notion of just or righteous warfare (or divinely sanctioned violence in any form) constitutes a double-edged sword with as many conceivable dangers as benefits. When wielded, such a weapon *must* be handled with utmost integrity if it is to avoid becoming a source of unnecessary injury and destruction. Nevertheless, since the destructive sword of unmeasured claims to divine sanction is flailed among us, it is expedient to consider the usefulness of a double-edged sword that measures such claims, advocating restraint and compassion in the face of any "necessary" destruction. If humanity is to avoid sinking into utter depravity in a world in which war has become dangerously depersonalized, a personal model of war, wherein individuals are deemed responsible for their actions and every human life is valued, must be reinstated in the absence of peace. In considering Jehanne's experience in which war was personal and immediate to all participants, and in looking to Jehanne as one who exercised conscience and compassion at all times and took full responsibility for her deeds, we might begin to recover some of the values essential to a thriving and respectful humanity for, although these values have been largely abandoned, they are not lost, and although it is easy to declare them irretrievable, such declaration is a sure path to evil.

Part One

Jehanne d'Arc

1

Jehanne d'Arc

Her Mission in Context

Approaching Jehanne

I have come here to the royal chamber to speak to Robert de Baudricourt, to ask him to escort me, or to have me escorted, to the King. But he pays no attention to me, or to what I say. But all the same, before mid-Lent I must be with the King, even if I have to wear my legs down to the knees. For there is no one on earth, be he king, or duke, or the King of Scotland's daughter, or anyone else, who can restore the kingdom of France, and he will have no help except through me, although I would much prefer to stay with my poor mother and spin, for this is not my station. But I must go, and I must do it, for my Lord wishes me to perform this deed.

—Jehanne d'Arc, testimony of Jean de Metz

Jehanne d'Arc was a powerful and forthright personality—a complex figure who cannot be contained within strict categories of interpretation or rigid structures. Nadia Margolis notes that Jehanne "is at the mercy of the intellectuals" and "has been subjected to all manner of appropriation . . . to the point of disappearance as a real person"[1] while Ann Pirruccello states that she "is claimed by so many that we do not know

---

1. Margolis, "'Joan Phenomenon,'" 281.

how to recognize her."[2] I attempt to present Jehanne's message as clearly as possible while imposing as little as possible upon her, (acknowledging that some imposition is inevitable). My approach is to observe, acknowledge, and evaluate material from the various testimonies and other historical records with minimal extrapolation or distortion. Moreover, I endeavor to emphasize what Jehanne apparently emphasized in the interest of identifying and understanding her purpose, and I attempt to eliminate selectivity based on personal agenda by incorporating relevant pieces of information whether or not they accord with my preconceptions of her, adjusting my interpretation to fit the evidence rather than adjusting the evidence to fit my interpretation! I seek to access something of Jehanne's transformative essence by weaving the pieces of her story so as to discern her apparent message and ongoing significance to humanity, which may be understood as God's message to humanity expressed through her, as a prophetic mystic. Through her particular style of military engagement and her martyrdom, Jehanne delivered a timeless message at the highest personal-temporal cost. The driving question of my investigation is, what insight or wisdom does Jehanne offer regarding claims to divine sanction in acts of war? She constitutes the starting point, the basis, and the main context of the enquiry. The goal of discerning rather than defining or manipulating Jehanne's message—of allowing her to speak for herself, insofar as possible—is based upon the conviction that, as one who was willing to die a harsh, unwelcome death at a young age in order to maintain the purity of her divine revelation while simultaneously forgiving those who wed her to the stake, hers is a message worth hearing.

We have inherited a wealth of historical information concerning Jehanne due, in part, to the intense scrutiny to which her public life was subjected. Although the record of the 1429 Poitiers interrogation (the first extensive theological examination of her character) has been lost or destroyed, the official conclusion of that examination and some eye-witness testimony concerning the process are preserved. The official record of the condemnation trial against Jehanne which took place at Rouen in 1431 is extant in the form of three Latin manuscripts translated from the original French and authenticated by notary signatures, and at least two known French manuscripts, the d'Urfé and Orléans manuscripts, both being possible copies of the original French trial minutes. The offi-

---

2. Pirruccello, "Force or Fragility," 278.

cial record of the nullification trial (also referred to as the rehabilitation trial) conducted in 1455–56, which investigated the legitimacy of the condemnation trial against Jehanne and overturned its verdict, is extant in the form of three original, authenticated manuscripts in Latin—with the exception of a single testimony in French (that of Jehanne's squire, Jean d'Aulon)—bearing notary signatures. Various collections and translations of historical documents pertaining to Jehanne including letters, chronicles, financial accounts, and the trial manuscripts are also available.

Jehanne's Mission in Historical Context

And if I were to be condemned and saw the fire lit and the wood prepared and the executioner who was to burn me ready to cast me into the fire, still in the fire would I not say anything other than I have said. And I will maintain what I have said until death.
—JEHANNE D'ARC, *TRIAL OF JOAN OF ARC*

Although the date of her birth is uncertain, it is generally accepted that Jehannette (Jehanne) d'Arc was born on or around January 6, 1412[3] in the village of Domremy (duchy of Lorraine),[4] France, during the Hundred Years' War between England and France (1337 to 1453). The climate of Jehanne's childhood was one of strife as the English had conquered the northern region of France and gained collaboration of that portion of the country known as Burgundy. Thus France was not only divided geographically, but French loyalties were divided by the war and also by papal schism. This lengthy war consisting of intermittent battles and troubled truces spanning 116 years created food shortages due to ravaged land and lack of means to transport goods as roads were unsafe. Villagers were terrorized by plunderers[5] and, in 1425, when Jehanne was thirteen, Domremy was torched by Anglo-Burgundians who thieved the

---

3. Jehanne testified in February, 1431 "that she was nineteen or thereabouts." Jehanne; in Scott, *Trial*, 65.

4. Domremy bordered France and the Holy Roman Empire. Although Lorraine owed allegiance to the Empire, due to shifting borders, it is uncertain to whom Domremy belonged, but it was generally regarded as constituting part of France at the time. Nash-Marshall, *Spiritual Biography*, 29, 178, n. 2.

5. Pernoud, *Retrial*, 11.

cattle.⁶ She, her family, and her neighbors periodically took refuge in nearby towns, as in 1428 when Burgundians attacked Domremy again and burned the crops, at which time Jehanne fled to Neufchâteau.⁷ The war took place almost entirely on French soil and revolved primarily around a lengthy and complex rivalry for the crown of France and long-standing contention over the land of Aquitaine, which both England and France desired to hold and control; however, many contributing factors had arisen between the two countries from as early as 1066.⁸ Tension and strife had thus persisted three and a half centuries when Jehanne eventually took up her sword.

A pivotal event occurred in May, 1418 when Burgundians under Duke John the Fearless and Parisian sympathizers took control of Paris, allowing the English entrance to the city and killing approximately two thousand French supporters. The dauphin, Charles VII, fled.⁹ In May, 1420, another major event transpired when the Treaty of Troyes was established by King Charles VI of France (who was suffering bouts of "insanity" and diminished power over his kingdom), Queen Isabeau of Bavaria (his wife), King Henry V of England, and Duke Philippe the Good of Burgundy. Under the treaty, Charles and Isabeau disinherited their son, Charles VII, in favor of Henry V who was to marry their daughter, Catherine. Moreover, they allocated the kingdom of France to Henry and his heirs *for all time*, anticipating that England would rule both England and France under a dual English monarchy.¹⁰ According to Deborah Fraioli, the treaty "was conceived as a diplomatic solution to end the Hundred Years War" on the supposition that peace would prevail under a single ruler. Since Henry and Catherine were expected to produce heirs combining the bloodlines, it was held that future kings would embody unity between England and France¹¹—unity, perhaps, but not equality since subsequent monarchs were to reign under the crown of England. Unity based on inequality (if unity can exist within a framework of inequality) is precarious and all did not accept the treaty,

6. Nash-Marshall, *Spiritual Biography*, 35.
7. Jehanne; in Scott, *Trial*, 66. Nash-Marshall, *Spiritual Biography*, 35.
8. Fraioli, *Hundred Years War*, xxvii.
9. Taylor, *La Pucelle*, 99, n. 67, 257, n. 42.
10. Fraioli, *Hundred Years War*, lx–lxiii, 144.

11. Ibid., 144. English ambition for such a dual monarchy dates back to at least 1340. Ibid., 18.

Charles VII being front and center among the dissenters. Supporters of the dauphinist claim to the French throne formed a military party whose goal was to drive the English from France permanently; they argued that neither could a royal heir be disinherited, nor could a French king "alienate his lands" since he reigned over but did not possess them.[12] Jehanne later informed Robert de Baudricourt, Captain of Vaucouleurs, "that the kingdom [of France] did not belong to the Dauphin but to her Lord, and that her Lord wished the Dauphin to be made king, and that He would give him His kingdom to rule."[13] Henry V and Catherine produced one son in December, 1421 and, with the deaths of Charles VI and Henry V in 1422, the infant Henry VI of England became contender for the French throne against Charles VII of France. And so the battle continued while the young Jehannette, still oblivious to her eventual, critical role in the affair, spun wool with her mother in Domremy.

Amid the general unrest caused by the war, the Great Schism of 1378–1417 within the Western Church saw up to three papal claimants vying simultaneously for authority. This instability within the Church placed additional strain on the conflict as divisions arose regarding which pope was legitimate, even after the Schism ended and into 1429.[14] Such strife no doubt heightened the attack response of some within the Church toward any further threat to ecclesiastical authority and stability and, as we shall see, Jehanne was haplessly to become such a threat.

This was the backdrop against which Jehanne, daughter of Jacques d'Arc and Isabeau Romée, grew up. Jehanne's family were reputable farmers who may have owned approximately fifty acres of land. Generally considered peasants, they were "neither rich nor poor."[15] Jehanne had three older brothers and a sister, and she sometimes tended the plough and cattle in addition to performing domestic tasks.[16] She received no

---

12. Ibid., 144–45.

13. Jehanne; quoted by Bertrand de Poulengy, squire, in Pernoud, *Retrial*, 102.

14. Craig Taylor indicates that Benedict XIII "defied the authority of the Council that tried to depose him" in 1417 and that "his successor, Clement VIII [antipope since 1423], did not ... resign until 26 July 1429." Taylor, *La Pucelle*, 122. In August, 1429, Jean IV, Count of Armagnac, questioned Jehanne concerning three claimants; in Taylor, *La Pucelle*, 122–23.

15. Pernoud and Clin, *Her Story*, 221.

16. Jean Moreau, Jehanne's godfather, (a merchant); in Pernoud, *Retrial*, 72. It is uncertain which daughter was oldest.

formal education; nonetheless, she spoke very well,[17] displaying "an admirable prudence in all her words."[18] Instructed by her mother in household and religious matters, she demonstrated a strong work ethic.[19] Jehanne was Catholic and voluntarily attended church frequently. She was reportedly of "sound morals, and ... such a good girl that almost everyone in Domremy loved her."[20] Pious and kind, she "tended the sick and gave alms to the poor,"[21] lending her bed to others while she slept by the hearth.[22] Jehanne's extreme piety earned her the teasing of friends as she frequently retreated from play into solitary prayer.[23] She even scolded the parish beadle for neglecting to ring the church bells but promised him a gift of wool or baked goods if he would reform the behavior.[24]

At age thirteen, Jehanne's spiritual life acquired a dimension with implications beyond the personal that altered the course of French and English history. She began experiencing what she described as visitations by heavenly beings, including Archangels Michael and Gabriel and Saints Catherine and Margaret, as well as unidentified angels on occasion, all of whom she understood to be messengers of God delivering divine revelation and counsel to her. The visitations consisted of voices, often accompanied by a powerful light. Initially frightened by the encounters, Jehanne's fear subsided once she felt confident of their divine nature; however, when her divine counsel endowed her with an astonishing mission to lift the siege of Orléans, she protested that she was merely "a poor girl," untrained in riding and warfare, but the voices persisted.[25] Overwhelmed by this daunting assignment, Jehanne eventu-

---

17. Albert d'Ourches, nobleman; in Pernoud, *Retrial*, 101.

18. Perceval de Boulainvilliers, king's councillor and seneschal of Berry; in Pernoud from Quicherat, vol. 5, 114–21, *Herself and Her Witnesses*, 98.

19. Jehanne stated "that her mother taught her the *Pater Noster, Ave Maria* and *Credo*" and taught her to sew and spin. Jehanne; in Scott, *Trial*, 65–66. Many nullification trial witnesses testified to Jehanne's work ethic.

20. Moreau; in Pernoud, *Retrial*, 71–72.

21. Simonin Musnier, farmer; ibid., 79.

22. Isabellette, wife of Gérardin d'Épinal, farmer; ibid., 84.

23. Jean Waterin, Jehanne's playmate; ibid., 87. Mengette, Jehanne's childhood friend; ibid., 81. Colin, son of Jean Colin of Greux; ibid., 79.

24. Perrin Drappier, beadle of Domremy; ibid., 78, and from Quicherat, vol. 2, 431; in Nash-Marshall, *Spiritual Biography*, 37.

25. Jehanne; in Taylor, *La Pucelle*, 141–42, 147–48, 152–54, 194–96. Although it is uncertain which Saints Catherine and Margaret Jehanne identified as her divine

ally accepted it. Saint Michael, she said, had explained the terrible plight of the kingdom of France and urged her to assist the French king, assuring her of God's help.[26]

Faithful to her divine counsel and having voluntarily pledged her virginity at age thirteen for "as long as it should be pleasing to God,"[27] Jehanne "*la pucelle*" (the Maid) left Domremy around January, 1429 at age seventeen to fulfill her mandate. Her initial task was to secure a means of traveling to Baudricourt. "She . . . went to find her uncle [Durand Laxart] and . . . told him that she wanted to stay with him for a short length of time; and she stayed there for about eight days. She then said . . . it was necessary that she go to Vaucouleurs and her uncle took her there. . . . And Joan said to Robert [de Baudricourt] that she had to travel to France. But Robert twice refused and dismissed her."[28] Jehanne sought from Baudricourt an escort to deliver her to the dauphin at Chinon that she might declare her mission to him, but Baudricourt advised Laxart to beat Jehanne and return her to her father.[29]

At that time, following a fourteen-year string of losses to the English, the dauphinist party, including Charles himself, was virtually hopeless of regaining French autonomy barring a miracle. The English had besieged Orléans and occupied most of the country north of the Loire including Paris and Rheims. "Surrounded by unscrupulous advisers, his coffers empty, . . . the Dauphin's fortunes were at their lowest ebb," writes W. S. Scott.[30] It is not surprising that prophecies which had circulated throughout France years earlier resurfaced in light of the compelling maiden proclaiming a divine mission. Jehanne identified with at least one of these, declaring to Baudricourt, "Have you not heard

---

counsel, many suppose them to be Catherine of Alexandria and Margaret of Antioch. Pernoud and Clin, *Her Story*, 113. While some scholars make scant or no reference to Gabriel as a member of her divine counsel, Jehanne makes several such references to him. Jehanne, March 3 and 28 and May 9, 1431; in Scott, *Trial*, 90, 140, 152.

26. Jehanne; in Scott, *Trial*, 120.

27. Ibid., 104.

28. Jehanne; in Taylor, *La Pucelle*, 142. In recording Jehanne's testimony, the notaries initially employed first-person discourse, later moving to third-person. (Some translators have retained the paraphrased responses while others have translated them back into first-person.) Laxart was actually Jehanne's first cousin's husband. The word "France" in medieval terminology designated the central area of the kingdom exclusive of peripheral regions. Pernoud and Clin, *Her Story*, 18, 112, 114.

29. Laxart; in Pernoud, *Herself and Her Witnesses*, 33.

30. Scott, *Trial*, 9.

the prophecy that France was to be ruined by a woman and restored by a virgin from the marches of Lorraine?" She had previously cited this to Laxart with great effect.³¹

Association of Jehanne with prophetic fulfillment persisted. Jean Érault, professor of theology and Poitiers examiner, identified her with a prophecy by Marie d'Avignon who claimed that a maid in armor would deliver France from misery.³² Also, a poem about Jehanne entitled *Virgo puellares*, presumably written by advisers of Charles VII in early 1429, was influenced by a prophecy attributed to Merlin which stated, "There will be a virgin who will ride in arms against the backs of the English archers, and her sex and the flower of her virginity will keep secret,"³³ although the prophecy originally stated simply, "A virgin ascends the backs of the archers / and hides the flower of her virginity."³⁴ During Jehanne's military campaign, a prophetic message foretelling a maid emerging from the Bois Chesnu and riding "on the backs of archers" against the English was transmitted to the imprisoned Earl of Suffolk.³⁵ The term *"Bois Chesnu"* ("Oak Wood") was interpreted as referencing a forest near Jehanne's childhood home. Although people associated her with this prophecy, Jehanne herself "put no faith in it."³⁶

On Jehanne's third appearance before Baudricourt, he granted her permission to travel to Chinon and supplied a group of men charged with conducting her there safely. Jehanne later recalled Baudricourt's parting advice: "Go, and let come what may," he said.³⁷ It was then, in late February, 1429, that Jehanne adopted male clothing appropriate to the task. "She said . . . that when she left Vaucouleurs, she took man's dress,

31. Jehanne; quoted by Catherine Royer, Jehanne's hostess at Vaucouleurs, in Pernoud, *Retrial*, 99. Laxart; in Taylor, *La Pucelle*, 273. The reference to France being "ruined by a woman" is commonly associated with Queen Isabeau who conspired in the Treaty of Troyes. Taylor, *La Pucelle*, 18, n. 56.

32. Jean Barbin, doctor in law; in Pernoud, *Retrial*, 115.

33. Berne MS 25; in Taylor, *La Pucelle*, 77, n. 21. Taylor, *La Pucelle*, 77. Fraioli, *Early Debate*, 63. Fraioli refers to Berne MS 205.

34. In Griscom, *Historia Regum Britanniae of Geoffrey of Monmouth*; in Fraioli, *Early Debate*, 62. The Merlin prophecy may have referred to opposition "between two zodiac signs, *Virgo* and *Sagittarius*." Fraioli, *Early Debate*, 63, n. 34.

35. Jean, Count of Dunois and Bastard of Orléans; in Pernoud, *Retrial*, 144. An oral version of the prophecy contained the locational reference extracted from a separate section of the Monmouth text. Fraioli, *Early Debate*, 63, n. 36.

36. Jehanne; in Scott, *Trial*, 76.

37. Ibid., 68.

and also a sword which Baudricourt gave her, but no other armour. And she said she was accompanied by a knight and four other men."[38] Jehanne and her escort traveled eleven days over enemy-occupied territory without incident—a feat considered remarkable by some—reaching Chinon on or around March 4. One imagines that an aura of the miraculous must have begun to surround her.[39]

Jehanne had prefaced her arrival at Chinon with letters to Charles VII requesting clearance to enter the city and stipulating that she would recognize him amid all those present there, which she accomplished.[40] After hearing her claim as to what she intended to achieve (i.e., the lifting of the siege at Orléans and the delivery of Charles to his coronation and anointing at Rheims[41]), Charles subjected Jehanne to two examinations assessing her credibility. The first was carried out by an ecclesiastical team at Chinon and the second, more extensive, inquiry took place at Poitiers.[42] Régine Pernoud notes that most of the former masters of the University of Paris were then at Poitiers since the English had infiltrated the University,[43] and it was from this group of academic theologians, lawyers, bishops, and other clergy that the Poitiers interrogators were drawn. The examination lasted approximately three weeks, yielding the conclusion that "no evil is to be found in her, only goodness, humility, virginity, devotion, honesty and simplicity." Furthermore, the examiners maintained that "to doubt her, or to dismiss her, without [her showing any] appearance of evil, would be to repel the Holy Spirit."[44] Thus, Jehanne's claim to a divine mission was officially sanctioned by the Church, but this would be completely ignored throughout the condemnatory process at Rouen.

Upon receiving approval at Poitiers and full support from Charles VII, Jehanne was thoroughly equipped and dispatched with an army

38. Ibid.

39. Several witnesses expressed astonishment that the group crossed such vast enemy territory safely. For example, Poulengy and Gobert Thibault, squire to the King of France; in Pernoud, *Retrial*, 103, 118.

40. Jehanne; in Scott, *Trial*, 69, 80–81. Moreau and Simon Charles, president of the royal treasury of France; in Pernoud, *Retrial*, 92, 108. Jean Chartier, chronicler; in Pernoud and Clin, *Her Story*, 22–23.

41. Reported by S. Charles; in Pernoud, *Retrial*, 107–8.

42. Jean, Duke of Alençon; in Pernoud and Clin, *Her Story*, 27.

43. Pernoud, *Herself and Her Witnesses*, 54.

44. Poitiers conclusion; in Taylor, *La Pucelle*, 73–74.

to Orléans where the raising of the siege on May 8 in a matter of days was considered miraculous given the nearly impregnable nature of the English forts erected there.[45] This victory constituted fulfillment of the first aspect of Jehanne's declared mission, and it was followed by a string of successes: the recovery of Jargeau on June 12, Meung-sur-Loire on June 15, Beaugency on June 17, and Patay on June 18. These victories cleared part of the route to Rheims, but Anglo-Burgundians still held many towns along the way. Despite the danger and, "although the King had no money to pay his army, all the knights, esquires, men of war and of the commonality" were willing to serve on the coronation "journey in the Maid's company, saying that wheresoever she went they would go."[46] A treaty was established with the town of Auxerre, and Troyes, Châlons, and Rheims surrendered to Charles, clearing the way for his anointment and coronation as King of France on July 17, 1429 and fulfilling the second element of Jehanne's mission. It is remarkable that, within two and a half months, nine towns were recovered by the French under Jehanne's inspiration and efforts and the dauphin was made King. Moreover, as the coronation party traveled a different return route from Rheims, additional towns pledged obedience to Charles. Incidentally, it was on Jehanne's approach to Rheims with the royal army that Pierre Cauchon, Bishop of Beauvais and counsellor to the child-king Henry VI of England, fled the city, and he was later displaced from his diocese when the Anglo-Burgundians were driven from Beauvais. It was Cauchon who subsequently took the lead in orchestrating Jehanne's demise.

On his coronation day, although Charles possessed an impressive military advantage, he began negotiating truces with the Duke of Burgundy and withdrawing support from Jehanne. Jehanne, however, imploring Burgundy to reconcile with Charles, understood that the Duke's lack of cooperation would necessitate continuation of the war.[47] "[P]eace," she maintained, "would not be found except at the end of a lance."[48] The statement does not indicate a preference for war on Jehanne's

45. Alençon; in Pernoud, *Retrial*, 155.

46. Alençon; in Pernoud, *Herself and Her Witnesses*, 120.

47. Jehanne's letter of July 17, 1429 to the Duke of Burgundy beseeched him to make peace with Charles and referred to a previous letter requesting the same, to which she had received no reply; in Taylor, *La Pucelle*, 95–96.

48. Jehanne; in Taylor, *La Pucelle*, 173.

part but a regrettable fact; she did not trust the Burgundians to honor their truces and correctly estimated that they would use any alleged truce period to strengthen their military capabilities. In fact, thirty-five hundred English reinforcements had entered northern France and were headed to Paris at the time of Charles's coronation, unbeknownst to the French party, arriving there on July 25. Pernoud deems the negotiations an act of "fraud" on the part of Burgundy and an act of "betrayal" by Charles against Jehanne and her companions-at-arms.[49] On August 5, 1429, Jehanne wrote to the city of Rheims:

> [I]t is true that the King has made truces with the Duke of Burgundy for fifteen days, by which he [Burgundy] must peacefully return the city of Paris at the end of fifteen days. ... No matter how many truces are made like this, I am not at all happy, and I do not know if I will keep them. But if I do, it will only be to protect the honour of the King, and ... I will keep together and maintain the army of the King so as to be prepared at the end of those fifteen days, if they do not make peace.[50]

Jehanne did not consider her mission completed; the English still constituted a formidable presence in France and would have to be expelled if the country was to unite under autonomous French rule. Although her suspicions toward Burgundy were validated as Paris was not handed over, Charles continued negotiating, undermining the royal army's efforts to recover Paris and the remainder of the kingdom. Paris had been fortifying since June 21 of that year in anticipation of an Armagnac attack,[51] and the longer that Charles stalled the effort to retake it, the stronger became the enemy's ability to defend it. Moreover, although several cities were eager to submit to Charles, he failed to approach them.[52] In late August, he ordered a truce at Compiègne and a four-month suspension of hostilities against Burgundians everywhere except Paris. He was soon to grant the Duke of Burgundy possession of Pont Saint-Maxence, Créil, Senlis, and Compiègne, the latter which refused to recognize the Duke's authority. These four towns had just recently surrendered to the King

---

49. Pernoud, *Herself and Her Witnesses*, 129.

50. Jehanne; in Taylor, *La Pucelle*, 118–19.

51. *Journal d'un Bourgeois de Paris*, 91–92; in Pernoud, *Herself and Her Witnesses*, 119–20. *Journal of the Siege of Orléans*; in Pernoud and Clin, *Her Story*, 62.

52. Enguerrand de Monstrelet, Burgundian chronicler; in Pernoud from Quicherat, vol. 4, 391, *Herself and Her Witnesses*, 133–34.

of France. Charles's behavior was odd and must have been particularly confounding, frustrating, and disappointing to those who had risked life and limb to further his cause.

Nonetheless, Jehanne pressed onward. On September 8, she and her companions attacked Paris but were met with strong resistance and retreated after nightfall, against Jehanne's will; an arrow had penetrated her thigh and, unable to walk, her comrades carried her away as they withdrew. She maintained that, had they prolonged the battle, they would have taken the capital that day.[53] Eyewitness and clerk of the Parlement of Paris, Clément de Fauquembergue, suggested that the inhabitants of Paris opposed the attempt to oust the occupying forces because Charles had abandoned them on fleeing the city eleven years earlier;[54] however, it is difficult to believe that all were of a single mind. The following day, Jehanne, the Duke of Alençon, and several other captains planned to resume the attack but were prohibited by their king who summoned them to Saint-Denis. Charles had contrarily ordered a bridge destroyed that Alençon had constructed in preparation for the assault; Jehanne and her party arrived there to find it demolished.[55] Charles ordered the assault abandoned on September 10 and, eight days later, extended the truce to include Paris.[56] On September 21, he dissolved the royal army. Moreover, Charles separated Jehanne and Alençon against their mutual will, sending the Duke to fight in the north—he was one of her most ardent companions-at-arms and the two never saw each other again. The remaining captains were scattered in various directions.[57]

53. Perceval de Cagny, chronicler for the Duke of Alençon; in Pernoud from Quicherat, vol. 4, 25–29, *Herself and Her Witnesses*, 137.

54. Fauquembergue, *Journal*; in Taylor, *La Pucelle*, 125.

55. Cagny; in Quicherat, *Procès de Condamnation*, vol. 4, 28.

56. That Paris was well-fortified did not exclude the possibility of it being taken by prolonged assault. Jehanne and some of the most experienced French military leaders (captain La Hire, Alençon, the duke of Bourbon, the counts of Vendôme and Laval, the lords d'Albreth, de Rais, and de Boussac, the two marshals of France, and captain Ponton de Xantrailles) believed it possible or would not have undertaken the endeavor. Kelly DeVries identifies the leaders. DeVries, *Military Leader*, 139. Moreover, had the French forces been allowed sufficient opportunity to demonstrate their strength, a significant portion of the Paris citizenry might have joined them. DeVries indicates that, the day following the battle for Paris, Jehanne was approached by "the count of Montmorency and fifty to sixty 'gentlemen'... who had defected from the city, wishing to fight with her and the French army against their former allies." Ibid., 146.

57. Alençon requested that Jehanne be allowed to fight with him in Normandy, but

Jehanne d'Arc

Prior to departing Saint-Denis, Jehanne deposited armor and a sword in the basilica there, an act which, although customary, might also suggest resignation on her part. Her wave of military victory in service to God and her country was receding. Jehanne was questioned about the matter at Rouen. "Asked why she offered these arms, she answered that this was out of devotion, according to the custom of men-at-arms when they were wounded; and because she had been wounded in front of Paris, she offered them to St Denis, because this was the [battle] cry of France,"[58] yet she had made no such offering with respect to a wound sustained at Orléans. "Montjoie Saint Denis" was the battle cry of the French royal army at the time and also "supposedly referred to the mound of stones" marking the site of Saint Denis' martyrdom.[59] Siobhan Nash-Marshall proposes that Jehanne's offering of arms in reference to the battle cry constituted a petitionary prayer requesting that she not be forced to abandon the battle for France,[60] but one cannot help wondering if Jehanne had inklings of her own upcoming martyrdom, hence her reference to the battle cry representing the martyred saint and her gesture at the basilica of Saint-Denis. The reference was uttered in association with a wound that had forced her withdrawal from the battle for Paris which, she maintained, had ultimately prevented French victory on that day, a day marking her sole opportunity to retake the capital and her first decisive military loss. Jehanne's reference was literally to the "cry of France," not "the [battle] cry of France" as interpreted by the translator.[61] Perhaps Jehanne intended the statement to carry a dual connotation, both as battle cry (a call to arms) and as "the cry of France," of a people and a land bloodied, ravaged, and burned under long-term foreign occupation and war. Jehanne undoubtedly understood that failure to regain Paris would prolong the war and suffering; hence, the "cry of France" was not only a battle cry—in this case, a call to defensive

---

the request was denied. Cagny; in Pernoud from Quicherat, vol. 4, 30, *Herself and Her Witnesses*, 141–42.

58. Jehanne; in Taylor, *La Pucelle*, 199.
59. Taylor, *La Pucelle*, 199–200, n. 119.
60. Nash-Marshall, *Spiritual Biography*, 116.
61. Pierre Tisset's French document reads, "le cri de France," and his Latin text reads, "clamor Francie." Jehanne; in Tisset and Lanhers, *Procès de Condamnation*, vol. 1, 171 and vol. 2, 141. The Orléans manuscript reads, "le cry de France." Jehanne; in Orléans MS 518, 137. The d'Urfé manuscript (ca. fifteenth century) accords with the Orléans manuscript. Doncoeur, *Minute Française*, 194.

war—but also a cry against injustice—against foreign occupation and offensive war. The "cry of France" expresses the dual nature of Jehanne's mission. In any case, the loss before Paris coupled with the stark orders issued by her king clearly indicated a turning point in Jehanne's mission. She had predicted six months earlier at Chinon that she would "last a year and scarcely more,"[62] suggesting that she was aware from the beginning of her campaign that her mission would be short-lived and the tide would somehow shift.[63] She might have been symbolically handing over the battle to those who would continue the fight after her. At any rate, Jehanne's ritual offering in the basilica suggests awareness of an imminent shift in fortune, a shift into the unknown.

Ordered back to the Loire, Jehanne was assigned the recovery of La Charité, which first required taking Saint-Pierre-le-Moûtier. The latter she accomplished; however, by November 9, Jehanne was in the position of requesting military supplies from the citizens of Riom. She wrote, "Dear and good friends, . . . with the help of God I intend to clear out the other places which are hostile to the king. . . . [A]nd because I and my men are poorly prepared to lay siege to La Charité, where we will be going shortly, I pray that you, for as much as you love the good and honour of the king and also that of all the others here, will wish to send aid immediately . . . gunpowder, saltpetre, sulphur, arrows, heavy crossbows and other military supplies."[64] When Jehanne and her small company arrived at La Charité, it was late November and cold. They remained there for a month before withdrawing due to lack of assistance from within the town[65] and lack of victuals from Charles.[66]

After being detained by the royal court throughout much of the winter of 1429, Jehanne left the king in late March or early April of 1430 and traveled to Lagny-sur-Marne to resume her military efforts independently.[67] She was accompanied by approximately two hundred men-

---

62. Jehanne; quoted by Alençon, in Pernoud, *Retrial*, 160.

63. Jehanne did not know exactly how long her military campaign would last, but she seemed to know it would be short. She anticipated freeing the Duke of Orléans from an English prison and recalled that her voices indicated it would take more than a year but less than three years. Jehanne; in Scott, *Trial*, 106–7.

64. Jehanne; in Taylor, *La Pucelle*, 130–31.

65. The Berry Herald (Jacques Bouvier); in Pernoud from Quicherat, vol. 4, 49, *Herself and Her Witnesses*, 145.

66. Cagny; in Pernoud, *Herself and Her Witnesses*, 145.

67. Jehanne was apparently holed up for at least part of the winter at the castle of

at-arms including her brother, Pierre, and her squire, Aulon.[68] In late April, Jehanne was positioned at Melun before proceeding to Crépy-en-Valois and, subsequently, to Compiègne in early May (which was under Burgundian siege).[69] At Melun, Jehanne's voices informed her of her impending capture by June 24 of that year without any recommendation on how she might avoid it. They reiterated the message "frequently, almost every day. And she begged . . . that when she should be taken prisoner she might die speedily, without suffering long imprisonment. And they told her that she should take it all in good part; and that it must happen so; but they did not tell her when." She was assured of God's help.[70] The unknown was gradually becoming known to Jehanne; the critical shift was about to occur. Jehanne lived in knowledge of her capture for a month before it occurred in late May, which must have been a powerful torment, yet she did not abandon the mission to which she felt divinely called. That she struggled during this period is certain. Jehanne maintained that, if her voices had revealed (as she often requested) the hour of her capture, "she would not have gone," clarifying that "she would not have gone willingly. Nevertheless she would have obeyed them in the end, whatever was going to happen to her."[71] Such painful willingness to sacrifice all personally for a divinely designated purpose constitutes utter dissolution of personal agenda, and it is such painful willingness to suffer, rather than enthusiastic willingness, that constitutes a useful marker in assessing claims to divine sanction.

Georges de La Trémoïlle (grand chamberlain in the court of Charles VII and chief negotiator with Burgundy) as she wrote letters from there. DeVries, *Military Leader*, 158–59, 224, n. 25. Pernoud and Clin, *Her Story*, 82, 190. Cagny indicates that Jehanne took leave without permission from the royal court. Cagny; in DeVries from Quicherat, vol. 4, 32, *Military Leader*, 162.

68. Jehanne's brothers, Jean and Pierre, joined her army at Tours in April, 1429. Pernoud, *Herself and Her Witnesses*, 126, 147.

69. Jehanne's army grew somewhat en route to Compiègne where she joined forces with the town's captain and citizens. DeVries, *Military Leader*, 162.

70. Jehanne's testimony indicates capture "before the feast of Saint John." Jehanne; in Scott, *Trial*, 99. Jehanne's request to die speedily suggests not that she desired death but that she considered her death inevitable once in English hands (as later confirmed by knight, Haimond de Macy) and wished to minimize her suffering. Macy; in Taylor, *La Pucelle*, 320. During a verbal exchange between Jehanne and the English at Orléans, they had threatened to burn her should she fall into their hands. *Journal of the Siege of Orléans*, 155; in Pernoud, *By Herself and Her Witnesses*, 84.

71. Jehanne; in Scott, *Trial*, 99.

It was during this period, on May 6, 1430, that Charles finally acknowledged publicly his error in having trusted the Burgundian peace ploy, but within two and a half weeks, Jehanne, his "greatest resource ... whom he had deprived of any effective means of action,"[72] was snatched from the battlefield for all time. She was captured by Burgundians at Compiègne on May 23 while defending the rear as her party retreated toward the town; it was Jehanne's custom to place herself in the most dangerous position, the vanguard on attack and the rearguard on retreat.[73] Jehanne's chivalry did not elude the enemy. A Burgundian chronicler wrote that "the Maid ... took all the brunt, and took great pains to save her company, remaining behind as captain and bravest of her troop." She was pulled from her horse by an archer and taken prisoner with her squire and her brother, Pierre.[74] Jehanne's willingness to place herself in greatest danger demonstrates full and direct engagement in her mission. Enguerrand de Monstrelet, also a Burgundian chronicler and *bailli* of Compiègne, noted that "the Burgundian party and the English were overjoyed ... [b]ecause they did not fear or dread any captain or commander as much as they had always feared this Pucelle until that day."[75]

Many have held that Jehanne was betrayed by the captain and defender of Compiègne, Guillaume de Flavy. It is suggested that he raised the drawbridge prematurely, not because the city was in imminent danger as it had several layers of defense of which the drawbridge was outermost, but with the intention of blocking Jehanne's retreat into the city.[76] The argument against Flavy rests primarily on the fact that it was not strategically necessary to close the drawbridge. He must have known that Jehanne was accustomed to defending the rear of her company and would retreat last. The boats that he placed on the Oise River to allow some of her men to escape served his own interests in

---

72. Pernoud and Clin, *Her Story*, 84.

73. Pernoud, *Herself and Her Witnesses*, 151.

74. Georges Chastellain; in Pernoud from Quicherat, vol. 4, 446–47, *Herself and Her Witnesses*, 151–52.

75. Monstrelet, *La chronique d'Enguerran de Monstrelet*; in Taylor, *La Pucelle*, 258.

76. Pernoud and Clin, *Her Story*, 87, 231–33. The Orléans manuscript mentions the possibility that Jehanne was betrayed by a "Frenchman" who hindered her retreat. In Scott, *Trial*, 46. In 1445, Flavy was accused of betraying Jehanne "in a trial set up by the descendants of Marchal Rieux whom Flavy had assassinated to take revenge for having been imprisoned by him." Olivier Bouzy, email, December 1, 2012. Bouzy does not favor the treason theory.

preserving them for the continued defense of Compiègne following her capture.⁷⁷ That boats were placed on the river does not mitigate the fact that it was unnecessary to raise the drawbridge. The lack of necessity coupled with the fact that Jehanne and her troops were defending his city renders it unlikely that she expected Flavy to behave in this manner. Unexpectedly disadvantaged, she would have been ill-prepared to deal with the situation.

What motive(s) might such betrayal have served? Some believe that several lords and captains within the French ranks were jealous of Jehanne's military accomplishments and orchestrated her downfall. It is also speculated that Flavy was motivated by financial gain.⁷⁸ She feared "nothing except treason," Jehanne declared en route to Rheims at the climax of her campaign,⁷⁹ a retrospectively foreboding statement in its tenor.

Upon capture, Jehanne was temporarily placed under guard at Margny. She was subsequently held in a castle at Beaulieu from which she nearly escaped before being transferred to Beaurevoir for four months. At Beaurevoir, Jehanne made her second escape attempt (this time against the command of her voices) by jumping from a seventy-foot tower, but she was again intercepted. Although she suffered injuries from this leap, which remarkably did not kill her, these quickly healed.⁸⁰

---

77. "In an endeavour to protect her retreating troops, Jeanne led a charge against Baudot and Luxembourg, thus giving time for the main body of the French to reach the boats which the Governor of Compiègne, one Guillaume de Flavy, had ready." Scott, *Jeanne d'Arc*, 80.

78. Scott maintains that Archbishop of Rheims, Regnault de Chartres, and Trémoïlle were "jealous" of Jehanne. Scott, *Trial*, 44, n.*. For three like-minded fifteenth-century accounts, including an accusation of monetary greed, see Pernoud and Clin, *Her Story*, 232–33.

79. Jehanne; quoted by Gérardin d'Épinal, in Pernoud, *Retrial*, 84.

80. Jehanne; in Taylor, *La Pucelle*, 187. Nash-Marshall places the height of the tower at seventy feet, whereas Scott stipulates eighteen meters. Nash-Marshall, *Spiritual Biography*, 134. Scott, *Jeanne d'Arc*, 85. Jehanne's captors obviously considered it high enough that she could not safely escape by jumping from it. Some have speculated that Jehanne did not jump from the tower but faltered in attempting to lower herself from it safely, but this contradicts abundant evidence. On March 3, 1431, Jehanne indicated that she jumped from the tower of Beaurevoir and that her captors initially thought she had died as a result. Jehanne; in Scott, *Trial*, 97–98. The March 14, 1431 trial session opened with the question of why Jehanne "leaped from the tower of Beaurevoir." She was also "[a]sked whether, when she leaped, she expected to kill herself" and was accused of having thrown "herself down from the tower." Scott, *Trial*, 111–12, 115.

In November, 1430, Jehanne's Burgundian captor, Jean de Luxembourg, sold her to the English who, in collaboration with Cauchon, held her enchained in a secular prison at Rouen, submitting her to an unjust trial without an advocate and condemning her to death by fire on May 30, 1431.

The myriad injustices of this condemnation trial were apparent to some from the earliest stages of the proceedings when several individuals strongly opposed the tactics of the Rouen court. Cleric, Jean Lohier, refused participation in the trial on the basis of its irregularities, injustice, and invalidity,[81] and Nicolas de Houppeville, Bachelor in theology, was denied participation and underwent imprisonment for his verbal stance against the inappropriate manner in which the trial was being conducted.[82] Vice-Inquisitor Jean Lemaître participated reluctantly in the proceedings. Jean Massieu, Jehanne's usher in the Rouen prison, testified that Lemaître was given to understand that death would visit him should he fail to take part in the process.[83] Trial notary Guillaume Manchon concurred that Lemaître strongly disapproved of the trial and participated as little as possible.[84] Throughout the proceedings, those who attempted to assist Jehanne or opposed the court were, at best, disregarded and, at worst, subject to the prospects of imprisonment, beat-

---

Article 41 of the initial seventy articles drawn up against Jehanne accuses her of attempting to commit suicide "by throwing herself down from the top of a tower. . . ." Murray, *Jeanne d'Arc*, 355. Article 37 states that Jehanne "jumped from the tower at Beaurevoir," and Article 64 indicates that she "cast herself from a high tower of the castle of Beaurevoir." Hobbins, *Trial*, 140, 153. The issue was deemed important enough for inclusion in the twelve final articles against Jehanne. Article 8 of these accuses her of throwing "herself from a very high tower, preferring to die . . ." Taylor, *La Pucelle*, 211. The charge reappeared on May 2, 1431 when Jehanne was officially admonished. Item 6 of the schedule of admonitions refers to "the sin she committed in leaping from the tower of Beaurevoir." Hobbins, *Trial*, 175. On May 23, 1431, when the schedule of Jehanne's alleged transgressions was read to her, Article 8 (above) was reiterated. Hobbins, *Trial*, 186. Had Jehanne attempted to lower herself from the tower safely, she would surely have raised this in refutation of the charge of attempted suicide repeatedly leveled against her. But she did not deny jumping from the top of the tower. Rather, she declared, "After leaping, I took confession and asked the Lord for forgiveness." Jehanne, March 14, 1431; in Hobbins, *Trial*, 104.

81. Lohier, retold by Guillaume Manchon, trial notary; in Pernoud, *Retrial*, 272–73.
82. Houppeville; in Pernoud, *Retrial*, 275, 277.
83. Massieu; in Taylor, *La Pucelle*, 332.
84. Manchon; ibid., 325. Other witnesses also testified to Lemaître's reluctance.

ing, or drowning.[85] Toward the end of the trial, three assessors submitted written reservations concerning the court's ability to judge appropriately the nature of Jehanne's revelations. Their opinion, presented "according to ... conscience," met with Cauchon's unambiguous disapproval.[86] On consultation, Jean de Saint-Avit (Bishop of Avranches) stated that, in the absence of certainty surrounding the legitimacy of Jehanne's claims, the case should be submitted to the pope, but Cauchon omitted this from the trial record[87] and Saint-Avit was subsequently imprisoned on the accusation of plotting to liberate Rouen.

Concerning the conditions of her imprisonment, Jehanne's cell was guarded by five Englishmen "of the lowest sort" who "mocked her." Three remained in her cell overnight and two were posted outside the cell entrance. "[A]t night she lay chained by the legs with two pairs of irons ... secured by another chain which passed through the legs of her bed and was attached to a great block of wood five or six foot [sic] long, by means of a lock."[88] It is widely asserted that, rather than being held by her enemies in a secular prison, Jehanne lawfully could—and should—have been kept in a more respectable, ecclesiastical prison guarded by women. Nonetheless, she was handled as a prisoner of war rather than an alleged heretic.[89] Such conditions would thoroughly crush the spirit of some but, no matter how physically or emotionally strained she might have been, Jehanne does not appear to have been spiritually crushed. She

85. Guillaume de la Chambre, assessor and physician at the Rouen trial, testified that Lohier and Houppeville were threatened with drowning for their lack of cooperation; in Pernoud, *Retrial*, 229–30.

86. The assessors were Richard de Grouchet, Pierre Minier, and Jean Pigache, Bachelors in Theology. Grouchet; in Pernoud, *Herself and Her Witnesses*, 198. Grouchet testified that the three participated in the trial only "out of fear, threats, and terror," and had considered fleeing; in Pernoud, *Retrial*, 207.

87. Isambart de la Pierre, Dominican friar and assessor at the Rouen trial; in Pernoud, *Retrial*, 282.

88. Massieu; in Pernoud, *Retrial*, 210.

89. Jehanne was captured as a prisoner of war but was tried in an ecclesiastical (Inquisitorial) court on charges of an ecclesiastical nature, not as a prisoner of war in a secular court. The vast majority of charges against her did not concern warfare but attempted to implicate her in acts of sorcery, heresy, idolatry, invocation of demons, boasting, lying, vanity, inciting others to worship her, seeking personal profit, promiscuity, attempted suicide, failing to submit to the Church Militant, blasphemy, falsely claiming divine sanction, violation of canon law in wearing and receiving the Eucharist in male clothing, and they concerned the nature of her divine counselors and revelations, her claim to discernment of spirits, and other "errors" of faith.

did not lose faith in her divine voices or the divinity of her mission, nor did she view personal comfort, safety, or happiness as necessary conditions of divine calling or support.

Why was Jehanne treated so harshly? During the fifteen months between her initial appearance at Chinon and her capture, circumstances in France had changed drastically. Not only had pro-French forces been revived and the siege of Orléans stunningly raised, but Anglo-Burgundian forces had suffered multiple defeats and lost considerable territory in France. Moreover, Charles VII had been anointed and crowned at Rheims. According to Scott, "[t]hat Jeanne should be brought to trial was a political necessity to her enemies: not only must it be shown that the Dauphin's coronation was invalid, but for the morale of the English army it was essential to prove that the French successes had a diabolic source."[90] Indeed, her enemies were determined that their most feared opponent would not see the light of freedom again. A letter from Henry VI to Cauchon dated January, 1431 stated the "intention to retake and regain possession of this Joan [from those in charge of trying her] if it comes to pass that she is not convicted or found guilty."[91] The English had nothing to worry about in this regard as Cauchon, who was instrumental in negotiating the Treaty of Troyes and twice fled the advancing French army, gladly took the lead in prosecuting and persecuting Jehanne.

There were two judges in the Rouen trial, namely Cauchon and Vice-Inquisitor Lemaître, a promoter named Jean d'Estivet, and approximately sixty assessors playing a consultative role. Among this handpicked panel were many masters and doctors of theology and canon law from the University of Paris who, in Pernoud's view, were intensely opposed to Jehanne because she defied their presumed wisdom.[92] Also, the University favored a dual monarchy under the English king and this was hindered by Jehanne's anointing and crowning of the French king at Rheims. Her accusers had reason to believe that, should they paint her as a heretic and witch, the dual monarchy might gain support.[93] Moreover, Jehanne had stepped beyond her allotted position in the social hierarchy and presented a compelling claim to divine sanction in support of a

---

90. Scott, *Trial*, 9.
91. Henry VI; in Taylor, *La Pucelle*, 136.
92. Pernoud, *Retrial*, 14.
93. Ibid., 203–4.

political mission; it is not surprising that she was met with multiple forms of rivalry and enmity.

In addition to the broader political agendas of the day, there are other conceivable reasons why Jehanne's enemies were as ardent as her supporters. Jehanne was a powerful individual, likely viewed as a threat by some members of a divided and floundering Church. In claiming unmediated communication with the divine realm, Jehanne inadvertently threatened the authority and power of the Church Militant and its representatives, comprised in part by those at Rouen who acted as her judges and assessors. The first of twelve final articles of accusation drawn up against her states, "[S]he ... refuses to submit herself, her actions and her words, to the Church militant. ... And ... she will not rely upon the decision or judgement of any living man but only upon the judgement of God."[94] This accusation reappears in the twelfth and final article, thereby framing and informing the entire body of accusations against her. Article 12 declares that "every faithful pilgrim in this world is bound to obey and to submit their actions and words to the Church militant, especially in the matter of faith and what concerns holy doctrine and Church laws." On the basis of this article, the Faculty of Theology at the University of Paris declared Jehanne "schismatic" and "apostate." The University's Faculty of Canon Law also condemned her as schismatic, defining schism as "unlawful separation, due to disobedience, from the unity of the Church," declaring that "this woman separates herself from the obedience of the Church militant."[95] The court demanded submission from Jehanne, citing it as her duty and doing everything within its power to coerce her; this included threat of torture and refusal to bury her in consecrated ground should she die imprisoned. Nonetheless, Jehanne refused to yield, not being deterred by any human. Fully committed to her mission founded on her claim to divine revelation, Jehanne permitted nothing to come between her and God.

Enigmatic and compelling, Jehanne's power defied logic. In fact, her achievements pointed directly to charism, something her enemies did not embrace in this warrior-maiden who swept the battlefields of France like a dynamic storm. Jehanne's confessor at Rouen asserted that, "had she gone over to the side of the English, she would not have been

---

94. Quoted in Taylor, *La Pucelle*, 208.
95. Ibid., 212, 214.

so [badly] treated,"[96] testifying to the fact that power, though often celebrated in friends, is usually condemned in foes.

Charism, in the theological sense, does not refer simply to a charismatic personality but to spiritual gifts in the form of grace bestowed by the Holy Spirit, such as the ability to prophesy or perform miracles (supernatural deeds).[97] At least three charismatic powers can be attributed to Jehanne, including discernment of spirits in the matter of her visitations, the ability to prophesy (as in the liberation of Orléans and the crowning of Charles VII at Rheims), and the apparently miraculous revival of an infant from death. In spring of 1430, Jehanne was called to Lagny to pray for an unbaptized child stillborn three days earlier. Several girls had been praying collectively for the child without apparent result; however, with Jehanne's participation, the infant revived long enough to be baptized before dying (again) and being buried in consecrated ground.[98] Many eyes were on the Maid and many words were spoken about her. A Burgundian chronicler reported "the great renown" of Jehanne and her reputation for performing miraculous deeds.[99] Such charismatic associations combined with her clarity of purpose, intelligence, independence, determination, courage, uncanny military expertise, and general popularity rendered her someone to be reckoned with. Anne Llewellyn Barstow indicates that, during Jehanne's time, the Church was attempting to eliminate folk religion and the spiritual powers of individuals while endeavoring to protect the exclusive spiritual power of the (male) priesthood established through the twelfth-century doctrine of transubstantiation. She notes that the bubonic plague of the previous century had diminished people's faith in the efficacy of the sacraments to protect.[100] Hence, when Jehanne emerged as protectress

---

96. Martin Ladvenu; in Pernoud, *Herself and Her Witnesses*, 230. Manchon was of like opinion. Manchon; in Pernoud, *Retrial*, 205. Rouen assessor and physician, Jean Tiphaine, quoted "a great English lord" as stating of Jehanne, "She really is a good creature. Why is she not English!" Tiphaine; in Pernoud, *Retrial*, 223.

97. Rahner, "Charism," in *Encyclopedia of Theology*, 184–86.

98. Jehanne; in Taylor, *La Pucelle*, 172. This event was not cited as a miracle in support of Jehanne's canonization since, in the canonization process, the Church scrutinizes all questions of miracle, employing medical professionals in issues of a physiological nature, and this was impossible with the Lagny incident which occurred approximately five hundred years earlier.

99. Jean Lefèvre de Saint-Remy, Burgundian chronicler; in Pernoud from Quicherat, vol. 4, 349, *Herself and Her Witnesses*, 153.

100. Barstow, *Joan of Arc*, 14, 18–19, 41.

of France and "daughter of God," as she was frequently addressed by her divine voices,[101] it is little wonder if certain members of the clergy became envious and considered their patriarchal power threatened, a power that resided in the unstable structure of the Church Militant. Whether one believed Jehanne's powers to be charismatic or diabolic, they appeared incalculable, uncontrollable, and intimidating, extending beyond ordinary human capability.

Envy, fear, and hostility toward Jehanne also lurked on the military front. The Burgundian archer who captured her was reportedly "angry that a woman ... should have surpassed so many valiant men."[102] Massieu testified that many felt animosity and fear toward her, particularly among the English.[103] Following the liberation of Orléans, letters were issued forbidding desertion by English soldiers, and sanctions were later ordered against any who refused to enter France due to fear of the Maid.[104] A Burgundian chronicler who fought against Jehanne at Patay wrote:

> By the renown of Joan the Maid, the courage of the English was much impaired. ... They saw ... their fortune turn its wheel sharply against them, for they had already lost several towns and fortresses which had returned to their obedience to the King of France, principally by the undertakings of the Maid, some by force, others by treaty; they saw their men stricken down and did not now find them of such or so firm and prudent words as they were wont to be. Thus they were all ... very desirous of withdrawing on to the Normandy marches, abandoning what they held in the country of France. ...[105]

Jehanne was feared because she was powerful, perhaps even more so because her power appeared inexplicable except by supernatural cause.

Jealousy contributed to resentment toward Jehanne in the French arena as well. Within the French royal court, Archbishop of Rheims and Chancellor of France, Regnault de Chartres, and Georges de La Trémoïlle, Grand Chamberlain of France and Charles VII's lieutenant

---

101. Jehanne; in Taylor, *La Pucelle*, 180.
102. Chastellain; in Pernoud and Clin, *Her Story*, 87.
103. Massieu; in Taylor, *La Pucelle*, 331.
104. Pernoud, *Retrial*, 133.
105. Jean de Wavrin; in Pernoud from Quicherat, vol. 5, 418, *Herself and Her Witnesses*, 112.

general for Burgundy, were notably hostile toward Jehanne, although Chartres initially supported her in his role as examiner at Poitiers.[106] These men, however, were involved in the false truces between Charles VII and Burgundy and, like Charles, had subsequently to face their folly, in contrast to Jehanne's wisdom. Incidentally (or perhaps significantly), Chartres was half-brother to Flavy who closed the drawbridge before Jehanne at Compiègne,[107] and he may have destroyed or otherwise suppressed the record of the Poitiers examination which favored her cause.[108] Jealousy is also thought to have motivated Charles's withdrawal of support from Jehanne. Burgundian chronicler Georges Chastellain wrote, "There were frequent and diverse changes all around his person, for it was his habit . . . when one had been raised high in his company . . . he began to be annoyed with him, and . . . willfully reversed that person from high to low."[109]

With powerful enemies on both sides, Jehanne was positioned precariously. A fifteen-year-old choirboy at Rouen cathedral overheard several canons who were taking part in the condemnation trial state "that a case must quickly be framed against her and that an excuse would be found for putting her to death."[110] Justice did not figure in the matter; therefore, when Jehanne requested of the Rouen court that her case be heard by the pope in Rome, the request was consistently denied.[111]

---

106. Chartres held Jehanne responsible for her capture, accusing her of pride, rejecting human counsel, disobeying divine command, and wearing rich garments. Chartres, from Quicherat, vol. 5, 168, in Taylor, *La Pucelle*, 21. One wonders if the archbishop's vestments were less luxurious than those of Jehanne who was given clothing in appreciation of military services rendered. DeVries notes that "[b]oth the *Journal du siège d'Orléans* (in Quicherat, IV:178–81) and the *Chronique de la Pucelle* (in Quicherat, IV:246–50) . . . decry at length La Trémoïlle's opposition to her." DeVries, *Military Leader*, 216–17, n. 9.

107. Pernoud and Clin, *Her Story*, 99, 178.

108. Pernoud, *Herself and Her Witnesses*, 67.

109. Chastellain; in Pernoud and Clin, *Her Story*, 79. Charles reportedly displayed jealousy even toward his son; "Every time that the dauphin Louis . . . won a victory, Charles would recall him immediately to court in order to neutralize his power." Pernoud and Clin, *Her Story*, 79.

110. Jean Riquier, priest; in Pernoud, *Retrial*, 202.

111. Jehanne asked on March 17 and May 2, 1431 to be delivered to the pope for questioning. On May 24, 1431, she requested that the trial documents be sent to the pope for review. Jehanne; in Taylor, *La Pucelle*, 202, 217; in Scott, *Trial*, 149. Pernoud maintains that Jehanne's request to have her case brought before the pope removes any doubt that she honored the Church Militant. Pernoud, *Retrial*, 289–90. Furthermore,

On the advice of assessor Isambart de la Pierre, she also offered submission to the Council of Basel on the understanding that it contained pro-French and pro-English representation, unlike the Rouen court, but this was also refused and the well-intentioned assessor was threatened with death by drowning.[112] Thus, Jehanne's case was not permitted to advance beyond the court staffed by her enemies.

On May 24, 1431, Jehanne was brought to the cemetery of Saint-Ouen where she allegedly abjured publicly under threat of immediate death by fire. As with other aspects of the trial, irregularities and peculiarities render the events that took place there and those that followed suspect. Two versions of the abjuration document exist (both copies as the original is not extant), a lengthy one of forty-seven lines in French (forty-four in Latin) and a short one of approximately six to eight lines. Massieu testified that, after a document of approximately eight lines was read by him to Jehanne and signed by her, it was substituted with a longer one which was declared official and forms part of the trial record. One of three trial notaries, Nicolas Taquel, also testified that the document signed by Jehanne consisted of approximately "six lines" in French script, and assessor and physician, Guillaume de la Chambre, confirmed that it contained "six or seven lines." Assessor Pierre Miget stated that it was the approximate length of a *Pater Noster*.[113]

Since a short document was read to and signed by Jehanne, it is reasonable to conclude that the long document contains a falsified signature. However, the latter bears the signature "Jehanne +," which is how she spelled her name in three extant letters containing her original signature, proving that, although illiterate,[114] she was able to sign her name and spelled it with consistency. The short abjuration document bears the signature "Jhenne +," an obvious misspelling of her name. Although this might lead one to consider the short document fraudulent and the long

---

when commanded to submit to the Church Militant, Jehanne undoubtedly understood the said Church to consist, in part, of the more or less corrupt ecclesiastical judges and assessors before her who were of the enemy.

112. La Pierre; in Pernoud, *Retrial*, 281. The Council of Basel, established in early 1431, sought conciliar power over the Roman papacy.

113. Massieu; in Taylor, *La Pucelle*, 334. Taquel and Chambre; in Pernoud, *Retrial*, 64. Miget; in Pernoud and Clin, *Her Story*, 233. Pernoud and Clin supply the length of the long document. Pernoud and Clin, *Her Story*, 131.

114. G. Thibault quoted Jehanne as stating that she "did not know A from B"; in Pernoud, *Retrial*, 118.

one legitimate, the contrary is more likely. Jehanne did not completely understand the contents or implications of the document presented to her at Saint-Ouen and requested that it be examined "by the clerks and by the Church in whose hands" she ought to be transferred so that they might advise her on the matter, but her accusers did not oblige. She was threatened with immediate burning if she refused to sign instantly[115] and the pyre was in view, the executioner waiting.[116] Jehanne protested that she was unable to read or write,[117] suggesting that she did not wish to sign since we know that she was capable of signing her name. Ordered to sign, she drew a mark on the document in mockery, after which an English official forced her into making a signature. Knight Haimond de Macy described the mark as circular, yet reproductions indicate only a signature and cross.[118] The fact that Jehanne's hand was forced, apparently by one who faltered in the spelling of her name in a state of haste and urgency before a jeering crowd, renders the short document more likely "authentic" than does the correct spelling of her name in the long document since the signature on the latter was not likely hurried, and care would have been taken in spelling Jehanne's name correctly in order to give it the appearance of legitimacy. Moreover, an Englishman forced Jehanne's hand, and he may not have known how to spell her (French) name correctly.

Jehanne laughed (or smiled) when signing.[119] This supports Macy's observation that she signed in mockery. Jehanne testified that she sometimes signed letters with a cross as an indication to "the person of her party to whom she was writing" that the letter should not be taken seriously.[120] Pernoud attributes Jehanne's laughter to irony, suggesting that she was forced by the enemy "to sign with a cross ... a document whose contents she considered false."[121] But perhaps Jehanne laughed at the

---

115. Jehanne; quoted by Massieu, in Pernoud, *Retrial*, 237–38. Manchon also testified that Jehanne was pressured to sign; in Pernoud, *Retrial*, 62–63.

116. Jean Monnet, professor of theology and canon of Paris; in Pernoud, *Retrial*, 238–39.

117. Macy; in Pernoud, *Retrial*, 195.

118. Ibid., 196. Massieu also indicated that Jehanne was forced to sign; in Taylor, *La Pucelle*, 334.

119. Manchon; in Pernoud and Clin, *Her Story*, 131. Guillaume du Désert, trial assessor, also stated that Jehanne laughed; in Pernoud, *Retrial*, 239.

120. Jehanne; in Taylor, *La Pucelle*, 160.

121. Pernoud, *Herself and Her Witnesses*, 217.

misspelling of her name which further invalidated the signature along with the cross of invalidation that she herself might have placed there as an indication of falsity since she reportedly made a mark on the paper prior to her hand being forced. At any rate, the evidence suggests that she did not view the abjuration entirely seriously. Nonetheless, it satisfied the court's purpose; according to Massieu, the document stipulated that she would henceforth wear only female clothing.[122]

The fact that the short document contained in the Orléans manuscript makes no reference to Jehanne's clothing further complicates the issue. However, in comparing the long and short documents at our disposal, one finds that the two are quite similar as the short document contains essentially the same beginning and ending as the long document with an intervening "etc." It appears, therefore, that this short document is simply an abbreviated reproduction of the official (and fraudulent) long document. No known copy seems to exist of the short document that was read to and forcibly signed by Jehanne, made reference to her clothing, and possibly contained the circle observed by Macy. We know that Jehanne adopted female clothing following the alleged abjuration and that her resumption of male clothing became central to her supposed relapse and final condemnation, which validates Massieu's recollection that the short document referenced Jehanne's clothing.

On signing, Jehanne was sentenced to life imprisonment, although the usual prison term for reformed heretics was then three years (though sentencing varied).[123] Hearing this, she requested transfer to an ecclesiastical prison as she was entitled, but Cauchon flatly refused.[124] On May 27, 1431, Jehanne resumed male clothing and was declared a relapsed heretic shortly thereafter. When asked to explain her behavior, she replied that she acted of her own accord, and that male attire was practical since she remained in the company of men. She renounced the alleged abjuration, indicating "that she never understood that she had made an oath not to resume . . . male clothing," nor had she intended to deny the voices of Saints Catherine and Margaret, and "all that she did [at the time of abjuration], she did out of fear of the fire." She reiterated that "she did

---

122. Massieu; in Taylor, *La Pucelle*, 334.

123. Pernoud and Clin, *Her Story*, 131. Perhaps it was on the expectation of eventually being released that Jehanne signed.

124. Manchon; in Pernoud, *Retrial*, 241. Convents often served as ecclesiastical prisons for female heretics. Nash-Marshall, *Spiritual Biography*, 19.

not understand what was in the schedule of abjuration."¹²⁵ According to Massieu, Jehanne reported that English guards had confiscated her female clothing and refused to return it, supplying her, instead, with male attire.¹²⁶ Several witnesses indicated that she claimed to have been treated violently by her guards and that an Englishman attempted to rape her, which prompted her change of clothing.¹²⁷ Perhaps it was anticipated that, in violating her sexually, Jehanne would recant the abjuration, choosing death over continued secular imprisonment, which would not have been an unlikely supposition since she had pledged her virginity to God. In fact, Jehanne cited as further cause for her "relapse" the fact that she had not been permitted to hear Mass or receive the Eucharist, nor had she been freed from leg irons following the abjuration—"she would rather die than" remain enchained. Furthermore, she explained, Saints Catherine and Margaret conveyed that God considered it an offense that she abjured to spare her life and that she had placed herself in a state of damnation.¹²⁸ Whatever the reason(s) for Jehanne's resumption of male clothing, Nash-Marshall points out that she "could not have had access to it unless someone had given it to her," and it is impossible to don leggings while chained at the ankles, so she would have required assistance in order to do so.¹²⁹

The evidence suggests that Jehanne's abjuration and relapse were orchestrated to entrap her since only a relapsed heretic could legally be burned, in which case the threat to burn her at Saint-Ouen was illegal and premature as she had not yet abjured or relapsed. The intent was

---

125. Jehanne; in Taylor, *La Pucelle*, 220–22. Paul Doncoeur points out that, when Jehanne was threatened with torture (nearly three weeks earlier), she denied in advance the validity of all confession that might be extracted from her through violence. Doncoeur, *Minute Française*, 49, n. 2. In recanting the abjuration, Jehanne denied the validity of that which was obtained via threat of immediate violence to her.

126. Massieu; in Taylor, *La Pucelle*, 335.

127. Ladvenu; in Pernoud, *Retrial*, 242, 279. Pierre Cusquel, mason of Rouen Castle in which Jehanne was imprisoned, and la Pierre provided similar testimony; ibid., 242, 281. It is uncertain why, if her male clothing was confiscated and a guard attempted to rape her, Jehanne did not apparently mention these matters to her judges but relayed them to others. It should be noted, however, that more than one individual testified that Jehanne was treated violently in her cell, and Jehanne's own testimony hints at the possibility. Moreover, an Englishman nearly struck assessor André Marguerie with a lance for inquiring as to why Jehanne resumed male attire. Massieu; in Taylor, *La Pucelle*, 335.

128. Jehanne; in Taylor, *La Pucelle*, 220–21.

129. Nash-Marshall, *Spiritual Biography*, 19, 162–63.

clearly to pressure her into abjuring. In the aftermath of the supposed relapse, Cauchon loudly declared to those English who were present, "Farewell, farewell, it is done. Be of good cheer!"—laughing as he did so.[130] Condemning her as relapsed supported the English cause in denouncing the legitimacy of Charles VII's kingship. Drawing this link publicly, Guillaume Érard had stated during his sermon preached to Jehanne at Saint-Ouen that the French king was a heretic and schismatic, like she who had helped him regain his kingdom.[131]

Jehanne was declared excommunicate, apostate, relapsed, heretic, and schismatic.[132] She was burned at the Old Marketplace of Rouen on May 30, 1431 before a secular sentence could be pronounced as a large crowd of spectators looked on.[133] She was not granted the customary "consideration" of being strangled by the executioner prior to the flames reaching her.[134] Jehanne's body was reportedly reduced to ashes save for her heart, which "remained intact and full of blood"; it was promptly thrown into the Seine with her ashes.[135] So it was that her enemies eliminated their most feared opponent, but only in body, and that not even completely.

It is unclear whether Charles VII attempted to ransom or rescue Jehanne; two of her comrades-in-arms may have tried. It is suggested that a failed campaign led by the Count of Dunois (Bastard of Orléans) toward Rouen during Jehanne's imprisonment there represented one

---

130. Ladvenu; in Pernoud, *Retrial*, 279. La Pierre provided nearly identical testimony. La Pierre; in Pernoud, *Retrial*, 281. Houppeville reported that Cauchon "spoke exultingly with great joy." Houppeville; in Pernoud, *Retrial*, 274.

131. Érard's words reported by la Pierre, Ladvenu, and Massieu; in Pernoud, *Retrial*, 236-37.

132. Final sentence; in Taylor, *La Pucelle*, 222-24.

133. Following pronouncement of an ecclesiastical sentence, the accused was normally handed over to the secular arm who would pronounce a secular sentence. Pernoud, *Herself and Her Witnesses*, 230.

134. Pernoud and Clin, *Her Story*, 198. According to Ladvenu, the executioner reported that the English had a high scaffold constructed for Jehanne which prevented him from reaching her and hastening her death; in Pernoud, *Retrial*, 280. Nash-Marshall notes that it was impossible for the executioner even "to place a faggot of green wood, whose smoke would have killed Joan before the flames, at her feet." Nash-Marshall, *Spiritual Biography*, 15.

135. Massieu, paraphrasing Jean Fleury, bailiff's clerk and scribe; in Pernoud, *Retrial*, 252. According to la Pierre, the executioner stated that he could not destroy Jehanne's heart and entrails by fire, despite applying oil, charcoal, and sulphur to them; ibid., 283.

such effort and that La Hire's attack on nearby Louviers constituted another.[136]

Though her life and military career were short, Jehanne's inspiration continued to thrive. She had managed to raise a despairing people to hope; she invigorated them and turned the tide of war in their favor. Once inspired, these people did not abandon their cause; the fighting continued long after the spectators departed and the coals from Jehanne's pyre quietly breathed their last. Although King Henry VI of England was crowned King of France in Paris on December 16, 1431 at age ten, he never achieved true victory in France. Peace was established between Philippe the Good of Burgundy and Charles VII in September, 1435 with the Treaty of Arras, marking the end of the civil war. The Anglo-Burgundian alliance finally broken, French and Burgundian forces reunited against the English who, by 1453, were completely driven from France except for Calais, (recovered in 1558).

With the return of Rouen to French rule in 1449, it became possible to access the 1431 trial records, question eye-witnesses to the proceedings, and assess the nature of Jehanne's condemnation. In February, 1450, Charles VII initiated an investigation into the Rouen trial but, since it was an Inquisitorial trial, only the Inquisition could overturn its ruling. An Inquisitorial trial based on an official request by Jehanne's mother and two surviving brothers (Jean and Pierre) ensued, considering the testimony of 115 witnesses in the form of approximately 160 statements. This trial, which opened in late 1455 and concluded in July, 1456, annulled Jehanne's condemnation. The nullification trial verdict pronounced that the trial of condemnation contained "deceit, slander, contradiction and manifest error of law and of fact."[137] Jehanne was canonized by the Roman Catholic Church in 1920, marking her as the only person to be canonized by the Church after being excommunicated and martyred by it.

Having been canonized, Jehanne meets the criteria for sainthood established by the Church, including the leading of a holy life and demonstrated ability to prophesy and perform miracles. "The exemplary

---

136. Pernoud, *Retrial*, 134. Étienne de Vignolles, nicknamed "La Hire," was a military captain and one of Jehanne's strongest supporters. At the time of her death, he was a prisoner of war, later ransomed with the assistance of Charles VII. Pernoud and Clin, *Her Story*, 187–88.

137. Verdict; in Taylor, *La Pucelle*, 349.

members of the Church are the saints,"[138] states Cardinal John Wright. Jehanne is thus classified among those viewed within the Catholic tradition as examples to be emulated, as models of life conducted in accordance with faith—*exemplary* models of *exemplary* life lived in *exemplary* faith. Exemplariness in humans, however, does not indicate absolute perfection as all humans are inherently flawed, though it implies a degree of perfection most high.[139] Such exemplariness warrants attention with respect to Jehanne's claim to divine sanction and her associated behavior.

Several aspects of Jehanne's story are particularly relevant. First, she believed strongly enough in the divinity of her mission that she accepted capture and martyrdom—both which she feared greatly—in order to honor it. Second, the body of information concerning her life and death includes much theological content and debate as the Poitiers examination, the Inquisitorial condemnation and nullification trials, and the beatification and canonization processes were all ecclesiastical. Third, Jehanne's military campaign is extensively documented, rendering a modern theological analysis possible. Fourth, one who familiarizes oneself with the details of Jehanne's life must concede that they are at least extraordinarily unusual and uncanny, if not miraculous, and openly invite meaningful interpretation. Finally, Jehanne was not an ordinary warrior by any account and one might hope that, if God sanctions participation in war, it would not be an ordinary occurrence but would stand out as clearly extraordinary so as to make evident the revelation that God presumably wishes to communicate through such sanctioning and to emphasize the exceptional nature of the occurrence.

Although one might recoil at the notion of a God who participates in violence, such notions are embedded in the Christian tradition from its Judaic roots to the Christian book of Revelation. Take, for example, the story of the destruction of Sodom and Gomorrah,[140] and also the representation of God as ultimately responsible for the violent death of His son as a fundamental element of Christianity. The concept that God

---

138. Wright, *Saints Always Belong*, 31. Canonization "infallibly declares the exemplariness of the saint's life" and is deemed "irrevocable." Molinari, "Canonization of Saints," 59, 61.

139. "Saints are canonized not only to intercede before the throne of God but also to afford those on earth models of perfection." Molinari, "Canonization of Saints," 61.

140. Gen 19:24–25.

sanctions violence is far from anathema to Christian theology despite its pacifist teachings. Moreover, anyone who espouses creationism cannot logically advocate for an entirely pacifist God given the violent nature of the food chain. Therefore, it is not surprising that medieval Christians conceived of God as participating in war, and one can easily (and often tragically) find evidence that it is not an uncommon perception today. It is critical to acknowledge and endeavor to understand this element of Christianity in historical context so that we might apprehend its implications and possibilities for the future of humanity.

Light must penetrate darkness in order to eliminate it. Amid the darkness of war, Jehanne entered the bloodied battlefield as a light of faith, sanctity, compassion, forgiveness, restraint, justice, individual responsibility, and respect for human life. She demonstrated a way through darkness, a way that called her to remain focused on divine light and to be a pillar of reflection beaming that light forth into a bleak corner of humanity. Sanctified light does not shun darkness but illumines it. This message transcends religious particularity and historical and geographical specificity and applies to situations past, present, and future.

2

The Theology of Jehanne d'Arc

Practical, Prophetic Mysticism

And she says that her revelations come from God,
without any intermediary.
—Notary, *Trial of Joan of Arc*

By virtue of her claim to divine revelation combined with her female gender, her male attire, her refusal to take oath in the manner demanded by the Inquisitorial court of Rouen,[1] and her refusal to submit to the Church Militant over God directly, Jehanne challenged the patriarchal, institutional power of the Church. Although she was a practicing Christian, devoutly attending Mass and participating in the sacraments, prayer, and pilgrimages, her focus was more directly on God than the Church. She respected the Church and the pope but placed God above them, which she cannot legitimately be faulted for, yet it was her confidence in divine revelation over ecclesiastics on which Jehanne was

---

1. From the first moment of her condemnation trial, Jehanne refused to reveal all in the courtroom, defying the command that she vow to tell the truth about all things asked of her, insisting that she did not have permission from her voices to divulge certain information concerning her revelations. This procedural controversy is recorded with respect to the trial sessions of February 21, 22, 24, 27, March 1 and 3, 1431. When the trial moved from public examination to private examination in Jehanne's cell on March 10, 1431, disagreement concerning the oath ceased to be recorded in the transcript; the request that she swear an oath is mentioned with respect to the first private session only.

faulted by her enemies. That the Church admitted such a gross error by canonizing her after burning her as a heretic strengthens Jehanne's implicit position that human fallibility exists within the Church. Jehanne was a mystic and, while identifying strongly with institutional Christianity, she also transcended it in claiming the right to spiritual autonomy, a right that the Church finally and fully acknowledged. Jehanne demonstrated that, although divine truth might reside within religious structures to an extent, it is not dependent upon them, or upon any human or thing—it is Truth in its own right.

This chapter explores Jehanne's relationship with the divine from a mystical theological perspective within the context of Jewish and Christian prophecy, while discerning her own mystical teachings. It focuses the mystical discussion, distilling its experiential, prophetic, and practical dimensions. Jehanne's mystical experience and response and the relevance of these to claims of divine sanction in acts of war constitute the main focus.

While the lives of mystics tend to be unusual in some aspect or another, and many are wont to categorize the state of unusualness as pathological, unusualness is merely a label that shifts according to majority rule and not a definitive marker of anything substantial. The fact that some are reluctant to admit the unusual into the realm of the acceptable demonstrates a narrowness of vision that might itself be deemed pathological should the majority shift, rendering the view a minority. Abraham Heschel holds that "[n]eurosis and psychosis are concepts" formulated upon the "cultural patterns" of a "particular society" and that what is perceived as mental disorder might actually constitute "a higher spiritual order."[2]

Since mysticism involves an experience of God, let us consider divine revelation, understood as God's concerned and loving communication to humans and involvement in human history.[3] Experientially, it is knowledge resulting "from a supernatural encounter with the divine."[4] Such encounters arise as grace, independent of human will; thus, "mysticism has its origin in God, in the action of the Holy Spirit."[5] If the divine

---

2. Heschel, *Prophets: II*, 184–85. For a medical analysis of Jehanne's psychological stability, see Preston Russell, *Lights of Madness*.

3. Vorgrimler, *Sacramental Theology*, 5–7.

4. Hvidt, *Christian Prophecy*, 126.

5. Watts, *Behold the Spirit*, xiv, 9.

nature is infinite, divine revelation and mystical experience are also potentially limitless, and the mystical literature demonstrates variation as well as consistency in descriptions of mystical experience, a prominent assertion being that mystical experience is essentially ineffable. For the mystic, God is ultimately—and ultimate—Mystery, unpredictable and uncontainable, revealed only partially and mysteriously through mystical experience.

Although mystical experience cannot be adequately expressed fully in the cataphatic (nor in the apophatic alone—it seems best, if insufficiently, expressed in a combination of the two), this does not mean that mystical experience is not itself cataphatic, or at least partially so. The apophatic characteristic applies largely to its essential ineffability (the inability to communicate the experience fully to a third party), not to the nature of the experience, except insofar as one can experience an apparent absence of God, yet the experience of absence—indeed, of anything—is itself cataphatic. Moreover, absence is experienced only in relation to presence, as lack of presence formerly experienced more fully but now experienced as memory, the memory of presence. John O'Donohue views absence not as "vacancy," but as "another form of presence."[6] The experience of absence is awareness of separation, not non-existence. Denys Turner acknowledges that "the apophatic is not to be understood as functioning in isolation, so that one could construct some such thing as an 'apophatic theology.' The apophatic . . . is intelligible only as being a moment of negativity within an overall theological strategy which is at once and at every moment both apophatic and cataphatic. If these things are so, then theology in so far as it is theology is 'mystical.' . . ."[7] Revelation is cataphatic and apophatic in that it reveals something, but not everything, of the divine.

There is currently a widespread trend placing "objective" experience, such as that purportedly involved in scientific observation, above "subjective" experience in the hierarchy of knowledge and truth, if the latter is granted a place at all. But can scientific experimentation be accorded objective status while founded upon the physical mechanics and individual thought processes of a mediating subject? It is more likely a matter of degree of subjectivity and objectivity that distinguishes various

---

6. O'Donohue, *To Bless the Space*, CD audio recording, session 1, section 2, track 24.
7. Turner, *Darkness of God*, 265.

types of knowledge as an absolute dichotomy is impossible,[8] and there is no proof that either category of knowledge ("subjective" or "objective") is superior to the other. Moreover, mystical experience is not necessarily more subjective than other forms of experience. Let us suppose that God is able to accommodate or transcend human limitation when conveying revelation such that it can be received and transmitted accurately by the recipient, that is, as God intends. This does not negate the assertion that revelation is mediated since to mediate is not necessarily to distort. Furthermore, although some revelation is conveyed through the mediating human body, Saint Teresa of Avila and Saint John of the Cross describe mystical experiences wherein divine revelation is impressed immediately upon the human soul supernaturally, during which time bodily senses and mental faculties are suspended by God.[9] This supports the notion that some mystical experiences are highly objective, calling into question popular conceptions of mystical experience as predominantly subjective. Saint John describes "formal" locutions in which "distinct" words are received by the soul, "not from itself." Such locutions are produced and impressed "supernaturally" upon the soul "without the use of the senses" and "without intervention of the soul."[10] While the limited capacity of language frequently renders (potentially unlimited) mystical experience ineffable, this is not so of divine messages formulated and received within linguistic bounds.

Mysticism accesses a type of knowledge distinct from mental knowledge. Mysticism, and theology in general, are more faith-based than evidence-based, which is not to deny revelatory phenomena as a form of evidence; however, as Nicholas Lash points out, "'personal experiences' are not repeatable in the way that optical experiments are."[11] Mystical knowledge differs from, but is no less valid than, scientific knowledge. Theological 'truths' are not necessarily verifiable or falsifiable, and any attempt at this is an attempt to eliminate the faith aspect of theology; to aim for epistemological certainty in this realm would

---

8. Alan Watts argues against the claim that human subjectivity stands in the way of knowledge, asserting that it is "the very condition of knowledge." Watts, *Behold the Spirit*, 120.

9. Teresa of Avila, *Collected Works*, vol. 1, 105, 121. Teresa of Avila, *Collected Works*, vol. 2, 164. John of the Cross, *Collected Works*, 187–88.

10. John of the Cross, 203, 208.

11. Lash, *Easter in Ordinary*, 28.

be futile, if not foolish. One who seeks to prove God's existence, holds Søren Kierkegaard, "has taken his position outside, he does not treat with God, but his is a treatise about God." Furthermore, he warns, there "comes fear enough when God comes and renders proofs superfluous."[12]

Practical Mysticism

Christ has no body now on earth but yours,
No hands but yours,
No feet but yours.
Yours are the eyes through which Christ's compassion
Is to look out to the earth,
Yours are the feet by which He is to go about doing good,
And yours are the hands by which He is to bless us now.
—SAINT TERESA OF AVILA (ATTRIBUTED)

Let us explore the practical component of mysticism. In Christian terms, mystical experience is "consciousness of the experience of uncreated grace as revelation and self-communication of the triune God."[13] As Dorothee Soelle explains, mysticism involves not only love of God for humans but mutual love between humanity and divinity.[14] She describes mysticism as experiential knowledge of God unlike that acquired through "instruction, tradition, books, and doctrines" and identifies two "ways of understanding God.... There is the ordered way, dogmatically legitimated and hierarchically directed, and the extraordinary one, resting on experiment and experience, which is incapable of being fully institutionalized." The latter, she notes, "represents a concession to the preecclesiastical and the extraecclesiastical reality of religious experience."[15] For Alan Watts, mysticism is essential to religion since religion lacking it "is only a futile straining to follow a way of life for which one has neither the power nor the grace, and there is no power in a merely theoretical grace." He asserts that "the realization of one's union with God... is *necessary*. It is not simply the flower of religion; it is the very seed, lying in the flower as its fulfilment and preceding the root as

12. Kierkegaard, *Stages*, 462.
13. Fischer, "Mysticism," 1004.
14. Soelle, *Silent Cry*, 1–2.
15. Ibid., 45.

its origin." Most individuals, he holds, fail to distinguish between "the meaning of religion" and "its form.... The form of Christianity consists of certain doctrines and precepts," whereas the "meaning is God himself, the ultimate Reality, not as an idea conceived but as a reality experienced. When apprehended . . . this meaning is a state of consciousness," a "mystical and nearly immediate experience of God."[16] Simone Weil similarly asserts that one who has not heard the divine "word, even if he adheres to all the dogmas taught by the Church, has no contact with truth."[17] "The love of institutional religion," she maintains, "although the name of God necessarily comes into it, is not in itself an explicit, but an implicit love of God, for it does not involve direct, immediate contact with him." For Weil, "contact with God is the true sacrament."[18]

Jehanne's notion of divinity appears consistent with these observations in that it transcended religious formulas and institutionalization, deriving primarily from mystical experience. She held her mystical knowledge of God above all, including the Church Militant. She did not oppose the Church itself and loved to hear Mass and partake in the sacraments—the issue was one of limitation and imposition. Her mysticism challenged the constraints of the Church.

Watts holds that those who misunderstand mysticism often "associate it with ecstatic trances, with the solitary life of the hermit, with purely negative conceptions of God, with keeping one's mind perfectly blank for hours on end, with vague reasoning, . . . with a distaste for action and concrete, physical life." On experiencing "consciousness of union with God," however, such conceptions arise only when God is viewed "as hostile to the world."[19]

Jehanne did not speak of ecstatic trances; if these comprised part of her mystical experience, they were treated as private or secondary, but there is no basis upon which to suppose that she experienced them. When pressed by her king and his associates on one occasion to speak of her divine encounters, Jehanne flushed and described a feeling of "great joy" and a desire "to be always in that state" which she experienced in the company of her divine counsel. In communicating the experience, she

---

16. Watts, *Behold the Spirit*, xvii, xxv, 15.
17. Weil, *Waiting for God*, 35.
18. Ibid., 117, 142.
19. Watts, *Behold the Spirit*, 5–6.

"exulted in a marvellous fashion, raising her eyes to Heaven."[20] Although she found moments of solitude when possible,[21] Jehanne did not retreat into a solitary lifestyle but placed herself at the center of the battlefields of France. She spoke very little in a descriptive manner about God, either apophatically or cataphatically, generally describing her divine counsel minimally when pressed to do so, usually in a cataphatic manner. She was far more inclined to speak of God's will, insofar as it was revealed to her, than of the divine nature. (Heschel notes "that the prophet rarely speaks of God as He is in Himself" but speaks of "God in relation to humanity, in relation to the world."[22]) Moreover, Jehanne's mind was far from blank, being occupied frequently with military strategy and the administration of assistance to those in need when not engaged in prayer. She demonstrated an impressive intellect, capable of reasoning with the best and astounding the Rouen court with the profound wisdom of her responses.[23] Jehanne uttered one of her most famous replies when asked whether or not she considered herself to be in the grace of God: "If I am not, may God put me there; if I am, may He keep me there. She said further that if she knew she were not in the grace of God, she would be the most miserable person in the world."[24] Her interrogators were "dumbfounded" by this most excellent response.[25] Jehanne did not possess a distaste for action but was always willing to do her part and urged others against reluctance. After persuading a procrastinating Charles to proceed to Rheims for coronation following the victory at Patay, she camped in a field for two days as an indication of her eagerness to depart.[26]

Thomas Merton asserts that theology, in order not to be devoid of sanctity, must be lived "fully, deeply, [and] in its totality."[27] "[E]xterior

---

20. Dunois; in Pernoud, *Herself and Her Witnesses*, 110.

21. Jehanne was known to retreat from battle intermittently in order to pray. Dunois; in Pernoud, *Retrial*, 139.

22. Heschel, *Prophets: II*, 215.

23. Nicolas Caval, Rouen assessor, noted the "considerable wisdom" of Jehanne's responses during the condemnation trial and her "very good memory," stating that "people were astonished" by these. Caval; in Pernoud, *Retrial*, 260–61.

24. Jehanne; in Scott, *Trial*, 73.

25. Boisguillaume, trial notary; in Pernoud, *Retrial*, 220.

26. Cagny; in Pernoud, *Herself and Her Witnesses*, 120.

27. Merton, *Christian Mysticism*, 16.

acts" must correspond to "interior intentions."[28] For Watts, "the meaning which saint and mystic express in idea and action is God. They think and act as they do because they are ... possessed by this life which is God.... God is pure life," he asserts, "and we are terrified ... because we cannot hold it or possess it, and we do not know what it will do to us."[29] "Mystical love for God holds together both what causes us to tremble in fright and what never ceases to fascinate us," explains Soelle,[30] while Kierkegaard maintains that "the expression of wonder is worship. And wonder is an ambiguous state of mind which comprises fear and bliss. Worship therefore is mingled fear and bliss all at once. Even the most refined and rational worship of God is blissfulness in fear and trembling, confidence in the face of mortal danger."[31] Jehanne loved and feared God[32] much in the manner of the following Kierkegaardian description:

> [W]as it not fearful ... that the object sought was so near thee that thou wast not seeking God but God was seeking thee; was it not fearful that thou couldst not move without being in Him, and not be so unobserved but, lo, thou wast in Him, ... nor say to Him, "Only an instant," seeing that He also was in the instant when thou didst say this; was it not fearful when the playfulness of youth and the immaturity of despair became seriousness at the instant when that which thou didst once point at and aspire after ... then came into existence, yea, was in existence everywhere about thee and embraced thee on every hand! But was it not blissful that the hand of the mighty [lowercase "m" suggests human, not divine, power] could block thee up in the darkest hole and yet not shut out God; was it not blissful that thou couldst fall into the deepest abyss where one can see neither sun nor stars and yet can see God; was it not blissful that thou couldst go astray in the solitary wilderness and yet at once find the way to God.... But he who leaves out fear, let him look well to it that he does not also leave out the finding.[33]

The passage parallels the persistence of Jehanne's divine counsel despite initial fear and hesitation on her part; they advised "her two or three

28. Merton, *Peace in the Post-Christian Era*, 133.
29. Watts, *Behold the Spirit*, 12, 57.
30. Soelle, *Silent Cry*, 127.
31. Kierkegaard, *Stages*, 458.
32. Multiple witnesses described Jehanne as God-fearing.
33. Kierkegaard, *Stages*, 462.

times a week that she must leave and go into France" and "that she must hurry."³⁴ Also, Jehanne abandoned youthful play, adopting a more serious nature, upon receiving divine revelation. "She . . . said that ever since she learned that she must come into France, she played very little, the least that she could."³⁵ Moreover, Jehanne never lost sight of God while suffering the torments of imprisonment or when led astray by the abjuration, nor finally throughout her martyrdom. It was the light of God that sustained her as she frequently received comfort from her divine counsel.³⁶ As Kierkegaard suggests that one does not effectively seek but is sought by God, Weil asserts that "[a]ctive searching" leads one away from the divine, whereas "waiting" for God in an attentive and consenting manner draws God to an individual who longs for God while renouncing all else. One "should do nothing but wait for the good and keep evil away," she advises.³⁷ Heschel remarks that "biblical religion" is characterized by "an awareness of a God who helps, demands, and calls upon man. It is a sense of being reached, being found, being sought after; a sense of being pursued."³⁸ Jehanne was attentive to God and claimed clearly to have been approached, called, pursued, and supported by the divine.

Mystical life requires courage in encountering God and the world. To be courageous is not to be devoid of fear but to confront fear and refuse to be immobilized by it. Courage cannot arise from an absence of fear and need not eliminate it. Where there is no fear, there is no possibility of courage, which is not to say that fearlessness does not have its own merit; perhaps it transcends fear and courage. At any rate, despite her fear of death by fire, Jehanne ultimately accepted it over the alternative of denying God. Her death, like her life, was marked by courage.

Mysticism as Involvement with the World

Jehanne practiced mysticism as a way of life, a way of involvement with the world. That is what the term "practical mysticism" refers to in this work, to fully living one's mysticism in the world, allowing mystical

---

34. Jehanne; in Scott, *Trial*, 67.
35. Ibid., 75.
36. Ibid., 103, 112, 121, 140–41, 152.
37. Weil, *Waiting for God*, 126–28.
38. Heschel, *Prophets: II*, 220.

experience and mystical consciousness to inform every aspect of one's life as the foremost impetus for thought and action. Jehanne embodied and exemplified practical mysticism, consistently applying her mystical sense to her activities, translating mystical experience and consciousness into divine servantship in the world. Even when she defied her divine counsel in leaping from a tower, Jehanne retained her mystical sensibility, commending herself to God in jumping and seeking divine forgiveness afterward.[39] Practical mysticism extends beyond the personal into the public realm; nonetheless, while mystics keep company with God in the world, mysticism is an ultimately solitary endeavor with respect to human relationships as it calls one to individual choice, responsibility, commitment, and endurance in living one's faith. Kierkegaard captures the solitary nature of mystical faith: "[T]he true wonder and the true fear one man cannot teach the other. Only when they constrict and expand the soul, thine, precisely thine, thine alone in the whole world, because thou art alone with the Omnipresent, only then do they truly exist for thee."[40]

Soelle views mysticism as "love for God" that is inconceivable "without political and praxis-oriented actualization . . . directed toward the world. . . . [N]o experience of God," she declares, "can be so privatized that it becomes and remains the property of one owner." Mystics, she holds, can relate to the world in a manner ranging from "withdrawal" to "transformation of the world through revolution." Whether practicing "renunciation, disagreement, divergence, dissent, reform, resistance, rebellion, or revolution," the mystic voices a distinct "No! to the world as it exists now. . . . For those who want the world to remain as it is have . . . betrayed the love of God and its restlessness before the status quo."[41] Jehanne's mystical life of action in the world proclaimed a powerful "No!" to foreign occupation and rule in France, to unjust warfare, to social stereotyping, to patriarchy, and to ecclesiastical interference with individual spiritual discernment. Soelle points out that mysticism, being available to all, stands as "the antiauthoritarian religion" against "power and dominance over" others. The mystical element of religion, she explains, "directs itself to the will and the action of love."[42]

39. Jehanne; in Scott, *Trial*, 111–12.
40. Kierkegaard, *Stages*, 463.
41. Soelle, *Silent Cry*, 2–4.
42. Ibid., 1, 36, 46.

The Theology of Jehanne d'Arc

Jehanne's mysticism contradicts the notion prevalent in some forms of mysticism that love of creature and involvement with the world must be transcended in order for a soul to advance toward God. Saint Teresa refers to "the nothingness of all things" and "the vanity of the world"[43] and speaks of such a strong desire to be with God alone that it produces detachment "from creatures" and "contempt for the world" along with a death wish mitigated only by God's desire that she continue to live.[44] She describes a type of mystical experience wherein "the whole world and its affairs give it [the soul] pain, and no created thing provides it with company, nor does it want any company but only the Creator; and it sees that having such company is impossible unless it dies."[45] Jehanne displayed love for others in all forms of activity in which she engaged in the world, including war, as an essential element of serving and loving God, and there is no evidence or reason to suppose that she was further from God than any other saint or mystic. For her, love of others and loving participation in the world were aspects of, not substitutes for, loving God. Jehanne demonstrated that such active love can prevent excesses of human violence and can serve toward mitigating, if not eradicating, human evil.

Jehanne refused to love evil and recognized the necessity of actively opposing it, even if such necessity demands employing it with restraint, conscience, responsibility, accountability, and compassion in order ultimately to defeat it. One must distinguish between loving an evildoer and loving evil itself whereby one might love an individual who commits an evil deed while refusing to love the deed. "By loving our neighbor," Weil maintains, "we imitate the divine love which created us and all our fellows. By loving the order of the world we imitate the divine love which created this universe of which we are a part."[46]

Jehanne demonstrated neither affinity for nor desensitization to violence or suffering but was deeply disturbed by these. She was "greatly distressed by such slaughter" of the English in the battle for Beaugency and, on witnessing an English prisoner being struck on the head and left for dead, she "dismounted [her horse] and received the Englishman's

---

43. Teresa of Avila, *Collected Works*, vol. 1, 63.
44. Ibid., vol. 2, 425–26.
45. Ibid., vol. 1, 429.
46. Weil, *Waiting for God*, 99.

confession, raising his head and comforting him as much as she could."[47] Soelle maintains that "resistance ... against becoming habituated to death" constitutes an aspect of the mystic's relationship to the world.[48] Jehanne was not a bloodthirsty warrior who willed the destruction of human life, not even that of the enemy, but she recognized the loss of some life as an inevitability of defensive war motivated toward the establishment of peace. Jehanne assured the dauphin that, "in God's name," she would bring him into the city of Troyes "by love or by strength and force,"[49] implying a preference for love over battle, the latter to be employed as a final resort should the enemy refuse to act in accordance with love.

Knowledge of God and Divine Mystery

In order to know and love God, Watts advises, one must relinquish all attempts to possess God. In mysticism, one allows oneself, in the manner of passive action, to "be possessed *by* God. . . . This is why there is no method, no formal technique, for attaining the mystical state and realizing union with God. For a method is an attempt to possess, and has its origin in pride and fear."[50]

Jehanne presumed very little about God and based her knowledge of divinity upon that which God revealed to her and religious instruction received as a child. She recounted her revelations without embellishment and did not claim elaborate understanding of God or divine motives, refusing to place restrictions on divinity, including restrictions implied by religious dogma or structure. When questioned regarding the ability of her divine counsel to speak given Jehanne's uncertainty as to whether or not they were fully embodied, she replied simply, "I leave that to God." Asked why God chose her above others to fight for the kingdom of France, she responded that it "pleased God so to do."[51] When Jehanne's assessors insisted that she submit to the Church Militant, she replied, "I submit myself to God who sent me, to the Blessed Mary and to all the saints of heaven. And it seems to me that God and the Church

---

47. Louis de Coutes, Jehanne's page; in Pernoud, *Retrial*, 179.
48. Soelle, *Silent Cry*, 4.
49. Jehanne; quoted by Dunois, in Taylor, *La Pucelle*, 283.
50. Watts, *Behold the Spirit*, 16–17, 93.
51. Jehanne; in Scott, *Trial*, 110.

The Theology of Jehanne d'Arc

are one, and no difficulty should be made about this. Why do you make difficulties about this?"[52] Asked if God hated the English, she answered that, "as to the love or hate that God has for the English, or what He would do for their souls, she knows nothing; but she is well assured that they will be driven out of France, except those who die there; and that God will send the French victory over the English." Asked if God supported the English when they were victorious in France, she responded "that she did not know whether God hated the French."[53]

Jehanne acknowledged and respected divine autonomy and mystery, making no attempt to define God but holding herself open to divine revelation at all times. She did not promote a particular doctrine of God but declared what she understood to be the will of God for her as conveyed through her divine counsel. Watts deems such behavior authentically mystical. He states, "[F]rom my present point of view, all doctrines of God—including atheism—are ultimately false and idolatrous, because doctrines are forms of words which can never be more than pointers to mystical vision, and not by any means the best pointers."[54] Soelle maintains that "[e]very idea we have of God fails God. Indeed, each idea produces a false familiarity with the divine."[55] Heschel agrees that objectification of God equates to falsification.[56] Jehanne's approach to divine mystery corresponds to prophetic perceptions of God. The prophet, Heschel explains, abstained "from any claim to comprehend God's *essence*, His inmost being, or even to apprehend His inscrutable thoughts, unrelated to history"; rather, the prophet insisted "upon the ability to understand His presence, expression or manifestation. The prophets experience what He *utters*, not what He *is*."[57] Kierkegaard adds that an individual whom "God appoints . . . to have divine authority" has such authority only "in relation to what was entrusted to him"[58] or her. Jehanne apparently recognized this and did not obscure the boundary

---

52. Jehanne; in Taylor, *La Pucelle*, 197.

53. Jehanne; in Scott, *Trial*, 123. This challenges Jane Marie Pinzino's thesis that Jehanne viewed the French as a people chosen by God like the Israelites. Pinzino, "Just War, Joan of Arc," 390–91.

54. Watts, *Behold the Spirit*, xviii.

55. Soelle, *Silent Cry*, 37.

56. Heschel, *Prophets: II*, 266.

57. Ibid., 264.

58. Kierkegaard, *Authority and Revelation*, 112.

between that which God elected her to do and that which she did of her own accord, between divinely revealed knowledge and knowledge otherwise acquired. In other words, she did not present herself as possessing divine authority in all matters, but only within a limited sphere.

The idea of union with the divine forms the essence of many, if not all, mystical formulations. To our knowledge, Jehanne did not employ mystical language; however, neither did she compose mystical treatises. While she is not known to have spoken of "union with God," Jehanne apparently lived it. Her active solidarity with God constituted union in the living of her life sacramentally, as a visible sign of invisible grace. Jehanne's will became united with divine will as she discerned it. The fact that she frequently took Communion with great devotion also indicates a desire for union with God through the Eucharistic sacrament. Alençon reported that Jehanne received the Eucharist twice weekly, often weeping at the sight of it.[59] Her confessor stated that "she confessed almost every day, and often took Communion."[60] Moreover, Jehanne declared that the only reward she sought through her divine counsel was "salvation of her soul."[61] Concern for her soul's salvation might be understood as desire for reciprocal love between herself and God, presuming that a soul's damnation would result from failure to love God adequately, constituting rejection of God's love. Salvation of the soul might thus be viewed as resulting from full participation in right-loving relationship with God. On this view, the desire for salvation is desire to be united in love with God. "[U]nity means love," states Heschel.[62] Accordingly, Watts notes that one who "discerns the activity of a living Spirit" understands salvation as complete "union with and acceptance of this mysterious Spirit."[63]

Salvation does not necessarily ensure freedom from suffering or from imminent death. In fact, salvation might not be the most appropriate or encompassing term to express the nature of divine action or intention toward humanity. Perhaps love is the most appropriate word to express this. Love does not ensure freedom from pain; the value of love resides in its own essence, which is independent of, if potentially present within, all human experience, including suffering. Of course, salvation

---

59. Alençon; in Pernoud, *Retrial*, 160.
60. Jean Pasquerel, Jehanne's confessor; in Pernoud, *Retrial*, 184.
61. Jehanne; in Scott, *Trial*, 69, 124.
62. Heschel, *Prophets: II*, 264.
63. Watts, *Behold the Spirit*, 127.

can be understood as referring exclusively to the soul, but this does not speak to divine presence or activity amid physical or emotional suffering, whereas love does. Love is conceivably the operative divine salvific principle in all human experience, including salvation of the soul. Let this be our working definition of salvation then, salvation as unity in right-loving relationship of an individual soul with the divine.

Watts holds that to seek for God implies that God is not already with us whereas "the indwelling Holy Spirit" resides within individuals perpetually, constituting the "gift of union with God." Hence, one does not "*attain* union with God; it is already given as an act of divine love."[64] Nonetheless, this gift can be rejected by an individual, the union broken. Niels Christian Hvidt asserts that "God through the prophet seeks . . . to lead" humans back to "original union with God."[65] This seems compatible with Jehanne's mysticism in that she did not apparently seek God by some method but understood God to be present and accessible always (even if not always clearly responsive) through prayer, the sacraments, and the Mass. Even when deprived of the sacraments, Mass, and prayerful solitude during imprisonment, Jehanne repeatedly encountered and responded to divine presence.[66] "God gives his life . . . in symbols and sacraments, but if that life is to be truly lively, it will not stay confined in those forms or in any others. It will use forms; it will express itself in forms; but it will not be held in forms," asserts Watts.[67] Accordingly, Jehanne declared that, even if her judges denied her permission to hear Mass, God had the "power to let her hear it without them, whenever it so pleased Him." She also stated "that Saint Catherine and Saint Margaret gladly heard her confession, each in turn."[68]

The darkness that mystics encounter in the experience of union with God must be noted. Watts cites as a requirement of the mystical life "sufficient faith" to enter an unknown realm experienced as "empty, arid and terrifying, an unaccustomed territory where all familiar landmarks

---

64. Ibid., 18, 76.

65. Hvidt, *Christian Prophecy*, 125.

66. While imprisoned at Rouen, Jehanne was denied the Eucharistic and confessional sacraments until the morning of her death. Ladvenu; in Pernoud, *Retrial*, 243. Jehanne; in Taylor, *La Pucelle*, 139, 180–81, 204–5. Massieu; in Taylor, *La Pucelle*, 335–36. Jehanne also requested to hear Mass while imprisoned but this, too, was denied. Jehanne; in Taylor, *La Pucelle*, 193–94, 197, 204–5.

67. Watts, *Behold the Spirit*, 56.

68. Jehanne; in Scott, *Trial*, 88, 135.

are left behind ... wherein one experiences bitter desolation and comes close to absolute despair." The experience frequently "involves temptations against faith."[69] The teachings of John of the Cross, who wrote a treatise on this "dark night of the soul" (frequently referred to simply as "the dark night"), are pivotal. He describes the soul's journey toward perfection in its "union with God through love," to the extent that such perfection is possible within the constraints of temporal life. According to John, the process by which a soul strives toward perfection consists in "two kinds of spiritual purgation: one, a purification of the sensory part; the other, a purification of the spiritual part." This process of purgation entails "affliction and torment" as well as illumination. He describes the night of sense as "a privation and purgation of all sensible appetites for the external things of the world, the delights of the flesh, and the gratifications of the will." Only by stilling the appetites, he explains, is one released from the pain caused by them. In aridity, the soul moves "with purity in the love of God" since its actions are no longer influenced by pleasure but by the desire to please God alone. The night of spirit, experienced as divine light or wisdom, is dark and painful because divine wisdom so greatly exceeds the soul's capacity to apprehend it that it overwhelms the soul and the intellect such that they become clouded or darkened. The soul "becomes a battlefield" for the conflict between its natural weakness and the infusion of divinity. Moreover, pain derives from the soul's recognition of its impurity revealed in contrast to the divine light.[70]

Jehanne underwent darkness characteristic of the dark night of the soul, leaving everything familiar including her home, family, friends, and traditional social roles, venturing into completely unknown roles and territories amid strangers and extreme dangers. Soelle speaks of "what ancient mysticism called 'being apart,' which is living out concretely one's farewell to the customs and norms of one's culture."[71] Jehanne exemplified this in adopting male attire and accepting a traditionally masculine role as military commander and knight, subjecting herself to much ridicule and scorn. It is little wonder that she preferred to remain in Domremy with her mother.[72] Darkness also descended upon

69. Watts, *Behold the Spirit*, 89–90.
70. John of the Cross, *Collected Works*, 74, 295, 326, 335–36.
71. Soelle, *Silent Cry*, 92.
72. Jean de Metz or de Nouillonpont, squire; in Pernoud, *Retrial*, 96.

Jehanne in the wake of Charles VII's coronation with the emergence of his contrary behavior toward her and her campaign, compounded with her first military defeat. Plunged further into darkness by foreknowledge of her captivity, the distress was intensified by her capture, imprisonment, failed escape attempts, corrupt trial, abjuration, recantation, and martyrdom. Jehanne's tribulations went from exceptionally difficult to extraordinarily difficult to unimaginably so. We have little to no record of how she felt throughout most of this, but we have enough to know that she suffered immensely and maintained her love of God, it being the means through which she endured martyrdom.

It seems that Jehanne's pledge of virginity to God reflected an instinctive understanding of and willingness to submit to the mystical process of sensory purgation since she pledged it on the occasion of her first divine visitation,[73] prior to learning of her mission and how virginity would serve it. Moreover, despite the intense activity and physical demands of military life, she consumed very little, being "moderate in eating and drinking" and "very abstemious," often eating "no more than a hunk of bread all day." She fasted most Fridays.[74] Jehanne sought neither fame nor personal glory and accorded all credit for her army's victories to God.[75] Regarding the matter of individuals kissing her hands, feet, and garments, she stated that "[m]any people gladly came to see" her but "kissed her clothing as little as she could help. But she said that the poor gladly came to her, because she did them no unkindness, but upheld and helped them as much as she could."[76] She earnestly attempted "to prevent the people from honoring and glorifying her"[77] and was "very upset and most displeased when some good women came to greet her and showed her signs of adoration."[78] "I would not know how to protect myself from such things," she declared, "if God does not protect me."[79]

---

73. Jehanne; in Scott, *Trial*, 104.

74. Raoul de Gaucourt, Grand Master of Charles VII's household; in Pernoud, *Retrial*, 117. Coutes; ibid., 177. Pasquerel; ibid., 188.

75. Jacques l'Esbahy, burgher and citizen of Orléans; ibid., 149. Seguin Seguin, professor of theology, Dean of the Faculty of Poitiers, Dominican friar, and one of the Poitiers examiners; ibid., 113.

76. Jehanne; in Scott, *Trial*, 94.

77. Esbahy; in Pernoud, *Retrial*, 149.

78. Simon Beaucroix, companion-at-arms to Jehanne; ibid., 121.

79. Jehanne; quoted by Barbin, in Taylor, *La Pucelle*, 303–4.

Jehanne requested "nothing from her king except good arms, good horses, and money to pay the people of her household. . . . [W]hat she had was her king's."[80] Squire Jean de Metz frequently gave her money which she, in turn, gave to others.[81] Moreover, there is no evidence or reason to suspect that Jehanne sought earthly privilege through her divine counsel but only advice and reassurance.[82] Such behaviors constitute an apparent inclination toward sensory purgation on Jehanne's part. That the process went beyond that which she desired is doubtless as she did not wish to be captured, although she consented to it in submission to divine will, resolving that, "seeing it so pleased Our Lord, it was best that she should have been captured."[83] The humiliations and hardships of captivity worked further sensory purgation in Jehanne, and her martyrdom effected the ultimate purgation of sense. One should note that the purgatory process does not suggest suffering inflicted by God but that pain is inevitable in the experience of a human soul drawing nearer to divinity.

Pertaining to Saint John's night of spirit, Jehanne's natural fear of imprisonment might be considered her "natural weakness" in contrast to the divine wisdom (exceeding human comprehension) that deemed her capture necessary.[84] The disturbing foreknowledge of her capture created a "battlefield" where conflict between Jehanne's natural weakness and the infusion of divinity took place. Nonetheless, Jehanne expressed an intense desire to serve God and lived and died by it. "[I]t is precisely the ability to stand above all personal dispositions, inclinations, and vested interests that marks the essence of prophetic consciousness," notes Heschel,[85] a consciousness with which Jehanne was abundantly endowed.

---

80. Jehanne; in Scott, *Trial*, 101. Although Jehanne requested nothing for herself personally from her king, she requested a tax exemption for the inhabitants of Domremy and neighboring Greux in recognition of her military services. In Pernoud and Clin, *Her Story*, 230–31.

81. Metz; in Taylor, *La Pucelle*, 273.

82. Jehanne; in Scott, *Trial*, 72.

83. Ibid., 103.

84. Jehanne; in Taylor, *La Pucelle*, 175–76.

85. Heschel, *Prophets: II*, 187–88.

The Prophetic as Mystical Calling

If they believe that I am sent from God, they are not deceived.
—Jehanne d'Arc, *Trial of Joan of Arc*

Jehanne was a practical mystic in that she applied her divine revelations to her actions in the world, but what of the prophetic element of her mysticism? In exploring the realm of prophecy, let us note that the prophetic relates to a particular type of divine calling founded in divine revelation. Liminal in nature, revelation is a threshold experience wherein boundaries are obscured and traversed. The Greek word, λιμήν,[86] meaning "harbor," suggests shelter as well as a place of possibility; it represents a meeting of worlds where exchange and communication can occur but also signifies a place of vulnerability to attack. This is the place of revelation where divine and human realms meet, where one stands in vulnerability and infinite possibility. It is the place of the prophet.

It is clear that revelation requires a witness or recipient since, without one, nothing is revealed. In the absence of witness, one might speak of occurrence or event, but not of revelation. According to Saint Teresa, God longs to reveal God's Self, but one must be willing to look at God in order for revelation to occur. "He is not waiting for anything else . . . than that we look at Him."[87] This resonates with Jehanne's experience as she, whose attention was always directed toward God, claimed to have seen angels frequently among individuals who did not see them.[88] While not requisite for the occurrence of revelation, recognition and comprehension are necessary to effective receipt of revelation, without which revelation might occur but remain ineffectual. One must recognize God in God's act of revelation in order that the divine message be understood. Herbert Vorgrimler agrees that individuals can be "blind to" or "misinterpret" God's presence, thereby interfering with its operation.[89]

While the mystic is a recipient of divine revelation and all prophets are necessarily mystics, not all mystics are prophets. According to Heschel, prophets receive revelation of the divine will, not the divine

---

86. "Limen" in English.
87. Teresa of Avila, *Collected Works*, vol. 2, 134.
88. Jehanne; in Taylor, *La Pucelle*, 180.
89. Vorgrimler, *Sacramental Theology*, 8.

self. Moreover, "[p]rophecy arises not from any sudden, spontaneous feeling awakened by an indeterminate, silent, and numinous image, but from an experience of inspiration which has its source in the revelation of a divine pathos."[90] The prophetic message is not solely for the prophet but is directed primarily toward others to whom the prophet "is sent with a mandate."[91] The prophet must not only deliver the message but "exercise authority."[92] "As a messenger," the prophet's "task is to deliver the [divine] word; as a witness, he must bear testimony that the word is divine."[93] In Merton's language, "[t]he prophet suffers inspiration, or vision. He shoulders the 'burden' of vision that God lays upon him. He bows under the truth and the judgments of God."[94] The prophet lives in "perpetual awareness of being perceived, apprehended, [and] noted by God."[95] Jehanne lived in such awareness and greatly feared erring, expressing deep concern over the possibility of displeasing her divine counsel.[96] "If a man is to understand his sin essentially," maintains Kierkegaard, "he must understand it because he remains alone . . . with the Holy One who knows all things. Only this fear and trembling is the true sort, only the sorrow which the remembrance of God awakens in a man, only the repentance His love fosters."[97] Merton describes the prophet as "one who lives in direct submission to the Holy Spirit in order that, by his life, actions and words, he may at all times be a sign of God in the world. . . . [The prophets'] submission to God is not merely a matter of charismatic accident but of perfect fidelity to grace. The prophet is a man of God . . . in the sense that he is consciously and freely obedient to the Holy Spirit, no matter what the price may be."[98] Jehanne, he observes, had "one of the most extraordinary charismatic missions of all time."[99] Heschel notes that it is not the fact that the prophet is "affected" that is

---

90. Heschel, *Prophets: II*, 265, 267.

91. Rahner, "Prophetism," in *Encyclopedia of Theology*, 1286–87.

92. Kierkegaard, *Authority and Revelation*, 118. Kierkegaard employs the term "apostle" rather than "prophet."

93. Heschel, *Prophets: Introduction*, 22.

94. Merton, *Disputed Questions*, 222.

95. Heschel, *Prophets: II*, 263.

96. Jehanne; in Taylor, *La Pucelle*, 147.

97. Kierkegaard, *Stages*, 464.

98. Merton, *Disputed Questions*, 223–24.

99. Merton, *Christian Mysticism*, 195.

paramount, "but the fact of his having received a power to affect others. . . . His sense of election and personal endowment is overshadowed by his sense of a history-shaping power."[100]

The prophet is a bearer of revelation, but Karl Rahner holds that forms of revelation vary significantly "according to the phase of the history of salvation in which the visionary lives and which he is intended to influence."[101] "The prominent theme" of the prophetic message "is exhortation, not mere prediction," explains Heschel. Although predictive accuracy is significant in establishing a "prophet's authority . . . , his essential task is to declare the word of God to the here and now; to disclose the future in order to illumine what is involved in the present."[102] Rahner adds that prophetic messages are not merely "doctrinal propositions but are to be translated into real action," which often renders the prophet a "leader and organizer of religious and social changes."[103] In fact, Walter Brueggemann holds that the "prophetic task" within an unjust social system "is to maintain a destabilizing presence." Prophetic destabilization "takes as its responsibility" the endeavor to oppose "forces of stabilization that are at work among the participants and benefactors of the [existing] social system,"[104] in Jehanne's case, the pro-English forces in France. The prophet exposes "false claimants to power who must be delegitimated." Prophets are motivated by the vision of "an alternative . . . social reality that they insist is true. . . . The contrast," notes Brueggemann, "may be between the rule of God who liberates and the rule of idols that enslave."[105] Heschel maintains that the prophet "is incapable of isolating the world" as there "is an interaction between [hu]man and God which to disregard is an act of insolence."[106] Hence, the prophet receives revelation and contributes to its fulfillment through prophesying and cooperating with the divine directives received. Anyone claiming divine sanction of his or her social activities ought to display characteristics of practical, prophetic mysticism in order to be considered credible—at least within Jewish and

---

100. Heschel, *Prophets: Introduction*, 21.
101. Rahner, *Inquiries*, 97.
102. Heschel, *Prophets: Introduction*, 12.
103. Rahner, "Prophetism," in *Encyclopedia of Theology*, 1287.
104. Brueggemann, "Destabilizing Presence," 223.
105. Ibid., 223–24, 238.
106. Heschel, *Prophets: Introduction*, 16.

Christian contexts—since the truly prophetic mission is synonymous with the legitimate claim to divinely sanctioned social activity.

Jehanne was a practical, prophetic mystic; she was a leader of social change based on her claim to divine revelation, which she openly and persistently proclaimed and devoutly obeyed. Like others who underwent a name change representative of divine calling,[107] "Jehannette" became "Jehanne *la pucelle*" upon leaving Domremy to embark on her divine mission.[108] Jehanne's "prophetic character," Pernoud and Marie-Véronique Clin observe, was born of her conviction that she clearly and precisely communicated a divine message without alteration.[109] Indeed, she reiterated her message clearly and consistently, even in her final moments.[110]

According to biblical tradition, prophetic revelation can occur while the visionary is dreaming or in an ecstatic state and manifests as voices and visions wherein God communicates via pictures, symbols, or angels.[111] Jehanne's revelations were communicated via visions and auditions and, although her divine counsel frequently appeared while she was awake, such as when the first voice addressed her in her father's garden,[112] they also communicated with her during sleep. At Orléans, Jehanne leapt from her bed in immediate response to a revelation directing her to attack the English.[113] She also testified that a divine voice awakened her during imprisonment and, although the voice spoke while she slept, she did not comprehend it until she awoke.[114]

Interpretation of Scripture is also linked to revelation. As a source of divine guidance, however, revelation in the form of direct, personal instruction is potentially more specific and detailed than that derived from Scripture. Perhaps it is also more powerful. Rahner emphasizes the relative clarity and specificity of private revelation over the generality and ambiguity of more generally available information in discerning

---

107. In biblical tradition Abram became Abraham, Sarai became Sarah, and Simon became Peter. Gen 17:4–5, 15; John 1:42.

108. Jehanne; in Scott, *Trial*, 64.

109. Pernoud and Clin, *Her Story*, 164.

110. Ladvenu; in Pernoud, *Retrial*, 249.

111. Rahner, *Inquiries*, 97.

112. Jehanne; in Taylor, *La Pucelle*, 141.

113. Aulon; in Pernoud, *Retrial*, 166.

114. Jehanne; in Taylor, *La Pucelle*, 146.

divine will in a given situation. "[P]ost-apostolic, private revelations," he asserts, constitute "imperatives" for action within the context of particular, "concrete historical situation[s]. . . . Because what God wishes to be done in certain given circumstances cannot be logically and unequivocally deduced from the general principles of dogma and morals, even with the help of an analysis of the given situation." Although "theoretical considerations may delimit the sphere of the correct and appropriate human action," they cannot determine "which of the various decisions within this sphere is in fact the one God wills at this moment, and how this one can be found. An opposite view would wrongly reduce the concrete and unpredictable character of free human action to universal patterns, and would degrade individual, spiritual reality to a mere instance of universal law."[115] In the absence of clear, divine directives such as those provided via prophetic revelation, moral discernment and moral action within specific social contexts, particularly those which are very complex, can be difficult and precarious.

Divine revelation affords us possible insight into the nature and will of God, but how might one recognize it and what constitutes sufficiently compelling evidence of divine revelation? As stated, "[I]t is not enough that someone claims purely and simply to be sent from God—this is the claim of all heretics—but it is necessary that he proves this."[116] Rahner holds that supposedly revelatory visions, if not substantiated by a mystical grace referred to as "infused contemplation," must be authenticated by an "external miracle," without which they cannot command assent from others.[117] He further states that the quality of humility in a visionary lends credence to supposed revelation.

---

115. Rahner, *Inquiries*, 108–9.

116. *De bono et malo spiritu*, written anonymously by a member of the University of Paris in September, 1429; in Taylor, *La Pucelle*, 126.

117. Rahner, *Inquiries*, 141–42, 162–64. Infused contemplation is generally understood as mystical experience wherein, without initiative on the part of a consenting recipient, God bypasses the bodily senses and acts directly upon a human soul to effect union with it. R. P. Aug. Poulain describes infused contemplation (also referred to as *"mystic union," "mystical . . . contemplation,"* or *"passive, extraordinary, or eminent"* contemplation) as a grace "of union with God" wherein "*God Himself*, and God alone, . . . manifests Himself" to an individual without the involvement of external objects. Poulain, *Graces of Interior Prayer*, 52–53, 60. Rahner describes the miraculous as "divine intervention which partly suspends the laws of nature." Rahner, *Inquiries*, 127. Saint Thomas Aquinas defines miracles as "all things that can be done supernaturally" by divine cause and, "just as the prophet's mind is moved by divine inspiration to know

> [Humility does] not so much imply a normal piety, veracity, modesty, discretion, etc., existing independently of the vision ... as a decisive transformation, a religious deepening of the person that comes with the experience and endures. This, for the investigator [of visions], is much readier and simpler evidence that the ... experience was accompanied by God's interior work of grace in the depths of the spirit, than any psychological description by the seer of his own vision.[118]

Hvidt cites the production of "good fruit" as an important criterion of "authentic prophecy." Obedience and strength, he adds, follow humility in the hierarchy of visionary qualities affirming revelation.[119]

In Jehanne, one observes qualities suggestive of infused grace. She was uncannily adept at military strategy, possessing all the skills of a military captain without ever acquiring them through formal training. Normally, a knight underwent "rigorous apprenticeship," receiving both military and moral instruction,[120] but Jehanne was appointed commander of war immediately upon gaining ecclesiastical approval. She "was very simple in all her actions," one witness remarked, "except in the conduct of war, in which she was altogether an expert."[121] Another testified that, "in the leading and drawing up of armies and in the conduct of war, in disposing an army for battle and haranguing the soldiers, she behaved like the most experienced captain in all the world, like one with a whole lifetime of experience."[122] Jehanne reportedly "took more admirable precautions [at Troyes] than two or three more experienced or famous" captains "would have done."[123] "I have seen her ride a horse and wield a lance as well as the finest soldier, and the soldiers themselves were most astonished by this," stated Marguerite La Touroulde.[124] Alençon observed that Jehanne was particularly adept at the strategic

---

something supernaturally, so too is it possible for the mind of the miracle worker to be moved to do something resulting in the miraculous effect which God causes by His power." Aquinas, *Summa Theologica*, vol. 2, q. 178, a. 1, 1924.

118. Rahner, *Inquiries*, 143–44.
119. Hvidt, *Christian Prophecy*, 129, 292–93.
120. Fraioli, *Hundred Years War*, 29–30.
121. S. Charles; in Pernoud, *Retrial*, 108.
122. Thibault d'Armagnac or de Termes, companion-at-arms to Jehanne; ibid., 121.
123. Dunois; in Taylor, *La Pucelle*, 283. Taylor employs the term "warlords" rather than "captains."
124. Touroulde, Jehanne's hostess at Bourges; in Pernoud, *Retrial*, 125.

placement of artillery.[125] Moreover, it was noted that she bore "the weight and burden of armour [weighing sixty pounds] incredibly well, to such a point that she . . . remained fully armed during six days and nights."[126] These are not small matters in light of the extensive training and experience normally required to accomplish many of the feats that Jehanne achieved apparently naturally—or supernaturally. It was also considered remarkable that the siege of Orléans was raised in three days under her efforts whereas such a task would ordinarily have taken over a month.[127] Jehanne also demonstrated great wisdom in response to interrogation. Jean Barbin, Royal Advocate in the Parlement of Poitiers and later Paris, testified that doctors of law and theology who examined Jehanne at Poitiers considered the wisdom of her replies evidence of "divine inspiration," given that she was uneducated.[128] With respect to the Rouen trial, Massieu expressed surprise at the effectiveness of Jehanne's responses to complex, difficult, "subtle and tricky questions," questions to which la Pierre indicated "the great clerics and learned people present would have found it hard to reply."[129] Moreover, before she was able to address a question, another examiner frequently introduced a second question so that "she was often hurried and troubled in her answers."[130] Manchon resolved that, given Jehanne's fatigue from relentless hours of examination, she "could not have defended herself before such great Doctors had she not been inspired," and Jehanne herself reported that Saints Catherine and Margaret counseled her with respect to how she ought to respond throughout the trial.[131] Margolis notes that Jehanne's "adamantly evasive and sometimes flippant answers rendered ridiculous" some of the questions asked of her, "making the judges, who sought to discredit her as a diabolical lunatic, look like infidels."[132] It is conceivable that Jehanne's multiplicity of uncanny abilities derived from an infusion of grace.

---

125. Alençon; in Pernoud, *Retrial*, 160–61.

126. Boulainvilliers, letter to the Duke of Milan; in Pernoud from Quicherat, v. 5, 114–21, *Herself and Her Witnesses*, 98–99.

127. Dupuy, *Collectarium historiarum*; in Taylor, *La Pucelle*, 90.

128. Barbin; ibid., 303.

129. Massieu; in Pernoud, *Retrial*, 217. La Pierre; in Murray, *Jeanne d'Arc*, 160.

130. Massieu; in Murray, *Jeanne d'Arc*, 171.

131. Manchon; ibid., 179–80. Jehanne; in Taylor, *La Pucelle*, 152.

132. Margolis, "Mortal Body," 16.

"[I]t was all for Our Lord," Jehanne declared.[133] Let us examine more closely the quality of humility in visionaries. Merton describes humility as "an emptiness of heart in which self-assertion has no place." One who "is not empty and undivided in his own inmost soul ... will be nothing more than an individualist. And in that case, his non-conformity is nothing but an act of rebellion: the substitution of idols and illusions of his own choosing for those chosen by society."[134] While Jehanne was certainly a non-conformist, she was neither an idolater nor an individualist in the sense described by Merton. Detachment and humility, according to Saint Teresa, go hand-in-hand since detachment involves "turning" from oneself as well as the world. One possessing these qualities, she maintains, "can easily go out and fight with all hell together and against the whole world and all its occasions of sin. Such a person has no fear of anyone. ... The only thing he fears is displeasing his God."[135] Jehanne, who fought fearlessly for the kingdom of France but feared displeasing God above all, demonstrated humility and detachment. She informed her Rouen assessors, "I am much more afraid of failing them [her divine messengers] by saying something that may displease these voices than I am of answering you."[136]

In fact, Jehanne displayed a healthy mixture of confidence and humility,[137] but her confidence derived from faith in God, not in herself, and she likewise exhorted others to "hope in God."[138] "[T]he courage of faith is the only humble courage," notes Kierkegaard.[139] While a healthy sense of national pride does not constitute arrogance (excessive pride), the English invasion of France and attempted usurpation of the French crown was commonly regarded as arrogant.[140] According to Saint Teresa,

---

133. Jehanne; in Scott, *Trial*, 125.

134. Merton, *Disputed Questions*, 184.

135. Teresa of Avila, *Collected Works*, vol. 2, 76–77.

136. Jehanne; in Taylor, *La Pucelle*, 147.

137. Confidence does not equate to arrogance, which opposes humility.

138. Jehanne; quoted by Jean Luillier, burgher of Orléans, in Murray, *Jeanne d'Arc*, 246. Jehanne repeatedly instructed her soldiers to place "all their confidence" in God. Coutes; in Murray, *Jeanne d'Arc*, 260.

139. Kierkegaard, *Fear and Trembling*, 87.

140. A French ballad of unknown authorship (ca. 1429) describes the English invaders as "too arrogant." *Ballade contre les Anglais*; in Taylor, *La Pucelle*, 85. A theologian wrote that God "humiliated the proud" by conquering the English through Jehanne. Dupuy, *Collectarium historiarum*; ibid., 90. Christine de Pizan wrote, "And so,

God will abandon a soul that has not attained genuine humility in order to teach it that "we have nothing we haven't received."[141] Humility, Weil maintains, involves "absolute acceptance of the possibility that everything natural in us should be destroyed."[142] Jehanne, as a contemporary observed, did not seek "her own interest with any guile" but exposed herself "to the supreme peril, in evidence of her faith."[143] Where self-interest predominates, one risks harming others whereas, as Soelle notes, "mystical power" seeks the empowerment of others.[144] "[A] person who has genuinely realized union with God is humble just because he sees no difference between himself and others," states Watts.[145] While Jehanne was lodged at the home of Touroulde, several women arrived at the house asking Jehanne to touch various religious objects, but she laughed and told Touroulde, "You touch them! They will be as good from your touch as from mine."[146] "[I]t is one thing to be admired," observes Kierkegaard, and "another to be a guiding star that saves the anguished."[147] Jehanne claimed to be "sent for the consolation of the poor and destitute."[148]

The Nature of Divine Revelation

While one can refer to a plethora of mystical treatises concerning various types of mystical experience and advising on the discernment of spirits, Saints Teresa and John are the main sources consulted in this work for descriptions of divine revelation deemed authentic by the Church. In fact, according to Hvidt, "mainstream prophetic theology" closely resembles Saint Teresa's theology in particular.[149] Teresa indicates that,

---

you English, . . . when you looked so fierce, you had no inkling that this would be so; but you were not yet treading the path upon which God casts down the proud." Pizan, *Le ditié*; ibid., 104.

141. Teresa of Avila, *Collected Works*, vol. 2, 187.
142. Weil, *Waiting for God*, 150.
143. *De mirabili victoria*, a contemporary treatise written about Jehanne; in Taylor, *La Pucelle*, 80. It was widely circulated and can reasonably be dated between March and September, 1429. Some believe theologian, Jean Gerson, to be the author. Taylor, *La Pucelle*, 78.
144. Soelle, *Silent Cry*, 158.
145. Watts, *Behold the Spirit*, 224–25.
146. Jehanne; quoted by Touroulde, in Pernoud, *Retrial*, 125.
147. Kierkegaard, *Fear and Trembling*, 21.
148. Jehanne; quoted by Touroulde, in Pernoud, *Retrial*, 125.
149. Hvidt, *Christian Prophecy*, 151.

when an authentic vision occurs, it is "clearly known,"[150] suggesting that divine visions possess a unique, divine quality which sets them apart from all visions not divine in nature. She describes a mystical state called "rapture of the spirit" in which, if one were to see saints, one would know "them as well as if he had often spoken with them" since "the eyes of the soul see much better than do we with bodily eyes . . . and without words understanding of some things is given."[151] She explains that, "[i]n just the difference between the light we see and the one represented there [in divine revelation], although all is light, there is no comparison; next to that light the sun's brilliance seems to be something very blurred." The imagination, Teresa asserts, is incapable of representing the nature of this divine light or anything of which God granted her knowledge. She indicates that, accompanying revealed knowledge, God "bestows . . . a delight so sublime as to be indescribable."[152] She therefore recommends "experience" over "learning" in recognizing authentic, divine visions[153] since "there is no appropriate comparison for supernatural things."[154]

John of the Cross categorizes revelation as a type of spiritual apprehension belonging to the "spirit of prophecy." It is "the manifestation of some [divine] secret or mystery, as when God . . . discloses" a "past, present, or future" divine deed or event, the mystery of the Trinity, "revelatory prophecies," divine "promises and threats," as well as "particular facts revealed . . . by God about the universe in general, and, in particular, about kingdoms, provinces, states, families, and individuals." Revelation can be conveyed through any or a combination of words, "signs, figures, images," or "likenesses."[155] One might note that Jehanne not only represented the fulfillment of pre-existing prophecy but embodied a prophetic revelation itself in the form of a promise of liberation to the French and a threat to the English—a double-edged sword conveying a dual message. In this instance, prophecy and prophet are one, a single instrument delivering, embodying, and fulfilling a divine message.[156]

150. Teresa of Avila, *Collected Works*, vol. 3, 141.
151. Ibid., vol. 2, 388–89.
152. Ibid., vol. 1, 330.
153. Ibid., vol. 3, 142.
154. Ibid., vol. 1, 249.
155. John of the Cross, *Collected Works*, 193, 200.

156. Fraioli observes that Jehanne's "entire mission could be considered a prophecy, her own role an integral part of the divine narrative she announced." Fraioli, *Early*

Saint John maintains that, in divine disclosure of "knowledge of the truth of things in themselves" or of human deeds and events, the information "is so embedded in the soul—without anyone telling it anything—that if someone were to assert the opposite, it would be unable to give interior assent even by force, for it has a spiritual knowledge of this truth which resembles clear vision. This knowledge pertains to the spirit of prophecy and to the grace" called "discernment of spirits."[157] Jehanne possessed this particular grace[158] and went to the stake on the basis of her certainty in this regard, whereas those falsely claiming divine sanction might be expected to falter under such circumstances. Jehanne unambiguously maintained that she was "sent by God,"[159] readily confirming that she had never consulted any ecclesiastic regarding her voices and visions.[160] She relied solely upon her own powers of discernment, something of which her adversaries did not approve, and the issue was raised throughout the condemnation trial.[161] However, the Poitiers examiners did not fault her on this matter, suggesting that the Holy Spirit was operational within her.[162] Hence, although Jehanne did not seek ecclesiastical opinion on the discernment of spirits, it was provided in the Poitiers commission's approval of her mission. Fraioli states that "the ecclesiastics at Poitiers handled their investigation of her according to the dictates of the church, as an occurrence appropriate to the application of *discretio*

Debate, 56.

157. John of the Cross, *Collected Works*, 196.

158. Jehanne's canonization confirms her power of discernment.

159. Jehanne; in Taylor, *La Pucelle*, 170. She reiterated this many times.

160. Jehanne; in Taylor, *La Pucelle*, 179. She may have done well to rely on her own discernment as Saint Teresa reports a period of twenty years in which she was unable to find a confessor who understood her. "This hurt me so much," she declares, "that I often turned back and was . . . completely lost." Teresa of Avila, *Collected Works*, vol. 1, 67. "It happened to me that I spoke about matters of conscience with a confessor who had gone through the whole course of theology, and he did me a great deal of harm by telling me that some matters didn't amount to anything. I know that he didn't intend to misinform me and had no reason to, but he simply didn't know any more. And the same thing happened to me with two or three others, besides the one I mentioned." Ibid., vol. 2, 59–60.

161. Of the initial seventy articles of accusation against Jehanne, Article 48 charges her with not seeking "spiritual advice" concerning the discernment of spirits; in Scott, *Trial*, 139–40. Article 11 of the twelve final articles reiterates the charge; in Taylor, *La Pucelle*, 211–12.

162. Poitiers inquiry conclusion; in Taylor, *La Pucelle*, 74.

spirituum," referencing the Hebrew and Christian Bibles and placing Jehanne within the prophetic realm of those traditions.[163] Jehanne's confidence in her divine revelations never wavered. She warned her Rouen assessors, "If you are well informed about me, you would wish that I were out of your hands. I have done nothing save by revelation."[164]

Jehanne's claim of operating under the direct command of God indicates that she drew no distinction between messages delivered by angels and saints and those received from God directly, these entities being of the divine realm and, therefore, of God. As Preston Russell observes, Jehanne's divine counsel "worked as plural manifestations from a singular above, always."[165] Others might consider Jehanne's revelations indirect, classifying her messengers as intermediaries, but one cannot deny her claim to direct contact with the realm of God on this basis. Accordingly, Rahner maintains that

> God as a free personal being can make himself perceptible to the created spirit, not only through his works but also by his free, personal word. And he can do it in such a manner that this communication of God is not simply himself in the direct vision of the Godhead, or in the dimension of a blessed intellect emptied of all that is finite, but also . . . in such a way that this communication is bound up with a particular place and time, with a concrete word or command, with a finite reality or truth, and so that it occurs with, or is connected with, the "apparition" of an object presented to the internal or external senses, which object represents and manifests God, his will, or the like.[166]

When urged to provide a sign validating her claim, Jehanne declared, "In God's name, I have not come to Poitiers to make signs. But lead me to Orléans, and I will show you the signs I was sent to make."[167] Victory alone, however, especially victory unaccompanied by any substantiated prophetic claim and devoid of miraculous quality, is not sufficient proof of divine sanction, and it is not uncommon for both sides in a conflict to experience some degree of victory. In the case of the Hundred Years' War, both the pro-English and French parties claimed divine fa-

---

163. Fraioli, *Early Debate*, 56.
164. Jehanne; in Scott, *Trial*, 66.
165. Russell, *Lights of Madness*, 169.
166. Rahner, *Inquiries*, 95–96.
167. Jehanne; quoted by Seguin, in Pernoud, *Retrial*, 113.

The Theology of Jehanne d'Arc

vor on occasion. In a letter to Charles VII, the Duke of Bedford asserted that, "by the grace of God," Henry VI was the "natural and rightful King of the kingdoms of France and England" and that the power of God stood behind the English forces against the French.[168] Moreover, a letter written by Philippe the Good, Duke of Burgundy, regarding Jehanne's capture declared, "And by the pleasure of our blessed Creator the thing thus came about and such mercy was vouchsafed us that she who is called the Maid was taken."[169] Such claims are problematic. Declaring the mere fact of Jehanne's capture a divine revelation amounting to more than the fact itself (i.e., amounting to an indication of divine support for the English) allows that any and all merely factual events might be legitimately construed as revelation indicative of some humanly imagined divine purpose transcending the fact itself. But this is untenable as divine revelation must differ from purely human occurrence in some way which renders it distinguishable from ordinary fact, such as through visions, auditions, or prophetic fulfillment.

That said, it is pertinent to note that, not only did the enemy view Jehanne's capture as divinely ordained, but she also viewed it thus and, therefore, as necessary. "[I]t had always been said to her [by her voices] that it was necessary that she should be a prisoner."[170] However, the fact of her capture does not indicate that God was against her and for the English, nor that the English invasion of France was divinely sanctioned. Divine sanction does not necessarily conform to human desire, and merely having what one wants does not constitute proof of divine favor or sanction. "[I]sn't it true . . . that those whom God blesses he damns in the same breath?" prods Kierkegaard, maintaining that "every privilege in the world of spirit . . . can only be purchased in deep pain."[171] "Over the life of a prophet words are invisibly inscribed: All flattery abandon, ye who enter here. To be a prophet is both a distinction and an affliction," Heschel remarks.[172] Saint Teresa declares that hearing the divine Voice "is a greater trial than not hearing it."[173] If these statements ring true, one

---

168. Duke of Bedford; in Taylor, *La Pucelle*, 119–20.

169. Philippe the Good; in Pernoud from Quicherat, v. 5, 166–67, *Herself and Her Witnesses*, 153.

170. Jehanne; in Taylor, *La Pucelle*, 175–76.

171. Kierkegaard, *Fear and Trembling*, 77, 99.

172. Heschel, *Prophets: Introduction*, 17–18.

173. Teresa of Avila, *Collected Works*, vol. 2, 298.

might suspect that persecution and surrender of personal will to divine will have much to do with the matter and that earthly persecution is as apt an indicator of divine sanction as earthly success. In fact, Hvidt notes a typical "convergence between the role of martyr and prophet."[174]

The most assured way of distinguishing mere fact from revelation is through the quality of experience involved in divine revelation, qualities such as those described by Saints Teresa and John which convey an authority known only to the recipient. For the outsider assessing another's claim to divine revelation, such assuredness is elusive and substantiation by previously mentioned indicators is required, such as the occurrence of corresponding external miracles (as in disclosure of hidden truths, performance of supernatural deeds, and knowledge of otherwise unknown past, present or future facts or events), production of good fruits, and qualities of humility, obedience, and strength in the claimant. Naturally, the greater the number of stipulated criteria satisfied by a claimant, the greater the apparent strength of the claim. For example, in evaluating the claim that Jehanne's capture indicated divine support for the pro-English cause in France, one must note that there was nothing apparently miraculous about her capture given the vast discrepancy in size of the opposing armies at Compiègne on that day[175] and the firm possibility of betrayal from within the French forces; capture was, therefore, neither unlikely nor inexplicable. Furthermore, the only aforementioned indicator that might apply to the pro-English claim of divine favor with respect to Jehanne's capture is production of good fruits; however, since the matter of what constitutes good fruits in war is too easily defined by the victor, this criterion cannot stand alone as an indicator of divine revelation.

After-the-fact indicators can be taken into account when evaluating claims to divine revelation. Martyrdom might be one *post factum* indicator; others include subsequent prophetic fulfillment and canonization, including posthumous miracles deemed necessary for canonization.[176] Such indicators, of course, are only useful after the fact with

174. Hvidt, *Christian Prophecy*, 106.

175. Monstrelet places the number of Burgundian combatants at approximately five thousand and Jehanne's army at between four hundred and five hundred. Monstrelet, *La chronique d'Enguerran de Monstrelet*; in Taylor, *La Pucelle*, 257–58.

176. Posthumous miracles attributed to Jehanne's intercession include two cancer cures, one tuberculosis cure, one cure of leg ulcers, and the cure of a hole in a woman's foot. Dispensation for a further miracle was granted on the basis that Jehanne had saved

respect to the claim from which they arise; however, they can reinforce the strength of prior indicators involved in a claim. Jehanne's canonization renders her a model of sanctity; therefore, in examining her words and deeds, key elements of her behavior can be identified as exemplary and formulated into a model of human agency applicable in the evaluation of other cases. It is impossible, however, to devise a system of evaluation enabling one to discern definitively what constitutes divine revelation in general and what does not.[177] To attempt this would be to endeavor to restrict God, but one cannot impose limits on the nature or content of divine revelation. Nonetheless, one can observe consistencies among cases officially deemed legitimate. For example, respects in which Jehanne's claim and experience correspond to those of biblical prophets and to those of Saints Teresa and John are instructive. What can be herein achieved is discernment of what apparently constituted divine revelation, divine sanction, and divine servantship in Jehanne's exemplary case. Incidentally, Weil ranks Jehanne among the "very few" individuals who can be rightfully "associated with real purity."[178]

Heschel indicates that "*divine attentiveness* [to] *and concern*" for humanity dominate prophetic consciousness; sharing in these, the prophet is driven to participate in God's involvement in human history, attempting to realize divine aspirations for the world.[179] The prophet, he asserts, "feels fiercely."[180] Prophets "care intensely about the moral shape of society," Brueggemann explains, "so they assault every social disorder."[181] Heschel elaborates: "The prophet's word is a scream in the night. While the world is at ease and asleep, the prophet feels the blast from heaven."[182] "God has thrust a burden upon his soul," for the "terror" of human agony is beyond human expression, yet prophecy "is the voice that God has lent to the silent agony, . . . to the plundered poor, to the profaned riches of the world. It is a form of living, a crossing point

---

France. Taylor, *Virgin Warrior*, 184, 238, n. 3 and n. 4.

177. Gerson states "that there is . . . no general rule or method that can be given always and infallibly to distinguish between revelations that are true and those that are false or deceptive." Gerson, *Early Works*, 335.

178. Weil, *Need for Roots*, 228.

179. Heschel, *Prophets: II*, 263.

180. Heschel, *Prophets: Introduction*, 5.

181. Brueggemann, "Destabilizing Presence," 221.

182. Heschel, *Prophets: Introduction*, 16.

of God and man."[183] Rahner describes the prophet as "the mouthpiece of God for" humans.[184] "It is sympathy with God," Heschel maintains, "that characterizes the total personality of the prophet, his inner state as manifested in his utterances, a state not limited to some moments, but affecting all his existence."[185]

In her childhood, Saint Michael informed Jehanne "of the misery that was in the kingdom of France" and urged her to assist the French king with God's help.[186] Corresponding to the divine sentiment of concern and intensity of feeling stipulated by Heschel, Jehanne's acceptance of this task and continued commitment to fight with minimal resources and without the support of her king during the final portion of her campaign demonstrated a deep, enduring concern for her oppressed people. Jehanne "heard it said that the people of Compiègne, all up to the age of seven years, were to be put to fire and sword"[187] and this was one of the reasons for her precarious leap from the Beaurevoir prison tower as she wanted to assist the inhabitants of the besieged city. Jehanne's inner prophetic state is also reflected in the testimony that "there issued from her lips no words that were not virtuous, edifying, and a good example to" others.[188]

"[S]he said that she never saw French blood without her hair standing on end."[189] Jehanne was partisan with the French—they were those whom she maintained God appointed her to help—but she displayed general concern for humanity. She respected and valued human life—her own and others'. She harbored no death wish and did not seek martyrdom but hoped to be freed from prison and twice attempted to escape. Upon hearing her death sentence, Jehanne "began to weep and lament in such a way that all the people present were themselves moved to tears."[190] Moreover, Jehanne preferred to interpret references by her

---

183. Ibid., 5.
184. Rahner, *Inquiries*, 97.
185. Heschel, *Prophets: II*, 189.
186. Jehanne; in Scott, *Trial*, 120.
187. Ibid., 111.
188. Gaucourt; in Pernoud, *Retrial*, 117.
189. Aulon; ibid., 167.
190. Orléans manuscript; in Scott, *Trial*, 173. Houppeville witnessed Jehanne "bathed in tears, leaving the castle to be taken to the place of execution"; in Pernoud, *Retrial*, 276. Two Rouen assessors, Jean Fabri and Miget, testified to Jehanne's tearful but pious end; ibid., 249–50.

divine counsel to her "martyrdom" as indicative of suffering but not death.[191] She wept at the sight of spilled blood, be it of friend or foe, and comforted dying soldiers, French and English alike. She agonized in the event of anyone dying without the sacrament of confession, demonstrating concern for the spiritual well-being of both French and English soldiers, and "when she saw them dying or wounded she had them confessed."[192] Jehanne did not glorify war but glorified God and the sanctity of human life. Honoring the sanctity of life is critical to preventing "unnecessary" violence and destruction; otherwise, life is treated as less consequential. Soelle suggests that "[t]he trivialization of life is perhaps the strongest antimystical force among us," whereas "mysticism is the radical substantiation of the dignity of the human being."[193] Wright asserts that saints sanctify society and preserve the world, being "magnanimous, great-souled people whose minds are big enough to include heaven and whose hearts are large enough to hold all the world—plus God."[194] Watts maintains that one who is united with God "will show mercy, love and consideration for others," being "aware of God in all human persons."[195] Righteousness and partisanship are not mutually exclusive and, although Jehanne's war, like all wars, was partisan, her righteousness was not. Her message extends beyond partisanship with any particular nation, culture, or religion to express solidarity with oppressed peoples everywhere at all times. Wright believes that Jehanne's "emphasis on vocation, on individual mission as the core of personality," renders her "as relevant . . . in an age of technology as ever she was to her own age. . . . She remains . . . the patron of the vocation and the dignity of the person in the face of all the . . . impersonal forces of a standardized culture threatening human personality. . . ."[196]

The prophet does not call upon God to engage in a particular task but is called by God, via revelation, to engage in a divinely appointed activity. "To the prophet, God is always apprehended, experienced, and conceived as a *Subject*, never as an object. He appears as One Who de-

---

191. Jehanne; in Taylor, *La Pucelle*, 189.
192. Pasquerel; ibid., 314, 316.
193. Soelle, *Silent Cry*, 13, 43.
194. Wright, *Saints Always Belong*, 36, 42.
195. Watts, *Behold the Spirit*, 224.
196. Wright, *Saints Always Belong*, 123.

mands, as One Who acts," notes Heschel.¹⁹⁷ This is not to say that, once called, a prophet cannot request divine assistance in carrying out a divine assignment. Jehanne sometimes presented requests to Saint Catherine, and Saints Catherine and Margaret reportedly transmitted these to God for response, but a response was not always forthcoming, such as when she inquired as to the date of her capture.¹⁹⁸ No one can effectively command revelation from God, but all are at the mercy of divine will to bestow it. While the prophet might seek direction or clarification, God is not compelled to oblige. Hence, the prophet is in darkness at times with respect to divine will, in which case action can, at best, be informed by conscience, moral discernment, and practical considerations. For example, when Jehanne's voices instructed her to attack the English at Orléans, she declared, "In God's name, my Counsel has told me that I must attack the English. But I do not know if I should go to their bastille or against Ffastolf, who is to revictual them."¹⁹⁹ This indicates that Jehanne was sometimes required to make her own military decisions without apprehension of specific, divine instruction, which leads to the issue of divine ambiguity discussed next.

Considering Divine Ambiguity

Beneath an overarching ineffability and mystery of God, divine revelation affords humans glimpses—limited knowledge—of the divine. In light of the dually cataphatic and apophatic nature of divine revelation, which produces ambiguity, it was necessary for Jehanne to negotiate gaps in order to apply the revelations received to her life. For example, she did not likely apprehend at the time of her alleged abjuration whether it was more in alignment with divine will that she continue to live—possibly to be freed and to continue fighting for the liberation of France—or that she give in to death rather than abjure since it was afterwards that her voices indicated that she had damned herself.²⁰⁰ Even then, the divine message was ambiguous. Did it imply divine punishment for denying

---

197. Heschel, *Prophets: II*, 265.
198. Jehanne; in Taylor, *La Pucelle*, 175, 188.
199. Jehanne; quoted by Aulon, in Pernoud, *Retrial*, 166.
200. "Elle répondit que Dieu lui manda par saintes Catherine et Marguerite la grande pitié de cette insigne trahison à laquelle elle, Jeanne, avait consenti en faisant l'abjuration et rétractation pour sauver sa vie, et qu'elle se damnait pour sauver sa vie." Jehanne; in Tisset and Lanhers, *Procès de Condamnation*, vol. 2, 345.

God? The voices did not declare that God had damned Jehanne, but that she, herself, did. The reference to damnation may not suggest divine punishment at all but that Jehanne had fallen into the snare set by Cauchon through which the court would damn her by committing her to suffer death by fire. Jehanne's voices had counseled her to answer her accusers boldly at Saint-Ouen[201] but, confused and terrified, she faltered and signed, clearing the way for her earthly condemnation. Her options were thus reduced to denying God or affirming God and being burned.

During her imprisonment, Jehanne's voices informed her that she would be "delivered" and would receive divine assistance.[202] "One day I must be freed," she stated.[203] Questioned as to whether or not her voices indicated that she would escape from prison, she responded, "Yes, indeed, they told me I should be delivered. But I know neither the day nor the hour. And [they told me] I must put a bold face on it."[204] Jehanne's testimony conveys that

> she did not know whether this meant being freed from prison or that, during her trial, some disturbance would arise that would allow her to be delivered. And she believed that it would be one or the other. And more often the voices told her that she would be delivered by a great victory, then saying to her: "Accept everything thankfully, and do not worry about your martyrdom; in the end you will come to the kingdom of heaven." And the voices told her this simply and definitely, that is to say without faltering. And she called this martyrdom on account of the pain and adversity which she suffered in prison; and she did not know whether she would suffer greater pain, but on this she committed herself to God.[205]

These statements point possibly to her escaping, being rescued from prison, or being liberated from her circumstances through death. They also reveal that Jehanne retained hope in the possibility of her survival while being fully aware that she might be put to death. Three weeks prior to her execution, Jehanne asked the voices if she would be burned, to which they replied "that she must wait on Our Lord" who "would help

---

201. Jehanne; in Scott, *Trial*, 169.
202. Ibid., 113.
203. Ibid., 87.
204. Ibid., 91.
205. Jehanne; in Taylor, *La Pucelle*, 189.

her."[206] The answer is elusive and Jehanne undoubtedly held hope and fear in precarious balance until the outcome became finally and dreadfully clear. She seems, however, to have been aware on some level from the start that her capture would lead to her demise. Under Burgundian imprisonment (prior to being sold to the English) she stated, "I well know that the English will put me to death, thinking to win the kingdom of France after my death."[207] Ambiguity nonetheless allowed Jehanne to maintain hope in an otherwise desperate situation. Had she known for three weeks or more that she was certainly to burn, one can imagine that this would have increased her torment considerably during that time. It is possible that ambiguity mitigated her suffering until it could no longer be mitigated. In a sense, Jehanne accepted her "fate" in advance of knowing what it would be by accepting her mission and continuing to fight in knowledge of her impending capture. Her moving lament on the morning of her death suggests that she did not view God as the instrument of her suffering but placed responsibility on her mortal enemies. "Bishop," she declared to Cauchon, "my death is your doing. . . . I appeal against you to God."[208] In appealing to God, as in all things, Jehanne referred the injustice of her cruel and excruciating death to the highest and only authority that she fully respected, honored, and trusted, suggesting that she anticipated some sort of final, divine vindication or justice, which one might suppose the nullification trial verdict followed by her beatification and canonization achieved.

While revelation and prophecy invite humans to more intimate relationship with God and constitute an offer of divine assistance in human affairs, God remains shrouded in mystery and apparent complexity. In fact, divine mystery is intrinsic to revelation since to reveal is to expose something previously unknown or unseen, something of the mysterious. Presuming divine infinity combined with perpetual divine desire to be apprehended by and involved with humanity, there is reason to posit continuation of divine revelation on the basis that infinite divine mystery can never be fully conveyed and the possibilities for revelation never fully exhausted in terms of content, quality, quantity, or frequency. It is plausible, however, that, through revelation, certain individuals

---

206. Jehanne; in Scott, *Trial*, 152.
207. Jehanne; quoted by Macy, in Taylor, *La Pucelle*, 320.
208. Jehanne; quoted by Jean Toutmouillé, friar, in Pernoud, *Retrial*, 245.

The Theology of Jehanne d'Arc

might afford humanity knowledge of God that was previously unknown or inaccessible.

Jehanne as Prophet

Jehanne's prophetic record is impressive, having prophesied accurately that she would raise the siege of Orléans, that she would have Charles VII anointed and crowned at Rheims, that the King of France would regain Paris, and that the Duke of Orléans would return from England[209] where he had been imprisoned since 1415. Also noteworthy is Jehanne's knowledge of a sword buried behind the altar in the church of Sainte-Catherine-de-Fierbois. She said that the "sword was in the earth, rusted, bearing five engraved crosses; and she knew that the sword was there through her voices. . . . She also said that immediately after the sword was found, the churchmen of that place rubbed it and the rust immediately fell off without effort."[210] Jehanne also accurately predicted her battle wound sustained at Orléans: "Rise tomorrow early in the morning," she advised her confessor, "and . . . be always at my side, for tomorrow I shall have much to do, and more than I ever had, and tomorrow the blood will flow out of my body above my breast."[211] Concerning the battle of Patay, she foretold that none or very few of the French would suffer injury or death there and, indeed, the French army suffered only one fatality[212] while enemy fatalities numbered two thousand.[213] At Chinon, Jehanne encountered a man who swore to God that she would not remain a virgin if he spent a night with her, to which she replied, "Oh, in God's name, do you take His name in vain when you are so near your death?"[214] and the man fell into a river an hour later and drowned.[215] It is noteworthy that many of Jehanne's prophecies foretold events of the im-

---

209. Seguin, G. Thibault, and Alençon; in Pernoud, *Retrial*, 113, 118, 160. Jehanne; in Scott, *Trial*, 135.

210. Jehanne; in Taylor, *La Pucelle*, 156.

211. Jehanne; quoted by Pasquerel, in Pernoud, *Herself and Her Witnesses*, 90. Jehanne also testified that she had made this prediction; in Taylor, *La Pucelle*, 158.

212. T. d'Armagnac; in Pernoud, *Retrial*, 121.

213. Pernoud takes the numbers from Burgundian sources which place the French death toll at three and English fatalities at two thousand. Pernoud, *Herself and Her Witnesses*, 119.

214. Jehanne; quoted by Pasquerel, in Pernoud, *Retrial*, 182.

215. Pasquerel; in Pernoud, *Retrial*, 182.

minent rather than distant future, rendering them almost immediately verifiable. Her prediction in March, 1429 that she would last barely more than a year also proved accurate as she was captured the following May. During the Rouen trial, Jehanne prophesied that the French "will soon win a great action which God will send to them; . . . it will shake almost the whole realm of France" and "before seven years are past the English will have lost a greater stake than they did before the town of Orleans, for they will have lost all they hold in France."[216] Although these latter prophecies remain ambiguous, they are possible allusions to the Treaty of Arras established in 1435, under which the Burgundians united with the French party, significantly diminishing English power in France, and to the liberation of Paris in 1436. That the recovery of the remainder of France took longer than seven years introduces the problematic inaccuracy (partial or complete) of some prophetic messages, a concern that we will revisit shortly. The aforementioned constitute only some of Jehanne's prophecies. She also claimed foreknowledge of her capture; however, since she did not share this revelation with anyone until after its fulfillment, it cannot be designated as prophecy. It is the sharing of the prophetic message that establishes the relationship between the prophet as prophet and others; it is ongoing concerned and faithful prophetic activity that sustains the relationship.

Hvidt includes Jehanne among the prophets of the Catholic tradition, stating,

> It is hard to consider the Catholic church without the prophetic tradition that has accompanied its entire history. Prophetic visions and divine instructions accompanied the founding of the vast majority of its religious orders. The same accounts for most pilgrimage sites, which usually became what they did after apparitions of Christ, of the Blessed Virgin, or of an angel to a privileged soul. Much Catholic hagiography has eminent prophetic traits, so that individuals such as Gertrude the Great of Helfta (†1302), Birgitta of Vadstena (†1373), Catherine of Siena (†1380), Joan of Arc (†1431), Julian of Norwich (†c.1416), and Margaret Mary Alacoque (†1690) all come across as classic Christian prophets.[217]

---

216. Jehanne; in Scott, *Trial*, 84, 122.
217. Hvidt, *Christian Prophecy*, 13.

Jehanne also has much in common with the Hebrew prophets as the bearer of a political-theological message, that is, a political message rooted in theological concerns. Hvidt states that, "in crucial periods in the history of the church, mostly women with a prophetic profile, such as Birgitta of Vadstena, Catherine of Siena, and Joan of Arc, stood up much like the Old Testament prophets and called the people of God to live in accordance with his Word."[218] He identifies the following prophetic characteristics within the Hebrew tradition:

1. Receipt of divine revelation.[219] (This correlates to Jehanne's visions and auditions.)

2. Critical moment of divine calling to a particular mission which "separates the prophet's life into 'before' and 'after.'"[220] (Jehanne abandoned childhood playfulness on receiving the divine command to go into France and left all familiarity on leaving Domremy. Upon departing Vaucouleurs, her life changed more drastically as she donned male clothing and became a warrior.)

3. Resistance to divine calling.[221] (Jehanne delayed before embarking on her divine mission; her voices urged her repeatedly to depart.[222])

4. Feelings of unworthiness to carry out the divine mission accompanied by assurance of divine assistance creating a dependency on God.[223] (Jehanne protested that she was merely a peasant girl and not qualified for the task but accepted it on the promise of divine assistance.[224])

5. Operates under obedience to divine authority.[225] (Jehanne considered her divine voices more authoritative than any other.)

218. Ibid., 305.
219. Ibid., 36–37.
220. Ibid., 37.
221. Ibid.
222. Jehanne; in Scott, *Trial*, 67. According to G. Thibault, Jehanne stated "that her Counsel had told her she should have gone more quickly to the King [dauphin]." Thibault; in Murray, *Jeanne d'Arc*, 265.
223. Hvidt, *Christian Prophecy*, 37–38.
224. Jehanne; in Taylor, *La Pucelle*, 142, 195–96.
225. Hvidt, *Christian Prophecy*, 38.

6. Functions as a friend of God, sharing in God's plans, happiness and sadness.[226] (Jehanne shared in God's alleged displeasure over the misery of France under foreign domination and applied herself to rectifying the situation.)

Based on Jehanne's example to this point, one might add the following possible prophetic characteristics:

1. Apparent absurdity. Liberation of the city of Orléans seemed impossible under the circumstances at the time, even more so by instigation of a militarily untrained and inexperienced peasant girl.

2. Prior lack of inclination, skill, or capacity to behave in the required manner. Jehanne was not normally violent and did not demonstrate any ambition to become a warrior prior to her divine calling.[227] She wept at the sight of spilled blood and was a most unlikely candidate, in practical terms, for the mission to which she was called—unlikely except with respect to her exceptional faith.

3. Risk to one's personal safety. The risk to Jehanne as a warrior is obvious, but she also risked her well-being as a lone female among thousands of armed men.

4. Necessity of faith and courage in accomplishing the task bestowed. Faith was required of Jehanne in order to believe in the absurd and seemingly impossible, and courage is required of all warriors.

Jehanne's courage in fulfilling her mission was remarkable given that she lived in a patriarchal society at a time when soldiering did not constitute a common social role for women and unattached female involvement with soldiers was generally regarded as promiscuous in the extreme. Moreover, Jehanne was not only expected to engage in military activity, but to *lead* her army to victory. Kelly DeVries notes that, previously, "[n]o troops of the Hundred Years War had ever followed a woman into battle, . . . and those few occasions in earlier medieval history of women leading soldiers were not well known, were thought to be mythological,

---

226. Ibid., 38–39.
227. Numerous witnesses reported that Jehanne was pleasant and kind.

or were, at best, a distant historical memory." DeVries maintains that he has uncovered "no evidence of late-medieval women warriors" except for Jehanne.[228] During the Rouen trial, when pressed for information concerning her revelations, Jehanne cited a popular saying that "people are often hanged for telling the truth."[229] The statement alludes to the inherent dangers of prophetic life,[230] dangers that, in Jehanne's case, were compounded with the dangers of an active military vocation and materialized in her martyrdom.

Answering the Call: Operative Elements of Practical, Prophetic Mysticism

The wars they will
be fought again
The holy dove
be caught again
bought and sold
and bought again;
the dove is never free.
—LEONARD COHEN, "ANTHEM"

The prophet is a disciple of God, and Jehanne's discipleship involved absolute obedience to the divine, regardless of personal cost, with a view to salvation of her country (as preservation and liberation from suffering) and possible salvation of her soul. The prophetic call urges improvement to the condition of humanity, thereby mediating salvation. In claiming freedom to obey God as she deemed appropriate, Jehanne's implicit challenge to the authority of the Church Militant threatened the view of salvation as mediated exclusively by the Church through the ongoing

---

228. DeVries, "Woman as Leader," 4, 13, n. 4.

229. Jehanne; in Scott, *Trial*, 73.

230. Marina Warner, acknowledging the dangers of a prophetic "vocation," asserts that the "Church has always found the rightful place of personal divine guidance a problem." Warner, *Joan of Arc*, 88. "[T]he function of the prophet cannot be institutionalized," states Joseph Ratzinger, "because the place of prophecy is eminently the place God reserves for Himself to intervene personally and anew each time, taking the initiative." Ratzinger, "Das Problem," 181; in Hvidt, *Christian Prophecy*, 80. "Prophecy is a corrective factor to the extent that institution and prophecy at times become opposite entities." Hvidt, *Christian Prophecy*, 173.

dispensation of grace via the sacraments.[231] Jehanne held that God alone delivers salvation, believing in the possibility of her own salvation even when excommunicated by the earthly Church,[232] suggesting that God might effect salvation in any manner God desires. If Jehanne's prophetic activities contributed to France's salvation, then she might be considered a mediator of grace functioning with a sacramental quality, as anyone who mediates divine grace might be viewed as operating sacramentally in the moment of mediation.[233] Hvidt states "that the experience of the prophet is . . . part of a larger ensemble of edifying operations of the Spirit—prophecy is never . . . without . . . grace backing its performance of the divine designs."[234] During the Poitiers examination it was suggested that, if God wished to liberate France, God did not require soldiers to accomplish it, to which Jehanne replied, "In God's name, the soldiers will fight, and God will give them the victory."[235] Pernoud and Clin note that "[e]xpertly trained theologians could hardly have given a better account of the delicate distinction between the action of grace and its temporal means."[236] "[I]f not for the grace of God," declared Jehanne, "she could do nothing."[237]

Two operative elements of the prophetic mediation of grace are faith and free will. Human free will has presumably existed as long as humans have, although we cannot arrive at a definitive account of it. It seems to be an innate capacity. The fact that our vocabulary contains terms such

---

231. Malcolm Vale notes that the "search for a more deeply personal relationship with God, mediated through the saints, was a common phenomenon in the later Middle Ages. Heretics [or those so deemed], while seeking such a relationship, erred in the eyes of the Church because too often the clergy were eliminated or their significance greatly reduced as sacramental mediators between man and God." Vale, "Courts and Cities in the North," 312.

232. On the morning of her execution Jehanne asked a theologian, "[W]here shall I be tonight?" He replied, "Do you not trust in God?" to which she responded that, with God's help, "she would be in Paradise." Jehanne and Pierre Maurice, to whom she put the question; quoted by Riquier, in Pernoud, *Retrial*, 250.

233. Whether divine revelation is received in mediated or unmediated form, the prophet nonetheless acts as a mediator of grace in delivering and acting upon the divine message.

234. Hvidt, *Christian Prophecy*, 293. Margolis acknowledges Jehanne's "sacramental role." Margolis, "Mortal Body," 12.

235. Jehanne; quoted by Seguin, in Pernoud, *Retrial*, 113.

236. Pernoud and Clin, *Her Story*, 29.

237. Jehanne; in Hobbins, *Trial*, 60.

The Theology of Jehanne d'Arc

as "choice" and "free will" suggests that these comprise aspects of human experience. Moreover, since to advocate the non-existence of free will is to abdicate the concepts of human responsibility and morality, and since life without freedom of choice would be apparently meaningless as people would be reduced to automatons, the position I take—in alignment with Jehanne's example—is that free will exists.

If human free will exists, then God presumably honors it, which leads to the question of whether or not the notion of human freedom can accommodate the concept of divine omnipotence. Thinkers such as C. S. Lewis and William of Ockham marry notions of divine omnipotence with divine Self-limitation, asserting that God, having once been omnipotent, eliminated certain available actions (e.g., controlling humanity and the world) by choosing others in the course of creation (e.g., granting humans freedom of choice in the world).[238] Such a view is compatible with a free will understanding of human evil, which holds that abuse or misuse of a good thing (human freedom) can produce evil[239]—compatible, that is, provided that one does not maintain the ongoing omnipotence of a benevolent deity in the face of divine Self-limitation. In fact, one is prompted to consider why notions of ongoing divine omnipotence persist. Perhaps anthropomorphism is at work through attribution to God of a human desire for power over others. Perhaps, also, the idea of divine omnipotence provides humans an escape route from the burden of responsibility for the misdeeds of humanity. Both may be true. At any rate, the tendency to attribute acts of human evil to an omnipotent deity must be questioned. Jehanne, while claiming divine sanction with respect to certain deeds, did not hold God accountable or responsible for all of her deeds or all human activity. "Everything good that I have done, I did by command of the voices," she maintained, excluding the divine from any wrongful deeds that she may have committed.[240] It is by acknowledging responsibility for our deeds and exercising moral accountability that humanity might end the self-inflicted plague of human violence. Sallie McFague agrees that the idea of an omnipotent God is "a very dangerous one" in that it supports a view of salvation as "sacrificial, substitutionary atonement" whereby humans are presumed forgiven for our sins and reconciled with

---

238. McGrath, *Christian Theology*, 209–11.
239. Ibid., 224.
240. Jehanne; in Scott, *Trial*, 106.

God[241] (rather than being called to account for our depravities); however, if God were omnipotent and humans essentially powerless, human sin would not exist in the first place. Furthermore, Soelle notes that the notion of an omnipotent, benevolent deity is incomprehensible in the face of suffering and promotes atheism, whereas an omnipotent "God who imposes suffering" would be "a sadist."[242] She favors a view of God as loving but not omnipotent, as One who, standing in solidarity with victims of human evil, is not impassible.[243]

Faith and Free Will in Light of the Shoah[244]

For many, the *Shoah* stands as one of the tallest, bleakest, darkest walls looming between humanity and God that one dare imagine, but one need not imagine it—it is real. Built from the bones of millions, the wall is darkened by the smoke and ash of millions more whose lives were snuffed out by the hand of human being upon human being. Now humanity stands before this monstrosity wondering what to make of it. Did God construct the wall from the deeds of humankind so that God might no longer look upon a humanity so bent on wretchedness? Did God construct the wall from our deeds in order to force humanity to confront our own depravity so that we might seek ways not of tearing down the wall, for what is done cannot be undone, but of scaling the wall and rising above it that we might retrieve God and once again incorporate divinity into our vision of life and the world? Or did humans construct the wall in a conscious attempt to sever God from the world so that human power might reign? Perhaps humans constructed the wall inadvertently, not troubling to realize that our actions amounted to a blatant rejection of God until it was done and we realized how dark our world had become, how shut off from the light we were. Or did God construct the wall together with humans, mutually declaring that there is no longer any common ground between us? Finally, one is compelled to ask, is there anything beyond the wall? Is there a place for God in a world

---

241. McFague, *Models of God*, 64.

242. Soelle, *Theology for Skeptics*, 64–65.

243. Ibid., 65–66.

244. *Shoah*, a Hebrew word meaning "catastrophe," is preferred by some over the term "Holocaust," meaning "burnt offering or sacrifice," to denote the massive, targeted destruction of Jewish people and other individuals under Adolf Hitler's Nazi regime.

capable of the *Shoah*, or is the *Shoah* evidence that no God exists? These are some of the questions smouldering among the ashes of Auschwitz.

Jewish theologians have responded diversely to these challenging but necessary questions. The following views support the notion of human free will as predominant. In response to the *Shoah*, Steven L. Jacobs rejects the idea of God as an active force in world history and proposes a divinity who became limited following the act of creation. Whether God chose limitation or otherwise acquired it is of little relevance to Jacobs. Through divine limitation, he postulates, humans acquired freedom to choose good or evil, rendering God incapable of preventing the *Shoah*. No appeal to God, he warns, "rational or emotional—will now overcome our technological fury" if we "choose to unleash it."[245] Irving Greenberg offers a theory of divine Self-limitation, suggesting that humans can move toward perfecting the world through the exercise of human freedom in emulating the divine. In order for a truly loving relationship to exist between God and humanity, he maintains, God must refrain from exercising greater power than humans are capable of as true love cannot accommodate an imbalance of power.[246] Michael Berenbaum also emphasizes the need for humans to work toward improving our world from which God seems absent, acting as our own redeemer. He rejects the notion of divine messianic intervention on the basis that a God who did not intervene in the *Shoah* "should be ashamed to act now."[247] This brings us to Peter Haas's observation that people often demand of God in relation to the *Shoah* what is otherwise not expected. "We are generally not prepared to assume that God will routinely intervene miraculously in individual human affairs," he asserts. "If I am flying an aircraft which I have failed to fill with sufficient fuel, the plane will crash.... None of us would either [1] expect a Divine miracle to occur... or [2] feel that God needed to be blamed or justified for the ensuing and totally foreseeable crash. Acts have consequences...." He notes that the *Shoah* consisted of "a series of individual decisions and acts, coordinated ... by a bureaucracy, but nonetheless individual acts which as a rule had precisely the outcome anybody would normally expect." Haas allows that "God may be benevolent and active in history in some way, but we ought to expect

---

245. Jacobs, "Judaism and Christianity," 2, 18.
246. Greenberg, "Voluntary Covenant," 78, 97.
247. Berenbaum, "World Without a Redeemer," 30–31.

our deeds to bear their natural consequences."[248] Heschel also refrains from holding God responsible for (or indifferent to) human iniquity since such practice amounts to conceiving of God "as a watchman hired to prevent us from using our loaded guns. Having failed us in this, He is now thought of as the ultimate Scapegoat."[249]

Haas maintains the apparent irreconcilability of an omnipotent and benevolent God with the "utter evil" of the *Shoah*, arguing that the removal of God "as an active force in the shaping of Western thinking" made the *Shoah* possible, the catastrophe itself reflecting an "eclipse ... of religion ... as a source of morality" such that the supposedly Christian institutions involved conducted themselves in a secular manner, "despite their claims to the contrary. They ... abandoned the moral field to the scientists, engineers, and bureaucrats of the secular Nazi ideology. God had, in effect, ceased to function as a meaning-generating concept for" many "despite the continuity of Christian bureaucratic institutions."[250] While both religious and secular individuals can behave morally or immorally, Haas points out that, when the divine is removed from one's ethical frame of reference, no place remains in which God can act.[251] "God is not silent," declares Heschel. "He has been silenced." Humans have "expelled" God from the world, betrayed God's truth and defied God's will. In Heschel's language, we have slammed the doors of the world on God. "*God is in exile.*"[252]

Faith, Free Will, and Jehanne

Let us consider the possible nature and origin of human free will. Beginning with the premise of divine Self-limitation, one might suppose that God was once omnipotent and chose to grant humans free will, relinquishing a portion of divine power. Perhaps God exchanged power for the possibility of reciprocal love between divinity and humanity. The

---

248. Haas, "Auschwitz," 115–16.

249. Heschel, "Hiding God," 378.

250. Haas, "Auschwitz," 108–9. Haas acknowledges the minority of "believing Christians" who rejected "the Nazi version" of reality and "risked life and limb to defy" it. Ibid., 109.

251. Ibid., 120. Greenberg suggests that fear of God can serve to restrain human immorality whereas, in the absence of such fear, "there are no limits." Greenberg, "Cloud of Smoke," 46–47.

252. Heschel, "Hiding God," 378–79.

notion that God remains omnipotent while Self-limited constitutes a contradiction in terms since to be limited in any sense is to be less than omnipotent. The idea that God, having chosen Self-limitation, might choose to reverse the decision is incoherent in that omnipotence cannot be exercised from a position of limitation, even self-imposed limitation. Rather, it seems that God remains limited in the presence of non-conforming human wills, unable forcibly to reclaim free will bestowed upon humans, assuming that human will is as powerful as divine will since, if it were not, it would be ineffective. On this view, God cannot appropriate human free will but it can be surrendered to God. Hence, the more that human will cooperates with divine will, the more that divine power is restored, which leads to the question of whether or not there is a tipping point at which divine power might become sufficiently strong to overpower and appropriate the balance of human power should God desire to do so. One can only speculate. It is conceivable that God would not wish to usurp human power since power that is willingly surrendered to God might be considered more justly acquired and, therefore, a more dignified form of divine power than omnipotent power exercised over humans against our wills. Voluntarily surrendered human power is theoretically preferable to both God and humans. Perhaps the ultimate, ideal, potential end of the free will dynamic is for humans voluntarily to restore divine omnipotence by surrendering human will to divine will, in which case humans would participate in divine "omnipotence" in paradoxical fashion.

Watts holds that human "freedom is a delegation of the very freedom of God. Evil is an act which the creature commits with God's own power. He must use God to refuse God."[253] Weil maintains that, "[o]n God's part creation is not an act of self-expansion but of restraint and renunciation. . . . God accepted this diminution. He emptied a part of his being from himself. . . . God denied himself for our sakes in order to give us the possibility of denying ourselves for him."[254] Divine dependence on humans resulting from the delegation of free will to humanity is presumably reversed at the moment of human surrender to divine will, at which point the human returns willingly to his or her original state in the divine-human relationship, that is, a state of dependence on God, except that the human is now voluntarily dependent on God. Such

---

253. Watts, *Behold the Spirit*, 68, n. 3.
254. Weil, *Waiting for God*, 89.

an understanding of the divine-human relationship wherein God seeks human cooperation but does not coerce is consistent with the prophetic perception of God as concerned for and intimately involved with human affairs. In any case, to claim that God is not omnipotent is not to declare God powerless but merely limited in the exercise of power. So long as human free will remains intact, the matter of its surrender is an ongoing human choice and divine concern. However, God's dependence on humanity is mitigated by God's freedom to dispense grace and to reveal God's Self to human beings at any time and in any way. Humans cannot control the revelatory event, only our response to it.

Some might argue that unsolicited divine revelation constitutes interference with human will by imposition of divine will in the act of revelation itself. Nonetheless, humans have the choice of accepting or denying God's revelation, of embracing or rejecting it, which clears God of the imposition charge and negates the interference theory, unless one considers the mere existence of something (i.e., revelation) and, therefore, of everything as constituting a form of interference with or imposition on human will. That, however, is not tenable. While humans are arguably influenced to varying degrees by everything that we consciously (and perhaps subconsciously) encounter, revelation cannot be said to interfere with human will on that basis since influence does not equate to interference, which has a negative connotation. Influence merely affects (and possibly informs) and can be positive or negative. The fact that we can ignore, reject, doubt, misinterpret, or fail to recognize divine revelation indicates that it cannot impose itself upon human will, but only upon human experience. The thing experienced does not dictate one's response to the experience.[255] Humans are capable of ac-

---

255. For example, an individual might have great difficulty in resisting a piece of cake offered by a friend while another might have no difficulty in declining it, although both enjoy cake; in neither instance does the existence of the cake diminish the freedom of the individuals in responding to it. In fact, a particular individual might accept cake in one instance and refuse it in another. Humans are free to interpret and respond to revelatory encounters in various ways in accordance with personal choice, values, understanding, or inclination, much like the way in which two people experiencing identical dreams might respond differently to them. One individual might believe that the dream is prophetic, that it relays an imperative to act in a certain manner, or that it is otherwise instructive or compelling and might take action based on this while the other might view the dream as completely insignificant and choose to ignore it. In both instances, the dream is experienced, but the human agents are free to respond to it in any manner chosen. Furthermore, in an extreme scenario, an individual might choose

tively opposing divine will at every moment whereas God cannot simultaneously grant human free will and violate it through active opposition. In granting humans free will, God does not eliminate divine will, but the divine right to enforce divine will, that is, to control human affairs, although God apparently retains the ability to participate in those affairs via revelation and grace. Hence, although prophetic revelation might urge and prompt in a powerful manner, it is not an explicit imposition of divine will over and against human will. Divine revelation might be regarded as an offering, an opportunity to experience God more fully by entering into more substantial relationship with God. "Act, and God will act," Jehanne prompted Alençon, her "gentle Duke," when he was once reluctant to engage in battle. "When God pleases, the hour is ripe."[256] If we accept the invitation to act in accordance with divine revelation, God can act through us but, unless we are willing conduits for the activity of divine grace, we can block its operation through us.

Human free will and divine omnipotence cannot be adequately discussed without considering the crucifixion event. Contrary to the teachings of traditional Christology, there is no compelling reason to suppose that God—if, in fact, God could do so—suspended human free will (temporarily or permanently) in the matter of the death of Jesus (or at any other time) in favor of a divine plan which was to arrive at inevitable fulfillment through divinely-coerced individuals. It seems more likely that the death of Jesus resulted from human choice and action in the exercise of free will. Jesus' plea on the cross, "Father, forgive them; for they do not know what they are doing," suggests that it was not by divine design that his executioners acted but by their own misguided wills; otherwise, there would be nothing for God to forgive with respect to this deed.[257] Perhaps misinterpretation of the crucifixion of Jesus and concomitant notions of salvation have created a theological worldview that has provided leeway for individuals to abandon, with relatively untroubled conscience, a sense of personal responsibility and accountability in the maintenance of social justice. Jacobs suggests that, as Judaism must rethink notions of God, covenant, "and the Jewish people," post-*Shoah* Christian theology should reevaluate the "notion of God the

---

to act in explicit contradiction to divine revelation on the basis that he or she worships Satan. In all of these instances, human freedom of choice remains intact.

256. Jehanne; quoted by Alençon, in Pernoud, *Retrial*, 157.

257. Luke 23:34.

Father, His Son Jesus the Christ, and the relationship of that Christ to this unredeemed world."[258] "[E]ven in historic Christianity the bitterness of the cross was not maintained in the recollection of believers or in the reality presented by the church," states Jürgen Moltmann. "[T]he more the church of the crucified Christ became the prevailing religion of society, and set about satisfying the personal and public needs of this society, the more it left the cross behind it, and gilded the cross with the expectations and ideas of salvation," he declares.[259] Soelle criticizes traditional Christology, stating that "[i]t is not difficult to establish sadistic traits in the picture of God . . . as it has been passed down . . . [wherein] the God who decrees suffering is praised. It has to be God himself there who crucifies poor Jesus or 'hands him over.' God can only forgive there when blood has flowed. In such theology the cross expresses above all the relationship between the Father and the Son; the fact that it was an instrument of the power of Imperial Rome is deemed incidental. . . . [W]e misunderstand the cross," she insists, "when we make it into a necrophilic, death-seeking symbol."[260] "It is not God who makes us suffer. But love has its price."[261] René Girard also rejects traditional Christological teachings and interprets the death of Jesus as a human act of murder rather than a sacrifice offered by God. "The Gospels," he asserts, "only speak of *sacrifices* in order to reject them and deny them any validity. . . . There is nothing in the Gospels to suggest that the death of Jesus is a sacrifice, whatever definition (expiation, substitution, etc.) we may give for that sacrifice." Moreover, Girard maintains, the Gospel texts contradict the "practice of making the deity responsible for all the evils that can afflict humanity." He believes that sacrificial interpretation of the crucifixion derives from a tremendous "misunderstanding" and human failure to comprehend, and accept responsibility for, our own violence. On Girard's view, while caused entirely by humans and not required or demanded by God, Jesus' death conveys a divine imperative to end sacrificial violence.[262]

Considering the possibility that humans perpetrated the crucifixion of Jesus with neither divine consent nor assistance, let us suppose that

258. Jacobs, "Judaism and Christianity," 20.
259. Moltmann, *Crucified God*, 40–41.
260. Soelle, *Theology for Skeptics*, 100, 103.
261. Ibid., 102–3.
262. Girard, *Things Hidden*, 180, 183, 210, 213.

The Theology of Jehanne d'Arc

Jesus' earthly purpose was to end humanly-inflicted suffering by teaching us to love one another as God loves us, but that humans, rejecting the message, freely killed Jesus[263]—and God could not prevent it. Thus, humanity continues to suffer at our own hands as we engage in acts of human evil, reenacting our rejection of the divine message of love. It is pertinent to recall that Jehanne did not hold God responsible for her martyrdom. God also conceivably suffers as a result of human godlessness and the crucifixion might be interpreted as representing mutual affliction between humanity and divinity. Free will allows humanity the ongoing possibility of self-redemption in choosing to end unnecessary violence[264] but, to the extent that human will is applied to contrary ends, all will suffer.

Lack of human cooperation with divine will might account for discrepancies between some prophecies and their fulfillment and for the ambiguity of some prophecy insofar as, in allowing human free will, God might offer tentative predictions about human events when the outcome is contingent upon human cooperation with divine will.[265] Jean Bréhal, Inquisitor of France at the time of Jehanne's nullification trial, suggested that, had her parents known of Jehanne's plan to leave Domremy, they might have contravened divine will by preventing or delaying her departure.[266] In fact, Jehanne's father was distressed over a prophetic dream that she "would go off with the soldiers," subsequent to which her parents guarded her very strictly, and "she greatly feared that they would lose their minds when she left" for Vaucouleurs.[267] Moreover, human will reportedly interfered with divine will in that, although Jehanne's voices instructed her to remain at nearby Saint-Denis follow-

---

263. Perhaps Jesus foresaw this (as Jehanne received indications of her upcoming martyrdom) and thus spoke of resurrection and the forthcoming gift of the Holy Spirit. Matt 16:21; John 14:26.

264. This does not rule out the possibility of employing minimal violence in ending violence.

265. John of the Cross advises that divine revelations whose outcomes "are dependent on human, changeable causes" should not be treated as literal predictions. John of the Cross, *Collected Works*, 171. Hvidt identifies "an 'if' that renders ... prophetic predictions plastic and open to human intervention.... Thus, the fulfillment of ... prophecy is always predicated on the free response ... from the faithful." Hvidt, *Christian Prophecy*, 110. Heschel agrees that "[t]he prophet's predictions can always be proved wrong by a change in" human conduct. Heschel, *Prophets: Introduction*, 16.

266. Bréhal; in Pinzino, "*Lex Privata*," 102.

267. Jehanne; in Scott, *Trial*, 105–6.

ing the battle for Paris, on account of her limited mobility due to injury, she was unable to prevent her comrades-in-arms from taking her with them as they returned to the Loire.[268] One cannot know how history would have unfolded had Jehanne remained near Paris—perhaps she would have retaken the city. She had advised Charles VII en route to Rheims that he would recover his entire kingdom *if* he proceeded boldly and courageously[269] but, in choosing to negotiate with Burgundy and to call a truce at Paris, Charles apparently delayed the complete recovery of his kingdom. Jehanne's example supports a view of God as either limited or supported by human will, but not as omnipotent. While dissenting human will might interfere with the fulfillment of divine will, assenting human will allows the suspension of human limitation through the operation of divine grace, permitting extraordinary events deemed miraculous to occur.

There is an important benefit to be derived from a degree of prophetic inaccuracy, which is that it discourages idolization or worship of humans. If prophets were completely accurate in their utterances, the fact that they are vehicles of God and not gods themselves might be overlooked. Our fallibility as humans, whose grace derives from a non-human source, might be forgotten. Such inaccuracies demand that human words and deeds always be thoroughly scrutinized and responsibly evaluated and that humans never be mistaken for gods.

Heschel states that the prophet "never finds in God a desire which does not bear upon man."[270] "Sympathy is the prophet's answer to inspiration, the correlative to revelation," he maintains, describing prophetic sympathy as "the assimilation of the prophet's emotional life to the divine, an assimilation of function, not of being." The prophet "lives not only his personal life, but also the life of God. The prophet hears God's

---

268. Ibid., 69. Also, Cagny; in Pernoud from Quicherat, vol. 4, 25–29, *Herself and Her Witnesses*, 137. Jehanne's divine counsel *permitted* her to depart Saint-Denis, but being permitted on account of her inability to exercise free will does not negate the fact that divine command was contradicted by the free will of her companions. Jehanne; in Scott, *Trial*, 139. That Jehanne's voices instructed her to maintain her position at Saint-Denis indicates that she was not without divine instruction (as some suggest) with regard to the latter part of her military campaign (post-coronation), at least with respect to movement.

269. S. Charles; in Taylor, *La Pucelle*, 319.

270. Heschel, *Prophets: II*, 265.

voice and feels His heart."[271] Weil maintains that, accepting God into one's life, God places a seed within us "without our knowing what" the seed contains. It eventually becomes apparent that, "[i]f we had known, we should not have said yes at the first moment" since "the growth of the seed within us is painful." In accepting the growth, she explains, one "cannot avoid destroying whatever gets in its way.... We can only consent to give up our own feelings so as to allow free passage in our soul for... love" of God. "That is the meaning of denying oneself," she insists. "We are created for this consent, and for this alone."[272] Weil's statement conjures Jehanne's proclamation: "I was born to do this,"[273] reflecting a single-hearted and single-minded dedication to divine mission.

Persistent in her claim to have obeyed God, Jehanne considered it

> impossible that she revoke what she had done or said, as declared to the trial, on the subject of her visions and the revelations that she said that she had had from God; and she would not revoke them for anything. She would not stop doing what God made, commanded and would command her to do for any man alive. And it would be impossible for her to revoke these ... ; and if the Church wished to make her do anything else contrary to the command that she said had been given by God, she would not do it for anything.[274]

So strongly was she compelled to act in accordance with divine will that, for Jehanne, to act contrarily was nearly inconceivable.[275] "The attention turned with love towards God (or in a lesser degree, towards anything which is truly beautiful)," states Weil, "makes certain things impossible for us. Such is the non-acting action of prayer in the soul. There are ways of behaviour which would veil such attention should they be indulged in and which, reciprocally, this attention puts out of the question."[276] Soelle quotes a pertinent passage from Lewis:

271. Heschel, *Prophets: Introduction*, 26.

272. Weil, *Waiting for God*, 79–80.

273. Jehanne declared that she was not afraid of encountering the enemy en route to Chinon as "she had God, her Lord, who would clear the way for her" since she was "born to do this." Jehanne; quoted by Henri Royer, husband of Catherine; in Pernoud, *Herself and Her Witnesses*, 36.

274. Jehanne; in Taylor, *La Pucelle*, 206.

275. As mentioned earlier, Jehanne disobeyed her divine voices in leaping from the Beaurevoir tower. Jehanne; in Scott, *Trial*, 121.

276. Weil, *Gravity and Grace*, 119.

> The odd thing was that before God closed in on me, I was in fact offered what now appears a moment of wholly free choice. . . . I became aware that I was holding something at bay, or shutting something out. . . . I felt myself being, there and then, given a free choice. I could open the door or keep it shut. . . . Neither choice was presented as a duty; no threat or promise was attached to either, though I know that to open the door . . . meant the incalculable. The choice appeared to be momentous but it was also strangely unemotional. I was moved by no desire or fears. In a sense I was not moved by anything. I chose to open. . . . I say "I chose," yet it did not really seem possible to do the opposite. On the other hand, I was aware of no motives. You could argue that I was not a free agent, but I am more inclined to think that this came nearer to being a perfectly free act than most that I have ever done. Necessity may not be the opposite of freedom, and perhaps a man is most free when, instead of producing motives, he could only say "I am what I do."[277]

That "[n]either choice was presented as a duty; no threat or promise was attached to either," corresponds to the initial moment of choice whereby one surrenders personal will to divine will from which unknown and "incalculable" consequences ensue with respect to which one may not be offered further choice, the consequences flowing naturally from and constituting part of the initial choice, or with respect to which any subsequent choice might not be entirely free (i.e., unbound by threat or promise).[278] Such acceptance of unknown consequences constitutes a significant aspect of faith. The experience of choosing while simultaneously feeling that it is impossible "to do the opposite" corresponds to Heschel's observation that the prophet "is both active and passive, free and forced. He is free to respond to the content of the moment; he is forced to experience the moment, to accept the burden of his mission. Thus the effect of the impact of inspiration is to evoke in him both a sense of freedom and a feeling of coercion, an act of spontaneity and an awareness of enforced receptivity."[279] Lewis's assertion that "[n]ecessity

---

277. Lewis, *Surprised by Joy*; in Soelle, *Silent Cry*, 23.

278. Heschel states that the event of prophetic inspiration, wherein God powerfully communicates a divine message to the prophet, contains "an element of will . . . expressed in the initial decision" of the prophet. The "subsequent direction and development is merely the unfolding of what is given in the moment of decision." Heschel, *Prophets: II*, 223.

279. Ibid., 225. To accept the burden of the mission does not equate to accepting

may not be the opposite of freedom" suggests that one is free to act in accordance with necessity when unbound by personal motives. "We have to consent to be subject to necessity," states Weil. "To be willing to go as far as possible is to pray to be impelled [by God], but without knowing whither." Weil characterizes operating from necessity not as "an action but a sort of passivity. Inactive action."[280]

Asked what her voices taught her with respect to the salvation of her soul, Jehanne replied that they first told her to behave well and attend church frequently and later instructed her to go into France and raise the siege of Orléans.[281] Since fulfillment of her mission was deemed necessary to the salvation of her soul, one wonders whether Jehanne exercised free will, submitted to divine will, or both. It is likely that Jehanne consented to do God's will prior to receiving instruction to go into France as the particulars of her mission were not revealed immediately. The mission would thus constitute an incalculable consequence stemming from an original choice. Jehanne voluntarily pledged her virginity—representing total commitment to God—on her first encounter with the voices; hence, it is reasonable to suspect that she committed herself to divine service at an early stage of the revelatory encounters. Having submitted to divine will, Jehanne would have considered it necessary that she cooperate once the particulars of her mission were unveiled, necessary at least to the accomplishment of divine will through her and to the salvation of her soul. Based on Jehanne's example, it seems possible for an individual to turn away from God having once submitted, but not without potential adverse consequences to the state of one's soul. Perhaps Jehanne could have avoided imprisonment and martyrdom had she chosen to abandon her mission and return to Domremy upon learning of her impending capture, but she might have suffered spiritual affliction as a result. Freedom and necessity are not opposites.

Jehanne did not claim that God requested anything of her but that God commanded her,[282] yet she did not apparently consider this relationship oppressive as she had consented to divine will. She stated, "I wait upon God my Creator in all. I love Him with all my heart.... I trust

---

the mission itself.

280. Weil, *Gravity and Grace*, 43–45.

281. Jehanne; in Scott, *Trial*, 67.

282. "Everything I have done is by the command of the Lord." Jehanne; in Taylor, *La Pucelle*, 154.

in my judge, that is the King of Heaven and earth."[283] Having accepted a divine call, Jehanne understood her role as divine servant. One "is called by a revelation to go out into the world to proclaim the word, to labor and to suffer, to lead an unremittingly active life as God's messenger," states Kierkegaard.[284] Jehanne was fully human, not superhuman, and, as such, she was immune to nothing within the realm of human experience, yet she surrendered her will fully to God. The essence of her spirituality was utter commitment to "God being served first" in all things.[285]

Reciprocity appears to be at work in the affairs of the world; as God conceivably limited God's Self in granting humans free will, we can likewise limit ourselves by giving our wills to God. In surrendering one's will to divine will, one does so in faith, faith that acknowledges human limitation. Jehanne declared to her Poitiers examiners, "There is more in our Lord's books than in yours,"[286] which speaks to her faith in the expansive mystery of God and awareness of the limitations of human knowledge. Although faith acknowledges human limitation, it does not advocate human powerlessness or thoughtlessness since one is not necessarily guided clearly, specifically, directly, and entirely by God at every breath and step of one's life, no matter how strong one's faith. In fact, Moltmann holds that "the greatest Christian saints were also the most profoundly abandoned by God."[287] Moreover, faith and surrender of personal will to divine will are perpetual choices requiring ongoing thought. Jehanne was clear, strong, and unshakable in her faith and also clearly thought for herself in accepting the divine call, formulating military strategy, twice attempting to escape imprisonment, responding to questions, and recanting the abjuration, to cite a few instances.

Jehanne's faith in her revelations was sufficiently strong that she was willing to place herself on the battlefields confident of victory. However, being confident of victory and being confident of one's personal survival are different matters, and Jehanne did not perceive herself as immune to death in battle. Confronted with the accusation that her courage derived from divine assurance that she would not die in combat,

283. Jehanne; in Scott, *Trial*, 148.
284. Kierkegaard, *Authority and Revelation*, 121.
285. Jehanne; in Taylor, *La Pucelle*, 206.
286. Jehanne; quoted by Touroulde, in Pernoud, *Retrial*, 124. "My Lord has a book in which no clerk has ever read." Jehanne; quoted by Pasquerel, ibid., 190.
287. Moltmann, *Crucified God*, 55.

The Theology of Jehanne d'Arc

Jehanne insisted that she had no more guarantee of this than any other.[288] In fact, she was wounded several times in battle. Nonetheless, Jehanne assured her army at Jargeau that they should not fear the English since "God was conducting their campaign. She said that if she were not sure that God was conducting their campaign, she would rather keep her sheep than expose herself to dangers like these."[289] This comes across more as a confession of faith and declaration that only God is worthy of such risk-taking than as a claim to divine protection. Upon incurring her first battle wound, Jehanne indicated that she knew she must die some day, but she did not know when, where, or how.[290] The only one to whom Jehanne promised invulnerability to death in his battles with her is Alençon, whom she vowed to return safely to his wife. Keeping her word, she warned him at Jargeau to move from a particular location in order to avoid being killed by a piece of artillery. The Duke heeded the advice and escaped untimely death, but a less fortunate man was killed in that place by the artillery indicated.[291] Jehanne participated in battles during the latter part of her campaign with respect to which she did not claim divine guidance,[292] although she apparently regarded these as supportive of her divine mission; in such instances, she had no grounds to presume herself subject to divine protection.

Jehanne displayed faith beyond reason. With respect to her first failed escape attempt, she resolved that it did not appear to be "God's will that she should escape."[293] Such faith embraces divine mystery and accepts chaos, paradox, and personal suffering as possible components of lived faith. Jehanne drew courage from the faith that sustained her. The personal consequences arising from her life of faith unfolded gradually

---

288. Touroulde; in Pernoud, *Retrial*, 124.
289. Jehanne; quoted by Alençon, in Pernoud, *Retrial*, 156.
290. Pasquerel; in Pernoud, *Retrial*, 189.
291. Alençon; ibid., 157.
292. The battle for Paris was not undertaken on the basis of Jehanne's revelations but at the discretion of herself and her comrades. Jehanne; in Taylor, *La Pucelle*, 186, 195. She participated in an assault at La Charité, not by the command of God, but on the recommendation of her companions-at-arms. Ibid., 173, 186, 195. She received no divine instruction to sally forth from Compiègne on the day of her capture. Ibid., 176. After learning of her impending capture, it became Jehanne's practice to defer to the military decisions of the other captains. Ibid., 186, 195.
293. Jehanne; in Scott, *Trial*, 117.

and frighteningly, yet she did not run from them, demonstrating that surrender cannot be partial but must be complete.

Kierkegaard on Faith and Violence

No theological discourse on faith and violence would be complete without reference to Kierkegaard's assessment of the nature of faith in his *Fear and Trembling*. In this work, Kierkegaard examines the *Aqedah*, the biblical account of Abraham's willingness to sacrifice his young son, Isaac, by divine command. According to the story, at the moment when Abraham is about to slay Isaac, an angel of God orders him to stop, sparing the boy.[294] The *Aqedah* exemplifies faith beyond reason and, whether or not one believes the tale, Kierkegaard's evaluation of it offers insight into the nature of faith, grace, and claims to divinely sanctioned violence.

For Kierkegaard, the *Aqedah* presents faith as a "monstrous . . . paradox capable of making a murder into a holy act well pleasing to God,"[295] capable, one presumes, depending upon the interpretation applied to the story. "The ethical expression for what Abraham did," he notes, "is that he was willing to murder Isaac; the religious expression is that he was willing to sacrifice Isaac; but in this contradiction lies the very anguish that can . . . make one sleepless."[296] Indeed, the words "murder" and "sacrifice" are merely two words for essentially the same deed, one word condemning the act, the other sanctifying it. "Can one speak unreservedly of Abraham," Kierkegaard asks, "without risking that someone will go off the rails and do likewise?" He points out, however, that "it is only in respect of faith that one achieves resemblance to Abraham, not murder."[297] Moreover, Joseph Blenkinsopp advises "that the ethical teaching of the prophets must . . . be explained with reference to the social contexts in which the message was uttered."[298] Hence, the particular divine directive received by the prophet is not necessarily to be construed as universal. Since a specific divine directive can apply definitively only to the specific individual to whom it is given in the specific context in which it is given, one cannot resemble the recipient of such a directive with respect to the

---

294. Gen 22:1–13. *Aqedah*, meaning "binding," is the name given in Hebrew sources to the story. Chilton, *Abraham's Curse*, 2.

295. Kierkegaard, *Fear and Trembling*, 61.

296. Ibid., 31.

297. Ibid., 32.

298. Blenkinsopp, *Prophecy in Israel*, 39.

directive itself unless one receives a similar divine directive. Otherwise, one can resemble one such as Abraham only with respect to his faith in receiving and responding to a divine directive. Likewise, the model of righteous warfare and human agency derived from Jehanne's claim to divine sanction in this work does not urge individuals to participate in war; rather, in addition to providing criteria against which claims to divine sanction might be measured, it encourages individuals who do engage in warfare to emulate her behavior in war grounded in her faith in God and divine revelation and its expression in terms of the divine concern for humanity revealed through the prophets, hence, its expression in compassion.

Abraham's action, Kierkegaard explains, suspends the ethical in relation to "a higher *telos*" residing outside the ethical and apart from the universal. When the ethical is teleologically suspended in an individual, that individual "exists as the particular in opposition to the universal." Hence, "the knight of faith renounces the universal in order to be the particular."[299] Hvidt explains that the prophet (who qualifies as a knight of faith) operates within the liminal and, within this realm, "exists apart from and does things differently from normal society [the universal]."[300] Moreover, the "classifications on which order normally depends are annulled or obscured—other symbols designate temporary antinomic liberation from behavioral norms and cognitive rules."[301] The "character of universality" is "lost" in the limen.[302]

"Someone who believes it is a simple enough matter to be the individual can always be certain that he is not the knight of faith," asserts Kierkegaard. "The knight of faith has only himself, and it is there the terrible lies ... [for] the knight of faith is alone about everything. ... The true knight of faith is ... the individual, absolutely nothing but the individual ... who, in cosmic isolation, hears never a [human] voice but walks alone with his dreadful responsibility."[303] Saint Teresa declares, "[I]n falling I had many friends to help me; but in rising I found my-

---

299. Kierkegaard, *Fear and Trembling*, 69, 72, 90.

300. Hvidt, *Christian Prophecy*, 265.

301. Turner, *Ritual Process*, 193; in Hvidt, *Christian Prophecy*, 265. This is consistent with Rahner's assertion that divine revelation can contradict universal law. Rahner, *Inquiries*, 108–9.

302. Toniolo, "Nostalgia delle Origini," 806; in Hvidt, *Christian Prophecy*, 265.

303. Kierkegaard, *Fear and Trembling*, 90, 94–96.

self so alone that I am now amazed I did not remain ever fallen. And I praise the mercy of God, for it was He alone who gave me His hand."[304] Although Jehanne had an army of followers, she stood alone before God and before her captors, judges, and executioner. "Only someone who finds the courage to be different from others can ultimately exist for 'others', for otherwise he exists only with those who are like him. And this is not much help to them," states Moltmann.[305]

According to Kierkegaard, faith manifests as paradox in the life of the individual who acts "on the strength of the absurd," the paradox itself constituting absurdity.[306] The paradox of faith, he explains, is

> that the single individual as the particular is higher than the universal, is justified before the latter . . . in such a way . . . that it is the single individual who, having been subordinate to the universal as the particular, now by means of the universal becomes that individual who, as the particular, stands in an absolute relation to the absolute. This position cannot be mediated, for all mediation occurs precisely by virtue of the universal; it is and remains in all eternity a paradox. . . . And yet faith *is* this paradox.[307]

Paradox, however, is not readily grasped by all, and faith is often perceived as madness, particularly to those devoid of faith. Kierkegaard characterizes Abraham, biblical "father" of faith, as "great in that hope whose outward form is insanity."[308] In what does this "insanity" consist? Suspending faith in human vision in favor of divine vision qualifies as madness defined in relation to that which the human mind ordinarily deems sane in the absence of divine considerations. Heschel describes the prophet as one "who suffers from a profound maladjustment to the spirit of society, with its conventional lies, with its concessions to man's weakness. Compromise is an attitude the prophet abhors," he maintains, as it contains great corruptive power.[309] This was evident in Jehanne's disapproval of Charles VII's negotiations with Burgundy through which pieces of France were voluntarily handed to the enemy. The prophetic

---

304. Teresa of Avila, *Collected Works*, vol. 1, 94.
305. Moltmann, *Crucified God*, 16.
306. Kierkegaard, *Fear and Trembling*, 65.
307. Ibid., 64. "[B]y means of the universal" suggests that one can only exist apart from the universal in relation to the universal.
308. Ibid., 16.
309. Heschel, *Prophets: II*, 188.

soul, Heschel asserts, is completely "insurgent against indifference to aberrations." Such "maladaptation" to society "may be characterized as *moral madness*" (as distinct from psychological madness).[310] Since the prophet (the knight of faith) lacks support from the universal, "the movement of faith must be made continually on the strength of the absurd,"[311] but, Kierkegaard advises, "no one has the right to . . . let others suppose that faith is something inferior or that it is an easy matter, when in fact it is the greatest and most difficult of all."[312]

What is the higher *telos* of the *Aqedah*? Peering through the madness of the story, which appears initially to sanction human sacrifice, one discovers that the *Aqedah* demonstrates divine prohibition of sacrificial violence—an angel stops Abraham from sacrificing the child. If God commanded Abraham to perform human sacrifice, the story suggests, it was in order to teach humanity *not* to do it. The *Aqedah* suggests itself as the only legitimate example of faith-based human sacrifice—legitimate only because it was pre-ordained *not* to succeed.[313] The *Aqedah* urges not only faith in God, but faith in the goodness of God. Paradoxically, the command to sacrifice Isaac has a revelatory purpose in condemning sacrificial murder as a human act displeasing to God rather than a holy act pleasing to God. If God sanctions violence, it is presumably out of necessity in engaging in human affairs in such a manner as ultimately to defeat human violence. On this view, divinely sanctioned killing is not considered sacrifice and is displeasing to God. Recall that it is faith, not murder, that constitutes the worthiness of Abraham's deed. Jehanne's mission, like the *Aqedah*, is paradoxical in condoning violent activity with a view to ending it. "[T]o express the sublime in the pedestrian absolutely," states Kierkegaard, "is something only the knight of faith can do."[314] Hence, in assessing claims to divine sanction, one might look for expression of the sublime absolutely in a claimant's activities—one might note Jehanne's undifferentiated compassion in warfare in this regard.

In considering "how it comes about that a new point of departure is created in relation to the established order," Kierkegaard suggests

310. Ibid.
311. Kierkegaard, *Fear and Trembling*, 41.
312. Ibid., 59.
313. Any other story following the same tenets would be viewed likewise.
314. Kierkegaard, *Fear and Trembling*, 45.

that it comes about by the fact that *the point of departure is FROM ABOVE, from God,* and *the formula is this paradox that an individual is employed.* Humanly understood, an individual ... is infinitely nothing in comparison with the established order (the universal), so it is a paradox that the individual is the stronger. This can be explained only by the fact that it is God who makes use of him, God who stands behind him; but just for this reason one sees God again, just because the situation is a paradox. When there are hundreds of men, what comes to pass is explained simply by the activity of the hundreds of men, but the paradox compels us (insofar as freedom can be compelled) to take notice of God, that he is taking part in it.[315]

Lex Privata, *Kierkegaard, and Jehanne*

The theological concept of *lex privata* as discussed in Jane Marie Pinzino's work on Jehanne is compatible with Kierkegaard's notion of a divinely sanctioned teleological suspension of the ethical. Pinzino describes the operation of *lex privata* upon and within an individual as an infusion of grace independent of conscience permitting personal suspension of public (and canon) law and commanding obedience to divine law revealed through "private, mystical experience."[316] This does not suggest that one does not engage conscience, but that conscience and prophetic revelation operate on different levels. In Jehanne's case, if conscience was not employed directly in the matter of discerning and obeying her divine instructions, it was apparently employed in her manner of carrying them out. Pinzino explains that, in the medieval application of *lex privata*, "chosenness ... increased one's personal responsibility rather than decreased it—[it was considered] a freedom *for* service to a greater mission rather than a freedom *from* the constraints of an onerous personal obligation. ... [It] demanded that an individual develop inward disciplines and capacities of moral discernment and sound judgment, forms of self-denial and strengths of ... character that bear fruit in the form of judicious actions serving the repair of the world. *Lex privata*," she observes, "emerged from the nullification trial discussion [of Jehanne] scarcely as an antinomian warrant, and more substantially as a self-sacrificial commitment to a greater cause and the common good." The understanding

---

315. Kierkegaard, *Authority and Revelation*, 192–93.
316. Pinzino, "*Lex Privata*," 86, 95.

of *lex privata* as arising from God distinguishes it from today's "secular individualism," she notes.[317] Jehanne's divine instructions may have corresponded to the dictates of her conscience to some extent, but the fact that the infusion of grace occurs independently of conscience suggests that it can contradict conscience. *Lex privata* does not appear to encourage suspension of conscience but to condone faith in revelation that transcends it. Although Jehanne was averse to bloodshed, the violence in which she participated did not necessarily contradict her conscience entirely if she viewed ending the war as a moral necessity. Jehanne's was a divine directive that one can more easily wrap one's conscience around than Abraham's in the absence of foreknowledge of the outcome.

Pinzino points out that, while *lex privata* transcends *lex publica*, it is still "a matter of law—divine law to be obeyed." Before the Rouen court, she observes, Jehanne "defended her illicit actions and behaviors as minor transgressions allowed by God ... for the sake of a greater cause. ... She explained that it was her primary obligation to obey the law directly mandated to her by heaven over the law of the Church, a law she normally upheld and obeyed." In so doing, Pinzino states, Jehanne demonstrated an "implicit sense of moral empowerment akin to the principle of *lex privata*."[318] Regarding her male clothing, Jehanne stated, "Since I do this by the command of God and in His service, I do not think that I am doing wrong; and this clothing will be set aside immediately when God chooses to command it."[319] The canonists at Jehanne's nullification trial cited *lex privata* in support of her activities, appealing to the irresistible workings of the Holy Spirit in compelling action in the faithful such that, in Jehanne's case, she "knew no alternative that would give her spirit rest."[320]

In terms of Kierkegaard's analysis, Jehanne viewed herself as standing in an absolute relation to the Absolute, refusing submission to the Rouen court over God. When instructed by her judges to choose one of her (enemy) assessors as advisor, Jehanne declared, "And for your offer of counsel, I have no intention of departing from the advice of Our Lord."[321] Moreover, the following is telling:

317. Ibid., 90, 95.
318. Ibid., 92, 95.
319. Jehanne; in Taylor, *La Pucelle*, 192.
320. Pinzino, "*Lex Privata*," 97.
321. Jehanne; in Scott, *Trial*, 131.

> She said also that she submits to God her Creator, Who caused her to do what she did; and refers it to Him in His own Person.
>
> Asked if she means that she has no judge on earth, and our Holy Father the Pope is not her judge,
>
> She replied: I will tell you nothing else. I have a good Master, Our Lord, in Whom I trust for everything, and not in any other.
>
> She was told that if she did not wish to believe in the Church . . . she would be a heretic . . . and that she would be punished by other judges who would sentence her to be burned.
>
> She answered: I will tell you nothing else.[322]

"No movement, no individual, ever had power without some kind of creed," declares Watts, "something believed so intensely as to be worth dying for. Ethical principles do not inspire such devotion, for the thing believed in must have far more reality than a mode of behaviour or an abstract social system."[323]

Several apparent contradictions in Jehanne's life and mission resonate with Kierkegaard's expression of the paradoxical or absurd. They are:

1. That she was both an active warrior and a compassionate saint.

2. That she was untrained in military matters and yet extremely adept militarily.

3. That she was a young peasant girl leading experienced men at arms in battle, turning the tide of war in favor of the French when they had all but lost conclusively.[324]

4. That she transcended the gender boundary while maintaining it by adopting a male role while self-identifying as Jehanne *la pucelle*, a distinctively female appellation.

5. That she was unschooled theologically or otherwise but was able to stump bishops and doctors of theology and law.

---

322. Ibid., 149.

323. Watts, *Behold the Spirit*, 10.

324. What occurred cannot be adequately attributed solely to "the activity of the hundreds of men" (to employ Kierkegaard's analysis) who fought with Jehanne since their efforts had not sufficed to that point. Orléans was on the verge of surrendering to Burgundy when Jehanne appeared in the city's defense. Pernoud and Clin, *Her Story*, 13.

6. That the Church was responsible for both her execution and canonization.

7. That she underwent the paradox of martyrdom itself, which is that the most faithful servants of God often die wretched deaths on account of their faith in a God who does not or cannot spare them their suffering. Leonard Cohen writes: "*Myself, I long for love and light, / but must it come so cruel, must it be so bright!*"[325] Paradox indeed.

"Faith is the highest passion in a human being," states Kierkegaard. "Many in every generation may not come that far, but none comes further."[326] Jehanne was a most faithful servant of God. For her, to fulfill her divine mission was to fulfill her life. Ridiculed, denounced, called a whore, wounded, betrayed, scorned, abused, and burned, Jehanne suffered and sacrificed all in the name of faith. She operated from a position of absolute persistence and conviction: "[S]he would rather die than turn back from what God had made her do."[327]

The Cost of Practical, Prophetic Mysticism

A soul that God permits to advance ... before the eyes of the world can well prepare itself for martyrdom at the hands of this world; because if it doesn't want to die to the world, the world will itself put it to death.
—SAINT TERESA OF AVILA, COLLECTED WORKS, VOL. 1

It was said that a change swept over many who watched and listened to Jehanne praying as she died, her eyes gazing through the flames upon the crucifix that she had pleaded to have held before her. "Being in the flames, she ceased not to call in a loud voice the Holy Name of Jesus, imploring and invoking without ceasing the aid of the Saints in Paradise."[328] Jehanne also beseeched the priests who were present to say Mass for her.[329]

---

325. Cohen, "Joan of Arc," *Stranger Music*, 148.
326. Kierkegaard, *Fear and Trembling*, 151.
327. Jehanne; in Taylor, *La Pucelle*, 198.
328. La Pierre; in Murray, *Jeanne d'Arc*, 161.
329. Fabri; in Pernoud, *Retrial*, 249.

She uttered pious and devout lamentations and called on the Blessed Trinity, and on the blessed and glorious Virgin Mary ... in her devotions, her lamentations, and her true confession of faith. Also she most humbly begged all manner of people, of whatever condition or rank they might be, and whether of her party or of the other, for their pardon and asked them kindly to pray for her, at the same time pardoning them any harm they had done her. This she continued to do for a very long time, perhaps for half an hour, and until the end. The judges who were present, and even several of the English, were moved by this to great tears and weeping, and indeed they wept most bitterly. Some, and several of these same English, recognized God's hand and made professions of faith when they saw her make so remarkable an end. ... When she was handed over by the Church, I remained with her, and she asked most fervently to be given a cross. And when an Englishman who was present heard this he made her a little one out of wood from the end of a stick, and handed it to her. She received it and kissed it most devoutly, uttering pious lamentations and acknowledging God our Redeemer. ... Then she put that cross on her breast between her body and her clothes and humbly asked me to let her have the crucifix from the church so that she could gaze on it continuously until her death. ... When it was brought, she embraced it closely and long and clung to it until she was tied to the stake. ... And ... while she was still uttering devoted praise and lamentations to God and the saints, she was led off and tied to the stake. And her last word, as she died, was a loud cry of "Jesus."[330]

The testimonies of Jehanne's death relate a profound and transformative demonstration of enduring faith, courage, and forgiveness.[331] She exhibited extreme piety, humility, and grace in extreme suffering. Indeed, the story of her martyrdom retains its force in the retelling nearly six

---

330. Massieu; ibid., 246–48. La Pierre confirmed that, in response to Jehanne's "pitiful, devout, and Catholic words" uttered at the execution scene, "those who saw her in great numbers wept, and ... the Cardinal of England and many other English were forced to weep and to feel compassion." He also confirmed Jehanne's request to have the crucifix within direct view and her calling upon the name of Jesus in her final moments. La Pierre; in Murray, *Jeanne d'Arc*, 161. Pierre Boucher estimated that "perhaps ten thousand" people were present. Boucher; in Pernoud, *Retrial*, 249. Chambre noted that, although many wept, "some of the English laughed." Chambre; ibid., 250.

331. The papal decree advancing the cause of Jehanne's canonization notes the transformative power of her martyrdom, stating that "Men then began to repent of the deed, and in the very place of execution to venerate the sanctity of the Maid"; in Warner, *Joan of Arc*, 29, 282, n. 72.

centuries later; condemnation of the innocent is a powerful phenomenon. "We are all lost," the King of England's secretary lamented after departing the execution scene, "for it is a good and saintly person that has been burned."[332] Moreover, the executioner confessed on the day of Jehanne's death that he considered himself damned for having "burned a saint."[333] So extraordinary was the event that trial notary Manchon wept for an entire month afterwards. "I never wept as much for anything," he declared. "With a part of the money that I was paid for the case, I bought a little missal, which I still possess, to remind me to pray for her."[334]

Jehanne's confessor at Rouen, Martin Ladvenu, testified that "[r]ight up to the end . . . she maintained and asseverated that the voices she heard were of God, and that all that she had done she had done at God's command, and that she did not believe that she had been deceived by her voices, and that the revelations she had received were from God."[335] Jehanne thus reasserted the validity of her divine revelations and mission before the crowd who had assembled to witness the spectacle of her death, communicating that which she regarded as the most significant message she could offer and nullifying for all time the alleged abjuration. Jehanne suffered an excruciating and humiliating public death in order to honor and sustain the truth of God's message delivered through her. "She let God use her in the world; she withheld nothing from him, neither action nor suffering," notes Ann Astell. For Jehanne, "the lonely fulfillment of her mission" constituted "a radical instrumentality" which was her "way of holiness."[336]

Martyrdom is "a perfect sacrifice of love, a total giving of oneself" to God.[337] For Soelle, "sacrifice does not mean that a God hostile to life and humans has to be placated with blood, or that a saving quality accrues to suffering as such. Rather, that concept [sacrifice] expresses the participation of humans who do not acquiesce but who, in mystical defiance, insist through their suffering that nothing become lost."[338] Sacrifice

---

332. Jean Tressard; quoted by Cusquel, in Pernoud, *Retrial*, 251.

333. Jehanne's executioner was Geoffroy Therage; quoted by la Pierre, in Pernoud, *Retrial*, 253, 283.

334. Manchon; in Pernoud, *Retrial*, 254.

335. Ladvenu; ibid., 249.

336. Astell, "Joan of Arc and Spirituality," 4.

337. Merton, *Christian Mysticism*, 43.

338. Soelle, *Silent Cry*, 148–49.

is inherently difficult in proportion to the degree of self-deprivation or pain contained within it. Kierkegaard maintains that it is only when one's action on behalf of God absolutely contradicts one's feeling that the action constitutes a sacrifice.[339] Martyrdom constitutes the ultimate self-sacrifice and the ultimate witnessing.[340] Jehanne did not desire martyrdom and struggled fiercely with accepting it, which renders hers a true sacrifice. "Death is always death despite all mysticism."[341] As she wept over the death of others, Jehanne was no happier with the prospect of her own demise.

> Alas, am I to be so cruelly and horribly treated that my pure and unblemished body, which has never been corrupted, must today be consumed and burned to ashes! Oh, I had rather be seven times beheaded than be burned like this. Alas, if only I had been in the prisons of the Church to which I have submitted, if I had been guarded by churchmen and not by my enemies and foes, I should not have come to this miserable end. Oh, I call upon God, the great Judge, to see the great wrongs and griefs that are done me.[342]

Jehanne loved both life and God, not viewing them as mutually exclusive (unlike those mystics who regard the material order and earthly life with disdain[343]). Weil asserts that "[w]e can ... be almost certain that those whose love of God has caused the disappearance of the pure loves belonging to our life here below are no true friends of God. Our neighbor, our friends, religious ceremonies, and the beauty of the world do not fall to the level of unrealities after the soul has had direct contact with God. On the contrary, it is only then that these things become real. Previously they were half dreams."[344]

---

339. Kierkegaard, *Fear and Trembling*, 88.

340. "Martyr" in Greek is synonymous with "witness." Feyerabend, "μάρτυς," in *Langenscheidt's*, 244.

341. Casaldáliga, "Mystik der Befreiung"; in Soelle, *Silent Cry*, 287.

342. Jehanne; quoted by Toutmouillé, in Pernoud, *Retrial*, 245. If any of Jehanne's prison guards attempted to rape her following the alleged abjuration, they were apparently unsuccessful in light of Jehanne's references to her physical purity. This does not rule out the possibility that she was otherwise violated.

343. Watts cites "Erigena, the Victorines, St Francis, Eckhart, Tauler, [and] St. Bonaventure" in this regard. Watts, *Behold the Spirit*, 38.

344. Weil, *Waiting for God*, 142.

While death is not unwelcome to all those classified as "martyrs," a distinction is herein drawn between those who seek martyrdom and those who reluctantly accept it as a necessary consequence of lived faith. On Jehanne's model, life is a means of serving God. The word "sacred" can mean "holy," or "set apart . . . for the service or worship of God."[345] Hence, if life is viewed as sacred, it might be understood as fundamentally designated for divine service or worship, or worship *in* service. Viewing life as sacred, one does not desire its destruction or treat it as something to be cast away, but as something to be sacrificed reluctantly and only out of necessity in the expression of, commitment to, and living of faith should such necessity arise. Therefore, when one chooses to end one's life not as a matter of absolute necessity in faith, one chooses to terminate one's service and worship of God as manifested in one's life; however, when one accepts unwelcome death as a matter of necessity in faith, one effects service and worship of God. On this understanding, death constitutes a sacrifice when the martyr recognizes life as sacred. The reluctant martyr is thus distinguished from those who orchestrate their own deaths in the name of faith. "In case a teacher is . . . enthusiastically conscious that he himself in his existence is expressing and has expressed by the sacrifice of everything the doctrine he preaches, this consciousness may well give him a sure and firm spirit, but it does not give him authority," asserts Kierkegaard. Real authority "is a specific quality which comes from another place and makes itself felt."[346] Watts cautions against "the danger that the imitation of Christ may become monkey business" and emphasizes the importance of "not so much the outward form of Christ as his inner spiritual state. Humanly speaking, his inner state, the cause of his outward glory, was precisely his realization of the inescapable presence . . . of God and union with him."[347] Perhaps sought martyrdom represents such a danger as it focuses on the outward event of Jesus' physical death while failing to recognize his aversion toward martyrdom expressed at Gethsemane.[348] "To seek out suffering," Watts holds, is to engage in "false moral heroics."[349] In the un-

---

345. "Sacred," in *New Lexicon Webster's Encyclopedic Dictionary*, 876.

346. Kierkegaard, *Authority and Revelation*, 110.

347. Watts, *Behold the Spirit*, 97–98.

348. "I am deeply grieved. . . . My Father," he pleads, "if it is possible, let this cup pass from me; yet not what I want but what you want." Matt 26:38–39.

349. Watts, *Behold the Spirit*, 245.

welcome death of a martyr it is the unwelcomeness that indicates faith. "[O]ne who does not know how to die does not know how to live," Watts maintains.[350] Viewing life as sacred, one is unable to commit murder or suicide lightly.

Without seeking it, the prophet is one upon whom considerable suffering almost inevitably falls since the prophet speaks with a powerful, polemical voice and is often feared, rejected, despised, and opposed by many, even when embraced by others. The prophetic "ministry of destabilization brings hostility as part of the territory," notes Brueggemann.[351] In light of the prophet's frequent persecution, the notion of physical well-being as an indication of divine sanction is not tenable. As Martin Le Franc argued, that one might die "shamefully" is no reliable indication of the state of one's soul, citing Jesus as a case in point.[352] The truly great, observes Kierkegaard, do not require admiration from the world and are not "relieved of the distress, the agony, and the paradox," but these stand at the heart of their greatness. "[E]veryone was great," he reflects, "in proportion to the magnitude of what he *strove with*. For he who strove with the world became great by conquering the world, and he who strove with himself became greater by conquering himself; but he who strove with God became greater than all."[353] Jehanne evidently strove with the world (her pro-English enemies), with herself (her fear of the fire), and with God (her forbidden escape attempt)—it is the path of the prophetic mystic. Reflecting on Kierkegaard's words, one understands that it is possible to conquer the world and oneself, but one does not conquer God; rather, one strives with God in conquering the world and oneself. Having conquered the world and oneself, there is nothing left to conquer—God alone remains. This seems a fitting interpretation of martyrdom.

Merton speaks of the prophet as "one who bears the burden of the divine mercy—a burden which is a gift to [hu]mankind, but which remains a burden to the prophet in so far as no one will take it from him."[354] It is in rejection of the divine gift that the prophet is sometimes martyred. Jehanne, whose divine gift of peace, justice, and compassion

350. Ibid., 25.
351. Brueggemann, "Destabilizing Presence," 242.
352. Franc, *champion des dames*; in Taylor, *La Pucelle*, 248–49.
353. Kierkegaard, *Fear and Trembling*, 15–16, 77.
354. Merton, *Disputed Questions*, 223.

was rejected by those who killed her, is such a case. In assessing claims to divine sanction, one might ask, what merciful gift does the claimant offer? If such a gift cannot be identified, one might rightly view the claim with suspicion.

Kierkegaard describes martyrs as

> those mighty dead who are able to do what no living man can do who lets men be cut down by thousands, what these mighty dead themselves could not do while they lived but are able to do only as dead men: to constrain to obedience a furious mob, just because this furious mob in disobedience took the liberty of slaying the martyrs.... [H]e conquers best who conquers last ... by being put to death—an eternally certain conquest! And this sacrifice is the sacrifice of obedience, wherefore God looks with delight upon him, the obedient man, who offers himself as a sacrifice, whereas he gathers his wrath against disobedience which slays the sacrifice—this sacrifice, the victor, is the martyr; for not everyone who is put to death is a martyr.[355]

Kierkegaard's account presents martyrdom as murder (by humans) of the faithful on account of their faith, murder that is not, in itself, pleasing to God. Rather, the faith in and love of God in the heart of the martyr which drives the martyr's decision to suffer and die over the alternative of betraying God is conceivably the most powerful gift that a human can offer the divine. On Kierkegaard's view, "God looks with delight upon" the martyr, but not the murder contained within martyrdom, upon the gift, but not the means.

Asked by the Rouen court on March 1, 1431 if her saints had promised her anything other than that "her King would be restored in his kingdom" and they would lead her to heaven, Jehanne replied that she would reveal the other promise to them "within three months."[356] She was martyred on May 30, 1431, just two days short of three months from the date when she made the prediction, which suggests that her martyrdom constituted the revelation to which Jehanne had alluded, although she may not have known it. When asked nine days later what sign convinced Charles VII of the legitimacy and divinity of her mission, Jehanne responded, "[T]he sign that you need is for God to deliver me from your hands and that is the most certain sign that He knows

---

355. Kierkegaard, *Authority and Revelation*, lix–lx.
356. Jehanne; in Taylor, *La Pucelle*, 163.

to send to you."357 Given that Jehanne's divine counsel referred to her martyrdom as deliverance, Jehanne's reference to her deliverance as a sign also conceivably alluded to her martyrdom, although she was likely still grappling with the intended meaning behind the word "deliverance" herself. Jehanne's statements reinforce the notion of martyrdom as a sign, as revelation, but I propose the term "inadvertent revelation" to denote a human event which, although not presumably initiated or condoned by God, inadvertently serves to reveal something of God via the martyr's witness. The martyr succumbs to death by persisting in faith and persists in faith by succumbing to death.

Martyrdom is a powerful phenomenon that engraves its message on the world almost indelibly. Without Jehanne's willingness to die for God, those inclined to portray her as a self-directed virago would have an easier time of it. Without the importance of Jehanne's mortal destruction to the enemy, those inclined to represent her as a token presence on the battlefield (contrary to eyewitness testimony) while others conducted the real business of war, would also have an easier time of it. Margolis holds that Jehanne's "lone mortal body, in war and in death, . . . offered the ultimate proof of her divine inspiration."[358] Jehanne's martyrdom strengthened the legitimacy of her claim to divine sanction and her message to the world. "[O]utside of martyrdom," states Jörg Splett, "every other form of saintly witness remains, in a sense, only partial. It has not the unequivocal finality of martyrdom."[359]

The message of Jehanne's martyrdom contains both vocal and visceral components. The message revealed through her final words is:

1. That God speaks to individuals.

2. That humans err and need forgiveness and that even those acting at God's command require divine and human forgiveness. (It is notable that Jehanne absolved those responsible for sending her to the stake when the fire was only moments from consuming her. She also requested forgiveness and prayers for her soul from these people, demonstrating awareness that her participation in war contributed to the suffering of others, even if it was considered "necessary" suffering, and acknowl-

---

357. Jehanne; ibid., 178.
358. Margolis, "Mortal Body," 10.
359. Splett, "Saints," 1497.

edging her personal responsibility toward God and others in her deeds.)

3. That physical suffering does not indicate an absence of God. (Jehanne invoked the Trinity and identified with Jesus in her suffering.)
4. That God suffers with humans, as suggested by Jehanne's request for and embracing of the crucifix.

The message delivered through Jehanne's burning body is:

1. That commitment to God does not provide immunity against earthly suffering.
2. That faith requires not only surrender of personal will to God but surrender to earthly consequences.
3. That no price is too high for the deliverance of divine Truth.
4. That God is worth dying for.
5. That love surpasses all.

Soelle asks if mystical love can "sustain itself . . . in suffering," in the apparent "midst of Godforsakenness."[360] Jehanne demonstrated that it can. Weil maintains that "[i]t is in affliction itself that the splendor of God's mercy shines, from its very depths, in the heart of its inconsolable bitterness. If still persevering in our love, we fall to the point where the soul cannot keep back the cry 'My God, why hast thou forsaken me?' if we remain at this point without ceasing to love, we end by touching something that is not affliction, not joy, something that is the central essence, necessary and pure, something not of the senses, common to joy and sorrow: the very love of God."[361] "Dying in the same way as Jesus died, for the same reasons as he did, the martyrs multiply the revelation of the founding violence," asserts Girard.[362] One wonders how many martyrs humankind requires before we recognize and heed the revelation of love. How many must we cut down before we raise ourselves up?

---

360. Soelle, *Silent Cry*, 133, 137.
361. Weil, *Waiting for God*, 43–44.
362. Girard, *Things Hidden*, 173.

Part Two

Righteous Warfare
and Its Applicability

3

Righteous Warfare and Human Agency

Whatever makes a soldier sad
will make a killer smile.
—Leonard Cohen, "The Captain"

In Jehanne's time, people paid attention to visionaries as there was general receptivity to mystical phenomena—even medieval kings consulted visionaries. Now heads of state speak the language of visionaries and prophets without accompanying prophetic or visionary characteristics and win widespread support, while anyone displaying visionary traits might be branded insane or absurd. There is a need for discernment. If one is to pay serious attention to appeals to divinely sanctioned violence—which ought to be viewed seriously given their demonstrated impact—one must acknowledge the possibility of legitimate mystical experience; otherwise, all such claims could be disregarded.

Secular-Theological Considerations Regarding Human Agency

If you want others to be happy, practice compassion.
If you want to be happy, practice compassion.
—14th Dalai Lama

I employ the term "secular-theological considerations" to denote areas of concern relevant to both theological and secular realms of understanding, such as human evil, ethics, chivalry, conscience, and compassion, considering specifically how these relate to human agency in warfare. Let us begin this exploration with the complex matter of evil.

While most individuals have some sense of the existence of evil, there is no general agreement with respect to its constitution; definitions, theories, and categories of evil abound. "[E]vil is not an abstraction; it is a powerful reality,"[1] states Lawrence S. Cunningham, engaging a longstanding debate. That evil is real appears self-evident, but reality and abstraction are not necessarily mutually exclusive; rather, reality and abstraction represent two aspects of evil—evil manifests concretely in experienced events and exists abstractly as a capacity, quality, or intention. On this view, evil is not reducible to pure abstraction. Nonetheless, the privation doctrine of evil holds that moral evil does not exist independently but only implicitly, as privation of goodness or "right order" resulting from a will turned away from God. Origen conceived of human evil in this way, and the concept was later propounded by Plotinus and Saint Augustine.[2] Hannah Arendt, however, considers it a "philosophical prejudice" to assert "that evil is no more than a privative *modus* of the good, that good can come out of evil; that, in short, evil is but a temporary manifestation of a still-hidden good. Such time-honoured opinions have become dangerous," she warns. "They are shared by many ... for the simple reason that they inspire hope and dispel fear—a treacherous hope used to dispel legitimate fear,"[3] fear of evil as an actual reality. Moreover, she maintains that violence "cannot be derived from its opposite"[4] and one might likewise suppose that evil cannot be derived from good. Furthermore, evil conceived as privation does not necessarily render it a nonentity. Darkness exists although it is an absence of light. It is equally true to state that light is an absence of darkness; therefore, one might argue that goodness is an absence of evil, turning the whole privation doctrine of evil on its head. Lack in opposites is a reciprocal inevitability. To be devoid of one thing is to be another; such absence does not entail utter non-existence, but only

1. Cunningham, *Catholic Heritage*, 25.
2. Copleston, *Medieval Philosophy*, 27, 84–85.
3. Arendt, *Violence*, 56.
4. Ibid.

non-existence of a particular quality in a given entity or phenomenon. Evil as a reality lacking the quality of goodness is a more useful concept than evil as a nonentity, as mere illusion, since nonentities cannot exert power. Evil conceived as a nonentity demands that all experiences of evil be denied validity, yet one can neither justifiably nor logically deny the existence of evil any more than one can justifiably or logically deny the existence of good. While evil might be characterized as lacking certain qualities, it cannot arise from utter lack since something does not arise from nothing. Evil can arise in conditions of lack and presumably requires certain conditions of lack for its existence, but it does not consist essentially or entirely in lack.

Peter van Inwagen distinguishes two categories of evil, one being "bad things" or "ordinary evil" (e.g., accidents, natural disasters, . . .) and the other being "the extreme reaches of moral depravity" or "radical evil." He notes that the predominant understanding of evil for centuries has been as "radical evil,"[5] and that is the form of evil addressed in this work. R. S. Downie defines human or moral evil as "suffering" caused by "morally wrong human choices, especially when the moral wrong is of an extreme kind." He identifies several types of moral evil. The "evil of fanaticism," he explains, arises when "sincerely held beliefs, such as political ideologies or religious fundamentalism," produce "evil effects" while ignoring the suffering of individuals. Downie also identifies "self-interest" as a potential form of evil. "The pursuit of self-interest at the expense of others," he explains, "is a common form of moral wrongdoing, but when the others are made to suffer in outstandingly bad ways," self-interest enters the terrain of "moral evil." Another type of moral evil is "the infliction of suffering for its own sake." This includes, but is not limited to, humiliation or dehumanization of others. Downie also cites "the will of political rulers" as a potential source of moral evil since "the social and political conditions of a regime" can encourage or permit evil deeds. He argues that "failure in moral imagination" constitutes a form of moral evil as well, such as when one fails to imagine the sufferings of a remote victim to one's actions.[6]

There is no evidence that Jehanne participated in any of the identified forms of moral evil. She neither inflicted suffering for its own sake nor treated anyone's suffering lightly. She forbade unnecessary violence.

---

5. Inwagen, *Problem of Evil*, 13–14, 17.

6. Downie, "Evil, human," 273.

She demonstrated an absence of self-interest and sought to align her will with divine will, operating first and foremost from that position rather than from the will of any political leader. In fact, she never hesitated to voice disagreement with those in authority, including the King of France. Consistently extending compassion to all victims, Jehanne was not lacking in moral imagination. On all counts, she defied moral evil, which might be summarily understood as the unnecessary (intentional or thoughtless) infliction of suffering.

An obvious manifestation of evil is the implementation of torture—obvious, yet still widely practiced and somewhat overlooked. Arendt reminds us that death is not the worst possible fate.[7] The fact that humankind employs torture ought to be the cause of gravest moral concern, yet there is a degree of acceptance with regard to this blatantly evil practice. Daniel Hobbins comments that the use of torture to extract confessions became "regulated ... in ecclesiastical trials after abuses occurred,"[8] betraying a startling disregard for the fact that all torture constitutes abuse, even "regulated" torture. The fact that something is permitted or regulated does not render it morally acceptable. The use of torture is not supported by Jehanne's model of behavior.

If humans possess free will, then everyone is capable of goodness and evil alike. This is heartening in the sense that, if human evil endures, human goodness can also endure. Jehanne represents the possibility of engaging evil actively from a position of goodness, with love and compassion. In this way, evil is denied free reign. In the presence of goodness evil is mitigated insofar as it must accommodate the good, even if only by conceding it space, so to speak. In such circumstances evil, rather than obtaining the upper hand, must contend with goodness, but where evil is overlooked it grows unchecked. The expectation that evil, if left to its own devices, will be transformed by example or by love alone has proven an unrealistic and unreliable strategy. Moral indifference (failure to be moved by moral evil) is also treacherous, and Heschel warns against it: "There is an evil which most of us condone and are even guilty of: indifference to evil. We remain neutral, impartial, and not easily moved by the wrongs done unto other people. Indifference to evil is more insidious than evil itself; it is more universal, more contagious, more dangerous. A silent justification, it makes possible an evil erupting

7. Arendt, *Eichmann*, 12.
8. Hobbins, *Trial*, 16.

as an exception becoming the rule and being in turn accepted."[9] Saint Teresa notes that "unrighteous persons are incited to make their evil known so that evil becomes so customary it seems socially justified."[10] Passivity, whether born of indifference or conviction, can contribute to the growth of evil whereas evil can sometimes be checked by combative force (counter-evil). For the prophet of God, recognition of and active opposition to evil are absolute imperatives.

> Indeed, the sort of crimes and even the amount of delinquency that fill the prophets of Israel with dismay do not go beyond that which we regard as normal, as typical ingredients of social dynamics....
>
> Their breathless impatience with injustice may strike us as hysteria. We ourselves witness continually acts of injustice, manifestations of hypocrisy, falsehood, outrage, misery, but we rarely grow indignant or overly excited. To the prophets even a minor injustice assumes cosmic proportions.
>
> ... But if such deep sensitivity to evil is to be called hysterical, what name should be given to the abysmal indifference to evil which the prophet bewails?[11]

Recognizing one's own capacity for and participation in evil, one might be less inclined to demonize others.

The importance of acknowledging all evil as pure and unqualified rather than separating it into categories of "greater" or "lesser" evil cannot be overstated since such qualification allows one to participate in evil while demonizing others as "more evil." Michael Ignatieff advances the idea of a "lesser evil." "To insist that justified exercises of coercion can be defined as a lesser evil is to say that evil can be qualified," he explains, but "it is essential to the idea of a lesser evil that one can justify resort to it without denying that it is evil, justifiable only because other means would be insufficient or unavailable." One either fights "evil with evil" or succumbs, he asserts; however, in resorting to this "lesser evil," Ignatieff reiterates, one "should act under a demonstrable state of necessity."[12] The terminology of a "lesser evil" is dangerous in that it diminishes ("lessens") awareness of the consistent degree of transparency, awareness,

---

9. Heschel, *Prophets: II*, 64.
10. Teresa of Avila, *Collected Works*, vol. 1, 93.
11. Heschel, *Prophets: Introduction*, 4–5.
12. Ignatieff, *Lesser Evil*, 18–19.

responsibility, accountability, and gravity with which all evil must be viewed. Moreover, the concept of degrees of good is inferred from the concept of degrees of evil which implies that, if an event or action is not purely evil (i.e., evil in the highest degree), then it is evil in part and must also be either partly good or partly neutral. This, however, is in league with the privation doctrine of evil and is susceptible to similar criticisms. As Weil maintains, "[g]ood is essentially other than evil."[13] To contemplate degrees of evil and degrees of good confounds the two and obscures the essential nature of each. Evil is, by its nature, unqualified.

It is consistent with Jehanne's example to view all war and all acts of human violence as inherently evil, whether or not participation in them might be considered divinely sanctioned or otherwise justifiable. As a warrior, Jehanne was not completely opposed to the use of violence, but she held restrictions on how and when it ought to be employed and was not indifferent to the violence in which she participated. Although she indicated that she liked a particular sword "because it was a good sword for war, useful for giving hard clouts," when questioned as to whether she preferred her sword or her standard, she replied that she preferred her standard by far, and that she carried it during battle "in order to avoid killing anyone," adding "that she had never killed anyone at all."[14] She indirectly consented to the killing of a Burgundian mercenary captain who had admitted to murder, theft, and treason—so long as he deserved it. Jehanne had proposed the man's exchange for a French prisoner; however, on learning that the latter was dead, she advised the *bailli* to do with the Burgundian whatever justice demanded. He was tried for two weeks by legal officials and judged guilty, so she did not play a direct role in the matter.[15] Nonetheless, in engaging in war Jehanne was involved in the business of killing, contrary to her aversion to bloodshed. In examining her conscience regularly, partaking in the sacrament of confession, and praying for forgiveness, she demonstrated acute awareness of the nature and implications of her deeds. Weil asserts that "[c]ontact with the sword causes the same defilement whether it be through the handle or the point. For him who loves, its metallic coldness

---

13. Weil, *Gravity and Grace*, 70.

14. Jehanne; in Scott, *Trial*, 82. Seguin's testimony accords with Jehanne's; in Pernoud, *Retrial*, 114.

15. Jehanne; in Taylor, *La Pucelle*, 190. Franquet d'Arras was the Burgundian captain in question.

will not destroy love, but will give the impression of being abandoned by God.... Murder freezes the soul of the man who loves only with a pure love, whether he be the author or the victim, so likewise does everything which, without going so far as actual death, constitutes violence."[16] Defilement comprises part of the unwholesome burden borne by one who employs divinely sanctioned violence. While Jehanne justified her actions on the basis of divine command, she did not attempt to qualify them or those of her soldiers—war was war, bloodshed was bloodshed, evil was evil, and accountability was accountability. She neither sought concealment of her deeds in collective anonymity nor raised her claim to divine sanction as a shield against individual responsibility. During sentencing at Rouen, Jehanne stated "that she charged no one with her deeds and words, neither her King nor anyone else; and if there were any fault, it was hers alone."[17]

Merton notes that

> [t]here are crimes which no one would commit as an individual which he willingly ... commits when acting in the name of his society, because he has been (too easily) convinced that evil is entirely different when it is done "for the common good." ... [Such individuals] have acquired a special deformity of conscience as a result of their identification with their group, their immersion in their particular society. This deformation is the price they pay to forget and to exorcise that solitude which seems to them to be a demon.[18]

Pernoud holds that the "amnesiac is no more a complete person than an irresponsible person is; neither one enjoys the full exercise of his faculties, which alone allow man true freedom without endangering himself or his peers."[19] Arne Johan Vetlesen maintains that the practice of "[c]ollectivizing human agency ... is tantamount to obliterating the morally and legally crucial distinction between individual and group,"[20] while Kierkegaard describes the effectiveness of vague, collective concepts in the advancement of political agendas. "'[T]he multitude,' an absurd monster or a monstrous absurdity, which nevertheless is physi-

---

16. Weil, *Gravity and Grace*, 63.
17. Jehanne; in Taylor, *La Pucelle*, 217.
18. Merton, *Disputed Questions*, 183.
19. Pernoud, *Terrible Middle Ages*, 173.
20. Vetlesen, "Genocide," 361.

cally in possession of power," is actually an "abstraction," he points out, "an inhuman something, the power of which is, to be sure, prodigious, but it is a prodigious power which cannot be defined in human terms, but more properly as one defines the power of a machine, . . . [as] horsepower. . . . This abstraction, whether you will call it the public or the multitude or the majority or the senseless people—this abstraction is used politically to bring about movement."[21] Jehanne did not operate from such collective abstractions, clearly identifying herself as Jehanne *la pucelle* and stating her purpose and method unambiguously.

George Kren identifies a common failure among late twentieth-century ethicists to come to terms with the notion of holding individuals responsible for evil actions committed under the official sanction of a nation or state.[22] "Where all are guilty, no one is," Arendt observes. "[C]onfessions of collective guilt are the best possible safeguard against the discovery of culprits, and the very magnitude of the crime the best excuse for doing nothing."[23] Kren notes, for example, that pilots who bomb cities are seldom, if ever, held responsible for the resultant deaths. Similarly, opponents of the death penalty criticize the law but do not normally hold executioners responsible for their deeds.[24] Arendt declares that "about nothing does public opinion everywhere seem to be in happier agreement than that no one has the right to judge somebody else. What public opinion permits us to judge and even to condemn are trends, or whole groups of people[;] . . . in short, something so general that distinctions can no longer be made, names no longer be named."[25] While one might argue that individuals do judge the actions of other individuals, such judgment is relatively inconsequential unless enacted in an official capacity, whereby it ceases to constitute individual judgment in the eyes of the public but becomes collective judgment under the law of a people as enforced by a state. Even judgment, then, is generally perceived as a collective behavior in that one is considered to be judged by legal systems. As Guy Adams and Danny Balfour point out, however, ethical behavior is not properly defined as "doing things" legally, efficiently, effectively, and professionally since this does not necessarily

21. Kierkegaard, *Authority and Revelation*, 193.
22. Kren, "Holocaust," 247.
23. Arendt, *Violence*, 65.
24. Kren, "Holocaust," 247–48.
25. Arendt, *Eichmann*, 296.

ensure "the well-being of individuals," particularly the most vulnerable.[26] Free will and individual responsibility go hand in hand—the former implies the latter—and individual responsibility cannot be appropriately or legitimately dissolved within collective precepts or notions of collective responsibility. Jehanne took seriously her personal role in the maintenance of social justice, acknowledging the ethical responsibility that rests upon individuals regardless of the general disposition of the society within which they operate. "[T]he lonely courage of Joan of Arc means that no one who simply follows the crowd can be said to follow her," asserts Astell.[27]

Another form of ethical failure is the attempt to conceal the true nature of evil deeds. Consider former American President George Bush's oft-repeated slogan that the United States of America and its allies had launched a "war on terror" by invading Afghanistan and Iraq following the 2001 attacks on the U.S.A. Countless individuals latched onto the term, drank it in and spewed it out without apparently pausing to acknowledge that war *is* terror! It is a nonsensical expression; the terror caused by Bush's directives is synonymous with the terror that he purportedly aimed to eradicate, but there was an apparent absence of clarity and honesty surrounding the affair. The contradiction in terms ought to be obvious to anyone giving the phrase a moment's thought but, unfortunately, a moment's thought seems more than many are willing to devote to destructive and consequential human activities, and therein lies much of the problem. Contrary to Bush's use of the word, Jim Forest cites Merton's frequent reference to "terrorism" not as indicating clandestine activities of a violent group, but as denoting "the acceptance by governments of tactics of war that result in large numbers of noncombatant" deaths.[28] There is obviously a case to be made that both forms of activity constitute terrorism. The purpose of this discussion is not to dispel the viable argument that it is sometimes acceptable to engage in violence in order to end it; it is to stress the need for clarity, honesty, and integrity in all such activities. Jehanne was forthright and honest; she did not attempt to convince anyone that what she engaged in was something other than what it actually was. She expressed her intentions clearly and

---

26. Adams and Balfour, *Administrative Evil*, 170.
27. Astell, "Joan of Arc and Spirituality," 4.
28. Forest, foreword to *Peace in the Post-Christian Era*, xix.

publicly, in plain language, employing a direct manner of speech; in fact, she is described as "disarming in her straightforwardness."[29]

The use of "poorly understood and emotionally loaded clichés" to justify belligerent actions[30] is also demonstrated by Bush's vague but influential term, "axis of evil," intended to demonize others in an attempt to legitimize further his country's offensive actions. Jehanne did not utilize such language or otherwise demonize the enemy. She did not claim French superiority (not even militarily as she attributed their military success to God) but simply identified the pro-English offenses committed in her country, demanded rectification, and declared it God's will that the English leave France. She did not portray the English as "other" in terms of the inhuman, subhuman, or demonic; rather, she fought an invader of her land and oppressor of her people, not one construed as an enemy in any other sense. "[W]ar becomes unlimited," suggests John von Heyking, "when participants view each other as unequal, whether as heretics, heathens, devils, or simply 'lesser breeds without the law.'"[31] Yet "[i]nternational human rights conventions" remind us "that even ... enemies have rights, which are not dependent upon reciprocity or good conduct," states Ignatieff.[32] Weil defines justice as "love for one's neighbor. . . . We have invented the distinction between justice and charity," she asserts.[33] Jehanne's charity is noted by George H. Tavard: "Jeanne's mission was to be a virgin soul. Only a virgin soul can engage in the struggle for justice without feeling hatred for the unjust, can obtain victory without taking pride in success, can be the innocent victim of a political and ecclesiastical machine bent on destroying her without acrimony toward those who have engineered her condemnation, can face the threat of torture with equanimity, and can go to death by fire with full confidence in God."[34]

"The supernatural virtue of justice" requires "behaving exactly as though there were equality when one is the stronger in an unequal rela-

---

29. Pernoud and Clin, *Her Story*, 224.
30. Merton, *Peace in the Post-Christian Era*, 19.
31. Heyking, "Taming Warriors," 15.
32. Ignatieff, *Lesser Evil*, ix.
33. Weil, *Waiting for God*, 24, 85.
34. Tavard, *Spiritual Way*, 51. "Virginity of soul is the *state of grace*, . . . a gift of God which is to be received and preserved with humility and trust." Benedict XVI, "Saint Joan," online.

tionship," states Weil,[35] but how might the notion of divine chosenness accommodate equality? Divine chosenness is not necessarily a matter of individual or collective favoritism or unconditional, perpetual selection, but it might be viewed as election to a cause—such as the cause of justice (and concomitant peace). Upon restoration of justice, the chosenness factor in such instances conceivably either dissolves or all become "chosen." This does not suggest that one can divest oneself of accountability for past deeds simply by altering one's course, but it discourages the casting of a people as good or evil based on claims to perpetual divine chosenness. Hence, the prophet might speak of election to a task and the oppressed of divine assistance without invoking the notion of chosenness, which can carry a connotation of permanence that is incompatible with Jehanne's treatment of the matter.

A further concern must be addressed. Against the sanctity of life, killing stands as intrinsically evil, but to what category of evil does killing in defense of self or others belong? It is not ordinary or natural evil, nor is it moral evil in any of the senses discussed. I propose that it be termed "morally necessary evil," designating necessary, minimal, defensive actions in accordance with conscience as well as divinely sanctioned actions in accordance with prophetic revelation. Needless to say, the term "morally necessary evil" ought not to be flaunted lightly and it is recommended that it be applied only in conjunction with the model of righteous warfare and human agency herein proposed.

It is not my purpose here to conduct a thorough evaluation of traditional moral systems, but it is expedient to note some insufficiencies and to consider a possible alternative or complementary form of morality. It is a mystical form of morality which transcends ordinary morality in certain extraordinary circumstances and corresponds to the idea of morally necessary evil. Mystical morality is not necessarily a morality applicable to all situations at all times, but it is applicable to claims of divine sanction since it is based on faith in and obedience to divine revelation. The human "sense of injustice is a poor analogy to God's sense of injustice," states Heschel.[36] While suspension of human morality is risky, morality itself is potentially dangerous since, in attempting to engage it, one risks erring. History demonstrates the ongoing failure of

---

35. Weil, *Waiting for God*, 87.
36. Heschel, *Prophets: II*, 64.

human morality. Certainly, no humanly constructed ethical system is infallible or entirely sufficient.

Teleological ethics specifies a desired outcome against which actions are judged to be right or wrong, assigning "a standard of value to the consequences of ... actions." Actions fulfilling the standard are deemed right while those deviating from it are considered wrong. It should be noted that teleological ethical systems define the consequences of an action as consisting in "*all* the effects which the action has in the future of the world." In circumstances where a consequence is judged as neither good nor bad but neutral, it is considered to have no bearing on the rightness or wrongness of the action from which it arises. However, even the slightest degree of goodness or badness in a consequence is to be factored into the calculation of whether the action which gives rise to it is considered right or wrong.[37] Immediately one apprehends absurdity in the assumption that humans are able even to approach accuracy in predictive calculations of this sort. Nevertheless, elements of a teleological ethical system known as utilitarianism are commonly employed.[38] According to utilitarianism, utility is the standard against which rightness or wrongness of an action is measured, wherein utility is considered to be the bringing about of "a *desirable* or *good* end," one with "*intrinsic value.*" Intrinsic value refers to the value of something as an end in itself, as valuable for its own sake, whereas that which is valuable as a means to an end is considered instrumentally valuable. In the latter instance, the means would not be considered valuable if the end were not so considered. Utilitarians acknowledge that things might possess one or both kind(s) of value.[39]

Since the fundamental principle of utilitarianism maintains that "*the right depends on the good*," it is necessary to assess the goodness or badness of the consequences of an action prior to performing it. According to utilitarianism, the "moral rightness of an act is not itself an intrinsic value," but "an act is right only when it is instrumentally good and its rightness consists in its instrumental goodness." As goodness in

---

37. Taylor, *Principles of Ethics*, 56.

38. The two main types of utilitarianism are act utilitarianism and rule utilitarianism. Act utilitarians hold that the consequences of each particular action determine its rightness or wrongness while rule utilitarians hold that right action conforms to a set of rules governing conduct which purport to bring about the best possible consequences for everyone when followed. Ibid., 63–64.

39. Ibid., 59–60.

the utilitarian sense refers to pleasure, happiness, or intrinsic goodness, right action is defined as that which promotes these states while wrong action is construed as that which promotes displeasure, pain, unhappiness, or intrinsic evil. On this view, "no act is [considered] morally wrong in itself. Its wrongness depends entirely on its consequences."[40]

One wonders among whom utility is to be calculated. While the utilitarian response is that "*everyone's* pleasure, happiness, or intrinsic good" must be equally considered,[41] such pan-inclusivity is impossible. Who, then, is to be excluded and on what basis? There is no simple answer. Moreover, the calculation is based on personal values which are highly subjective; we do not all share the same definition of pleasure, happiness, or intrinsic goodness. Consequently, the universally representative calculation that utilitarians aim to achieve is impracticable, if honorable.

The basic utilitarian formula for ethical evaluation recommends the following:

1. Consider all possible courses of action.

2. Calculate as accurately as possible the likely consequences of each possible course of action. This involves estimating, for each alternative, the quantity or degree of probable positive and negative consequences to everyone affected.

3. Compare the predicted consequences of each action in order to determine which one points to the greatest overall amount of pleasure, happiness, and intrinsic goodness and the least overall amount of displeasure, unhappiness, and intrinsic evil.

4. Act in accordance with the action deemed likely to yield the maximum intrinsic value and the least intrinsic disvalue; this act is considered the only morally acceptable one.[42]

---

40. Ibid., 60, 62. In citing pleasure, happiness, and intrinsic goodness and their opposites (pain, unhappiness, and intrinsic evil) as possible standards of value (or disvalue) against which acts might be judged as ethical or unethical, Paul W. Taylor incorporates Jeremy Bentham's "hedonistic utilitarianism," John Stuart Mill's "eudaimonistic utilitarianism," and G. E. Moore's "agathistic utilitarianism" in his treatment of the subject. Ibid., 60.

41. Ibid., 61.

42. Ibid., 61–62.

That the calculation is to be performed completely impartially[43] represents an obvious difficulty since it is highly unlikely and probably impossible that one will maintain impartiality on both conscious and subconscious levels while conducting such an assessment. Hence, it is reasonable to suspect that the utilitarian formula is most likely to be applied with partiality, in which case it can be used to "justify" anything depending on one's perspective; it could even "justify" opposing positions in a single dilemma. Michael Walzer considers the utilitarian approach adopted by the United States government in detonating two atomic bombs over Japan in 1945 with the purported goal of ending World War II.[44] Walzer notes that, "had the Japanese exploded an atomic bomb over an American city, killing tens of thousands of civilians and thereby shortening the agony of war, the action would clearly have been [considered] a crime" by the American government[45] rather than an acceptable utilitarian means to an end. Furthermore, one is prompted to ask why two atomic bombs rather than one were employed if the aim was to demonstrate the capacity for destruction possessed by the American forces and to instill fear for the purpose of terminating all opposition. One such horrific bomb would surely have accomplished that as effectively as two—which is not to condone the use even of one but to cite an obvious weakness in the rationale offered for the attacks on Hiroshima and Nagasaki. Acknowledging that detailed utilitarian calculations are cumbersome and not easily applied to all possible ethical dilemmas arising in everyday life, utilitarians advocate acting in accordance with habit derived from past experience when precedents are available.[46] The problem is that precedent does not always serve morality—take, for example, the nuclear bombing of Japan mentioned above; even in retrospect, some people maintain that it was necessary and, on utilitarian grounds, would condone repetition of similar atrocities in kind or scale. Moreover, deference to precedent can too easily become habit, a lazy or convenient way of avoiding responsible ethical decision-making.

In light of the problem of identifying with certainty, or even probability, all who would be affected by a given action and what the various effects would be in the future of the world, one must consider over what

43. Ibid., 61.
44. Walzer, *Just and Unjust Wars*, 263–68.
45. Ibid., 264.
46. Taylor, *Principles of Ethics*, 62.

period of time (how many generations) effect might reasonably be calculated, but this is an arbitrary decision at best. If one had attempted to calculate in advance the total or net effect of Hitler's "final solution," would the (questionable) guilt assumed by subsequent generations of Germans have been factored into the calculation? And what of the Jewish children (born and unborn) who were murdered, and the unconceived progeny of those who died? The value of that which is not permitted to come into existence or develop cannot be accurately estimated. Moreover, quantity is not necessarily more valuable, desirable, or advantageous than quality. What if the one person killed to save the many in a given situation might have (or might have produced a child who might have) helped save the world or found a cure for cancer or a solution to poverty, environmental devastation, or war for that matter had he or she survived? Such possibilities cannot be factored into the utilitarian equation since what might be cannot be attributed certainty or even expectability, and it is sometimes the unexpected that has the most intrinsic or instrumental value. "Predictions," states Arendt, "are never anything but projections of present automatic processes and procedures, that is, of occurrences that are likely to come to pass if men do not act and if nothing unexpected happens; every action . . . and every accident necessarily destroys the whole pattern in whose frame the prediction moves and where it finds its evidence."[47] "It is the function . . . of all action," she points out, "to interrupt what otherwise would have proceeded automatically and therefore predictably."[48] "Since the end of human action . . . can never be reliably predicted, the means used to achieve political goals are more often than not of greater relevance to the future world than the intended goals."[49]

The fact that utilitarianism fails to provide certainty in ethical calculation is not its most outstanding danger since legitimate certainty is seldom, if ever, attainable in moral evaluation except, perhaps, in hindsight. What is more dangerous is the *illusion* of certainty in performing ethical calculations, that is, supposition that one can accurately predict outcomes and oblivion to or disregard for the possibility—indeed, the likelihood—of error. Utilitarian ethics, with its notably mathematical language of formula, calculation, net utility, positive result, negative re-

47. Arendt, *Violence*, 7.
48. Ibid., 30–31.
49. Ibid., 4.

sult, greatest number, least number, problem, and solution, is susceptible to illusions of certainty, precision, accuracy, completeness, and appropriateness, whereas human ethical calculation is never as precise or reliable as mathematics. We need only recall the implications of the term "final solution" during World War II in order to grasp the potentially insidious power lurking within such mathematical language employed in the field of moral reasoning. One of the dangers of predictive theories, Arendt warns, is that "they have a hypnotic effect; they put to sleep our common sense, which is nothing else but our mental organ for perceiving, understanding, and dealing with reality and factuality."[50] Merton observes that scientifically objective consideration of moral issues, which "reduces human persons to statistical anonymity . . . and calculates how many millions we can lose 'and still get along,' . . . contributes to the . . . blunting of humane and moral sensibility and it accustoms minds to" indifference. Moral reflection based on "pragmatic principles" is not only "vague" and "fluid," he insists, but also produces "opportunistic choices based on short term guesses of possible consequences."[51]

In the context of these observations, let us return to the concept of "lesser evil," which is utilitarian in nature and similarly flawed. It is a notably mathematical term which suggests precision of calculation and, like other utilitarian claims, the possibility of accurately and objectively measuring evil in its past, present, and future manifestations but, as previously pointed out, this is impossible to accomplish. The evaluation of "greater" and "lesser evil" is skewed by human subjectivity, which is to say that one seldom counts the destruction of oneself or one's people as a lesser evil than that of a perceived enemy, or even as an equal evil, regardless of the numbers involved. This clearly hinders moral reasoning.

Although we have explored just one form of ethics, it is sufficient to establish awareness of the potential for gross miscalculation inherent in human ethical systems; hence, it is not terribly unnerving to contemplate a teleological suspension of the ethical as described by Kierkegaard in situations involving divine sanction. In fact, temporary suspension of the appeal to ethical systems seems not only appropriate but morally desirable in situations of divine revelation since it is neither expedient to apply moral laws to nor to derive them from individual mystical directives that are case specific. Nonetheless, case specific directives might

---

50. Ibid., 8.
51. Merton, *Peace in the Post-Christian Era*, 14, 65.

serve a general pedagogical moral purpose when properly understood in context and applied to subsequent events; they might, for example, suggest emulation of some aspect of attitude or behavior, such as the aspect of faith in the *Aqedah* (not murder).

Kierkegaard's notion of a teleological suspension of the ethical in obedience to divine revelation qualifies as an ethic of faith, contrary to purely utilitarian ethics, which is not to suggest that it is devoid of utilitarian purpose but that it is derived from and grounded in faith; any utilitarian purpose that it might serve would presumably be a divine purpose which may or may not accord with a humanly conceived purpose. Watts's claim that "[m]orality is a by-product of union with God"[52] supports the notion of such a teleological ethical suspension. One must, of course, employ utmost discretion in interpreting and applying the notion of ethical suspension in order to avoid misappropriating it. For example, moral vacuity employed to evil ends such as genocide constitutes teleological suspension of the ethical but is not likely representative of Kierkegaard's knight of faith who, in teleologically suspending the ethical, does so on the basis of faith from a position of absolute relation to the Absolute and all that this entails. It is the absolute relationship of absolute faith in the Absolute that constitutes the fundamental pedagogical element of Kierkegaard's teaching on the subject and that must be assessed in considering claims to divine sanction involving teleological suspension of the ethical. One who suspends the ethical but does not stand in an absolute relation to the divine while claiming to do so constitutes a false knight of faith. The model of righteous warfare and human agency derived from Jehanne in this work can assist in distinguishing between the true knight of faith (the prophet) and the false knight of faith (the false prophet).

While teleological suspension of the ethical cannot serve alone as an indicator of divine sanction, it constitutes a possible aspect of divine sanction. Heschel explains that the "prophets did not conceive of the ethos as an autonomous idea, as a sovereign essence, higher in the scale of reality than God Himself, standing above him like a supreme force. God to them was more than a moral principle. . . . [T]he relation between God and man cannot be simply equated with the value of the moral idea."[53] It was observed during Jehanne's active military career and with

52. Watts, *Behold the Spirit*, 187.
53. Heschel, *Prophets: Introduction*, 217.

respect to it that, "when divine virtue operates, it establishes the means according to its aim; hence, it is not safe to disparage or to find fault ... with those things which are from God."[54] During the Rouen trial, Jehanne insisted "that she came from God, and ought not to be [t]here; and ... that they should remit her into the hands of God, from Whom she came."[55] The statement suggests that she ought not to be judged by human standards of morality or tried in human courts since she was an agent of God subject to divine law and judgment. At Jehanne's nullification trial, several canonists upheld the "authority of divine revelation over established legal codes in the obedience required of every Christian in meeting the demands of faith."[56] *Dignitatis Humanae* declares that everyone is "bound to obey" his or her conscience and must answer to God in such matters. It also notes that the apostles "were not afraid to speak out against public authority when it opposed God's holy will: 'We must obey God rather than men' (Acts 5:29)," it recommends. "This is the path which innumerable martyrs and faithful have followed through the centuries."[57] Since *lex publica* is humanly constructed, it is subject to error or omission and presumably inferior to *lex privata* if the latter is genuinely divinely sanctioned, constituting divine law (*lex divina*). As private divine revelation can beneficially impact the public domain, to disregard it on the basis that it might contravene *lex publica* could endanger public welfare. Wright cites it as a "duty to follow that vocation which comes to each of us from God."[58]

The concept of duty can be viewed in a threefold manner in terms of duty to God, duty to self, and duty to others, the latter two being conceivably embedded in the first such that, in fulfilling one's duty to God, one fulfills one's duty to self and others. Duty to God is thus granted supremacy as its fulfillment ensures the fulfillment of all duty. Kierkegaard describes duty as "the expression of God's will" such that the ethical might exist paradoxically in a manner which "can cause the knight of faith to give his love of his neighbour the opposite expression to that which is his duty ethically speaking"[59] (i.e., that which would nor-

54. *Mirabili victoria*; in Taylor, *La Pucelle*, 83.
55. Jehanne; in Scott, *Trial*, 71.
56. Pinzino, "Lex Privata," 87.
57. *Dignitatis Humanae*, a. 11; in Flannery, *Vatican Council II*, 808–9.
58. Wright, *Saints Always Belong*, 121.
59. Kierkegaard, *Fear and Trembling*, 70, 83.

mally be considered his or her ethical duty under a universal ethic). For example, when Jehanne raised her sword, allegedly by divine command, the ethical precept to refrain from killing was paradoxically overridden by her individual ethical duty to participate in war. Ending the suffering caused by the war through restoration of peace and justice constituted a benefit served by the higher ethic of Jehanne's mission, but one might also consider the more subtle benefit potentially derived by the English from her campaign, which is that it prevented them from "sinning" indefinitely in the invasion of France, that is, from committing further acts of violence and oppression, arguably not divinely sanctioned, for which they might be held accountable before God. It is conceivable that, while risking defilement of her soul through participation in violence, Jehanne (wittingly or unwittingly) assisted the enemy by intercepting the self-inflicted defilement of their souls.[60] Jehanne also fulfilled her duty to the enemy by warning Cauchon of the risk to which he exposed his soul in judging her. "You say that you are my judge; take care what you are doing because, in truth, I have been sent by God and you put yourself in great danger."[61] She later added, "And I warn you so that if God punishes you, I am doing my duty in telling you this."[62]

If one were to set aside all considerations of divine sanction, a reasonable moral argument could still be constructed for Jehanne's case of going to war, most notably on the basis of self-defense and defending the wrongly oppressed. Moreover, Jehanne adhered to an ethical code of chivalry, an honor-based behavioral code formulated around the mid-twelfth century among feudal knights which, although it changed through time, consistently forbade any knight ever to take "unfair advantage of another knight."[63] The code governed the "capture, treatment and ransoming" of knights.[64] Common chivalric values included honor, courtesy, generosity, courage, loyalty, piety, defense of the weak, respect for women, protection of the king, and maintenance of social order.

---

60. Nash-Marshall believes the English were aware that, if Jehanne's mission was divinely sanctioned, then the English "attempt to seize the French throne was not only doomed, it was also sinful, and put their eternal souls in peril." Nash-Marshall, *Spiritual Biography*, 140.

61. Jehanne; in Taylor, *La Pucelle*, 146.

62. Ibid., 188.

63. Backman, *Worlds of Medieval Europe*, 179.

64. Bellamy, *Just Wars*, 1.

The Church supported chivalric knighthood insofar as it promoted justice, protected the poor, and defended the faith.[65] Pernoud notes that it "would be naïve to believe that all knights respected this high ideal," but the ideal thrived "for at least three centuries."[66] However, at the commencement of Jehanne's military career, chivalry was on the decline,[67] as demonstrated in the murders of Louis of Orléans and John the Fearless of Burgundy in 1407 and 1419 respectively.[68] A major factor in the decline of chivalry was that military innovations at the turn of the fourteenth century rendered certain chivalric practices outmoded and impractical. As more cunning strategies were employed, chivalry gave way gradually to a different type of warfare, such as the reinstatement of raids and siege warfare, which increased civilian suffering and casualties.[69] Jeremy duQuesnay Adams notes that "the restraints of chivalric warfare ... had sought profitable prisoners rather than mere bloodshed."[70]

Jehanne refused to yield to the decline in chivalric practice, maintaining that God was moved by pity to assist the people of Orléans and would not tolerate enemy possession of both "the Duke [of Orléans] and his town"—an act which flouted chivalric ethics.[71] When the English took one of her heralds prisoner although heralds were to be treated with immunity, Jehanne did not hesitate to cite the transgression and request his return.[72] Moreover, in accordance with chivalric custom, she entreated the English several times to leave France peacefully, warning of her impending attack should they not comply. "You Englishmen, who

---

65. Backman, *Worlds of Medieval Europe*, 180.

66. Pernoud, "Epilogue," 290.

67. Pizan (ca. 1410) states, "[N]o longer are the noble early rights preserved that the valiant warriors observed. Those who follow the military custom in the present time abuse it through the enormous greed that overcomes them." Pizan, *Deeds of Arms*, 177.

68. While on his way home, Louis of Orléans was ambushed and brutally murdered by John the Fearless of Burgundy. John the Fearless was murdered in turn by an agent of Charles VII during an encounter between them that was supposed to be friendly; Charles was blamed for the crime. Fraioli maintains that he was disinherited by his parents for this reason. Fraioli, *Hundred Years War*, lxi, lxiii, 144. In denouncing him, Charles's opponents seem to have overlooked the murder of Louis of Orléans.

69. Fraioli, *Hundred Years War*, 32–39.

70. Adams, prelude to *Her Story*, 4.

71. Jehanne; quoted by Dunois, in Murray, *Jeanne d'Arc*, 234.

72. Pasquerel; in Taylor, *La Pucelle*, 84.

have no right in this realm of France, the King of Heaven commands and bids you by me, Joan the Maid, to leave your forts and return into your own country. Otherwise I will give you such a harrying that no one will ever forget it. This I write to you for the third and last time, and I shall not write again."[73] She also offered the besiegers of Jargeau a chance to leave peacefully rather than be "taken by assault."[74] Jehanne did not permit "her company [to] loot anything"[75] and refused to eat food that she knew to be stolen, even when food was scarce,[76] nor did she "allow immoral women" to keep company with the soldiers, driving them away unless the men were willing to marry them.[77] Jehanne not only forbade her soldiers and the other captains to swear,[78] but she forbade anyone to swear or otherwise denounce God. A citizen of Orléans reported, "I remember well to have seen and heard . . . a great lord, walking along the street, begin to swear and blaspheme God; which, when Jeanne saw and heard, she was much perturbed, and went up to the lord who was swearing, and, taking him by the neck, said, 'Ah! master, do you deny Our Lord and Master? In God's Name, you shall unsay your words before I leave you.' And then, as I saw, the said lord repented and amended his ways, at the exhortation of the said Maid."[79] It was said that the "soldiers considered her a saint, for she behaved in such a godly way when with the army, both in her deeds and her words, that no one could have uttered a reproach against her."[80] While passing through the town of Sainte-Catherine-de-Fierbois en route to Chinon, Jehanne heard Mass

---

73. Jehanne; quoted by Pasquerel, in Pernoud, *Retrial*, 187.
74. Jehanne; in Taylor, *La Pucelle*, 158.
75. Beaucroix; in Pernoud, *Retrial*, 120.
76. Pasquerel; in Taylor, *La Pucelle*, 316. Also, Beaucroix; ibid., 302.
77. Beaucroix; in Pernoud, *Retrial*, 120. Alençon witnessed Jehanne chasing such a woman from the army with sword drawn, maintaining that her sword was [somehow] broken in the incident. Alençon; in Taylor, *La Pucelle*, 309. Jehanne's page described what is likely the same event, adding that "she did not strike this woman" but warned her never to be found among the soldiers again. Coutes; ibid., 298.
78. Seguin, Beaucroix, Alençon, and Coutes; in Pernoud, *Retrial*, 114, 120, 160, 179–80.
79. Reginalde, a widow of Orléans; in Murray, *Jeanne d'Arc*, 251. T. Douglas Murray cites two further testimonies to the same incident. Murray, *Jeanne d'Arc*, 251.
80. Barbin; in Pernoud, *Retrial*, 115.

three times in one day,[81] and she regularly encouraged her soldiers to attend as well.

Jehanne modeled chivalric courage, but hers was an exceptionally faithful courage corresponding to her courageous faith. Upon sustaining her first battle wound in which an arrow penetrated "for a depth of six inches" in the area of her lower neck or shoulder, "she did not retire from the battle and took no remedy against the wound."[82] She refused to allow the practice of a customary healing charm, declaring a preference for death over that which she considered sinful.[83] Later, in knowledge of her impending capture, Jehanne continued to assume battle positions that enabled her to protect her comrades-in-arms but endangered herself. She also charged into battle highly visible (and thus vulnerable) by her banner and colorful clothing which facilitated her capture as the enemy reportedly "dragged her to one side by her cloth-of-gold cloak and pulled her from her horse, throwing her flat on the ground."[84] A "tabard [tunic] was worn [over armor] so as to be recognized by soldiers of one's own company and to weaken the sun's blinding reflections."[85] Nash-Marshall suggests that Jehanne maximized her visibility so that her soldiers could easily locate her if in need of instruction or courage.[86] "[I]t goes against the very nature of self-interest to be enlightened," observes Arendt.[87]

Let us look more closely at the role of conscience in Jehanne's life. Like "evil," "conscience" is an ambiguous term. Merton describes it as "the light by which we interpret the will of God in our ... lives."[88] "Without [an engaged] conscience," he asserts, "freedom never knows what to do with itself."[89] For Merton, a properly-functioning conscience is grounded in love, compassion, charity, and benevolence. Such "an in-

---

81. Jehanne; in Taylor, *La Pucelle*, 155.

82. Dunois; in Pernoud, *Retrial*, 138. Pasquerel indicated that a crossbow bolt pierced through her shoulder "from one side to the other." Pasquerel; in Taylor, *La Pucelle*, 316. Jehanne testified that "she was wounded in the neck by an arrow." Jehanne; in Scott, *Trial*, 83.

83. Pasquerel; in Pernoud, *Retrial*, 189.

84. Chastellain; in Pernoud from Quicherat, vol. 4, 446–47, *Herself and Her Witnesses*, 151.

85. Pernoud and Clin, *Her Story*, 195.

86. Nash-Marshall, *Spiritual Biography*, 129.

87. Arendt, *Violence*, 78.

88. Merton, *No Man Is an Island*, 30.

89. Ibid., 27.

ner ground of deep faith and purity of conscience" requires self-sacrifice, without which self-interest remains an impediment, he explains.[90]

> Deep within his conscience man discovers a law which he has not laid upon himself but which he must obey. Its voice, ever calling him to love and to do what is good and to avoid evil, tells him inwardly at the right moment: do this, shun that. For man has in his heart a law inscribed by God. His dignity lies in observing this law, and by it he will be judged. His conscience is man's most secret core, and his sanctuary. There he is alone with God whose voice echoes in his depths. By conscience, . . . that law is made known which is fulfilled in the love of God and of one's neighbor.[91]

Dignitatis Humanae asserts that humans are "bound" to God "in conscience but not coerced."[92] Nonetheless, the workings of conscience can be a compelling force, and Jehanne preferred to die than act against divine will.[93]

Conscience might be viewed as a faculty of human awareness that enables receptivity to promptings by divine grace which serve to inform and instruct individual human behavior in all instances of moral decision-making provided it is not blocked by some aspect of the individual. On this view, conscience (unless it is suppressed) guides morality, functioning as a vehicle through which divine impulses, urgings, and inclinations are received and processed. Moral disposition thus comprises one's response—in the form of thought, emotion, decision, and deed (action or inaction)—to the revelations of conscience. From this perspective, conscience is not equated with moral discernment but facilitates it. Rudolf Hofmann agrees that "[c]onscience itself cannot be taken as being equivalent to moral evaluation or moral knowledge." He asserts that "[t]heology must reject all attempts to restrict the understanding of conscience to the sphere of the moral, even though this can in fact set the limits for the experience of conscience by the unbeliever. The conscience of the Christian will fulfil its function only when every dawning value is deeply experienced as a gracious approach of the divine perfection and every situation of decision as . . . a gift and a call of

90. Merton, *Peace in the Post-Christian Era*, 149–51.
91. *Gaudium et Spes*, a. 16; in Flannery, *Vatican Council II*, 916.
92. *Dignitatis Humanae*, a. 11; ibid., 807.
93. Jehanne; in Taylor, *La Pucelle*, 198.

God, as a possibility of Christian loyalty in the presence of the divine 'Thou.'[94] Thus Christianity has often conceived of "conscience as the site of the encounter between the individual and God, or of conscience as the voice of God."[95] Conscience therefore represents an ongoing experience of revelation calling forth human behavior aligned with divine aspirations for the world. It is a mystical force and therefore liminal in nature. Like other forms of revelation, it can be obeyed or rejected. To operate from an engaged conscience does not entail always or inevitably choosing the good, but it entails the experience of guilt, shame, and/or fear of God (i.e., a "bad conscience") in cases where the good is not chosen and enacted. Suppression of conscience consists in a turning away from conscience such that the divine is no longer engaged through it and morality no longer informed by it. So long as conscience is engaged in the process of moral discernment, it need not be recognized as divinely informed in order to serve effectively. In other words, the activity of conscience is not contingent upon human comprehension of its source or its functioning; an individual can operate from an engaged conscience regardless, reflecting and serving divine aspirations for the world.

Participation in war, even if divinely sanctioned or morally necessary, requires cleansing of conscience since war is presumably not ultimately aligned with divine aspirations for humanity but is an inherently evil human activity.[96] Prophetic revelation might override the "usual" dictates of conscience by sanctioning participation in war, but it does not eliminate conscience which continues to inform one's behavior in warfare. Jehanne did not go to war on the basis of conscience but on the basis of prophetic revelation, yet her conscience was not suppressed and presumably served to reinforce the fact that war is intrinsically evil. Merton holds that, "whether in warfare or in pacifism the Christian is bound to act according to . . . conscience. There are very strict limits set upon his exercise of the right to defend himself and his nation by force, and there are also strict limits upon his willing submission to [the use of] evil and violence. . . . The Christian is not only bound to avoid certain evils, but . . . is responsible for very great goods. . . . [N]o Christian

---

94. Hofmann, "Conscience," 286.

95. Hogan, *Confronting the Truth*, 23–24.

96. "Higher experiences of the spiritual life move often at the margin of the certain conscience." Hofmann, "Conscience," 287.

is ever allowed to be indifferent to man's fate."[97] Accordingly, Jehanne exemplified the necessity of always engaging conscience and acknowledging that violent self-defense constitutes a form of evil demanding restraint, that one's responsibility to God and to others includes a commitment to benevolence, and that the dignity and sanctity of all human life must be recognized and respected everywhere and at all times. Wright maintains that Jehanne's death testified "to the Christian concept of conscience and to the Christian idea of personal vocation," citing her as proof that conscience "binds us to a duty, summons us to an obligation, commands us to a martyrdom." Jehanne, he asserts, "reminds us that neither conscience nor authority amount to anything except as means to an end greater than either or both, and that end is *sanctity*, the sanctity that *conscience* must *seek always* and that *authority* must always serve."[98]

Conscience and the sacrament of confession were vital to Jehanne. She maintained that one could not cleanse one's conscience too much and confessed regularly when possible, believing that her divine counsel would not speak to her if she were in a state of mortal sin.[99] "She was accustomed, before going to an assault, to take account of her conscience," observed one witness.[100] Jean Pasquerel testified that Jehanne was very pious and confessed and took Communion frequently,[101] while another confessor stated that she "had a good soul and tender conscience."[102] Jehanne also frequently urged her companions-at-arms to confess.[103] At Orléans, she regularly had her company of priests assembled to lead the army in singing antiphons and hymns but allowed only those who first confessed to take part in the gatherings, making priests available to all who wished to participate.[104] On Ascension Day at Orléans, "she ordered that no one should go out of the town to the attack ... without first

---

97. Merton, *Peace in the Post-Christian Era*, 10.

98. Wright, *Saints Always Belong*, 127, 129, 130.

99. Jehanne; in Scott, *Trial*, 73–74, 114.

100. Charlotte, daughter of Jacques Boucher in whose home Jehanne was lodged at Orléans; in Murray, *Jeanne d'Arc*, 251.

101. Pasquerel; in Taylor, *La Pucelle*, 312. Also, Orléans manuscript; in Scott, *Trial*, 40.

102. Robert Baignart; quoted by T. d'Armagnac, in Murray, *Jeanne d'Arc*, 293.

103. Numerous witnesses testified to this.

104. Pasquerel; in Pernoud and Clin, *Her Story*, 37.

making confession."[105] Jehanne, like Soelle, apprehended that attending to conscience cannot "be postponed to a later day."[106]

Saint Teresa describes the false peace experienced by one who is not remorseful. She maintains that, in order to advance toward God, a soul must understand its error and experience interior conflict as a result. She allows that it is "impossible for us to be angels here below because such is not our nature. In fact," she states, "a soul doesn't disturb me when I see it with great temptations. If love and fear of our Lord are present, the soul will gain very much.... If I see a soul always quiet and without any war ... I always fear even if I do not see it offending the Lord."[107] This corresponds to Arendt's suggestion "that a 'good conscience' is enjoyed as a rule only by really bad people, criminals and such, while only 'good people' are capable of having a bad conscience."[108] Lack of a fully-engaged conscience and a consequent lack of remorse enable one to commit offenses against God, others, and one's own soul without suffering the pangs of discomfort or anguish that would afflict one with a fully-engaged conscience. The distinction is not between possessing and utterly lacking conscience, but the variable consists in the state of one's conscience, in whether or not it is engaged and the extent to which it is engaged. "We do not have to create a conscience for ourselves," states Merton. "We are born with one, and no matter how much we may ignore it, we cannot silence its insistent demand that we do good and avoid evil."[109] While all are arguably born with a conscience, Merton's assertion that it cannot be silenced is debatable since people who willingly commit repeated atrocities would not likely be able or willing to do so without a suppressed conscience. Silencing of conscience differs from the act of ignoring it—in order to ignore, one must first be aware and then choose to disregard, whereas silencing involves suppression such that conscience is no longer perceived. Silencing, in this sense, has a numbing effect. Hofmann maintains that "the ordination to the good, which is present in the structure of conscience, can, through faulty training, not indeed be made false in itself, but weakened to the point of

---

105. Pasquerel; in Murray, *Jeanne d'Arc*, 286.
106. Soelle, *Silent Cry*, 267.
107. Teresa of Avila, *Collected Works*, vol. 2, 222–23.
108. Arendt, *Life of the Mind*, one-vol. ed., vol. 1, *Thinking*, 5.
109. Merton, *No Man Is an Island*, 41–42.

being practically ineffective."¹¹⁰ Silencing of conscience likely produced the false peace observed by Saint Teresa, but the problem is not specific to her time. "In a world of power politics, there is no question that conscience is a great nuisance," states Merton,¹¹¹ and Heschel warns against the insidious nature of widespread suppression of conscience:

> Modern thought tends to extenuate personal responsibility. Understanding the complexity of human nature, the interrelationship of individual and society, of consciousness and the subconscious, we find it difficult to isolate the deed from those circumstances in which it was done. But new insights may obscure essential vision, and ... conscience grow scales: excuses, pretense, self-pity. Guilt may disappear; no crime is absolute, no sin devoid of apology. Within the limits of the human mind, relativity is true and merciful.¹¹²

Suppression of conscience is facilitated by societies that systematically displace it. Rainer Baum asserts that "modern society" fails "to generate demand for the exercise of conscience" and actually "discourages" it. He explains that, in a society which compartmentalizes labor, "[c]onscientiousness can take the place of conscience very easily." The division of labor, he suggests, "generates moral indifference" in that one is not generally expected to concern oneself "with consequences of action that reverberate beyond" one's "specific sphere of competence and control," based on the assumption that "other relevant experts" will attend to such considerations.¹¹³ Moltmann asserts "that in a technocratic society all human relationships are reduced to the level of things, and general apathy is spreading on an epidemic scale."¹¹⁴ Wright expresses concern that "poetry and prayer, love and thought may become casualties of the intellectual and spiritual paralysis of a civilization depersonalized, automated, seduced by statistics and controlled by computers, with a consequent fatal enfeebling of the sense of the spiritual, the meaning of the person, the thrust of vocation."¹¹⁵ Indeed, in a 2010 interview, American Judge David Cobos described monitoring devices affixed by

110. Hofmann, "Conscience," 284.
111. Merton, *Peace in the Post-Christian Era*, 48.
112. Heschel, *Prophets: Introduction*, 14.
113. Baum, "Holocaust," 56–59, 81.
114. Moltmann, *Crucified God*, 62.
115. Wright, *Saints Always Belong*, 122.

truant officers to delinquent school children in Midland, Texas as serving the purpose of "an electronic conscience."[116]

A society that interferes with the operation of conscience by any means, including the use of deceptive language, places itself at risk of moral collapse. Consider the term "collateral damage," prominent in modern military discourse, which serves to diminish linguistically the significance and severity of destruction involved in the actualities to which it refers. The word "damage" constitutes an understatement when referring to death, and "collateral" frequently denotes property, often of secondary significance. It is defined in one instance as "odds and ends of trash: rubbish" and as "a miscellaneous clutter of personal belongings."[117] Such connotations diminish the value of that which is destroyed under the umbrella of "collateral damage."

Thoughtlessness also facilitates suppression of conscience by permitting deception, flawed judgment, and indifference with respect to whether a situation constitutes a matter of conscience or not. Situations in which the voice of conscience is normally heard might be discarded as morally irrelevant. However, Arendt insists that, if the ability to distinguish between right and wrong is connected to the ability to think, "then we must be able to 'demand' its exercise from every sane person, no matter how erudite or ignorant, intelligent or stupid" that individual is,[118] thought being one of the few possessions of which one cannot easily be robbed if one is committed to retaining it. Hence, it is the responsibility of individuals to exercise thoughtful discernment with respect to the engagement of conscience. While thoughtfulness is no guarantee of benevolence, Arendt suggests that thoughtlessness creates conditions in which evil can easily take root.[119] John Mackie maintains that a vice requires distorted understanding for its existence and is unable to withstand honest reflection on its own nature.[120] Although many evil deeds are thoughtfully planned, it is moral thoughtlessness that apparently enables their planning and facilitates their performance.

---

116. The monitors are used to track the movement of students who are under court order to attend school. Cobos, interview by Tremonti, December 2, 2010.

117. "Collateral," in *Webster's Third New International Dictionary*.

118. Arendt, *Life of the Mind*, one-vol. ed., vol. 1, *Thinking*, 13.

119. Ibid.

120. Mackie, "Virtue," 225–26.

One might wonder what role thought plays in obedience to conscience or other forms of divine revelation. Since few individuals claim the type of clear, direct, specific divine guidance that Jehanne claimed, most rely on conscience or on independent moral discernment as a guide to moral behavior. However, even in cases involving a claim to specific divine instruction, the claimant does not dispense with thought, but thought plays a potential role in discerning the authenticity of revelation. For example, had Jehanne's voices instructed her to perform deeds which completely violated her moral sensibilities, she might have rejected them. However, since the mission to which she was called accorded with her notion of justice, she was able to proceed with confidence and a clearer conscience than had she been called to act in a manner which she regarded as unjust.[121] One chooses whether or not to be receptive to divine revelation and to act in accordance with it in each instance. Jehanne neither ignored nor suppressed conscience but engaged it. Heschel contrasts those who neglect conscience with the prophets who live so keenly by it:

> So many deeds of charity are done, so much decency radiates day and night; yet to the prophet satiety of the conscience is prudery and flight from responsibility. Our standards are modest; our sense of injustice tolerable, timid; our moral indignation impermanent; yet human violence is interminable, unbearable, permanent. To us life is often serene, in the prophet's eye the world reels in confusion. The prophet makes no concession to man's capacity. Exhibiting little understanding for human weakness, he seems unable to extenuate the culpability of man.[122]

Justice is central to the prophetic mission, but the prophet's commitment to justice triggers resentment among perpetrators of injustice. The words of the prophet "burn" in others "where conscience ends," states Heschel;[123] hence, the characteristic persecution of the prophet.

Considerations of justice lead to debate over pacifism and violence. Pacifism in its extreme form of unmitigated refusal to employ aggressive

---

121. Jehanne believed in her apparitions of Saint Michael because he provided "good counsel, comfort and sound doctrine." Jehanne; in Scott, *Trial*, 121. She wrote to the citizens of Tournai, "May God watch over you and grant you grace to uphold the just cause of the kingdom of France." Jehanne; in Taylor, *La Pucelle*, 94.

122. Heschel, *Prophets: Introduction*, 9.

123. Ibid., 10.

and sometimes violent means against evil can amount to a form of evil itself—the evil of willing complicity. Therefore, whether one opposes evil with evil or passively refuses to confront evil, one effectively participates in evil, the distinction being one of kind, between active and passive evil or active and passive participation in violence. Charles Guthrie and Michael Quinlan point out that the decision not to challenge by force the 1994 genocide in Rwanda did not constitute a "morally neutral" choice on the part of the international community.[124] A more viable understanding of pacifism includes the possibility of actively combating evil by its own means, as minimally and justly as possible, as a last resort, and with a view to peace. "Non-violence is no good unless it is effective," Weil concedes. However, one ought to "strive" toward non-violence, she advises, acknowledging that this depends on the adversary as well.[125] Merton relinquishes a purely pacifist stance against war, maintaining that "a 'just war' is at least a theoretical possibility" where self-defense is required. He asserts that one is not morally obliged to render oneself "helpless in the face of an overwhelming enemy power."[126]

Jehanne was a "pacifist-warrior," that is, a warrior by necessity and a pacifist at heart. She declared to the citizens of Troyes that she and the royal army would "enter, with God's help, all the towns that should belong to the holy kingdom [of France], and establish a good, firm peace there."[127] Thus her goal of peace was pronounced—war was the means, not the end. Questioned as to whether or not she was present at a particular battle in which some of the English died, Jehanne replied, "Yes, in God's name, I was. . . . Why did they not leave France and go home to their own country?"[128] One senses a deep sincerity in the question. Had the English withdrawn peacefully from French soil there would have been no need to vanquish them.

The pacifist-warrior as manifested in Jehanne operates from compassion. O'Donohue identifies compassion as "the dividing frontier between barbarity and civility."[129] To be actively compassionate is not necessarily to spare another's suffering but to be genuinely sympathetic,

---

124. Guthrie and Quinlan, *Just War*, 24.
125. Weil, *Gravity and Grace*, 85–86.
126. Merton, *Peace in the Post-Christian Era*, 4, 17.
127. Jehanne; in Taylor, *La Pucelle*, 95.
128. Jehanne; quoted by Tiphaine, in Pernoud, *Retrial*, 223.
129. O'Donohue, *Beauty*, CD audio recording, disc 3, session 6, track 10.

to attempt to alleviate the suffering of others, and to provide comfort insofar as possible. One might exercise compassion in war by causing minimal destruction, permitting retreat or taking prisoners for exchange as preferential to killing, refraining from targeting noncombatants, and refusing to engage in acts of torture or other forms of cruelty—in essence, by conducting defensive war as humanely as possible. Jehanne's undifferentiated compassion among the soldiers marks her as an exceptional warrior. Indeed, one wonders how many warriors or war-mongers actually engage compassionately with their victims. She was greatly afflicted on account of the many English who died without confession at the fort of Saint-Loup, after which she confessed immediately and compelled her entire army to do likewise and to thank God for the victory on threat of her otherwise abandoning them.[130] On another occasion, Jehanne declared to an English commander, "You have called me a whore, but I have great pity for your soul and your men's souls." Shortly afterward, the commander and his soldiers fell fully armed into a river and drowned, and Jehanne wept because they died without confession.[131] Moreover, as the English army fled Orléans with the French in pursuit, Jehanne ordered, "Let the English go, do not kill them. They are going. Their flight is enough for me."[132] "Christian identification with the crucified Christ means solidarity with the sufferings of the poor and the misery both of the oppressed and the oppressors," asserts Moltmann.[133] One does not merely speak compassion, one experiences it and extends it. Weil offers an interesting perspective; in the act of compassion, she states, one is voluntarily "diminished by concentrating on an expenditure of energy" which does not increase one's personal power but confers "existence" upon another individual.[134] Thus there is an element of self-sacrifice in the act of compassion. O'Donohue maintains that compassion humanizes the person who receives it,[135] and I would suggest that it also humanizes the one who extends it. Weil explains that compassion "is not a compensation for, but a spiritualization of, the suf-

130. Pasquerel; in Pernoud, *Retrial*, 186.

131. Jehanne; quoted by Pasquerel, in Pernoud, *Retrial*, 189.

132. Jehanne; quoted by Beaucroix, in Taylor, *La Pucelle*, 301. Dunois provided similar testimony; in Murray, *Jeanne d'Arc*, 237.

133. Moltmann, *Crucified God*, 25.

134. Weil, *Waiting for God*, 90.

135. O'Donohue, *Beauty*, CD audio recording, disc 3, session 6, track 10.

ferings being undergone; it is able to transfigure even the most purely physical sufferings."[136] "Generosity and compassion are inseparable," she asserts, "and both have their model in God."[137]

This brings us to the subject of charity and Jehanne's expression of it. According to Weil, "[p]reference for some human being is necessarily a different thing from charity. Charity does not discriminate. If it is found more abundantly in any special quarter, it is because affliction has chanced to provide an occasion there for the exchange of compassion and gratitude."[138] When asked whether or not she hated the Burgundians, Jehanne replied that she did not like them since she learned that God supported the King of France.[139] She stated that she had known only one Burgundian in Domremy, "whose head she would have wished to be cut off, that is, if this had pleased God."[140] The Burgundian was a farmer named Gérardin d'Épinal who testified that, just prior to her departure for Vaucouleurs and apparently alluding to her mission, Jehanne said to him, "Friend, if you were not a Burgundian, there is something I would tell you." She subsequently met Épinal on the road to Rheims with others from Domremy who were attending Charles's coronation, and it was to him that she confided her fear of treason.[141] The testimony suggests that Jehanne was on very friendly terms with this man and it appears unlikely that she wished literally for his beheading. It also seems that he was not staunchly committed to the Burgundian cause given that he

136. Weil, *Need for Roots*, 172.
137. Weil, *Waiting for God*, 90.
138. Ibid., 131.

139. Jehanne; in Taylor, *La Pucelle*, 149. The Orléans manuscript reads: "Interroguee se la voix luy dist en sa jeunesse qu'elle hayst les Bourguygnons, respond que, depuis qu'elle entendit que les voix estoyent pour le roy de France, elle n'a point aymé les Bourguygnons." Orléans MS 518, 77. Bouzy notes that, although the word "aymé" might refer either to love or friendship, it is likely that Jehanne confessed a dislike—not a lack of love—for the Burgundians. He supposes that, had Jehanne declared a lack of Christian love, the Rouen judges would have employed such a statement against her, and we have no indication of this occurring. Bouzy, conversation with author, May 7, 2011. Although a definitive translation eludes us, the University of Paris, unlike the trial judges, did accuse Jehanne of transgressing "God's commandment to love one's neighbour" in the context of the statement. Censure of the University of Paris, Article 10 of the twelve final articles drawn up against Jehanne; in Scott, *Trial*, 158.

140. Jehanne; in Taylor, *La Pucelle*, 149.

141. Jehanne; quoted by Épinal, in Pernoud, *Retrial*, 84. Burgundians eventually captured Jehanne and fatally sold her to the English.

attended the dauphin's coronation. While Jehanne was displeased with Épinal's Burgundian sympathies, she considered him a friend and made no motion toward harming him. Jehanne also threatened Dunois with beheading should he fail to inform her of the arrival of the English captain, Ffastolf, at the siege of Orléans[142] but did not follow through when he failed to do so. It is evidently an expression that she employed without literal intent.[143] "The words of the prophet are stern, sour, stinging. But behind his austerity is love and compassion for [hu]mankind."[144] As far as we know, Jehanne never declared hatred toward anyone.

Jehanne's occasionally harsh words seem more aligned with righteous anger than hatred, an anger conceivably necessary to the accomplishment of her mission. Heschel reminds us that anger may be "reprehensible when associated with malice, [but] morally necessary as resistance to malice." There are situations in which "anger alone can conquer evil," he asserts. "It is after mildness and kindness have failed that anger is proclaimed." (Anger is, in effect, a double-edged sword.) Its total suppression in the face of evil might qualify as "surrender and capitulation" and serve to stultify "moral sensibility. Patience," explains Heschel, is "a quality of holiness, [but it] may be sloth in the soul when associated with the lack of righteous indignation." On the other hand, unrestrained anger can also prove disastrous.[145] Heschel notes that, in the prophetic model of divinity, anger and mercy function inseparably. "The prophet . . . holds God's love as well as God's anger in his soul, enraptured or enfevered." Divine anger, he insists, "must not be treated in isolation, but as an aspect of the divine pathos . . . aroused by" human sin. "The prophet's angry words cry. The wrath of God is a lamentation."[146] "Divine sympathy for the victims of human cruelty is the motive of [God's] anger." Moreover, divine anger is an ephemeral condition, not "a habit or a disposition" and, "beyond . . . [this] anger lies the mystery of compassion."[147] Soelle maintains that the "nausea caused by this world of injustice and violence ought at least to be perceptible; it ought

---

142. Aulon; in Pernoud, *Retrial*, 166.

143. A similar expression today is, "I'll have your head if . . ."

144. Heschel, *Prophets: Introduction*, 12.

145. Heschel, *Prophets: II*, 61, 77. Heschel defines righteous indignation as "impatience with evil." Ibid., 63.

146. Ibid., 62–64, 77, 92.

147. Ibid., 67–69.

to increase to the point of physical vomiting, as is told about so many highly gifted women from Catherine of Siena to Simone Weil. That kind of nausea is an experience of compassio[n]."[148] The statement suggests that violently inflicted suffering is so contrary to essential human nature that the true witnessing of it automatically induces a purgative, cathartic process. In Jehanne's case, weeping apparently constituted that process. "This kind of suffering is not imposed," notes Soelle, "nor is it chosen. . . . It arises from a relationship to the world that is not immersed in the I [ego] alone."[149] "The world is full of evil," states Merton, "and it is our duty to fight evil and teach truth."[150] Heschel reassures us that nearly "every prophet brings consolation, promise, and the hope of reconciliation along with censure and castigation,"[151] and this dual message is reflected in Jehanne's famous (first) letter to the English:

> King of England, . . . [h]and over to the Pucelle, who is sent from God the King of Heaven, the keys of all the towns which you have taken and ravaged in France. She is come here on God's behalf to restore the blood royal. She is quite ready to make peace, if you are willing to do right, that is, to leave France, and to make amends for the injuries you have done, and to hand back the monies you have received all the time that you have been here.
>
> And you, archers, soldiers, gentlemen and others who are now besieging the town of Orleans, get you back in God's Name into your own country. And if you will not do so, then expect to hear from the Pucelle, who will shortly encounter you, to your very great hurt.
>
> King of England, if you do not do so, . . . wherever I find your people in France, I shall fight them and drive them out; and shall make them go, whether they will or no; and if they will not obey, I shall have them put to death. I am sent here by God the King of Heaven to fight them and to drive them out of France. And if they will obey, I will have mercy on them. And do not think that you will stay here any longer, for you do not hold the realm of France from God the King of Heaven, son of the Virgin Mary. For he who will thus hold it is Charles, the true heir, for God the King of Heaven so desires. And it is revealed to him by the Pucelle that very shortly he will enter Paris with a good company. And if

---

148. Soelle, *Silent Cry*, 140.
149. Ibid.
150. Merton, *Run to the Mountain*, 460.
151. Heschel, *Prophets: Introduction*, 12.

you do not believe the message of God and the Pucelle, I inform you that wherever we find you, we will fight you, and will make so great a to-do [*hay-hay*] there that not for a thousand years has France had one so great. And firmly believe that the King of Heaven will send such strength to the Pucelle that neither you nor your soldiers will be able to repel either her or her forces. And when it comes to blows we shall see who has the better right.

And you, Duke of Bedford, who now besiege Orleans, the Pucelle begs that you will not compel her to destroy you. . . .

And I beg you, if you desire to make peace, to answer me in the city of Orleans, where we hope to be very shortly; and if you do not do so, you will remember it by reason of your great sufferings.[152]

"There is a cruelty which pardons," notes Heschel, "just as there is a pity which punishes. Severity must tame whom love cannot win."[153] The relationship between compassion and violence as embodied by Jehanne can serve as a paradigm in instances wherein violence is deemed divinely sanctioned or otherwise necessary. Compassion might be one of humanity's best defenses against self-destruction since it involves sympathy which contradicts insidious indifference that allows individuals to commit horrendous acts of violence while retaining the ability to sleep undisturbed.

Just War Theory

We asked for signs
the signs were sent:
the birth betrayed,
the marriage spent;
the widowhood
of every government—
signs for all to see.
—Leonard Cohen, "Anthem"

The theory of just war dates back approximately two thousand years and is diversely rooted in Judaism, Christianity, Islam, Hinduism, Confucianism, ancient Greece, Rome, and Egypt. Just war theory seeks

152. Jehanne; in Scott, *Trial*, 30–31.
153. Heschel, *Prophets: II*, 76.

to delineate what constitutes morally justifiable war. My intention in discussing it is to assess how the fundamental components of just war theory correspond to or contradict Jehanne's example and to determine whether or not anything can be gained from her example that might be useful in addressing current insufficiencies in the just war model.

Merton describes just war theory as supposing "a *defensive* war in which force is strictly limited and the greatest care is taken to protect the rights and the lives of noncombatants and even of combatants."[154] Henrik Syse and Gregory Reichberg explain that the term "just war" does not refer simply to a theory or set of rules but encompasses "an ideal of the 'just warrior'" as expressed through medieval notions of chivalric honor and virtue. This ideal pertains not only to military personnel, but to all individuals "who make decisions and perform fateful actions as the use of armed force is being contemplated or actually takes place."[155] Two major aspects of just war theory are *jus ad bellum*, concerning that which is deemed just reason for engaging in war, and *jus in bello*, concerning that which is considered just behavior (right conduct) in war. The number and arrangement of criteria stipulated within each category vary and, recently, some have recommended inclusion of a third category, *jus post bellum*, intended to address the after-effects of war, suggesting that aftermath conditions ought to factor into the decision of whether or not to go to war.[156] *Jus post bellum* is also concerned with post-war behavior of victors.[157] According to just war theory, all criteria within the designated categories must be satisfied for engagement in war to be considered just, but Alex J. Bellamy notes that the criteria are seldom weighted equally in practice, and it is questionable whether or not all criteria are satisfied in all cases to which the notion of just war is applied. Some theorists stipulate that *jus in bello* criteria are irrelevant unless *jus ad bellum* criteria are first satisfied.[158]

Jus ad bellum stipulates that war is to be undertaken by a lawful or sovereign authority, not by individual citizens. This traditionally refers to the authority of a sovereign ruler or governing body without a superior. On this precept, it rests upon the authoritative individual or body

---

154. Merton, *Peace in the Post-Christian Era*, 68.
155. Syse and Reichberg, *Ethics, Nationalism, and Just War*, 2.
156. Guthrie and Quinlan, *Just War*, 26, 43.
157. Bellamy, *Just Wars*, 121.
158. Ibid., 121–22, 128.

to discern "just cause, to avoid evil intentions, and to achieve the end of peace" and the common good,[159] but this is problematic as sovereign authorities do not always behave lawfully or justly and do not necessarily serve the collective good, which is subjectively defined. Contrarily, an individual or group lacking lawful authority might behave rightly in opposing a corrupt sovereign authority, thereby providing a great moral service to the community. Human authority is not synonymous with justice; therefore, to insist that just war can be undertaken only by an earthly sovereign is untenable given the potential for abuse of lawful authority. Since every free person is responsible for his or her behavior and conscience, each bears the responsibility of choosing whether or not to support the decisions of lawful authorities. Ultimate moral accountability resides with the individual.

While Jehanne's military endeavors enjoyed lawful support from the dauphin, she also claimed support from the most sovereign authority possible—divine authority.[160] In fact, from a theological perspective, God might be considered the only sovereign authority, in which case divine sanction of warfare might be held as the only (or at least most) legitimate sanction of warfare. With respect to the just war tradition's interpretation of legitimate authority, Cicero (106–43 BCE) maintained that certain pagan priests of Rome were able to discern the will of the gods with respect to warfare and could authorize the Roman senate to declare war. Ambrose (340–97 CE) asserted that the right to wage war rested with the state rather than the Church but allowed that the Hebrew prophets had legitimately proclaimed war by divine command. Both Ambrose and Augustine (354–430 CE), however, relegated this prophetic role to the distant past and viewed earthly sovereigns as divine representatives in matters of war.[161] Gratian of Bologna held (ca. 1140 CE) that God can directly command war through the voice of the pope in defense of the Church both materially and doctrinally.[162] Hence, the possibility of God sanctioning participation in warfare through prophetic figures was abandoned by mainstream just war theorists long before Jehanne proclaimed her mission. Although some theorists acknowledge two types of justice—"objective or true justice (knowable to God)" and

159. This interpretation of lawful authority derives from Aquinas. Johnson, "Thinking Morally," 6.
160. Jehanne declared God her "sovereign Lord." Jehanne; in Scott, *Trial*, 92.
161. Mattox, *St. Augustine*, 16–17, 74, 77.
162. Bellamy, *Just Wars*, 32–33.

"subjective justice (knowable to humans)"[163]—they do not address the possibility that lay individuals might acquire knowledge of objective justice directly through divine revelation. Jehanne's situation, wherein an "ordinary" citizen of humble social status and a member of the Church laity raised her sword against a political enemy in the name of God, does not apparently conform to the general expectation of just war theorists with respect to legitimate authority, although the fact that her military campaign was approved by the heir to the throne of France does.

It is highly unlikely that Jehanne would have been moved to military action by royal authority alone as she considered it "better to obey and serve her sovereign Lord, that is God, than men."[164] Jehanne agreed to fight on the basis of direct divine authority and the dauphin's approval was sought later, also by divine instruction. Since it might have been difficult for her to gain support from the soldiers initially without political and financial backing from Charles VII, it was a practical matter as well as a customary matter which accorded due respect to earthly sovereignty in accordance with chivalric practices and a medieval worldview.

Jus ad bellum also holds that war is to be undertaken with just and proportionate cause, but the criterion of just cause is ambiguous since it does not clearly specify what constitutes just cause.[165] Commonly declared cases for just cause in warfare are self-defense and defense of an ally against unwarranted aggression. Punishment has sometimes been cited as just cause,[166] but this is certainly questionable.

One might wonder what the primary commitment of just war is, whether it be to justice or to peace. For Augustine, the primary objective of war is peace.[167] Arendt states that "[t]he end of war—end taken in its twofold meaning—is peace or victory; but to the question And what is

---

163. Ibid., 122.

164. Jehanne; in Scott, *Trial*, 92.

165. Some maintain that just cause is to be assessed relatively such that it becomes "sufficient cause"; rather than determining just cause, one is thereby required to establish a "more or less" just cause, that is, "sufficiently just cause to legitimize the actions" intended. Bellamy, *Just Wars*, 123. Note that sufficiency as a qualifier relates to quantity whereas justice as a qualifier relates to quality.

166. Mattox, *St. Augustine*, 9, 74.

167. Augustine, *City of God*, vol. 6, 165. John Mark Mattox lists "peace as the ultimate objective of war" as a separate *jus ad bellum* principle/criterion. Mattox, *St. Augustine*, 10.

the end of peace? there is no answer. Peace is an absolute."[168] Since notions of justice are highly perspectival and debatable, it is difficult if not impossible to establish justice as the central goal of war in a generally applicable sense. Peace, on the other hand, is more uniformly understood and can be broadly designated as a goal of war. This is not to assert that justice plays no role in just war; rather, justice is implicit in peace since true peace cannot exist without justice. Therefore, to establish peace is to achieve justice as well. Augustine distinguishes between "the just peace of God" and the "peace of the unjust," which is no peace at all.[169] A peaceful society demands more than an absence of war; it requires the presence of justice. Jehanne's declaration that peace in France would only be achieved at the point of a lance[170] expresses her ultimate purpose (peace), her means of achieving it (by lance), and the necessity of the means in that it was the only effective option available (last resort). Her commitment to justice and her pursuit of peace were components of a single endeavor. That she aimed to oust a longtime invader in defense of her country and its citizens places Jehanne's mission firmly within the realm of just cause.

Although just cause and proportionate cause are often treated separately, given that disproportionate cause is unjust, proportionate cause seems an inevitable aspect of just cause. The criterion of proportionate cause requires that the proportion of good to be achieved (intended) outweighs the proportion of evil manifested in achieving it. Guthrie and Quinlan note, for example, that it would not constitute proportionate cause if a nation were to wage war on another for robbing one of its citizens, insulting its flag, or offending its head of state.[171] Jehanne demonstrated proportionate cause by engaging in an existing war, employing weapons already in use by the offending party, and refraining from violence in excess of that which she sought to eliminate. The good that she aimed to achieve—an end to war that had persisted over ninety-two years and the establishment of lasting peace—outweighed the minimally necessary (albeit considerable) violence employed.

168. Arendt, *Violence*, 51.

169. Augustine, *City of God*, vol. 6, 171. Conquerors often seek "to impose" on their newly-acquired subjects "the laws of their own [brand of pseudo-]peace." Ibid., 167.

170. Jehanne; in Taylor, *La Pucelle*, 173.

171. Guthrie and Quinlan, *Just War*, 12.

In many instances, estimation of proportionate cause is difficult in the same manner in which all utilitarian calculation is difficult, the problem being uncertainty. Expected outcomes do not always correspond to actual outcomes, and calculation of proportionality runs the risk of subjectivity and partiality. We need not revisit these issues in detail at this time but must acknowledge them and note that Jehanne's faith in divine revelation eliminated such problems of uncertainty for her.

Jus ad bellum indicates that war is to be undertaken as a last resort. This requires not that every other possible option be exhausted prior to engaging in war, but that every other potentially effective option be first considered and tried, if possible. "Last," in this context, indicates least-preferred.[172]

France was on the verge of being lost entirely, and perhaps permanently, to England when Jehanne undertook her military campaign. Many regarded her involvement in the war as France's only hope. Certainly, ample time had elapsed for the conflict to be resolved, but this had not come to pass. Moreover, Jehanne delayed acting upon the instructions of her voices before finally departing for Vaucouleurs.[173] Furthermore, she thrice entreated the enemy to leave France peacefully rather than compel her to engage in battle. She clearly approached warfare as a last resort.

Jus ad bellum also demands that a formal declaration of war be issued, allowing the opponent opportunity to correct the offensive behavior. The requirement of advance warning or ultimatum by means of formal declaration supports the criterion of last resort. As we have seen, Jehanne's ultimatum to the English (comprised of several letters) declared her unambiguous intention to attack should they refuse to leave France and, in fact, exhorted them to do so.

Also under the rubric of *jus ad bellum* is the stipulation that war must be undertaken with reasonable probability of success. Success is not, in this context, measured in terms of military victory alone, but in terms of the total consequences of a particular action. For instance, an enemy might not be entirely defeated but might be significantly weakened or prevented from succeeding in a very destructive endeavor.[174] In calculating likely outcomes and reasonable probability of suc-

---

172. Ibid., 13, 33.
173. Jehanne; in Scott, *Trial*, 67. G. Thibault; in Murray, *Jeanne d'Arc*, 265.
174. Guthrie and Quinlan, *Just War*, 32.

cess, the utilitarian problem of impossible accuracy again rears its head. Moreover, as Merton points out, in an era of nuclear weaponry (and biological and chemical weaponry as well) it is increasingly difficult to measure, or even hope for, favorable outcomes in war,[175] rendering the criterion somewhat obsolete.

Jehanne defied the criterion of reasonable probability of success since the likelihood of an untrained and inexperienced young woman leading an army and paving the way to victory for a party that was almost completely defeated in a seemingly interminable war was, by all reasonable assessment, almost nil. Hence, Jehanne's example testifies to the serious inadequacy of utilitarian calculation of probability. Because her case for engaging in war was founded on faith rather than reason, her situation was not bound by the limitations of human reason and the miraculous was free to occur. Human activity directed by reason alone can impose restrictions on the activity of grace, blocking its operation through a refusal to engage it.

Finally, *jus ad bellum* insists that war must be undertaken with right intention. The issue of right intention is complex, but it is generally agreed that one who acts in the name of peace, justice, and the common good acts with right intention, whereas one who acts for the sake of hatred, revenge, oppression, or the extension of one's power or territory acts with wrong intent. There is obviously a strong connection between right intention and just cause, as well as between last resort and right intention. According to Guthrie and Quinlan, right intention aims "to create a better, more just and more lasting subsequent peace" for all involved than if war is not undertaken.[176] Again, terms such as "better" and "more just" are subjective and problematic, but what Guthrie and Quinlan seem to suggest is that peace without justice is not true peace and that true peace is the aspiration of right intention. It must be noted that, not only is it difficult to discern others' intentions,[177] but governments often act with partiality rather than in the interest of all concerned as recommended by the concept of right intention. Furthermore, states Bellamy,

---

175. Merton, *Peace in the Post-Christian Era*, 142.

176. Guthrie and Quinlan, *Just War*, 12–13, 24–25.

177. Bellamy holds that "something approximating intentions" can be ascertained from the actions of others. Bellamy, *Just Wars*, 125. This, however, is not infallibly the case.

"[s]ocieties tend to expect their governments to expend more energy protecting fellow citizens... than protecting foreign non-combatants."[178]

As we know, Jehanne was very explicit about her intentions in going to war. She was not motivated by vengeance and did not seek to expand, but to restore, the kingdom of France. Moreover, she attempted to eliminate, not to engage in, oppression and sought nothing from the enemy but freedom. Jehanne's goal was to establish enduring peace and its necessary component, justice. In the process, she displayed respect and concern for all.

According to *jus in bello*, war must be practiced with discrimination, which deems it impermissible to attack noncombatants deliberately, and risk to noncombatants must be completely minimized.[179] This becomes complicated when there is no clear division between the geographical position of combatants and noncombatants. Targeted destruction of property, monuments, religious buildings, food, and water supplies is also prohibited but, unfortunately, mass bombing often eliminates such distinctions in matters of destruction. Harm to captives, ambassadors, or those seeking asylum is forbidden, as is violation of corpses, and the rights of conscientious objectors and religious professionals are to be respected. Minimal force is not to be exceeded.

Jehanne did not target noncombatants[180] and forbade pillaging.[181] She also granted asylum to religious professionals.[182] Moreover, given the extent of her piety, it is unthinkable that she would have allowed the destruction of religious buildings, and it is equally inconceivable in light of her character and her compassion toward the wounded enemy that she would have permitted the violation of corpses. There is no evidence of transgressions such as these on Jehanne's part, and even her most hateful, disparaging, and determined accusers in Rouen did not charge her with anything of this nature.

Corresponding to the *jus ad bellum* requirement of proportionate cause, *jus in bello* requires that proportionality be observed such that the means of war is proportional to the end. The means of war must not

---

178. Ibid., 119.

179. Guthrie and Quinlan, *Just War*, 14, 39.

180. This is not to claim that noncombatants did not sometimes die inadvertently as a result of battles in which she participated.

181. Beaucroix; in Pernoud, *Retrial*, 120. Pasquerel; in Taylor, *La Pucelle*, 316.

182. Coutes; in Murray, *Jeanne d'Arc*, 262.

constitute greater evil than that which it seeks to eliminate, but more good than evil must be the fairly estimated result of the action. All foreseeable incidental harm should be factored into the evaluation and only minimal necessary force is permitted.[183] At the risk of monotony, it must be observed that such utilitarian predictions are impossible to perform with certainty and constitute cause for concern. This criterion prohibits the use of torture and traditionally placed restrictions on types of weaponry deemed acceptable.[184] The points cited with respect to Jehanne's military campaign in relation to proportionate cause (*jus ad bellum*) pertain to proportionality *in bello* as well. The destruction caused by medieval warfare was more containable than that caused by modern bombs and, as warfare technology advances, proportionality *in bello* is increasingly difficult to estimate and achieve.[185]

Evidently, several aspects of just war theory rely heavily upon utilitarian calculation, which is inherently flawed, rendering application of the theory problematic and its reliability questionable.[186] "Every act," Weil recommends, "should be considered from the point of view not of its object but of its impulsion. The question is not 'What is the aim?' It is 'What is the origin?'"[187] "We should not take one step, *even in the direction of what is good*," she advises, "beyond that to which we are irresistibly impelled by God."[188] While extreme, Weil's position reflects awareness of the fallibility of human moral evaluation. Technological advances have stymied the potential efficacy of just war theory in important respects since every war must now consider the possibility that chemical, biological, or nuclear weapons might be launched, the consequences of which are inestimable short of total destruction. Let us not forget that the atomic bomb has been intentionally detonated twice over civilian populations. When such weapons are employed, the distinction between combatant and noncombatant is impossible to observe, as is

183. Guthrie and Quinlan, *Just War*, 14, 39–41.

184. Mattox, *St. Augustine*, 10.

185. Augustine includes "good faith" as a *jus in bello* criterion, stipulating that pledges (including those to the enemy) must be honored but that it is otherwise acceptable to employ deceptive military strategy against an enemy. Cicero and Ambrose espouse variations of this criterion. Ibid., 11, 64–65, 84.

186. Bellamy notes that "*jus ad bellum* criteria" in particular "afford considerable latitude to political leaders." Bellamy, *Just Wars*, 131.

187. Weil, *Gravity and Grace*, 45.

188. Ibid., 44.

proscription against the destruction of food, water, religious buildings, monuments, and property. In Jehanne's day, "the means of defence were ... superior to the means of attack,"[189] but this is no longer true. The means of attack in modern warfare often far exceed the means of defense, not only in that there is no reliable defense against nuclear, biological, or chemical weapons and little to no means of limiting their devastation once unleashed, but also in that civilians do not normally have access to weapons akin to those employed against them. Arendt asserts that "[t]he very substance of violent action is ruled by the means-end category, whose chief characteristic, if applied to human affairs, has always been that the end is in danger of being overwhelmed by the means which it justifies and which are needed to reach it."[190] Consequently, Merton advises that, "[s]ince any large scale war is likely to turn ... into a global nuclear cataclysm, we can no longer afford to ignore our obligation to work for the abolition of war."[191] The problem remains, however, that war exists and demands response.

Despite its shortcomings, Guthrie and Quinlan maintain that just war theory serves as "a systematic reminder of moral questions which we ought to think about when we consider embarking upon armed conflict or when we engage in it."[192] Although this is true, it is not sufficient; an alternative, more comprehensive theory of acceptable warfare is needed. Jean Bethke Elshtain notes that current just war theory assumes "the existence of universal moral dispositions, if not convictions—hence, the possibility of a nonrelativist ethic," as well as "the need for moral judgments of who/what is aggressor/victim, just/unjust, acceptable/unacceptable," and also "the potential efficacy of moral appeals and arguments to stay the hand of force." She refrains from passing judgment on whether or not the assumptions are reasonable or realistic,[193] but it should be noted that Jehanne's example demonstrates possible suspension of a universal ethic, deference of human judgment to divine judgment, and a declared necessity for violence in opposing a particular aggression. What Elshtain offers is her opinion that, in times of war, it appears "likely that many" just war criteria "will go unheeded. They

---

189. Pernoud, *Herself and Her Witnesses*, 107.
190. Arendt, *Violence*, 4.
191. Merton, *Peace in the Post-Christian Era*, 5.
192. Guthrie and Quinlan, *Just War*, 46.
193. Elshtain, "Epilogue," 324–25.

may have sufficient force," she allows, "to give war-makers a bad conscience, and they offer men and women a 'voice' in and through which to register their objections and their moral distress." Nonetheless, she cautions against "the crusading impulse lurking in the interstices of just-war discourse. The language of good and evil, just and unjust, may . . . turn people out as judges who sometimes become executioners. Should this happen, the preponderant force of 'official' just-war discourse may not have sufficient strength to hold in check the 'heretical' crusading offshoot."[194]

Just war theory does not address individual claims to divine sanction, yet amid the excessively destructive weaponry of today, perhaps divinely sanctioned warfare is the only conceivably justifiable warfare. "Every creature which attains perfect obedience [to God] constitutes a special, unique, irreplaceable form of the presence, knowledge and operation of God in the world," states Weil.[195] Perhaps the key to abolition of war, or at least reduction or mitigation of evil in war, lies in the essential values manifested in Jehanne's conduct as divine servant in war. It is worth considering in light of what is at stake.

Daughter of God: Constructing a Model of Righteous Warfare and Human Agency

She showed pity not only to the French, but also to the enemy. I know that, for I was with her for a long time. . . .
—Simon Beaucroix, Nullification Trial

Jehanne represents the reconciliation of warrior and saint. As a warrior-saint, she was no ordinary warrior but an extraordinary one, a warrior *par excellence* by virtue not only of her remarkable military proficiencies but also by virtue of her saintliness, her exceptionally virtuous character. Yet Jehanne was fully human and, as such, not immune to human susceptibilities, but she surmounted these, excepting the inevitable insurmountability of death. As fully human, Jehanne serves as a potential model for others.

---

194. Ibid., 329–30.
195. Weil, *Gravity and Grace*, 48.

Jehanne's life and death demonstrate the nature, significance, and impact within human history of a deeply lived divine-human relationship. The task before us, insofar as possible, is to delineate Jehanne's divinely-mandated prophetic agency within this relationship. Jehanne did not simply fight a "just war"—a war deemed just by human reasoning (although it might be reasonably considered just)—but she fought a war allegedly by divine command. This places her agency in a category that I have chosen to define as righteous in order to distinguish it from the just war category, which does not necessarily refer or appeal to divinity, although it has at times done so indirectly,[196] and to distinguish it as a model based on Jehanne specifically. Within the model of righteous warfare and human agency herein proposed, divine sanction figures as the central characteristic and righteousness as a defining and necessary behavioral quality; human conduct is prescribed in accordance with presumed divine principles as apprehended through Jehanne's example. While just war theory rests on human ability and willingness to distinguish between moral and immoral behavior, the notion of righteous warfare rests primarily on faith in a form of morality discerned through processes of ongoing divine revelation. Since war thrives unchecked in the absence of righteousness, righteousness in matters of war can serve to mitigate or discourage warfare. Of course, we are speaking of righteousness and not self-righteousness; the latter honors the ego, whereas the former, in the sense that we employ it,[197] denies it.

A distinction must be drawn between "righteous warfare" and "holy war." Whereas "holy war" is directed against a perceived religious enemy, Jehanne did not view the English or Burgundians as religious enemies since they, like the French royalists, were Christian. In fact, she granted immunity to English ecclesiastics at Orléans.[198] Her purpose in fighting was neither religious conversion nor elimination of a religious group; hence, she did not engage in "holy war."[199]

---

196. In such instances, the Church, or the pope specifically, were often regarded as divine representatives or spokespersons on behalf of war. Bellamy, *Just Wars*, 33, 35, 42, 44, 46–48.

197. Righteousness, in the context of righteous warfare herein described, derives from faith in the divine and commitment to divine servantship, hence, surrender of ego-based personal will to divine will.

198. Coutes; in Murray, *Jeanne d'Arc*, 262.

199. In a letter written and signed by Pasquerel, he presumes to write in Jehanne's voice against the Hussites, but it is obvious that she did not author the letter whose

Righteous Warfare and Human Agency

There is no such thing as a truly just war since war inevitably contains elements of injustice, although it might contain elements of justice or justifiability as well. While righteous warfare as herein defined might be considered just in many respects, it is not characterized fundamentally by justice but by righteousness, which presumably corresponds to divine justice. Since human notions of justice and morality are elusive (fluid and subjective), all theories based fundamentally on these concepts are somewhat deficient and tentative, although necessary, useful,

---

language and style are notably inconsistent with nine extant letters dictated by Jehanne. Moreover, the letter presents her as threatening to abandon her domestic campaign in order to embark on a holy war elsewhere—a highly unlikely scenario given Jehanne's utter devotion to her mission in France. Also, Jehanne was signing letters in her own hand by the time Pasquerel's letter was written and none of her extant letters is signed in his name. Furthermore, Taylor observes that Pasquerel's letter was composed in Latin (a language in which Jehanne was presumably unskilled) whereas Jehanne's letters were dictated in French. Taylor, *La Pucelle*, 132. A statement in Jehanne's first letter to the English is sometimes interpreted as a reference to crusade despite the fact that it is extremely vague, making no explicit reference to crusade or war, and any interpretation of it is inevitably and entirely speculative. She once uttered a crusade-related comment in a letter to the Duke of Burgundy, but the comment is peripheral to the main thrust of the message, which is that Christians ought not to war against each other. The letter reads, "High and dread prince, duke of Burgundy, the Maid calls upon you by the King of Heaven, . . . to make a firm and lasting peace with the king of France. You two must pardon one another fully with a sincere heart, as loyal Christians should; and if it pleases you to make war, go and wage it on the Saracens. . . . I pray you, . . . make war no more on the holy kingdom of France." Jehanne, July 17, 1429; in Pernoud and Clin, *Her Story*, 67. The statement can be interpreted as an approbation of crusade activity for those inclined to war; however, if Jehanne did not utterly disapprove of crusade (and we do not know what the movement represented to her), she did not, according to existing evidence, declare it divinely sanctioned and did not participate in it or express any explicit desire to do so. Nor is there any testimony suggesting that she actively rallied others to that end. Taylor interprets Jehanne's reference to the Saracens as a warning or taunt. Jehanne's letter goes on to declare that the Duke of Burgundy will not win any further battles against the French royalists, who have Jesus on their side; hence, Taylor infers, the duke would fare better fighting the Saracens. He categorizes the statement as military "crusading rhetoric" "typical" of the time. Taylor, *La Pucelle*, 4, 19–20, 76, n. 20. In fact, all evidence relating Jehanne directly to war does so in the context of expelling the English from France by order of that which she apprehended as very specific divine command. Since all accounts of her divine purpose are devoid of any reference to crusade, there is no compelling reason to suppose that she would have undertaken such a campaign. Rather, testimony indicates that Jehanne longed to return to her peasant life in Domremy once her military mission in France was fulfilled. Following the coronation of Charles VII, she declared, "[P]lease God my Creator that I may now retire, and lay down my arms, and go to serve my father and mother and keep their sheep, with my brothers and my sister, who will be glad to see me again." Jehanne; quoted by Dunois, in Pernoud, *Retrial*, 144.

and potentially meaningful. In righteous warfare, one appeals to divine justice, to a higher authority than human authority and, in so doing, engages divine mystery, agrees to play by divine rules—which one is not necessarily privy to—and follows a path which could lead to martyrdom.

Documentary evidence portrays Jehanne as one who was authentic and constant. She was authentic in that she simply was who she was, no matter what she was engaged in or in whose company. Her behavior was not rooted in pride, self-importance, or a desire to impress others. She was not given to pretense and did not put on airs. She possessed a genuine essence that predominated. Pernoud and Clin observe that Jehanne was transparent; "she had a particular limpidity, a clear reflection of that invisible world with which she felt herself in touch."[200] Yet there is an ineffable quality to Jehanne as well; perhaps Robert Bresson touched it in stating (with respect to her) that one "does not explain greatness, [but] one tries to attune oneself to it."[201] "[W]hatever truly is great is available equally for all,"[202] maintains Kierkegaard, so no-one is off the hook in terms of the demands on individual character. "It is against my nature," he reflects, "to . . . talk inhumanly about the great as though some thousands of years were a huge distance; I prefer to talk about it humanly as though it happened yesterday and let only the greatness itself be the distance that either exalts or condemns."[203]

Jehanne's exemplary teaching by means of lived witnessing of faith reveals how one rises to the occasion of serving God in the context of war, for surely there are means of serving God in all human contexts. Heschel points out that the content of legitimate prophetic messages often directly opposes the "hopes and inclinations" of the prophet.[204] That Jehanne continued to fight in knowledge and fear of her impending capture demonstrates an obvious absence of personal agenda. She fulfilled the requirements of practical, prophetic mysticism in all its unpredictable, uncompromising, unyielding, solitary, and terrifying aspects as well as its ultimate, intrinsic dignity, sanctity, and beauty. Anyone claiming divine sanction in acts of war whose behavior does not correspond

---

200. Pernoud and Clin, *Her Story*, 163–64.

201. Robert Bresson, French film producer; in Pernoud, *Herself and Her Witnesses*, 277.

202. Kierkegaard, *Fear and Trembling*, 96.

203. Ibid., 37.

204. Heschel, *Prophets: II*, 208.

to Jehanne's behavior cannot be considered in league with her, nor with the Jewish and Christian prophetic traditions in which she participates. In fact, such a one might be suspected of false prophecy, at least within the parameters of those traditions.

Since arbitrary evidence in support of divine sanction cannot reasonably command credence from others, random claims to isolated incidents as constituting evidence of divine sanction must be held in suspicion. This is not to say that God cannot sanction whatever God wishes in whatever manner God wishes, but it is to state that, based on Jehanne's model, multiple related identifying characteristics were present and, while an isolated event might very well be divinely sanctioned, isolated incidents simply do not provide sufficient evidence upon which others can formulate sound judgment with respect to a given claim.

While there is no definitive proof of divine sanction, Kierkegaard suggests that willingness to suffer [at the hands of others] constitutes a divinely elected apostle's strongest evidence of his or her claim, with respect to which "his speech will be brief: 'I am called by God; do with me now as you will, scourge me, persecute me; but my last word is my first: I am called by God, and I make you eternally responsible for what you do to me.'"[205] The words fit Jehanne like a glove. Recall that she held Cauchon responsible for her death and accountable to God.[206] Moreover, on being threatened with torture, she responded, "Truly, if you were to tear me limb from limb and make my soul leave my body, I would not say to you anything else. [And if you force me to do so], then afterwards I shall say that you made me say so by force."[207] With respect to her mission, Jehanne's last word was, indeed, her first, that she was called by God.

It cannot be concluded from Jehanne's example that God sanctions indiscriminate warfare or war in and of itself. She was involved in a specific war for a specific purpose under specific circumstances and conducted herself in a specific manner. In order to apprehend what God conceivably sanctioned through her conduct, a comprehensive model derived from Jehanne, stipulating criteria that might be considered collectively as representative of righteous warfare and human agency, is

---

205. Kierkegaard, *Authority and Revelation*, 117–18.
206. Jehanne; quoted by Toutmouillé, in Pernoud, *Retrial*, 245.
207. Jehanne; in Scott, *Trial*, 151.

necessary so that individual elements of her behavior and circumstances are not misapplied in isolation from other crucial aspects.

From the foregoing examination of Jehanne's life and death, one hundred criteria emerge as essential to or potentially indicative of divine sanction in accordance with her claim. Since it is conceivable that divine call and response might vary, not all criteria are designated as essential, yet it is important that no criterion be overlooked in applying the model. It is expedient to divide the criteria into three categories as follows:

1. Twenty-two criteria (twelve essential and ten non-essential) indicative of divine, prophetic calling.
2. Sixteen criteria (all essential) indicative of divinely sanctioned righteous warfare.
3. Sixty-two criteria (forty-seven essential and fifteen non-essential) indicative of divinely sanctioned human agency.

In the interest of clarity, functionality, and practicality, the criteria are presented in table form as an appendix toward the end of the book. This clear, concise, user-friendly appendix serves as an accessible, simple, portable tool for evaluating claims to divinely sanctioned violence. The shaded enumerations indicate criteria of critical importance designated as essential while unshaded enumerations represent typical, and therefore highly indicative, non-essential criteria. The numbers themselves do not designate priority.

As Jehanne did not teach by doctrine primarily but demonstrated a way, the model distills one hundred significant characteristics of her way which might be considered divinely sanctioned. "[T]he main task of prophetic thinking is to bring the world into divine focus," states Heschel,[208] while Hvidt indicates that the prophet calls people from a wayward path by demonstrating "the right one."[209] The model provides a method for reflecting upon prophetic claims in the context of indicative aspects of Jehanne's prophetic task. It is prescriptive as well as evaluative, meaning that it is instructive both in terms of evaluating claims to divine sanction and in suggesting how one ought to behave in warfare if it is to be considered righteous. It is not essentially a predictive model, which is to say that it does not rely on human predictive capabilities as

---

208. Heschel, *Prophets: Introduction*, 24.
209. Hvidt, *Christian Prophecy*, 161.

does utilitarianism. (The model contains prophetic elements, but these are not grounded in human predictive capabilities, and it demonstrates aspects of proportionality, but this does not constitute the basis for going to war in view of the model.)

It is crucial to emphasize that sporadic satisfaction of criteria is insufficient to render a claim legitimate under the model. Rather, all essential criteria in a given category must be either met, indeterminate, or inapplicable in order for that category to be considered satisfied with respect to a particular claim; moreover, a majority of these must be met rather than indeterminate or inapplicable in order for an evaluation to be considered authoritative. Even though it is not possible in every situation (due to lack of available information) to determine whether or not all essential criteria are met, application of all available information to the model enables one to discern a certain degree of conformity or lack of conformity of a claim to Jehanne's example. Moreover, blatant violation of any essential criterion is sufficient to establish illegitimacy of a claim under the model regardless of limited information. Even if all pertinent facts are known in applying the model, which can be used to assess one's own potential deeds as well as those of others, it is unlikely that conformity to all essential criteria will be established in most cases. Nonetheless, the assessment can assist in evaluating the extent to which a claim appears to be aligned with divine aspirations for the world against the extent to which it does not.[210] The model thus serves to facilitate evaluation of diverse claims within diverse contexts and can assist one in developing an informed response to any claim. If one chooses to support a claim that does not satisfy all essential criteria,[211] then one ought to endeavor to increase the level of overall conformity by striving to conduct oneself in accordance with the prescribed model and by urging other participants to do likewise. In responding supportively to a claim of divine sanction, one should view such a response as a commitment to live in witness to one's faith and all that it entails, in full recognition of one's personal choice and responsibility in the matter. Therefore, in following

---

210. While divine aspirations cannot necessarily be invariably known to humans, apparent divine aspirations can be reasonably extrapolated from the examples of saints and prophetic figures, or allegedly divine figures such as Jesus.

211. This is not a recommendation that one do so, but simply an acknowledgment that one might do so.

another, one ought first to determine whether or not the particular act of following is in accordance with one's own path as faithful witness.

The model does not provide scientific grounds for the evaluation of claims to divine sanction since no definitive proof exists with respect to evaluating such claims; it does, however, offer a comprehensive and reasoned approach to discerning the apparent strength or weakness of a claim. Not sanctioning warfare in any general sense, the model sanctions only that which might be considered divinely sanctioned based on Jehanne's example, thereby serving as a potential guide to righteous behavior in warfare and in general. Since Jehanne's claim was founded upon mystical experience and, given that mysticism constitutes a component of many religious traditions, the model might prove useful not only within Judaic and Christian contexts but within other religious contexts as well. Moreover, it is so comprehensive as to contain minimal potential for abuse. It is likely less susceptible to abuse than just war theory, utilitarianism, or the concept of lesser evil, all of which are commonly employed with little to no acknowledgment of the significant potential for and history of abuse associated with them. It is critical to discern who is calling whom in claims to divinely sanctioned violence. Is God calling a prophet, or is a false prophet invoking the name of God?

4

Applying the Model

And draw us near
and bind us tight,
all your children here
in their rags of light;
in our rags of light,
all dressed to kill;
and end this night,
if it be your will.
—Leonard Cohen, "If it Be Your Will"

Theological exploration of Jehanne's claim to divinely sanctioned violence in previous chapters has yielded a comprehensive model of righteous warfare and human agency against which other such claims might be measured in order to ascertain degree of conformity to her. It has been determined that Jehanne's claim and related behavior place her within the Jewish and Christian prophetic traditions; hence, she can be classified as a practical, prophetic mystic. Indeed, anyone claiming divine sanction of violent activity is presumably either a prophet or a false prophet, and it is the purpose of the model to help distinguish between these. In this chapter, practical application of the model in the form of two case studies demonstrates its proper use and usefulness in assessing the call to violence and in responding to such a call, bearing in mind that inaction is also a response. The criteria stipulated in the model are applied first to the activities of Adolf Hitler and his Nazi regime during

World War II and, secondly, to those of Dietrich Bonhoeffer who conspired to have Hitler assassinated. The first case study evidences voracious, unrestrained violent activity while the second involves reluctant, restrained violent action, both within a shared context and both employing references to divinely inspired motivation. While neither Hitler nor Bonhoeffer claimed clear and direct divine instruction with respect to their activities in question, their invocation of and/or appeal to divinity is readily discernible. Since claims to explicit divine revelation with respect to warfare or other forms of violence are quite rare, it is critical to assess implicit examples such as these in order to ascertain how they operate and their potential effects. Moreover, the cases demonstrate the model's applicability both to state-sanctioned violence and to political violence against a state. Since both cases are historical and ample information exists on which to perform relatively thorough assessments, they are optimally useful in demonstrating how each criterion within the model ought to be applied. The fact that pertinent information has come to light since occurrence of the events offers the opportunity to conduct potentially more accurate assessments than might have been conducted at an earlier stage. Clearly, the more information at one's disposal when performing an evaluation, the more potentially effective the assessment will be. However, this does not mean that only retrospective evaluations can be performed effectively since each case is different and there will always be information available upon which a claim can be assessed. Regarding Hitler, for example, although many details of his case emerged publicly following the war, much of the evidence upon which his case is assessed was available prior to or during the war—most notably his publications, speeches, aggressive military campaigns, and numerous atrocities, which means that a quite thorough and useful analysis could have been performed via the model had it existed at that time. Moreover, it is possible that information available historically might subsequently become lost; hence, in some situations, more information will be available to contemporaries than to posterity. In fact, the model is useful in determining whether or not sufficient information exists to evaluate a claim effectively, identifying gaps in the available information and suggesting areas of inquiry that might be pursued in order to conduct a more complete assessment. If adequate information is not available to conduct a proper assessment, then one might withhold judgment and refrain from acting upon a claimant's agenda, if possible, until sufficient information is obtained to assess a majority of criteria in each category. Nonetheless, even evaluation of minimal information or of a single category can be tentatively useful pending further investigation (provided it is not construed as thorough and definitive) as all assessments are informative. Although minimal information could readily yield a definitive verdict of disqualification, in order for an affirmative verdict to be reached, a great quantity of evidence is required. This constitutes an intrinsic strength of the model.

As with Jehanne, the evaluations of Hitler and Bonhoeffer are based largely on primary source material supplemented with secondary sources. The first case study draws heavily from Hitler's speeches and publications, and also from the testimony of various members of his Nazi regime. The second case study draws heavily from Bonhoeffer's correspondence and other published works (including books, sermons, and lectures), and also from testimonials of those who knew him, as well as from Eberhard Bethge's definitive biography. The criteria are addressed in enumerated form corresponding to the appendix in order to facilitate reference between the appendix and the case studies, and also to enable convenient comparison between the two cases. All bold-typed enumerations represent essential criteria (corresponding to those shaded in the appendix).

Case Study One—Adolf Hitler *et al.*

Can't run no more
with that lawless crowd
while the killers in high places
say their prayers out loud.
But they've summoned up
a thundercloud
They're going to hear from me.
—Leonard Cohen, "Anthem"

"*Gott mit uns*" ("God is with us") reads a belt buckle worn by German soldiers under the bloody dictatorship of Adolf Hitler, while a medallion of the "Holy German Reich" proclaims, "One Reich, One People, One Führer."[1] Hitler was born in Braunau am Inn, Austria in 1889.

---

1. Pia, *Nazi Regalia*, 15, 110. Hitler employed the term "Holy German Reich" as a matter of course.

From youth he deeply desired to become an artist but was rejected by the Vienna Academy's school of painting, an experience which struck him like a thunderbolt (according to his own description), so certain was he of his artistic ability. His interest turned to architecture, but a lack of credentials ruled out this path of study.[2] After spending five years as a laborer in Vienna following the death of his parents, Hitler moved to Germany in 1913, a man in his early twenties. He served as a German soldier throughout World War I and Germany's loss in that war impacted him greatly as he considered it a "degradation of a great people to a second class nation."[3] He eventually joined the National Socialist German Workers' Party (NSDAP or Nazi Party) despite his preference for founding a political party of his own.[4] In 1923, he unsuccessfully attempted to seize state power by means of a putsch and was consequently imprisoned in 1924 but served only eight months of a five-year sentence.[5]

While imprisoned, Hitler composed and dictated most of the first volume of his two-volume work, *Mein Kampf*,[6] expounding his racial theory and political ideology. He sought alignment of the entire German people—as defined by race, not population—under his will and power so that this unified people might conquer other nations out of excessive self-interest:

> [T]ransformation of a general, philosophical, ideal conception of the highest truth into a definitely delimited, tightly organized political community of faith and struggle, unified in spirit and will, is the most significant achievement, since on its happy solution alone the possibility of the victory of an idea depends. From the army of often millions of men, who as individuals more or less clearly and definitely sense these truths, and in part perhaps comprehend them, *one* man must step forward who with apodictic force will form granite principles from the wavering idea-world of the broad masses and take up the struggle for their sole correctness, until from the shifting waves of a free thought-world there will arise a brazen cliff of solid unity in faith and will.[7]

2. Hitler, *Mein Kampf*, 9, 17, 19–20.
3. Hitler; in Halasz, *Hitler*, 8.
4. Hitler, *Mein Kampf*, 220, 224.
5. Romane; in Domarus, *Essential Hitler*, 833–34.
6. Hitler, *Mein Kampf*, vii. Also, Heiden, introduction to *Mein Kampf*, xvii.
7. Hitler, *Mein Kampf*, 381.

Hitler viewed the "Aryan race"[8] (which he identified with German National Socialists) as supreme, as "the founder of all higher humanity," that is, as the creator of "human culture, ... art, science, and technology,"[9] and he sought to promote this "master race"—which he represented as uniquely sacred—at the expense of all others. "Human culture and civilization on this continent are inseparably bound up with the presence of the Aryan. If he dies out or declines, the dark veils of an age without culture will again descend on this globe.... Anyone who dares to lay hands on the highest image of the Lord [i.e., the Aryan] commits sacrilege against the benevolent creator of this miracle and contributes to the expulsion from paradise."[10] Racial purity was the cornerstone of Hitler's ideology. With his characteristically skewed application of theological concepts, he had no qualms about claiming that *"[b]lood sin and desecration of the [Aryan] race are the original sin in this world and the end of a humanity which surrenders to it."* Moreover, in Hitler's ideology the "mightiest counterpart to the Aryan is represented by the Jew."[11] "[I]n his vileness he becomes so gigantic that no one need be surprised if ... the personification of the devil as the symbol of all evil assumes the living shape of the Jew," he asserted.[12] It is difficult, if not impossible, to imagine a harsher anti-Semitism than that to which Hitler gave expression in voice and deed.

In 1925, Hitler reorganized the NSDAP. Gradually gaining prominence, he became Chancellor of Germany in 1933 and also assumed the office of President in 1934, thereby securing autocratic rule. He subsequently launched an aggressive military campaign for the expansion of German territory, initiating World War II. His intentions were to address overpopulation in Germany and to support aspirations for an expanded

---

8. In Hitler's usage, the term "Aryan" indicates one who is "non-Jewish, Polish, or Czech or 'alien,' 'non-Marxian' (i.e., non-social democratic, non-communist, non-trade unionist)." Brady, *German Fascism*, 150. In addition to these disqualifying criteria, Hitler did not generally associate the term "Aryan" with anyone of non-German blood. Heather Pringle explains that the Aryans—conceived of as "a tall, slim, muscular master race with golden hair and cornflower blue eyes"—are actually "a mythical race" with a lengthy history pre-dating Nazi Germany. Pringle, *Master Plan*, 27–28.

9. Hitler, *Mein Kampf*, 290.

10. Ibid., 383.

11. Ibid., 249, 300.

12. Ibid., 324.

German race[13] with a view to exterminating non-Aryans.[14] He was opposed to assimilation of conquered populations based on his theory that interbreeding weakens victors and causes their defeat.[15]

In the interest of accomplishing his agenda, Hitler implemented the "psychological preparation" of the people. "The aim of this leadership is to mould the people in accordance with the political beliefs and principles of National Socialism," he explained, observing that "[i]t is often much more difficult for a nationalist to bring his nation to a sense of reason than to do the contrary." Hence, Hitler injected religious symbolism into much of his public discourse. For example, his proclaimed mission was to guarantee the German people their "daily bread,"[16] to ensure their "resurrection" in the aftermath of World War I, to bring about "salvation of the Reich,"[17] and to prove the "eternal" worth of German culture,[18] thus to accomplish a "miracle."[19] While Hitler feigned to encourage reason among the German populace,[20] his propaganda actually bred unreasoned hatred, indifference, and brutality toward others.

While the foregoing historical sketch is brief, further details of Hitler's life and mission will emerge as the model of righteous warfare and human agency is applied to him and his regime. Let us proceed with application of the first segment of the model pertaining to divine, prophetic calling.

Divine, Prophetic Calling Criteria

1. Receipt of divine revelation (e.g., visions, auditions) calling one to a specified task—*criterion not satisfied*

Hitler's claim to divine sanction was implicit, resting on mere belief and devoid of reference to divine revelation. "I believe that it was . . . God's

---

13. Hitler; in Halasz, *Hitler*, 48.
14. Hitler; in Domarus, *Essential Hitler*, 400–401, 405, 410.
15. Hitler; in Halasz, *Hitler*, 17.
16. Ibid., 16–17, 20–21, 74.
17. Hitler; in Domarus, *Essential Hitler*, 200, 211. Also, Hitler; in Halasz, *Hitler*, 37.
18. Hitler; in Halasz, *Hitler*, 35.
19. Hitler; in Domarus, *Essential Hitler*, 200. Also, Hitler; in Halasz, *Hitler*, 36–37, 73–74.
20. Hitler; in Halasz, *Hitler*, 21.

will that from here [Austria] a boy was to be sent into the Reich, allowed to mature, and elevated to become the nation's Führer," he stated.[21] "Hence today I believe that I am acting in accordance with the will of the Almighty Creator: *by defending myself against the Jew, I am fighting for the work of the Lord.*"[22] "I follow the path assigned to me by Providence with the instinctive sureness of a sleepwalker. ... [T]his has not been the work of man alone."[23] "I have a right to believe that Providence has chosen me to fulfill this task."[24] Hitler had a "right," but no compelling reason, to believe in the divinity of his mission since success alone is not indicative of divine sanction. A right to believe does not constitute the substance of divine calling. In fact, Hitler spoke as one who calls God to a human task rather than one called by God to a divine task. "Where will and faith so fervently join forces, Heaven cannot withhold its approval," he asserted, claiming that "it cannot be that Providence will allow this Volk [the German nation] to perish."[25] Hitler's ideology and theology were thus egocentric and ethnocentric rather than theocentric. National Socialism "places the Volk at the center of its entire way of thinking," he declared. "For it, this Volk is a revelation conditioned by blood, in which it recognizes the God-given building block of human society."[26] But he provided no basis for considering the *Volk* a revelation. "[W]e believe our actions correspond to the will of the Almighty," he stated, while also declaring that "he who personifies Germany's highest peak receives his calling from the German Volk and is obligated to it alone!"[27] Hitler thus responded to a human calling which he construed as being aligned with divine will, relegating God to a back seat.

2. Discernment of spirits (charism)—*indeterminate*

Since Hitler did not operate on a claim of spirit communication (visions, auditions, and the like), this criterion cannot be assessed with respect to him.

21. Hitler; in Domarus, *Essential Hitler*, 22, 162.
22. Hitler, *Mein Kampf*, 65.
23. Hitler; in Domarus, *Essential Hitler*, 22, 153.
24. Ibid., 408.
25. Ibid., 22, 161.
26. Ibid., 150.
27. Ibid., 153, 256.

3. Offers oneself as an instrument of God and willing conduit for divine grace (decision aspect)—*criterion not satisfied*

Hitler declared, "I will bow to one single commandment only, a commandment that has compelled me ever since I was born: Deutschland!"[28] He thereby shunned the Decalogue and any notion of personal divine command. "It is in this [German] Volk that we believe, for this Volk we fight; and ... to this Volk that we are willing ... to commit ourselves body and soul," he emphasized.[29] Hitler did not apparently offer himself as an instrument of God or conduit for grace but painted his will and earthly successes in the colors of religious faith. With respect to his successful war campaigns, he proclaimed, "Providence blessed our work time and time again. The more brave we were, the greater were the blessings accorded us by Providence. And within the last six years, Providence was constantly on our side[;] ... such great works cannot be accomplished without its approval. ... I myself bore profound testimony to the workings of Providence which stands by mankind and assigns it missions to be fulfilled."[30] Hitler regularly declared himself an instrument of God before and for the German people but provided no compelling evidence in support of the claim or any indication that he understood the requirements and implications of divine servantship. Yet he audaciously designated the physical manifestation of his will, embodied in the Third Reich, "the new German kingdom of greatness and power and glory and justice. Amen."[31]

4. Actively engages in divine servantship, operates under willing obedience to divine (vs. human) authority, surrender of personal will to divine will, views oneself as being in an absolute relation to the divine—*criterion not satisfied*

Hitler demonstrated no inclination to surrender his will but frequently invoked God publicly. "May God give us that greatness of spirit which will enable us to formulate our plans in a manner worthy of our national

---

28. Ibid., 157.
29. Ibid., 300.
30. Ibid., 161.
31. Ibid., 146.

greatness," he stated,³² granting no concession to divine plans. "[B]ehind us there stands not merely the *weltanschauung* [worldview] of a movement that is master of Germany but also our will."³³ "Who can deny that the National Socialist Movement has become the omnipotent master over the German Reich?" he asked,³⁴ displacing all notions of divine power. "Trust in a leadership that knows only the thought of winning this battle, that subordinates all other concerns to this, that is suffused with the fanatical will to do everything and to risk everything for success in this battle, . . . [;] at the helm of the Reich there stands a leadership which . . . knows only the one thought: to force victory under any circumstances!"³⁵

Hitler's megalomania is notorious. "Today we have the absolute power to enforce our will everywhere," he declared. "All power lies in the authority of the Reich." As leader of the Reich, Hitler demanded "absolute obedience" to his "absolute authority,"³⁶ but only God has absolute authority in the eyes of the divine servant. "I cannot conceive of any task on this earth more marvelous and glorious than to serve this Volk," Hitler declared,³⁷ suggesting that he could not imagine anything more delightful than serving his own purpose since the *Volk* was subject to his will. "My will . . . is your faith!" he rallied the people, encouraging them to maintain a position of "zealous blind will."³⁸ "More than ever before it is necessary that the entire party stand behind the leadership in blind obedience as one man."³⁹ The only absolute relationship with the divine that was apparently conceivable to Hitler was the notion that his absolute will reflected divine will absolutely, but there is nothing of the mystical sense of an absolute faith-based relationship with God in that, wherein one takes one's instruction from God, not vice versa.

32. Hitler; in Halasz, *Hitler*, 88.
33. Ibid., 81.
34. Hitler; in Domarus, *Essential Hitler*, 308.
35. Ibid., 201–2.
36. Ibid., 254, 316.
37. Ibid., 139.
38. Ibid., 139, 316.
39. Ibid., 380.

5. Submits to divine judgment and lives in constant awareness of this judgment—*criterion satisfied*

With respect to World War I, Hitler wrote, "I had so often sung '*Deutschland über Alles*' [Germany above all] and shouted '*Heil*' at the top of my lungs, that it seemed to me almost a belated act of grace to be allowed to stand as a witness in the divine court of the eternal judge and proclaim the sincerity of this conviction."[40] If Hitler genuinely believed in divine judgment and considered himself subject to it throughout the Second World War, he must have conceived of an extremely lenient and/or violent God or been unperturbed by or oblivious to the possibility of divine condemnation as a result of his blood lust.

---

6. Shares in God's happiness, sadness, concern, sympathy, and aspirations for the world, active concern for humanity—*criterion not satisfied*

Hitler's concern was not for humanity but for his notion of the German *Volk* specifically. Following the invasion of Poland, he had nearly two million Poles slaughtered in order to clear land for German settlement.[41] He maintained that "God continues to bestow His grace only on him who continues to merit it. But whoever speaks and acts in the name of a people, which is a part of God's handiwork, will continue to discharge his mandate only so long as he does not sin against the existence or future of that part of God's creation that has been entrusted to his care."[42] Hitler thereby distinguished between peoples against whom he presumed it acceptable and unacceptable to sin.

---

7. Destabilizing presence in an unjust social system, exhortation to improve condition of humanity, serves the repair of the world and the common good—*criterion not satisfied*

While he was certainly a destabilizing presence, Hitler and his Reich *constituted* an unjust social system. His notion of improvement involved

---

40. Hitler, *Mein Kampf*, 163.
41. Romane, preface to *Essential Hitler*, xvii.
42. Hitler; in Halasz, *Hitler*, 75.

Applying the Model 175

exterminating a large portion of humanity; he did not strive for the common good but for the distinctly German good at the expense of others. "The earth is there for him who takes it. It is a challenge cup that is taken from those peoples who become weak," he asserted. "Strength determines right on this soil."[43] So reads the law of Hitler. The concept of a common good extending beyond the German people (i.e., those who were strong and able) eluded him completely.

Brueggemann explains that social systems organize social power by ordering, defining, valuing, and legitimating life and seeking "to contain and monopolize all social meanings and all social possibilities." The social system "inclines to be effective at delivery of a 'good life' for those who participate in and support the system" and "works well for all those who accept its definitions of reality." It purports to solve all social needs and aspirations to such an extent that the system itself may be "assigned ontological status as the embodiment of" divine intention. Any alternative concept of reality threatens such a system whose "managers" and "benefactors" seek to stabilize it "so that it is not noticed that it is a system, so that it seems it is the only . . . possible, thinkable reality. And if no other social reality is thinkable or possible, then criticism of this one tends to be precluded."[44]

Brueggemann's description reflects the nature of the Third Reich. Hitler repeatedly declared his social system an embodiment of divine intention: "It was not the point of the actions of Providence that have accompanied and blessed our miraculous [National Socialist] path that now . . . the fruits of this struggle should be lost."[45] Moreover, Hitler tolerated no critics of his rule but sought "to install an authority to which each and every man submits in joyful obedience,"[46] thereby displacing individual obedience to conscience or to God directly. On June 30 and July 1, 1934 Hitler ordered numerous executions in an event known as the "Röhm Purge" or "Night of the Long Knives." At least twelve leaders of the SA (Nazi storm troopers) were among the victims who numbered in excess of two hundred.[47] Afterward, Hitler warned, "Every person

43. Hitler; in Domarus, *Essential Hitler*, 192.

44. Brueggemann, "Destabilizing Presence," 222–23. The concept of social system as solution conjures Hitler's "Final Solution to the Jewish question," an extermination program forming part of his unjust social system.

45. Hitler; in Domarus, *Essential Hitler*, 312.

46. Ibid., 258, 261.

47. Domarus, *Essential Hitler*, 72, 258. Also, Romane; in Domarus, *Essential Hitler*,

should know for all time that, if he raises his hand to strike out at the state, certain death will be his lot."[48]

8. Lived witnessing of faith in God—*criterion not satisfied*

Despite his claims to divine assistance, Hitler advocated faith in himself and the *Volk* over faith in God. "German Volk, I have taught you to have faith, now give me your faith!" he demanded. "Our Volk is the only thing on which we can depend. The only thing upon which we can build. Everything we have accomplished to date we owe only to its quality, its capabilities, its loyalty, its decency, its diligence, its sense of order."[49] Hitler's pronouncement of faith in the German people (himself included) omitted any mention of God. "[W]e should once more declare our belief in our nation with all our hearts," he recommended. "We cannot often enough renew our confession of faith that it is our desire to belong to this nation and to serve it."[50] "[T]he Party must have full belief and confidence in itself," he asserted.[51] Moreover, he indicated that "[r]everence for great men [not God?] must be instilled . . . in German youth as a sacred inheritance."[52]

9. Courage (inner strength) in responding to divine directive (accomplishing task)—*indeterminate*

A case can be made that it required courage on Hitler's part to campaign boldly, to rise to power from obscurity, and to lead his country in aggressive war against other nations, but his courage failed when Germany's military defeat became inevitable and he chose to end his life rather than fall to the enemy. The courage that he possessed was not unfailing. Moreover, since Hitler conveyed the impression of following his own

---

258. Hitler acknowledged seventy-seven deaths but the Ministry of Justice placed the figure at 207. Julius Rieger; in Bethge, *Biography*, 373.

48. Hitler; in Domarus, *Essential Hitler*, 258.
49. Ibid., 23, 138.
50. Hitler; in Halasz, *Hitler*, 65.
51. Ibid., 75.
52. Hitler; in Domarus, *Essential Hitler*, 230.

directives, it is difficult to perform a reliable assessment of his courage in response to a divine directive.

10. General attentiveness—*criterion not satisfied*

While Hitler was attentive to many details,[53] leading an unprecedented campaign of mechanized mass murder, he was not generally attentive toward others. Moreover, it was crucial to the accomplishment of his task that his collaborators be grossly inattentive to many blatant facts and critical details. The following comment by a Nazi regarding the crematorium at Auschwitz extermination camp is revealing: "There was a horrible smell," he recalled, "[b]ut you get so used to it that you eat your sandwiches in there too."[54] In fact, Richard Overy indicates that "[n]othing was denied more vehemently in the interrogation rooms at Nuremberg than the persecution of the Jews."[55] In Hitler the Nazis had a model of inattentiveness to factual reality and many of his supporters apparently ignored the fact that he lied habitually. "We ourselves have experienced the dreadfulness of war. None of us wants it," Hitler claimed. "None of us wants foreign property."[56] These were obvious falsehoods in light of the fact that he launched an aggressive military campaign in order to secure foreign lands for Germany. Moreover, Patrick Romane notes that Hitler's "account of the National Socialist Revolution ignored the fact that many people had simply disappeared or somehow ended up dead. Nevertheless, Hitler was clear: the enemies of National Socialism simply faded away—and no one should mention them again!"[57] Hitler's racial ideology is replete with generalizations and assumptions based on extremely scanty or absolutely no factual evidence, betraying a blatant inattentiveness to reality. His claim that the Jewish people sought "the extermination of all European and Aryan peoples"[58] exemplifies this negligence. Clearly, Hitler was selectively attentive, not generally so.

---

53. Albert Speer attests to Hitler's sharp memory for detail. Speer, *Inside the Third Reich*, 231.

54. Eugen Horak, interpreter with the Reich Security head office; in Overy, *Interrogations*, 199.

55. Overy, *Interrogations*, 178.

56. Hitler; in Domarus, *Essential Hitler*, 164.

57. Romane; in Domarus, *Essential Hitler*, 178.

58. Hitler; ibid., 33.

11. Humility—*criterion not satisfied*

Hitler lacked humility, presenting himself as a god figure and presuming to grant Germany "absolution for the sins of the past"—those originating prior to his rule—and to consecrate the flags of the SA and SS (Nazi paramilitary).[59] "May Heaven be our witness: the guilt of our Volk is extinguished, the crimes punished, the disgrace blotted out!" he declared.[60] Hitler presented himself as master of destinies: "The Führer is the Party and the Party is the Führer . . . and as the supreme master of German destinies, it is the mission of the Party to supply the Führer for the Nation and therefore for the Reich."[61] Hitler derived great personal pride from the Party he had fashioned to serve him, calling it "the greatest organization man has ever built!"[62] "Who can take it amiss if all of us who have shared in this work gaze in proud satisfaction on these achievements," he asked.[63] "[W]e are able . . . proudly [to] acknowledge: there is no Volk better on this earth than the German one."[64] In light of Hitler's braggadocio, his occasional claim to absolute humility seems false. "We stand in complete and unconditional humility before the divine laws as revealed to man," he stated. "These laws we respect, and our prayer is one of brave fulfillment of the duties entailed."[65] In reality, Hitler operated from his own dictatorial laws.

12. Production of good fruit—*criterion not satisfied*

Charles W. Syndor, Jr. speaks in the opinion of many when he writes of Hitler that "[n]o other figure in modern history had such a profound, and profoundly malevolent, influence upon humankind, or came nearly as close to achieving the destruction of civilization as he did,"[66] while Romane maintains that Hitler instigated "more deaths than any other

---

59. Domarus, *Essential Hitler*, 146–47.
60. Hitler; in Domarus, *Essential Hitler*, 147.
61. Hitler; in Halasz, *Hitler*, 76–77.
62. Hitler; in Domarus, *Essential Hitler*, 184.
63. Hitler; in Halasz, *Hitler*, 36.
64. Hitler; in Domarus, *Essential Hitler*, 199.
65. Ibid., 160.
66. Syndor, foreword to *Essential Hitler*, v.

person in history." His was "a campaign of destruction."[67] Baum describes the *Shoah* as "state-administered destruction of politically designated surplus populations, . . . mass murder . . . accomplished as work."[68]

13. Initial hesitation, reluctance, resistance, fear, doubt—criterion not satisfied

Hitler did not hesitate to publish his shocking racial ideology and agenda in *Mein Kampf* for the world to read. He expressed no doubt about the correctness of his views or his objectives but propagated them unhesitatingly and rigidly. Consider the following passages from his work:

> With satanic joy in his face, the black-haired Jewish youth lurks in wait for the unsuspecting girl whom he defiles with his blood, thus stealing her from her people. . . . It was and it is Jews who bring the Negroes into the Rhineland, always with the same secret thought and clear aim of ruining the hated white race by the necessarily resulting bastardization, throwing it down from its cultural and political height, and himself rising to be its master.[69]

> *What we must fight for is to safeguard the existence and reproduction of our race and our people, the sustenance of our children and the purity of our blood, the freedom and independence of the fatherland, so that our people may mature for the fulfillment of the mission allotted it by the creator of the universe.*
>
> Every thought and every idea, every doctrine and all knowledge, must serve this purpose. And everything must be examined from this point of view and used or rejected according to its utility.[70]

Hitler did not doubt the validity of his convictions, method, or purpose (i.e., his "mission") and did not hesitate to act on them. Nor did fear apparently restrain him from embarking on his agenda. He eventually feared that someone would usurp his power,[71] but anyone suspected of it was dealt with harshly.

---

67. Romane, preface to *Essential Hitler*, xiv–xv.
68. Baum, "Holocaust," 58.
69. Hitler, *Mein Kampf*, 325.
70. Ibid., 214–15.
71. Domarus, *Essential Hitler*, 273.

14. Apparent absurdity requiring faith in God—*criterion not satisfied*

In Jehanne's example, faith is required by one called to a divine mission in order that he or she might believe in the feasibility of the absurd and seemingly impossible task to which he or she is called, whereas Hitler's proclaimed mission did not appear absurd to him but completely reasonable and feasible. In fact, he believed that his Reich would endure for a millennium. "There will not be another revolution in Germany for the next thousand years!" he proclaimed.[72] Moreover, Hitler dismissed that which he perceived as absurd. "You cannot expect or demand of one that he abide by principles that seem absurd," he stated.[73]

The absurdity in Hitler's aggressive campaign of destruction consisted in his assumption that the world would comply with his objectives or simply be defeated. The degree of compliance and complicity with which his objectives were met within Germany was also absurd—tragic, but absurd. Nonetheless, the absurdity to which this criterion points is apparent absurdity of the task apprehended by the individual called to fulfill it, not utter absurdity of the task to which the individual called is oblivious or absurdity of the response of others to the task.

15. Prior lack of inclination, skill, or capacity to behave in required manner—*criterion not satisfied*

Robert Gellately maintains that, throughout Hitler's early years, he displayed "little or no indication of the fanatical nationalist, rabid anti-Semite, and heartless warmonger he was to become." Gellately holds that no conclusive evidence of Hitler's anti-Semitism existed prior to 1919 but that it developed as a result of the First World War.[74] Lack of indication, however, does not necessarily entail lack of inclination and there are indications that racial intolerance and aggression emerged much earlier. Hitler's self-description indicates that, as a boy, he was inclined to certain behaviors for which he would become notorious as dictatorial leader of Germany. For example, he claimed that his "oratorical tal-

---

72. Hitler; in Domaras, *Essential Hitler*, 308.
73. Ibid., 181.
74. Gellately, *Lenin, Stalin, and Hitler*, 81–82.

ent was being developed in the form of more or less violent arguments with ... schoolmates. I had become a little ringleader," he boasted. He described himself as a "pugnacious," "persistent," "recalcitrant" boy, as "anything but 'good' in the usual sense of the word," and as refusing to be swayed from his own will. "Neither persuasion nor 'serious' arguments made any impression on my resistance," he noted.[75] Decades later, one of his military generals stated, "If you talked for two hours [to Hitler] and you thought that finally you had convinced him of something, he began where you had started just as if you had never said a word."[76] Hitler also relayed how, as a child, he became enamored with war after discovering books and periodicals on the subject in his father's library; it became his favorite reading material. "It was not long before the great heroic struggle had become my greatest inner experience," he wrote. "From then on, I became more and more enthusiastic about everything that was in any way connected with war."[77]

It was during his secondary school years that Hitler identified as a "fanatical 'German Nationalist'" and began engaging in pro-German activities, becoming a "revolutionary" according to his own assessment.[78] During this period he perceived "the poison of foreign nations" that "gnawed at the body of ... German nationality,"[79] this being an obvious indication of early racial intolerance and xenophobia on Hitler's part. During his time in Vienna (1908–13) he developed a disdain for "Marxism and Jewry."[80]

In terms of skill, Konrad Heiden indicates that, when he wrote *Mein Kampf* (in the 1920s), Hitler "lacked the experience, the responsibilities, [and] the knowledge" that he would later acquire as Führer.[81] But it would be remiss to overlook the fact that, during his five years in Vienna, Hitler spent most of his free time educating himself through extensive reading.[82] After moving to Munich and joining the NSDAP,

75. Hitler, *Mein Kampf*, 6, 8.
76. Ewald von Kleist, general field marshal of the German army; in Goldensohn, *Nuremberg*, 347.
77. Hitler, *Mein Kampf*, 6.
78. Ibid., 10, 12–13, 15.
79. Ibid., 15.
80. Ibid., 21.
81. Heiden, introduction to *Mein Kampf*, xix–xx.
82. Hitler, *Mein Kampf*, 22, 35, 37.

his involvement with the Party undoubtedly allowed him to acquire political experience and to develop political skills gradually prior to attaining a position of power within the German government, so he was not entirely unprepared.

16. Feelings of inadequacy—*indeterminate*

Desiring to engage in political leadership and contemplating whether or not to join the National Socialist German Workers' Party, Hitler expressed concern over the possibility of being viewed by others as inadequate for the task. He was "poor and without means," unknown in the realm of national politics, and relatively uneducated. How would the formally educated world "confront" him?[83] Whether or not Hitler regarded himself as inadequate is uncertain, but it seems likely given his "two days of agonized pondering and reflection" on the matter.[84] Had he felt completely confident in his ability to prove his potential detractors wrong, the decision presumably would not have presented such difficulty. At any rate, if he did experience feelings of inadequacy, they were apparently short-lived. In fact, Albert Speer indicates that Hitler demonstrated a "growing belief in his superhuman abilities."[85]

17. Feelings of unworthiness to carry out the mission, accompanied by assurance of divine assistance and creating a dependency on God—*indeterminate*

Hitler did not normally express feelings of unworthiness before God but felt assured of "the blessing of Providence" provided that he fought his battle relentlessly and courageously.[86] While he sometimes claimed dependency on God in political achievements, Hitler provided no compelling evidence of divine assistance, merely citing the attainment of his goals as indicative of divine support. Without the "blessings" of "Providence," he reasoned, he "would never have been able to set out on the path leading . . . across so many hurdles and through so many attacks

---

83. Ibid., 222–24.
84. Ibid., 224.
85. Speer, *Inside the Third Reich*, 243.
86. Hitler; in Speer, *Inside the Third Reich*, 555, n. 13.

to the takeover of power and, finally, to this struggle ... crowned by victories ... but ... also ... weighed down by many worries which would have broken many weaker characters."[87] That which seemed advantageous to Hitler he generally credited to Providence while attributing his troubles to "the devil."[88] Jehanne, however, attributed to divine will even events which seemed disadvantageous to her, such as her capture and failed escape attempts, drawing on divine support in times of trial. Whatever Hitler's notion of divine assistance, it did not apparently correspond to feelings of unworthiness, nor did his claim to dependency seem tied to such feelings, but we cannot be certain.

18. Severe disruption to, or break from, previous lifestyle— *criterion satisfied*

Hitler's rise to autocratic power, surrounded by millions of supporters, constituted a drastic change in lifestyle as he was relatively unknown previously. "I was a lonely and unknown man," he recalled.[89] He became the center of attention, securing a place in world history, and also rose from meager financial means to considerable wealth.

19. Personal risk, encounters hostility and/or persecution as a result of prophetic ministry—*criterion satisfied*

Anyone who engages in controversial politics publicly places him- or herself at risk of hostility and persecution, and Hitler was no exception as several attempts were made on his life. Hitler attempted to minimize risk to himself, employing brutality against those who opposed him or were suspected of it. In July, 1944 he had "thousands of Germans who were under suspicion" hanged in relation to a failed assassination attempt against him.[90] Utilizing the event to his advantage, Hitler declared his survival a "miraculous rescue" indicative of "the warning finger of God" directed at others.[91]

   87. Hitler; in Domarus, *Essential Hitler*, 408–9.
   88. Hitler; in Speer, *Inside the Third Reich*, 555, n. 13.
   89. Hitler; in Domarus, *Essential Hitler*, 407.
   90. Domarus, *Essential Hitler*, 129.
   91. Hitler; in Domarus, *Essential Hitler*, 129.

20. Experiences intense solitude, stands as the particular against the status quo—*criterion not satisfied*

Hitler transformed the status quo in accordance with his will, employing psychological conditioning to influence the masses. He gained millions of supporters in this way. "The [National Socialist] Movement will continue to present its ideas to the people over and over again until they are under our spell," he resolved.[92] As leader of the Reich, Hitler always had committed supporters who stood by him "in devoted faithfulness" and loyalty.[93] He did not stand alone, not even in death as he and his bride, Eva Braun, committed suicide together.

21. Ability to prophesy (charism)—*criterion not satisfied*

Addressing domestic opponents prior to his rise to power, Hitler stated, "I have been a prophet so often in my lifetime, and you have not believed but instead ridiculed and mocked me. Once again, I will be a prophet."[94] "And I desire to be nothing other than what I have been in the past: the warner of my Volk, the instructor of my Volk, the Führer of my Volk!"[95] Hitler cast himself as a prophetic figure, frequently attempting to prophesy but failing miserably as his predictions were generally inaccurate, such as in the case of his annual New Year's forecasts.[96] Moreover, he declared, "I predicted . . . —and I am careful to refrain from rash prophecies—that . . . the result of this war will be the annihilation of the Jewish race."[97] Thankfully, he was wrong despite his considerable strides in that direction. Hitler also predicted failure of the allied landings in northern France in 1944,[98] but this was a blatant miscalculation. Hitler's prophecies typically failed, and one might conclude that they were not divinely inspired but mere declarations of his will stated as inevitable fact—a mark of the false prophet.

92. Ibid., 145.
93. Ibid., 409.
94. Ibid., 134. See also 399.
95. Ibid., 157.
96. Domarus, *Essential Hitler*, 32, 48, 61, 119, 122, 317.
97. Hitler; in Domarus, *Essential Hitler*, 33. See also 319, 399.
98. Domarus, *Essential Hitler*, 129.

22. Ability to perform miracles (charism)—*criterion not satisfied*

There is nothing apparently miraculous about Hitler's achievements—shocking, but not miraculous. No laws of nature were suspended in the accomplishment of his goals. Hitler's ability to influence the masses of German people—his techniques being largely ineffective in moving the international community[99]—was primarily a result of carefully calculated, rehearsed, and perfected processes of manipulation. He utilized all means conceivable to him of manipulating an audience. For example, he considered the location and "temperature of the venue" of his speeches, preferring to speak later in the day when people's "mental resistance had waned" and they were less likely to be alert and independently critical.[100] "The outstanding oratorical art of a commanding Messianic figure will more easily succeed in winning over for a new cause people whose powers of resistance have already been weakened in the most natural way, than those who are still in full possession of their spiritual and mental resilience," he advised.[101] It was artifice, not miracle, that served Hitler in this regard. Nevertheless, he deemed it miraculous that many convened to support him.[102]

Summary Assessment—Divine, Prophetic Calling

Of the twenty-two criteria indicative of divine, prophetic calling, Hitler satisfies three (one essential and two non-essential), he fails to satisfy fifteen (nine essential and six non-essential), and four are indeterminate (two essential and two non-essential). Of the twelve essential criteria, only one is met. Of the ten non-essential criteria, two are met. On this assessment, Hitler's case cannot be viewed as representative of divine, prophetic calling in accordance with the model. Let us continue in order to determine how he fares in the other two categories.

---

99. Halasz, introduction to *Hitler*, 2.
100. Ibid. Also, Domarus, *Essential Hitler*, 56.
101. Hitler; in Domarus, *Essential Hitler*, 56.
102. Hitler; in Domarus, *Essential Hitler*, 151.

Divinely Sanctioned Righteous Warfare Criteria

1. Appeal to most sovereign authority (divinity)—*criterion satisfied*

Hitler considered himself sovereign over the German people but invoked God in support of his agenda. "All power and authority in the state is now in the hands of this organization [i.e., the National Socialist Party]," he declared. "Millions of people voluntarily subjected themselves to it, and millions of others were brought into line."[103] "God formed this Volk, and it has become what it should according to God's will, and according to our will, it shall remain, nevermore to fade! . . . Work such as ours that has received the blessings of the Omnipotent can never again be undone by mere mortals," he claimed.[104]

Hitler's public prayers were often petitionary, of the wish fulfillment variety, and he viewed fulfillment of his wishes as answered prayers. "It is our unshakable will to restore . . . inner unity of the nation. . . . For fifteen years this goal has been all at once our wish, our prayer, and our idea, and today we can say that our prayer has been answered, our wish fulfilled. . . . Today those around us are talking about terror in Germany, about violence. That is neither terror nor violence; it is destiny."[105] Such "prayer," however, does not seek direction from the divine but lays one's personal agenda on God. Hitler appealed to his desires which he attempted to qualify through invocation of divine authority.

---

2. Defensive, not offensive—*criterion not satisfied*

Hitler declared, "I have never waited for others to begin the offensive; I myself initiate the attack."[106] He falsely claimed to fight a defensive, spiritual war: "Jews, Freemasons, and their allies, the ideological opponents of National Socialism, are the authors of the war presently directed against the Reich," he declared. "The systematic spiritual struggle against these powers is a necessary war mission."[107] Moreover, Hitler believed

---

103. Ibid., 176.
104. Ibid., 22, 152.
105. Ibid., 164.
106. Ibid., 303.
107. Ibid., 402.

that all people of German blood belonged within German borders and that, should Germany be too small to accommodate this, then it would be her "moral right to acquire foreign soil" in order to mitigate the "distress" of the German people.[108]

3. Not pre-emptive—*criterion not satisfied*

Prior to attacking Russia, Hitler stated, "If the United States and Russia enter the war, [it will create] a very great burden for our military. So any possibility of such a threat must be precluded."[109] Even in situations dominated by other motives for aggression, Hitler claimed pre-emption as justification. Regarding forthcoming invasions of Luxembourg, Belgium, and Holland in order "to gain as large an area as possible" to serve "as a base for conducting a promising air and sea war against England," he maintained that "[t]he cover explanation ... must be that they are merely precautionary measures in view of the threatening concentration of French and English forces on the French-Luxembourg and French-Belgian borders."[110] Hitler frequently characterized his aggressive actions as pre-emptive.

4. Last resort, entreats the enemy to leave or desist peacefully, issues ultimatum. Not killing for its own sake (i.e., killing as an end in itself)—*criterion not satisfied*

Hitler did not operate on the principle of last resort. Aggression and violence were the primary methods by which he pursued his goals. "You either stick a fellow into a concentration camp or you kill him," he advised. "These days, the latter is more important for the sake of deterrence. If you want to set an example, you must also hit all fellow travelers!"[111] Hitler advocated killing as a first resort, not the last. He offered no ultimatum or opportunity for the alleged enemy to withdraw peacefully, and it was a punishable offense to safeguard Jewish people or help them escape Germany and the Nazi death camps. However, Hitler

108. Hitler, *Mein Kampf*, 3.
109. Hitler; in Domarus, *Essential Hitler*, 747.
110. Ibid., 724–25.
111. Ibid., 284.

did not normally employ killing for its own sake but as a means to an end, on the basis of some motivation such as deterrence, vengeance, the desire to eradicate populations in order to acquire living space and to ensure blood purity of the German race, or to eliminate opposition to his power. He often proceeded from fear, hatred, or a combination of the two. "Hitler was always afraid: his fears revolved around his obsession that a vast secret conspiracy of all Jews was in control of most governments," Romane explains.[112] Whereas the two components of this criterion are expected normally to support each other, the fact that Hitler refrained from killing for its own sake did not ensure that he killed only as a last resort, which is the main thrust of the criterion.

5. Aims to establish just peace—*criterion not satisfied*

"If we have said it once, we have said it a hundred times: we want peace with the rest of the world."[113] Despite his words, Hitler proved a tremendous threat to world peace and was, in fact, a warmonger. "The programmatic principles of my party are its doctrine on the racial problem and its fight against pacifism and internationalism," he asserted.[114] The only kind of "peace" that Hitler aspired to was unjust peace—peace established and enforced on his iniquitous, dictatorial terms—which is no peace at all. He considered it a "fact . . . that ultimate justice resides in power,"[115] that might is right.

6. Proportionate cause—*criterion not satisfied*

Baum points to the "utterly unprecedented disproportionality between the evil committed and the motivation leading to it" that characterized the actions of Adolf Eichmann, who organized the transportation of millions of Jewish people to concentration and extermination camps, and others of the Hitler regime.[116] Josef Goebbels, Hitler's propaganda minister, described the situation from a Nazi perspective:

112. Romane, in Domarus, *Essential Hitler*, 372.
113. Hitler; in Domarus, *Essential Hitler*, 164.
114. Hitler; quoted by Heiden, introduction to *Mein Kampf*, xx.
115. Hitler; in Domarus, *Essential Hitler*, 314.
116. Baum, "Holocaust," 55.

Jews are now being deported to the east. . . . Here will be used a fairly barbarous method that one can't come close to describing; not much will remain of the Jews themselves. On the whole, it can be determined that sixty percent of them will have to be liquidated, only forty percent being usable for the purposes of labor. The former district leader of Vienna, who is in charge of the action, is showing a good deal of circumspection in following a method that does not attract a lot of attention. Justice is being meted out to the Jews; although it is barbarous, they fully deserve it. . . . If we did not defend ourselves against the Jews, they would destroy us.[117]

Hitler bred the evil of genocide on the basis of mere suspicion that the Jewish population was internationally organized politically, was determined to destroy Germany (and the world), and was capable of doing so.[118]

---

7. Does not operate from vengeance or hatred—*criterion not satisfied*

Hitler hated many people, including Communists, Jews, Gypsies, Poles, Serbs, Russians, and the French,[119] and aimed to eliminate them. He also operated from vengeance, having people who opposed him murdered. "[W]e want to . . . ensure that those who attempt to injure the German Volk receive their due," he explained.[120] When the Reichstag (German legislative building) was burned, Hitler vowed "to avenge this crime as quickly as possible by having the [allegedly] guilty arsonist and his accomplices publicly executed!"[121] "In the future," he asserted, "high treason and betrayal of the Volk will be ruthlessly eradicated."[122] Moreover, in planning his offensive against England, Hitler stated, "I reserve for myself the decision on terror attacks as a means of reprisal."[123]

---

117. Goebbels; in Domarus, *Essential Hitler*, 403–4.
118. Hitler referred to "the Jewish-international enemy of the world" bent on destroying Europe and exterminating its nations. Hitler; ibid., 425.
119. Romane, preface to *Essential Hitler*, xv.
120. Hitler; in Domarus, *Essential Hitler*, 222.
121. Ibid., 226.
122. Ibid., 231.
123. Ibid., 744.

8. Does not seek to acquire new territory but might protect or recover rightful lands—*criterion not satisfied*

A main goal of Hitler's military campaign was "to gain space for the German Volk in the East."[124]

9. Does not seek domination of others (oppression)—*criterion not satisfied*

Hitler implemented laws that not only violated the German constitution but effectively eliminated parliament as well,[125] which contradicted his pledge to "rule strictly in compliance with the constitution" and to "amend it in a strictly constitutional manner!"[126] Hitler's oppressive tactics extended beyond German borders as he aspired to establish Nazi Germany as "lord of the earth."[127] The statement represents his aspirations for a National Socialist state of which he was then aspirant leader and "lord."

10. Does not engage in holy war—*criterion not satisfied*

Hitler despised and imprisoned Jehovah's Witnesses, stipulating that only a signed renunciation of their faith could secure their release. Of approximately ten thousand who were imprisoned, 25 to 50 percent died.[128] Such activity constitutes an act of holy war. One might suppose that Hitler also waged holy war against the Jewish people if it were not for the fact that he did not regard them as a religious group but as a race. "[T]heir whole existence is based on one single great lie, to wit, that they are a religious community while actually they are a race. . . . The Jew

---

124. Ibid., 812.
125. Domarus, *Essential Hitler*, 265–66, 292.
126. Hitler; in Domarus, *Essential Hitler*, 301.
127. Hitler, *Mein Kampf*, 688.
128. Romane, preface to *Essential Hitler*, xvii. Rudolf Höss (Hoess), commandant of Auschwitz concentration camp, testified to the internment of Jehovah's Witnesses there. Höss; in Goldensohn, *Nuremberg*, 313.

has always been a people with definite racial characteristics and never a religion," he maintained.[129]

11. Formal declaration of intent to engage in war, warning— *criterion not satisfied*

Hitler frequently attacked countries without first declaring war or issuing any warning, such as in the invasions of Denmark, Norway, Belgium, the Netherlands, and Luxembourg.[130] In fact, Hitler issued only one "formal declaration of war," that against the United States of America.[131]

12. Employs minimal appropriate force (proportionality), minimal bloodshed, forbids unnecessary evil or excessive force— *criterion not satisfied*

Hitler vowed that his regime would "break terror with ten-times-greater terror" and would "exterminate traitors no matter who they might be."[132] He perpetrated unrestrained violence, promising to "employ every means" in support of his cause.[133] "In questions of foreign policy," he declared, "I shall never admit that I am tied by anything."[134] Max Domarus notes that Hitler's "campaign aiming at ... eradication of the Polish intelligentsia, ... the Polish Catholic clergy, and ... the Polish Jews ... surpassed anything the world had previously seen. ... It was on Hitler's orders that his cohorts in the SS indulged in an unprecedented murder spree among a small people left virtually defenseless" under German occupation.[135] As Heiden points out, all paths leading from Hitler led to bloodshed. It required minimal or no provocation for Hitler to employ maximum, murderous force with alarming "light-heartedness."[136] As

---

129. Hitler, *Mein Kampf*, 232, 306.
130. Domarus, *Essential Hitler*, 106–7.
131. Ibid., 118.
132. Hitler; in Domarus, *Essential Hitler*, 409.
133. Hitler; in Halasz, *Hitler*, 12.
134. Hitler; quoted by Heiden, introduction to *Mein Kampf*, xx.
135. Domarus, *Essential Hitler*, 278–79.
136. Heiden, introduction to *Mein Kampf*, xx.

Wilhelm Frick, Hitler's minister of the interior, put it, Hitler "recognized no limits."[137]

13. Does not target noncombatants—*criterion not satisfied*

Hitler had millions of noncombatants (men, women, and children) systematically murdered, including approximately six million Jews, two million Poles, up to half a million Gypsies, up to a quarter of a million people whom he categorized as genetically inferior, and thousands of others.[138]

14. Does not employ torture—*criterion not satisfied*

The Nazis conducted infamous medical experiments and unnecessary operations on thousands of prisoners without anesthetic, inflicting unnecessary, inhumane suffering. These included "freezing experiments" which utilized prisoners in the testing of potential hypothermia treatments, "bone-grafting experiments," subjection to "mustard gas in order to test possible antidotes," and so on ad nauseam.[139]

15. Does not inflict suffering for its own sake—*criterion not satisfied*

One might argue that, since the immense suffering caused by the implementation of Hitler's agenda was largely a by-product of the killings ordered by him which were apparently conducted for reasons other than killing for its own sake, then the resultant suffering was not inflicted for its own sake but for the same reasons that the killings were conducted. However, the absolute cruelty with which so much of the killing was carried out suggests otherwise. If one wanted to murder people as a means to some practical (albeit reproachable) end, one could do so without first

---

137. Frick; in Goldensohn, *Nuremberg*, 44.
138. Romane, preface to *Essential Hitler*, xvi–xvii.
139. United States Holocaust Memorial Museum, "Nazi Medical Experiments." For details concerning the experiments and unnecessary operations performed on prisoners, see affidavit of Franz Blaha, Dachau concentration camp doctor; in Overy, *Interrogations*, 374–81. Various conspirators against Hitler were tortured in Nazi prisons. Bethge, *Biography*, 900, 907.

humiliating and taunting them or inflicting additional physical suffering as the Nazis frequently did. Take, for example, this (shocking) testimony:

> I was once present in Vienna when they were loading up people for one of those mass evacuations. Hundreds were crammed into the waggons, which normally took a couple of cows. And they were thoroughly beaten up as well. I went up to a young SS man and asked if the beating up was really necessary. He laughed and said they were only scum anyway. . . . What was the purpose of that beating up? I have nothing against the gas chamber. A time can come when it is useful for the race to eliminate certain elements. Extermination is one thing, but there is no need to torture your victims beforehand.[140]

16. Forbids looting—*criterion not satisfied*

Hitler exploited populations and territories that he conquered, forcing people to perform labor for a pittance in Germany or their own conquered lands.[141] The Nazis confiscated and placed in galleries hundreds of paintings from primarily Jewish owners.[142] Jewish capital was also confiscated by the Nazis in Denmark.[143] Moreover, concentration and extermination camp prisoners were often stripped of personal belongings. Once killed, even their gold teeth were extracted. Oswald Pohl, who was in charge of the SS economic and administrative main office, testified that such articles as rings, watches, money, and gold bars were confiscated and deposited in the Reichsbank.[144]

---

140. Horak; in Overy, *Interrogations*, 198–99.
141. Martin Bormann, Hitler's Chief of Staff; in Domarus, *Essential Hitler*, 364–65.
142. Speer, *Inside the Third Reich*, 178.
143. Goldensohn, *Nuremberg*, 379.
144. Pohl; in Goldensohn, *Nuremberg*, 401. Gold eyeglass frames were also seized. Goldensohn, *Nuremberg*, 90–91. In the hurried preparations for their wedding, the gold bands that Hitler and Braun were to exchange "were found in a small locked treasury belonging to the SS. They had probably been torn off the fingers of dead Jews in one of the concentration camps," Robert Payne surmises. Payne, *Life and Death of Hitler*, 552.

Summary Assessment—Divinely Sanctioned Righteous Warfare

Of the sixteen criteria—all essential—indicative of divinely sanctioned righteous warfare, Hitler satisfies only one, consisting in his appeal to divine authority. He fails to satisfy fifteen. He cannot be construed as having engaged in divinely sanctioned righteous warfare on the basis of this model. One category remains on which to assess Hitler's claim. Let us proceed in that direction.

Divinely Sanctioned Human Agency Criteria

1. Undifferentiated compassion, mercy, forgiveness—*criterion not satisfied*

Speer describes Hitler as possessing a "general contempt for all persons."[145] Hitler demonstrated extreme lack of compassion toward others and vowed to declare "merciless war" on perceived enemies,[146] most notably Communists and Jews,[147] insisting that the German state be "merciless against all adversaries, against all religious fragmentation, [and] against all fragmentation into parties."[148] "Those who base their politics on subversive activities shall be mercilessly exterminated," he warned.[149] Forgiveness seemed foreign to Hitler.

---

2. Honors the sanctity of life—*criterion not satisfied*

Hitler described "the Jew" as "only and always a *parasite* in the body of other peoples."[150] Such dehumanization fails to respect the sanctity of human life, as does any policy of extermination. "When I ... look at

---

145. Speer, *Inside the Third Reich*, 94.
146. Hitler; in Domarus, *Essential Hitler*, 212.
147. Domarus notes that, for Hitler, "[i]f it was not the Jews, then it was the Communists who were the source of all evil." Domarus, *Essential Hitler*, 218. In fact, Hitler sometimes conflated them, declaring, "[W]e know what the Jewish Bolshevist menace is, as it threatens the world to-day [sic]." Hitler; in Halasz, *Hitler*, 92.
148. Hitler; in Domarus, *Essential Hitler*, 314.
149. Ibid., 165.
150. Hitler, *Mein Kampf*, 304.

the intellectual classes we have—unfortunately, I suppose, they are necessary; otherwise one could one day, I don't know, exterminate them," Hitler reflected.[151] His opinion concerning people for whom he had no use was that they ought to be exterminated. "[A] human life was not worth much in his eyes," Hermann Goering recalls.[152]

3. Respects the dignity of the person—*criterion not satisfied*

According to Hitler, "[a]ll who are not of good race in this world are chaff."[153] "When we read of the concentration camps, the gulags, the police states, and the death squads, we see forces which attack the very nature of human dignity and truth," notes Cunningham.[154] A former prisoner of the Nazis, Simon Wiesenthal, reports that "every day there were deaths in the camp; Jews were strung up, trampled underfoot, bitten by trained dogs, whipped and humiliated in every conceivable manner. Many who could bear it no longer voluntarily put an end to their lives."[155]

4. Fully-engaged conscience—*criterion not satisfied*

Hitler asserted that, "[o]nly when an epoch ceases to be haunted by the shadow of its own consciousness of guilt will it achieve the inner calm and outward strength brutally and ruthlessly to prune off the wild shoots and tear out the weeds [read 'non-Aryans']."[156] Engaged conscience played no role in Hitler's ideology; rather, he represented conscience as something that could be determined by the will of another person, implicitly denying that conscience impresses itself upon individuals directly. "The Party represents the political conscience and the political will," and the people must be brought into line with these, he asserted.[157] Hitler promoted the notion of collective conscience with considerable

---

151. Hitler; in Domarus, *Essential Hitler*, 18.
152. Goering, president of the Reichstag; in Goldensohn, *Nuremberg*, 112.
153. Hitler, *Mein Kampf*, 296.
154. Cunningham, *Catholic Heritage*, 25.
155. Wiesenthal, *Sunflower*, 11.
156. Hitler, *Mein Kampf*, 30.
157. Hitler; in Halasz, *Hitler*, 74.

effect; Eichmann confirms that "the most potent factor in the soothing of his... conscience was the simple fact that he could see no one... who actually was against the Final Solution."[158]

---

5. Operates from a driving force of love—*criterion not satisfied*

Syndor notes that "[h]atred was the emotion most natural to Hitler, the staple of his character. His capacity for hatred was unlimited and was never satiated."[159] Hitler actively and intentionally bred hatred; it was the driving force from which he operated. "Anti-Semitism will be fed in every prisoner-of-war camp, in every family," he insisted.[160] "*Social activity must never and on no account be directed toward philanthropic flim-flam.*"[161]

---

6. Genuine distress concerning all bloodshed, not desensitized to violence or suffering—*criterion not satisfied*

"I do not want to be misunderstood," Hitler asserted. "[I]f the course of this [National Socialist] revolution was bloodless [which it was not[162]], it was not because we were not men enough to stand the sight of blood. For four years, I was a soldier in the bloodiest war of all time. I never once lost my nerve throughout, no matter what the situation or what I was confronted with."[163] Hitler "pronounced death sentences with the greatest calm and without a trace of sentiment."[164] Given the millions who were tormented and whose blood was needlessly shed at his command, it is evident that Hitler consorted comfortably with murder.

---

158. Arendt, *Eichmann*, 116.
159. Syndor, foreword to *Essential Hitler*, vii.
160. Hitler; in Domarus, *Essential Hitler*, 401.
161. Hitler, *Mein Kampf*, 29–30.
162. Romane, in Domarus, *Essential Hitler*, 178.
163. Hitler; in Domarus, *Essential Hitler*, 178.
164. Hjalmar Schacht, president of the Reichsbank; in Overy, *Interrogations*, 213.

7. Sense of duty to God, God served first in all things—*indeterminate*

In strengthening the German army, Hitler purported to operate from a sense of responsibility to God and his own conscience, citing the army as a symbol of "honor" and its restoration as a providential event.[165] Hitler viewed himself as "the most independent man, beholden to no one, subordinate to no one, owing thanks to no one, answerable to" his "conscience alone." But he also stated, "There is but one commander of this conscience of mine—namely, the nation—the German nation and the pick of it that is united in the Movement, in the National-Socialist Party. In everything that I do this is the only commander [not God] to which I feel myself responsible." He also maintained that "the only duty" citizens "owe is to the nation."[166] It is unclear whether Hitler believed he acted from a sense of duty to God or whether this was a piece of propaganda.

8. Love of God, piety—*indeterminate*

"I may be no pious churchgoer," Hitler declared, "but deep within me I am nevertheless a devout man."[167] Hitler did not demonstrate exceptional piety but occasionally participated in religious practices. Romane suggests that he "willingly appeared to be religious at times but ... saw organized religion as a threat to his power."[168] To assert that Hitler did not love God or was not devoted to God would be to impose a particular concept of God on the interpretation; it is possible that he loved and was devoted to God as he defined God and as he claimed to, even if his notion of God does not conform to any commonly accepted notion of God. Domarus holds that Hitler "actually believed in a god, but it was not the same God who has been worshipped by the peoples of this planet for millennia as the preserver and protector of all life: it was even less the God whose highest commandment requires one to love one's neighbour."[169]

165. Hitler; in Halasz, *Hitler*, 14–15.
166. Ibid., 58–59.
167. Hitler; in Speer, *Inside the Third Reich*, 555, n. 13.
168. Romane, in Domarus, *Essential Hitler*, 426.
169. Domarus, *Essential Hitler*, 21.

9. Fear of God—*criterion not satisfied*

Since Hitler presumed his will to be one with divine will and his deeds to be backed by divine approval, there is no compelling reason to suppose that he feared God. He did not demonstrate any such fear. When his war failed to progress as planned, Hitler assumed that "he who fights valiantly obeying the laws which a god has established and who never capitulates but instead gathers his forces time after time and always pushes forward—such a man will not be abandoned by the Lawgiver. Rather, he will ultimately receive the blessing of Providence."[170]

10. Permits nothing to come between self and God, accepts no human deterrent—*criterion satisfied*

This is true if Hitler genuinely believed the goals of National Socialism under his dictatorship to be divinely inspired and ordained, as he claimed. He willingly accepted no human deterrent from his declared mission but vowed "to employ all means—down to the last—" in his struggle to establish a thriving German *Volk*.[171]

11. Mystical relationship transcends institutionalization or religious formulas, mystical defiance—*criterion not satisfied*

Hitler rejected mysticism. "[W]e have no desire of instilling in the Volk a mysticism that transcends the purpose and goals of our teachings," he declared. National Socialism "does not advocate mystic cults" but concerns itself with "considerations of an exclusively racial nature." Hitler stressed that his Party would "not tolerate subversion by occult mystics in search of an afterlife." Such individuals, he asserted, represent something that has "nothing to do with" National Socialism. Mysticism, he maintained, produces "mysterious dark forces" that violate "the will of man" while National Socialism represented "a cool and highly-reasoned approach to reality based upon the greatest of scientific knowledge and its spiritual expression."[172]

---

170. Hitler; in Speer, *Inside the Third Reich*, 555, n. 13.
171. Hitler; in Domarus, *Essential Hitler*, 746.
172. Ibid., 158–59.

Nonetheless, Nazi leaders Alfred Rosenberg and Heinrich Himmler advocated an allegedly mystical ideology,[173] employing the term "mystical" loosely. Soelle writes that "[t]he Nazis ... seized upon many traditions of German mysticism ... [and] had their own revelations and sacred writings, rituals and consecrated places; they had the cults of blood and soil, fire and wind, martyrs, gurus, and the *Führer*."[174] Heschel notes, however, that "the prophet speaks with derision of those who combine ritual with iniquity,"[175] and Soelle recognizes "Nazi-mysticism" as "false mysticism."[176] Nevertheless, I would caution against the term "Nazi-mysticism" and propose "Nazi pseudo-mysticism" instead, lest the boundaries become blurred. At any rate, Hitler defied Himmler's "mystical" notions: "What nonsense!" he insisted. "Here we have at last reached an age that has left all mysticism behind it, and now he wants to start that all over again. We might just as well have stayed with the church. At least it had tradition. To think that I may some day be turned into an SS saint! Can you imagine it? I would turn over in my grave."[177] He likewise denounced Rosenberg's attempts at a mystical interpretation of National Socialism and German history.[178] "God have mercy on him who attempts to subvert our Movement and our state by insisting upon convoluted orders or introducing vague mystical elements to them,"[179] the Führer warned his stray sheep.

12. Conviction, determination, persistence, endurance, uncompromised, singular commitment to declared mission— *criterion not satisfied*

Hitler demonstrated these qualities except with respect to his suicide. "My will is tough, unrestrained, and unshakable," he declared.[180] He asserted that the "future of a movement is conditioned by the fanaticism, ... the intolerance, with which its adherents uphold it as the sole cor-

---

173. Domarus, *Essential Hitler*, 158.
174. Soelle, *Silent Cry*, 53.
175. From Heschel's commentary on Amos. Heschel, *Prophets: Introduction*, 31.
176. Soelle, *Silent Cry*, 53.
177. Hitler; in Speer, *Inside the Third Reich*, 94.
178. Speer, *Inside the Third Reich*, 95–96.
179. Hitler; in Domarus, *Essential Hitler*, 160.
180. Ibid., 303.

rect movement, and push it past other formations of a similar sort."[181] "[T]he Party must have full belief and confidence in itself and must not allow itself to be deflected from its line of action by any criticism or doubts as to the correctness of the undertaking on which it is engaged."[182] "Persevere and above all be persistent,"[183] he advised. Although Hitler did not persevere in the end but took his own life, he held firm until the last minute, when "enemy shells literally exploded on the doorstep of the Reich Chancellery" building that housed his bunker.[184] Nevertheless, he bailed out in that most critical of moments wherein one is pushed either to stand firm as witness to one's faith or bear testimony to a lie.

13. Does not engage in or encourage suicide, does not seek suffering or martyrdom—*criterion not satisfied*

On April 30, 1945, when defeat was inevitable, Hitler committed suicide in his Berlin bunker. It was not a rash decision; he had stated as early as 1932, "If the party ever falls apart, I will take a gun and end it all in a minute."[185] Furthermore, Hitler provided poison to his secretaries in order that they might also commit suicide.[186]

14. Reluctantly accepts suffering or martyrdom if necessary to mystical witnessing—*criterion not satisfied*

According to his own testament, Hitler killed himself "in order to escape the disgrace of a deposition or surrender,"[187] and also because he feared more serious repercussions should he fall into enemy hands. "The consequences would be unimaginable," he remarked to his pilot, Hans Baur, "if they [the Russians] captured me alive."[188] Hitler thereby failed to demonstrate mystical witnessing.

181. Hitler, *Mein Kampf*, 349–50.
182. Hitler; in Halasz, *Hitler*, 75.
183. Hitler; in Domarus, *Essential Hitler*, 204.
184. Domarus, *Essential Hitler*, 131.
185. Hitler; in Domarus, *Essential Hitler*, 66.
186. Domarus, *Essential Hitler*, 811.
187. Hitler, Personal Testament, April 29, 1945; in Domarus, *Essential Hitler*, 809.
188. Hitler, one day prior to his suicide; quoted by Hans Baur, in Payne, *Life and Death of Hitler*, 564.

15. Steadfast faith in God and divine revelation—*criterion not satisfied*

Hitler declared belief in God—a god fashioned after his own ideals; he was not unlike many in this regard. However, it is not apparent that his faith was steadfast, and he did not actually claim receipt of divine revelation. When Hitler committed suicide, he thought it possible that the war and the National Socialist state might persist; he appointed a successor and named an entire cabinet to carry out the work of the Reich following his death.[189] If he believed it his divine mission to lead the German nation, it seems that he abandoned this mission prematurely when the situation failed to develop as planned. Hitler asked and ordered his appointed successors not to commit suicide with him, but to hold firm and continue the struggle in his stead.[190] There is no indication of steadfast faith in such behavior. Moreover, both his final Political Testament and his final Personal Testament, signed only hours before his premeditated suicide and comprising several pages, are devoid of any reference to God. Apparently, God had no significance to Hitler in death; at least he gave no public testimony to his alleged faith during his final hours. He did not bear witness to God in death.

16. Apprehension of the intrinsically evil nature of human violence and war, does not attempt to qualify evil—*criterion not satisfied*

Hitler apparently failed to apprehend the intrinsically evil nature of human violence and war, given that he unreservedly authored so much of both unnecessarily. In fact, Nazism associated killing with honor rather than evil. This is apparent in the "Blood and Honour" inscription on the knife carried by members of the Hitler Youth (National Socialist youth movement), and an SS service dagger bore the inscription, "My honour is my pledge."[191] "[T]he gilt... Cross of Honour of the German Mother" was instituted by the Nazi regime recognizing "the outstanding achievement of a mother who had borne eight or more children to serve the

---

189. Hitler's final Political Testament; in Domarus, *Essential Hitler*, 806–8.
190. Ibid., 806–7.
191. Pia, *Nazi Regalia*, 17, 20.

Nazi state." Six or seven children fetched a silver cross while bronze was awarded for four or five offspring.[192] Honor was thus associated with the provision of able-bodied people to carry out Hitler's agenda of aggressive war and mass murder. Such "honor" was not only considered laudable but was sanctified by Hitler who stated, "The national honour, the honour of our army and the ideal of freedom must . . . become sacred to the German people!"[193] Since he failed to recognize evil, it would be pointless to discuss qualification of evil in relation to Hitler who did not draw such fine ethical distinctions.

17. Recognition of personal defilement sustained through the use of violence—*criterion not satisfied*

Hitler did not display hesitation or regret, nor did he attribute guilt or defilement to himself, with respect to the violence that he orchestrated. In his final Political Testament, he blamed the Jewish people for the war and the resultant destruction and suffering,[194] neglecting to mention that he had an estimated six million of them, all civilians, slaughtered throughout the course of the war. "It is untrue that I or any other person in Germany wanted war in the year 1939," he claimed. "It was desired and instigated exclusively by those international statesmen who are either of Jewish origin or work for Jewish interests."[195]

18. Deep sensitivity to evil vs. indifference—*criterion not satisfied*

Hitlerism produced a tremendous degree of indifference to evil, particularly in Nazi Germany. Hitler's "deadly cocktail of uncritical prejudice, moral abdication and reflexive violence produced a casual indifference to suffering and an easy familiarity with the pervasive morbidity of the [concentration and extermination] camps," notes Overy.[196] A mem-

---

192. Wykes, "Symbols of Tyranny," 5–6.
193. Hitler; in Halasz, *Hitler*, 12.
194. Hitler; in Domarus, *Essential Hitler*, 804–5.
195. Ibid., 804.
196. Overy, *Interrogations*, 198.

ber of Hitler's propaganda team, Hans Fritzsche, admitted as much. "Unfortunately," he stated, "too many of us were indifferent."[197]

19. Impatient with injustice, prone to righteous anger—*criterion not satisfied*

Hitler engaged in tremendous injustices and was prone to self-righteous anger, but not apparently to truly righteous anger. His fits of rage toward anyone who defied him were notorious, although they were sometimes reportedly staged.[198]

20. Righteous character (not self-righteous), ethical code of conduct (e.g., chivalry), moral discernment, holds self and others to high ethical standard of behavior—*criterion not satisfied*

In contemplating future leadership of the German *Volk*, Hitler denounced morality. "As a social phenomenon this new selection of leadership has to be divorced from the numerous prejudices that I can only term phony and profoundly nonsensical social morals," he declared. "[T]he Reich government intends to undertake a thorough moral purging of German society," he advised,[199] rejecting "the loathsome humanitarian morality."[200] "There can be no talk of humanitarianism regarding the Jews," he asserted. "Jewry must be thrown to the ground."[201] Hitler's might is right stance advocated that "visible success is ultimately decisive for the correctness of a principle," and he boasted that the German state observed "no . . . social morals."[202]

---

197. Hans Fritzsche, propaganda official; in Goldensohn, *Nuremberg*, 67.
198. Speer, *Inside the Third Reich*, 97–98.
199. Hitler; in Domarus, *Essential Hitler*, 181, 229.
200. Hitler, *Mein Kampf*, 42.
201. Hitler; quoted by Goebbels, in Domarus, *Essential Hitler*, 413.
202. Hitler; in Domarus, *Essential Hitler*, 137, 182. Hitler likewise declared that there "is no attitude that does not have its ultimate justification in the resulting advantages for the community." Ibid., 181.

21. Teaches by example over doctrine—*criterion not satisfied*

Hitler declared it the mission of the National Socialist Party "to construct and consolidate its own internal organization and make it an impregnable and enduring shrine of National-Socialist doctrine" and "to educate the entire nation along the lines of that doctrine."[203] He thrust his doctrine upon the nation and demanded conformity; doctrine was paramount to his impact on others and his success. Since his example corresponded to his doctrine, one could assert that Hitler taught by example as well as doctrine, but doctrine provided context and gave meaning and power to his example without which the latter would likely have been impotent. Indoctrination convinced many of the legitimacy of Hitler's cause and proved effective in gaining their cooperation. Rudolf Höss, commandant of Auschwitz extermination camp, approved of the events that transpired there on the belief that "if the Jews were not exterminated at that time, then the German people would be exterminated for all time by the Jews," echoing Hitler's main thesis.[204] Goebbels cited the same as justification for persecution of the Jewish people.[205] Hence, it is reasonable to conclude that the power of Hitler's teaching was rooted in doctrine.

22. Service-oriented, work ethic, disinclination toward idleness or sloth—*criterion satisfied*

Hitler was committed to work and service and created a state in which all were expected to work toward the concrete manifestation of his ideals, and he also worked tirelessly in that direction. "In this state, everyone is called upon to fight and work in some way or another," he advised. "The earth is not there for cowardly peoples, not for weak ones, not for lazy ones. The earth is there for him who takes it and who industriously labors upon it and thereby fashions his life." At the end of his life, Hitler wrote, "In these three decades, all my thoughts, actions, and life have been guided by my love for and loyalty to the Volk. . . . I have used up

---

203. Hitler; in Halasz, *Hitler*, 76.
204. Höss; in Goldensohn, *Nuremberg*, 296.
205. See criterion 6, Divinely Sanctioned Righteous Warfare category.

my time, my working power, and my health in these three decades."[206] Goering testified to the deterioration of Hitler's health, indicating that his "nerves were kaput. His left hand trembled and he was physically rocked."[207]

23. Seeks to empower the disenfranchised, partisan with the wrongly oppressed—*criterion not satisfied*

Hitler's philosophy was unequivocal and simple: "He who cannot assert himself does not deserve to live."[208] He was an oppressor and despiser of many and moved to have disadvantaged peoples such as "the chronically ill, the lame, [and] the deformed," eliminated.[209] He considered them a "heavy burden" and believed that they threatened the German *Volk* with "gradual disintegration." If anyone should "fail" or "become weak" in the "struggle for survival," he maintained, "Providence will not rush to his aid. Instead, it will sentence him to death. And rightly so. Other men will come. The space will not remain empty. . . . And life continues . . . without consideration for the weakling."[210] On the occupation of Poland, Hitler "underlined that there must be but one master for the Poles, and this is the German. . . . Never must we elevate them to greater heights." Under Hitler's order, all "Polish 'masters'" were to "be killed."[211]

24. Honors personal responsibility in maintenance of social justice—*criterion not satisfied*

Hitler violated social justice on many counts. "There is a divine will, and all we are is [*sic*] its instruments," he asserted,[212] implicitly denying human freedom of action and personal responsibility. Group membership often permits and encourages—sometimes commands—one to refrain from thinking independently and taking responsibility for one's actions,

206. Hitler; in Domarus, *Essential Hitler*, 170, 195, 804.
207. Goering; in Goldensohn, *Nuremberg*, 112.
208. Hitler; in Domarus, *Essential Hitler*, 195.
209. Romane, preface to *Essential Hitler*, xv.
210. Hitler; in Domarus, *Essential Hitler*, 195–96, 257.
211. Bormann; ibid., 363–64.
212. Hitler; ibid., 162.

and many of Hitler's accomplices operated in such fashion. For example, Eichmann stated that the fact that so many others supported the "Final Solution" created a "Pontius Pilate feeling" that freed him from any sense of guilt.[213] Kren notes that the *Shoah* would have been impossible without people willing to abdicate ethical discernment to those in authority.[214] It was Hitler's claim to absolute authority which demanded submission from others that allowed gross irresponsibility and large-scale social injustice to occur under his rule.

25. Protects, defends others at potential cost to self—*criterion not satisfied*

Hitler claimed to act in defense of the German people,[215] but he did not protect or defend millions who were his intentional, innocent victims, including Germans not considered of Aryan stock and those who opposed him, whether or not they fit the "Aryan" bill. His alleged goal was to safeguard the Aryan race,[216] but such a race as Hitler conceived it did not exist.[217] Moreover, by inciting aggressive war, Hitler subjected millions of German soldiers to death, and his war brought air raids upon German cities causing considerable civilian deaths while he withdrew to his bunker.

26. Direct participation in mission in a position of vulnerability—*criterion not satisfied*

Hitler amassed power and governed through delegation (although, as he became increasingly obsessed with his work and power, he delegated less administratively).[218] He did not engage directly in combat[219] or extermi-

---

213. Eichmann; in Arendt, *Eichmann*, 114.
214. Kren, "Holocaust," 255.
215. His declared purpose was "equality of rights" for Germany. Hitler; in Halasz, *Hitler*, 13.
216. "This fight will not end with the planned annihilation of the Aryan but with the extermination of the Jew in Europe." Hitler; in Domarus, *Essential Hitler*, 410.
217. Pringle, *Master Plan*, 27–28.
218. Speer, *Inside the Third Reich*, 294.
219. We are speaking of WWII, not WWI.

nation. Apart from occasional visits to the front, Hitler issued orders from a relatively safe distance to be carried out in the camps and on the battlefields,[220] despite the fact that he declared himself invincible. "I ... have the conviction and the certain feeling that nothing can happen to me, for I know that Providence has chosen me to fulfill my task," he stated.[221] Nonetheless, Hitler had the added security of a bunker. Moreover, from mid-March until mid-July of 1944, while the war that he initiated raged throughout Europe, Hitler vacationed in the Alps.[222]

27. Refuses to love evil, actively opposes evil—*criterion not satisfied*

Hitler is frequently characterized as "evil incarnate" or "the personification of evil," and there is hardly a case to be made that he in any way opposed it; he labeled his victims evil, but unjustifiably. Hitler orchestrated and commanded some of the most horrific, calculated, pervasive, and extensive evil known—he not only embodied evil but enthusiastically bred it and created conditions in which it thrived. He was obsessed with it and possessed by it, yet he did not apparently recognize it. Hitler projected his own evil onto others in a tremendous act of scapegoating. In discussing the *Shoah* with Goebbels, he stated, "One should not get sentimental here. The Jews deserve the catastrophe that they are experiencing today. With the annihilation of our enemies, they will experience their own annihilation. We must speed up this process with cold brutality. With this, we render mankind an invaluable service, since it has suffered under and has been tortured by Jewry for millennia."[223] He displayed no remorse over his actions but only pride. Perhaps in externalizing his evil, Hitler subconsciously believed he could control it.

---

220. Speer and General Schmundt, Hitler's armed forces adjutant, proposed "bringing young frontline officers to Hitler, in order to introduce a little of the mood of the outside world into the stale, hermetic atmosphere of the headquarters." Speer, *Inside the Third Reich*, 295.

221. Hitler; in Domarus, *Essential Hitler*, 303.

222. Domarus, *Essential Hitler*, 128–29. Speer indicates that, even when Hitler took vacations, he relocated his headquarters to the holiday location and remained fully involved in his work. Speer, *Inside the Third Reich*, 294. It is difficult to ascertain whose perspective is more accurate, that of Domarus who disapproved of Hitler, or that of Speer who was devoted to Hitler. That Hitler took a "working vacation" seems plausible.

223. Hitler; in Domarus, *Essential Hitler*, 401.

28. Prefers peace to war and non-violence to violence—*criterion not satisfied*

Hitler's claims to embrace peace cannot be believed given his extensive warmongering activities. "Our love of peace is perhaps greater than that of other nations. . . . No one of us has the intention of threatening anybody," he declared.[224] "The nation is united in a yearning for peace and determined to defend German liberty. We want nothing but to coexist with other peoples in mutual respect. We do not wish to threaten the peace of any people."[225] Contrary to his words, however, Hitler demonstrated a strong propensity for and commitment to war and violence.

29. Does not glorify violence or war—*criterion not satisfied*

Hitler regarded his soldier's uniform as "the holiest and dearest."[226] He was not averse to violence or war, nor did he hesitate to glorify them:

> Our soldiers have emerged victorious from this greatest battle of all time. In a few weeks, we have taken over 1.2 million enemies as prisoners of war. Holland and Belgium have capitulated. The British Expeditionary Force has been largely destroyed, the remainder either taken prisoner or driven from the continent. Three French armies no longer exist. The danger of enemy penetration into the Ruhr territory has been eliminated for good. German Volk! Your soldiers have fought bloodily for this most glorious deed in history. . . .[227]

Hitler reveled in the destruction of war and encouraged others to aspire to military glory.[228]

30. Concern for spiritual welfare of self and others, apprehends spiritual implications—*criterion not satisfied*

Hitler advised the German Churches, "[L]et one thing be quite clear: the churches may determine the fate of the German being in the next world,

---

224. Hitler; in Halasz, *Hitler*, 13.
225. Hitler; in Domarus, *Essential Hitler*, 135.
226. Ibid., 618.
227. Ibid., 737–38.
228. Hitler; in Domarus, *Essential Hitler*, 206.

but in this world the German nation, by way of its leaders, is determining the fate of the German being." He insisted on this "clear and clear-cut division,"[229] apparently conceiving of no consequential relationship between earthly life and any possible afterlife. In other words, Hitler demonstrated no awareness of, or concern for, spiritual consequences deriving from earthly deeds. "The religions and the churches will maintain their freedom," he asserted. "But we are in charge of politics."[230]

31. Benevolence, kindness; does not engage in cruelty—*criterion not satisfied*

Hitler engaged in enormous cruelties, demonstrating extreme deficiencies in kindness and benevolence. Suffice it to note that approximately twenty thousand mentally and physically challenged children were starved to death by the Nazis under his rule.[231]

32. Generosity, charity—*criterion not satisfied*

Hitler was not of evidently charitable disposition and "was progressively self-centered as time went on."[232] He displayed an insatiable lust for blood and power and considered it justifiable to rob other countries and peoples of everything—their land, their dignity, their very existence—in order to benefit the German nation and feed his drives. Anticipating victory in Russia, Hitler remarked, "We'll be getting our granite and marble from there, in any quantities we want."[233]

33. Rejects personal glorification and idolization—*criterion not satisfied*

Hitler glorified himself and sought glorification from others. "I fought as a decent German soldier," he declared. "Then ... I went on my way through Germany and won this dearest land of all for myself, finding

---

229. Ibid., 315.
230. Ibid., 430.
231. Yahil, *Holocaust*, 309.
232. Erhard Milch, general field marshal and armaments chief of the German air force; in Goldensohn, *Nuremberg*, 364.
233. Hitler; in Speer, *Inside the Third Reich*, 180.

hundreds of thousands and millions who believed in me because I ... believed un [sic] them. At a time when all began to have doubts of Germany ..., I was proud to be a German, I clung fast to this people, I fought and struggled for it, and won its confidence.... [M]y name will remain as that of one of the greatest sons of this country.... I now proclaim for this land [Austria] its new mission."[234] Hitler presented himself as godlike in assigning a mission to others. He also declared his "ambition to establish a memorial" to himself,[235] confirming his desire for preservation and idolization in history. "We ... have been chosen by fate to make history in the loftiest sense of the word. What millions of people are deprived of has been given to us by Providence. Even most distant posterity will be reminded of us by our work.... One day, a page in world history will be devoted to us, the men from the National Socialist Party and the German army.... One day we will stand ... immortalized in the pantheon of history...."[236] The word "pantheon" suggests divine qualities.

34. Is not motivated by self-fulfillment or material gain—criterion not satisfied

Hitler strove single-mindedly and relentlessly toward the acquisition of power and fulfillment of his will. "I thought originally when Hitler came to power that he was thoughtful about the people's welfare," stated an air force chief. "But soon it became obvious that Hitler cared about nothing except more and more personal victories."[237] The situation was similar with Eichmann who, according to Arendt, "had no motives at all" for participating in mass murder, apart from "an extraordinary diligence in looking out for his personal advancement."[238]

Hitler became wealthy through his racial ideology and position as Führer, deriving income from sales of *Mein Kampf*[239] and from schemes

---

234. Hitler; in Halasz, *Hitler*, 26–27. Hitler declared it Austria's mission to become part of Germany. Ibid., 27.
235. Hitler; in Domarus, *Essential Hitler*, 28.
236. Ibid., 310–11.
237. Milch; in Goldensohn, *Nuremberg*, 362.
238. Arendt, *Eichmann*, 287.
239. Heiden, introduction to *Mein Kampf*, xix.

such as claiming royalties for reproduction of his image on postage stamps.[240]

35. Refuses to benefit from anything unjustly acquired—*criterion not satisfied*

Hitler's war campaign consisted in a program of expansion of German territory and exploitation of peoples in the form of slave labor and of other foreign resources. "Dunkirk has fallen!" he exclaimed. Forty thousand "Frenchmen and Englishmen have been taken prisoner. . . . Immeasurable amounts of material have been taken."[241] "In order to establish the conditions necessary for the final conquest of England, I intend to continue the air and naval war against the English homeland more intensively than heretofore," he announced. It was also Hitler's intention to invade Russia for the purpose of acquiring land "by the German sword" for the German nation.[242] "Once Russia is defeated, . . . [t]he master of Europe and the Balkans will . . . be Germany," he maintained.[243]

36. Clarity of purpose—*criterion satisfied*

Hitler demonstrated clarity of purpose, first delineating his intentions in *Mein Kampf* and then carrying them out unwaveringly to his utmost ability. His goals were clear and rigid. Domarus notes that, by age thirty, Hitler "had a clear picture of his foreign policy plans and refused to the end to relinquish or revise these aims."[244] "[W]e National Socialists must keep an unshakable hold on our political aims, namely of securing the land and soil rightfully belonging to the German Volk on this earth," Hitler advised.[245]

---

240. Speer, *Inside the Third Reich*, 87.
241. Hitler; in Domarus, *Essential Hitler*, 738.
242. Ibid., 44, 743.
243. Hitler; quoted by Franz Halder, Colonel General, in Domarus, *Essential Hitler*, 742.
244. Domarus, *Essential Hitler*, 41.
245. Hitler; in Domarus, *Essential Hitler*, 41.

37. Sincerity, authenticity—*criterion not satisfied*

Hitler orchestrated and rehearsed the delivery of his speeches in order to convey a specific impression to his audience, taking pains even to alter his accent depending on which German audience he was addressing.[246] Syndor indicates that "[h]e wrote all his own speeches, the important orations requiring days of elaborate preparation. He developed and rehearsed exaggerated but powerfully effective techniques that included operatic gestures, alternating cadences of speech, levels of voice, sarcasm and irony, and the uncanny timing that charged his performances with electrifying tones of menace, fury, and hatred."[247] Hitler did not, therefore, present himself naturally and authentically publicly; rather, the public forum was his theatre and Hitler the star actor.

Hitler was frequently hypocritical, misrepresenting himself and National Socialist aims publicly. "Germany wants nothing for herself which she is not prepared to give to others," he claimed. "Germany desires nothing except an equal right to live and equal freedom."[248] Yet his drive for ultimate superiority of the German Aryan nation over all others was necessarily exclusive; his goal was superiority rather than equality. Furthermore, Hitler denounced the employment of religion for political purposes but created a state-ruled German Christian Reich Church. German Christians attempted "a synthesis between Nazism and Christianity, identifying religious aims with national aims."[249] The German Christian Church permitted Aryan membership exclusively and operated under a national Reich Bishop approved by Hitler; the position of Reich Bishop was an allegedly spiritual authoritarian office.[250] This Church promoted Hitler's racist ideology under the guise of religion, proclaiming a "godless fellow-countryman . . . nearer to" it "than one of another race, even if he sings the same hymn or prays the same prayer."[251] Hitler expected the Reich Church to replace the existing

---

246. Domarus, *Essential Hitler*, 54–55, 57.
247. Syndor, foreword to *Essential Hitler*, vii.
248. Hitler; in Halasz, *Hitler*, 12.
249. Busch, *Karl Barth*, 224.
250. Barth, *Theological Existence*, 30–35, 48–49.
251. Joachim Hossenfelder, German Christian leader; quoted by Franz Hildebrandt, in Bonhoeffer, *No Rusty Swords*, 205–6.

Protestant Church;[252] his practice thus contradicted his assertion that "[w]orst of all ... is the devastation wrought by the misuse of religious conviction for political ends. In truth, we cannot sharply enough attack those wretched crooks who would like to make religion an implement to perform political ... services for them. ... For a single political swindle ... they are willing to sell the heart of a whole religion. ..."[253]

38. Integrity—*criterion not satisfied*

Hitler lacked integrity. "May no man doubt my determination to put my plans once conceived into action no matter how," he announced,[254] believing that his ends justified any means. He was not averse to breaking his word. "We National Socialists ... have no desire for our Army to be used to force on other nations something that they have no wish for," he declared prior to launching aggressive war on numerous countries.[255] Hitler also violated signed agreements, such as his non-aggression treaty with the USSR, and his regime contravened international law[256] as evidenced by the International Military Tribunal at Nuremberg.

39. Treats God as a Subject, not an object to be bent to one's will—*criterion not satisfied*

Hitler spoke frequently on God's behalf, apparently from his own convictions rather than from any claim to divine revelation or the tenets of any religious tradition. He stated, "I believe in God, and I am convinced that He will not desert 67 million Germans who have worked so hard to regain their rightful position in the world."[257] He unhesitatingly declared racial interbreeding a "sin against the will of the eternal creator" and the "original sin of racial poisoning,"[258] distorting the traditional doctrine of original sin. The state must "begin by raising marriage from the level of

252. Hitler; in Domarus, *Essential Hitler*, 430.
253. Hitler, *Mein Kampf*, 268.
254. Hitler; in Domarus, *Essential Hitler*, 50.
255. Hitler; in Halasz, *Hitler*, 16.
256. Domarus, *Essential Hitler*, 191–92.
257. Hitler; in Domarus, *Essential Hitler*, 21.
258. Hitler, *Mein Kampf*, 286, 405.

a continuous defilement of the [Aryan] race," he asserted, "and give it the consecration of an institution which is called upon to produce images of the Lord [the pure Aryan] and not monstrosities halfway between man and ape."[259] The would-be artist thus fashioned an Aryan image of the divine which he sought to impress upon the world and impose upon God.

40. Does not define or claim elaborate understanding of God, accepts divine mystery—*criterion not satisfied*

Hitler did not appear to approach God in an inquiring manner, seeking to ascertain the divine position on a given matter, but expressed his convictions concerning God with little to no reservation. Hitler's god seemed quite predictable. "If we adhere to this path, decent, industrious, and honest, if we do our duty so bravely and loyally, it is my belief that the Lord will help us again and again in the future," he asserted. "He does not abandon decent people for any length of time! While He may sometimes put them to the test or send them trials, in the long run He will always allow His sun to shine upon them and ultimately give them His blessing."[260] "[T]he fruits of human labor are . . . transitory if they are not blessed by the Almighty," Hitler stated, assuring the people that no earthly enemy could deprive them of their God-given success. Concerning his intention to secure foreign lands for the German people, Hitler declared, "[T]his action is the only one which, before God and our German posterity, would allow an investment of blood to appear justified."[261] He deemed the concept of basic equality among human beings "a sin against the will of the Eternal Creator."[262] Hitler spoke assuredly about the divine nature, divine motives, and divine judgment but did not speak of or apparently apprehend divine mystery.

259. Ibid., 402.
260. Hitler; in Domarus, *Essential Hitler*, 155.
261. Ibid., 41, 152.
262. Hitler, *Mein Kampf*, 430.

41. Does not hold God responsible for human evil—*criterion not satisfied*

Hitler proclaimed his evil desires to be the will of God but did not apparently view them as evil. That which he represented as evil he deemed offensive to God, such as racial interbreeding or breeding between healthy and unhealthy individuals,[263] but we cannot take Hitler's perception of evil as the ground for our assessment. While he did not attribute to God that which he regarded as evil, Hitler did attribute to God that which he did not consider evil but which constitutes evil according to commonly accepted definitions of the word—that is, his own deeds.

42. Does not claim divine sanction with respect to all of one's actions but only those founded on divine revelation—*criterion not satisfied*

Hitler demonstrated the converse of this criterion, indiscriminately claiming divine sanction of his activities and agenda while not claiming receipt of divine revelation specifically.

43. Exercises personal responsibility and accountability before God and others—*criterion not satisfied*

Hitler *declared* himself "responsible to God and . . . [his] own conscience"[264] but frequently failed to *exercise* responsibility and accountability for his deeds. For example, he denied responsibility for the events of November 9 and 10, 1938 (known as *Kristallnacht*) when the Nazis wreaked destruction on Jewish property throughout Germany, arrested thirty thousand Jewish citizens, and killed at least ninety-one. Hitler blamed his storm troopers (SA) and the general public for the affair,[265] contrary to his (later) assertion that "[i]t is one of the most uplifting tasks of leader-

---

263. Ibid., 402–3.
264. Hitler; in Halasz, *Hitler*, 14.
265. Domarus, *Essential Hitler*, 279, 394–95. Gellately, *Lenin, Stalin, and Hitler*, 326, 635, n. 44.

ship to allow one's followers to mark only the victory, and to take upon oneself the entire responsibility at critical moments."[266]

Hitler did not generally condone individuality, individual responsibility, or individual conscience but urged the German people to submission. "[M]ay you one and all forget what life has made out of you as individuals, may you remember that . . . you are members of the one nation, and that you are so not by human will but by God's will."[267] "It is of no importance whether the individual among us lives—what must live is our Volk!"[268] Pleased with his success in swaying millions to this point of view, Hitler observed, "[W]e have convinced this nation that it can only exist as a nation and not as a collection of individuals,"[269] as a machine, in other words, not as a group of free-thinking, responsible people. The "unity of a nation's spirit and will are worth far more than the freedom of the spirit and will of an individual," he maintained.[270] Hitler sought to establish Germany as a nation under a single authority and will to which all were expected to submit. All were "to move as one man" when ordered to do so.[271] It is not surprising that Speer, Hitler's Minister of Armaments and War Production, was the only senior officer of the Reich at Nuremberg to accept responsibility for his deeds. Nonetheless, Linda Hogan notes that, while acknowledging his personal responsibility, Speer attempted "to deceive himself and others about the extent and nature of his involvement" in the *Shoah*.[272] The commandant of Treblinka extermination camp, Franz Stangl, declared his conscience clear, noting that he had never hurt anyone himself.[273] Höss estimated that two and a half million Jewish people were executed at Auschwitz, yet when asked if he ever protested, he indicated that he had to accept the order given him. "Don't you have a mind or opinion of your own?" asked the interrogator. "Yes," replied Höss, "but when Himmler told us something, it was so correct and so natural we just blindly obeyed it."[274]

266. Hitler; in Domarus, *Essential Hitler*, 205.
267. Hitler; in Halasz, *Hitler*, 66.
268. Hitler; in Domarus, *Essential Hitler*, 202.
269. Hitler; in Halasz, *Hitler*, 39.
270. Ibid., 62.
271. Ibid., 39.
272. Hogan, *Confronting the Truth*, 158–59.
273. Kren, "Holocaust," 248.
274. Höss; in Goldensohn, *Nuremberg*, 296. The interrogator was the author, psychiatrist, Leon Goldensohn.

Hitler's will was thus served by the Nazi machine which completely disregarded individual responsibility and moral accountability.

44. Accepts unknown consequences, uncertainty—*criterion not satisfied*

Whether or not he harbored doubts, Hitler frequently claimed certainty with respect to outcomes. "I do not doubt for a second," he stated, "that we will secure our vital rights outside the country in exactly the same way as we were able to lead it onwards within."[275] Jehanne claimed certainty with respect to the outcome of particular events based on her apprehension of divine revelation, but she accepted imminent capture without foreknowledge of the consequences, and this is the type of acceptance that is relevant in evaluating claims to divine sanction; that is, acceptance of unknown personal consequences—of an undisclosed cost to self. Hitler did not accept such unknown personal consequences but escaped them through self-inflicted death.

45. Exercises independent thought—*criterion satisfied*

Although Hitler exercised independent thought, he relied upon others to abandon free thought and surrender willingly to his ideas. Speer writes, "My inclination to be relieved of having to think, particularly about unpleasant facts, helped to sway the balance [in deciding to join the Nazi Party]. In this I did not differ from millions of others. Such mental slackness above all facilitated, established, and finally assured the success of the National Socialist system."[276] Eichmann allowed others to think for him, claiming merely to have followed orders and denying that he was "master of his own deeds."[277] The fact remains, however, that Hitler was an independent thinker.

---

275. Hitler; in Domarus, *Essential Hitler*, 46.
276. Speer, *Inside the Third Reich*, 20.
277. Eichmann; in Arendt, *Eichmann*, 136.

46. Offers a merciful gift, promise of a better future—*criterion not satisfied*

Hitler self-identified as a messianic figure, as creator and leader of a new age. "The new age has already come," he proclaimed, "and we welcome its arrival: the new age is the new German Volk that we have created!" He predicted that, following extermination of the Jewish people, "a long era of international understanding, and therefore of true peace, will come over the suffering world. . . . What used to be our party program is now the basis of a new and improving world." While Hitler promised "a new and better order,"[278] that which he offered was not merciful or better in the eyes of moral humanity. He delivered death and destruction while refusing, as Domarus notes, "to acknowledge authorship of the unheard-of catastrophe into which he had plunged Germany and the entire world."[279]

47. Normally upholds customary moral laws—*criterion not satisfied*

The Nazis fabricated and enforced a code of conduct that violated traditional and customary moral laws. As Adams and Balfour point out, Hitler created a "morally inverted" order.[280] Morality was turned on its head such that, where it would normally be expected to operate, there existed instead a moral vacuum. Acts of kindness (e.g., protecting Jews) were condemned whereas acts of evil (e.g., murdering Jews) were praised.

48. Does not proclaim divine condemnation of others—*criterion not satisfied*

Hitler condemned those whom he perceived as foes and claimed divine support in his condemnatory activities.[281] He warned against "the devil-

---

278. Hitler; in Domarus, *Essential Hitler*, 261, 301, 319.
279. Domarus, *Essential Hitler*, 131.
280. Adams and Balfour, *Administrative Evil*, 167.
281. The first criterion with respect to divine, prophetic calling above provides examples of this.

ish plan of the Jewish international criminals" that he maintained could bring about the destruction of "all European peoples."²⁸² "After the death of his victim," Hitler fantasized, "the vampire [the Jew] sooner or later dies too." He held that Karl Marx "recognized in the morass of a slowly decomposing world the most essential poisons, extracted them, and, like a wizard, prepared them into a concentrated solution for the swifter annihilation of the independent existence of free nations on this earth. . . . Marxism . . . systematically plans to hand the world over to the Jews" who "made a pact with the devil," he insisted.²⁸³ Such characterization of others as devilish, vampiric, as sorcerers dealing in poison, and as committed to the devil is typical in Hitler's parlance.

---

49. Possible temporary suspension of universal ethic in some regard in relation to a divinely sanctioned higher *telos*— criterion not satisfied

Hitler did not aim to suspend a universal ethic temporarily but to obliterate it permanently in favor of his own laws by which he intended, for one thing, to exterminate European Jewry. "I believe in the eternity of this Reich," he declared.²⁸⁴

The notion of a teleological suspension of the ethical has been viewed in the context of suspension of *lex publica* in favor of *lex divina*. However, when Hitler suspended *lex publica* in Germany, he simply created a new *lex publica*. The National Socialist Party, he stated, was "a corporation under public law" whose statutes were "to be determined by the Führer"²⁸⁵ (not God). Nevertheless, Hitler invoked the notion of a teleological suspension of the ethical in favor of a divine *telos*. "The Almighty has allowed us to take this wonderful path and will continue to bless us," he announced. "For we are fighting here for a higher right, for a higher truth and for a higher human decency."²⁸⁶ "[A] man who feels it his duty . . . to assume the leadership of his people is not responsible to the laws of parliamentary usage or to a particular democratic concep-

---

282. Hitler; in Domarus, *Essential Hitler*, 407.
283. Hitler, *Mein Kampf*, 311, 327, 382.
284. Hitler; in Domarus, *Essential Hitler*, 495.
285. Ibid., 255.
286. Ibid., 312.

tion, but solely to the mission placed upon him."[287] "Here I believe in a higher and eternal justice. It is imparted to him who proves himself worthy of it."[288]

Hitler's claim to divinely sanctioned teleological suspension of the ethical is not supported by compelling evidence of his having been in an absolute relation to the Absolute (to employ Kierkegaard's terminology), which is essential if any such suspension is to be considered divinely inspired. Moreover, Hitler's claim to divine sanction and his ethical suspension were broad and general, supposing that whatever Hitler succeeded in doing was *ipso facto* a result of Providence, whereas teleological suspension of the ethical in favor of a divine *telos* is typically represented as more finely focused and specifically directed.

It must be emphasized that, within the context of the model, teleological suspension of the ethical might be considered indicative of divine sanction only when all essential criteria are satisfied (unless indeterminate or not applicable). The criterion must never be cited as indicative on its own. In fact, no single criterion should ever be considered sufficient in assessing a claim favorably.

---

50. Charism, spiritual gifts, uncanny abilities (including but not limited to those cited under the category of Divine, Prophetic Calling), mediates grace—*criterion not satisfied*

Hitler had charisma among the German people, but mere social or political charisma falls short of theological charism which is traditionally linked with Christian virtues.[289] One might argue that Hitler's oratorical strength was charismatic but that he abused it by isolating it from Christian virtues; however, divorced from virtue, such ability cannot be deemed truly charismatic. A spiritual gift is not presumably charismatic in and of itself but only when employed in a virtuous manner under the power of divine grace. Moreover, psychiatrist Leon Goldensohn refers to the "myth of the magnetism of Hitler" which sprang from the Nuremberg trials,[290] which suggests that Hitler did not possess a genu-

---

287. Hitler; in Halasz, *Hitler*, 37–38.
288. Hitler; in Domarus, *Essential Hitler*, 161.
289. Rahner, "Charism," 185.
290. Goldensohn, *Nuremberg*, 184.

inely magnetic personality but that such characterization was fabricated by Nuremberg defendants in an attempt to obtain exemption from personal accountability on the pretext that they involuntarily succumbed to some supernatural force. Moreover, Hitler not only lacked charismata but seems to have denied their existence, asserting that "[n]o one can ever master what he has not already learned and trained himself up to."[291]

51. Honest disposition, transparency—*criterion not satisfied*

Hitler was a pathological liar whose speeches are replete with falsity. "National Socialism does not harbour the slightest aggressive intent towards any European nation," he declared[292] before invading Austria, Czechoslovakia, Poland, France, Denmark, Norway, Belgium, the Netherlands, Luxembourg, and Russia. Hitler also stated, "The German Reich government … will … scrupulously comply with every treaty signed,"[293] but his invasion of Russia proved this false.[294]

52. Straightforward, honest language, forthrightness—*criterion not satisfied*

Hitler implemented deceptive language rules that aimed to conceal, disguise, and deny the depravity of Nazi activities by addressing them in relatively benign terms; carefully selected words cloaked hideous truths with more palatable lies. Arendt points out that the "term 'language rule'" was itself deceptive and intended to mask that which is ordinarily termed lying. Expulsion was called "forced emigration," concentration camps were spoken of "in terms of 'administration'" and extermination camps "in terms of 'economy,'" and "the official code name for extermination was … 'Final Solution.'" The words "evacuation" and "special treatment" denoted killing, the phrase "granting … a mercy death" referring explicitly to death by gassing which was construed as "the humane way" of killing and avoiding "unnecessary hard-

---

291. Hitler; in Halasz, *Hitler*, 78. As we know, Jehanne was a military expert having undergone none of the training and experience ordinarily required for that vocation.
292. Hitler; in Halasz, *Hitler*, 16.
293. Hitler; in Domarus, *Essential Hitler*, 88.
294. Domarus, *Essential Hitler*, 657.

ships." Deportation to the camps was referred to as "change of residence, ... resettlement, ... and labor in the East." Gassing centers were called "Charitable Foundations for Institutional Care." This was all considered "objective" as opposed to "emotional" language.[295] The Nazis apparently had no tolerance for the emotional which they stifled through deception. "I could not have carried on as an administrative officer if I had let myself be swayed emotionally," stated Pohl.[296] Sixteen years after the fact, Eichmann's defense lawyer still believed that the murder of millions by gas constituted a "medical matter."[297] The term conveys an attempted sanitization of murder rather than outright denial. In fact, Arendt asserts that the language rules did not deceive the Nazis about what they were doing but kept them from associating it "with their old, 'normal' knowledge of murder and lies."[298] Berel Lang explains that, as with all lies, the perverse vocabulary was accompanied by knowing affirmation of what was false and constituted a moral violation consisting not in the falsity itself but in the activities that it facilitated. Falsity, Lang concedes, is not necessarily unethical depending on its purpose and the circumstances in which it is employed.[299]

53. Unambiguous public statement of purpose and method—*criterion satisfied*

Before rising to power, Hitler declared his agenda publicly in his book, *Mein Kampf* (first published in 1925), clearly exposing his racist political ideology and intentions. Heiden states that, "in its pages Hitler announced ... a program of blood and terror in a self-revelation of such overwhelming frankness that [he supposes] few among its readers had the courage to believe it."[300]

---

295. Arendt, *Eichmann*, 43, 69, 84–85, 108–9.

296. Pohl; in Goldensohn, *Nuremberg*, 408.

297. Eichmann's lawyer, Robert Servatius, had never been a Nazi. Arendt, *Eichmann*, 69.

298. Ibid., 86.

299. Lang, "Language and Genocide," 350.

300. Heiden, introduction to *Mein Kampf*, xv.

54. Reliability, consistency, constancy—*criterion not satisfied*

Hjalmar Schacht observed that Hitler was extremely unreliable, frequently doing "the exact opposite to what he ... said before and [he] did not consider himself tied by any promises or agreement."[301] Again, Hitler's assertion that Germany would not "wage wars of aggression" or "rob other nations of their freedom"[302] serves as an example. Moreover, Hitler claimed, "The German Reich government is guided by the hope of possibly being able to bring about ... a framework within which the German Volk would be in a position to establish tolerable relations with the Jewish people."[303] Meanwhile, he had been declaring for ten years that the Jewish people ought to be exterminated and proceeded to act unremittingly on the conviction.[304] Furthermore, Hitler had an erratic personality. "[H]e would be most friendly and affectionate on one day," stated Joachim von Ribbentrop, "and the very next time I saw him he would criticize me and even accuse me of betraying him."[305]

55. Strives with the world, with self, and with God—*indeterminate*

Hitler obviously strove against the world. Whether or not he strove with himself is indeterminate. He does not seem to have striven earnestly with God but presumed God's will (and everyone else's) subject to his own. He declared himself in right relationship with God and did not appear to entertain the possibility that the situation might be otherwise, but we cannot be entirely certain since he would not likely have confessed such inner struggles if they existed.

---

301. Schacht, president of the Reichsbank until 1939; in Overy, *Interrogations*, 213.
302. Hitler; in Halasz, *Hitler*, 15.
303. Hitler; in Domarus, *Essential Hitler*, 269.
304. Hitler, *Mein Kampf*, 169.
305. Von Ribbentrop, Hitler's foreign minister; in Goldensohn, *Nuremberg*, 190.

56. Expression of the sublime absolutely in the pedestrian—*criterion not satisfied*

While there was something ostensibly subliminal about Hitler's effect on the millions who threw their support behind him, it was more likely due to his psychological tactics (e.g., brainwashing and fear mongering) than to the expression of sublime qualities on his part. In fact, Hitler lacked the sublime qualities of compassion, humility, charity, and sanctity, but he was a master of manipulation who recognized "the importance of physical terror toward the individual and the masses. Here, too, the psychological effect can be calculated with precision," he explained. "*Terror at the place of employment, in the factory, in the meeting hall, and on the occasion of mass demonstrations will always be successful unless opposed by equal terror.*"[306] Hitler introduced terror, not subliminal qualities, to the pedestrian. It permeated the most ordinary aspects of human life such that taking a shower might produce fatal poisoning and labor might involve extracting gold teeth from corpses.

57. Wisdom, sound judgment—*criterion not satisfied*

Hitler repeatedly demonstrated poor judgment with respect to foreign politics, grossly miscalculating international response to his National Socialist agenda. His expectation of an alliance with Britain proved unrealistic;[307] in fact, Britain vowed "to destroy Hitler and every vestige of the Nazi regime."[308] Moreover, he failed to anticipate accurately the result of his campaign against Russia, which refused to surrender according to his plan.[309] Hitler's Russian offensive also lacked wisdom as German troops were ill-prepared for the harsh winter conditions encountered there.[310] "The Russians were five times superior to us . . . Germans, both in numbers and in the superiority of their equipment," explained one of Hitler's generals. "My immediate commander was Hitler himself. Unfortunately, Hitler's advice in those critical periods

---

306. Hitler, *Mein Kampf*, 44.
307. Domarus, *Essential Hitler*, 109–13, 276.
308. Winston Churchill; in Domarus, *Essential Hitler*, 115.
309. Domarus, *Essential Hitler*, 117–18.
310. Ibid., 722, 726.

was invariably lousy."³¹¹ Furthermore, his campaign of expansion failed to recognize Germany's limited resources for maintaining control of conquered lands.³¹² Domarus concludes that Hitler held a "distorted" view of international politics and that all "his theories and ideas with which he had operated since 1919" were "wrong without exception." When members of the Reich realized that "Hitler was merely improvising," several fled Germany, committed suicide, or sought an alternate exit route.³¹³

58. Undergoes mystical "dark night," struggle with pain and suffering—*indeterminate*

Hitler may have avoided much pain and suffering by ending his life before it became unbearable, although the decision to take his life was likely painful. He also suffered the gradual failure of his regime, though he was reluctant to acknowledge it. As the war progressed, Speer indicates that Hitler suffered from "[o]verwork and isolation [which] led to a peculiar state of petrifaction and rigor. He suffered from spells of mental torpor and was permanently caustic and irritable."³¹⁴ We have little indication that Hitler's struggles were mystical in nature, but the following statement interprets them in that context: "I often feel that we will have to undergo all the trials the devil and hell can devise before we achieve Final Victory," Hitler stated.³¹⁵ Our information is insufficient to assess reliably the nature of Hitler's inner struggles.

59. Demonstrates grace in extreme suffering—*criterion not satisfied*

Again, it must be noted that Hitler killed himself in anticipation of extreme suffering. While he undoubtedly suffered the hardships and humiliations of defeat in the aftermath of World War I, he failed to dem-

---

311. Kleist; in Goldensohn, *Nuremberg*, 345–46.
312. Domarus, *Essential Hitler*, 282.
313. Ibid., 112, 131, 276.
314. Speer, *Inside the Third Reich*, 294.
315. Hitler; quoted by Speer, *Inside the Third Reich*, 555, n. 13.

onstrate grace in that context but sought to dominate the world at all costs in retaliation.

60. Embodies paradox—*criterion not satisfied*

Hitler did not evidently embody any striking paradox; he despised and sought to oppress others and acted accordingly, moving to eliminate and/or subdue them by manipulation or ruthless force. He was not a man of light navigating darkness, but a man of dark intentions who carried them out darkly.

61. Canonization, holiness, posthumous miracles—*criterion not satisfied*

Hitler has not been canonized, has not been attributed posthumous miracles, and is not generally associated with holiness.

62. Identification with a particular, well-established prophecy—*criterion satisfied*

Hitler has been associated with the cryptic prophecies of sixteenth-century French seer, Nostradamus (Michel de Nostredame). Moreover, Hitler associated himself with Friedrich Nietzsche's notion of the *Übermensch* (Superman or Overman who embodies raw power and transcends human nature) and identified his ideological Aryan race with a race of world rulers prophesied by Nietzsche.[316] Furthermore, Nietzsche penned a prophecy that reads, "I know my fate. One day my name will be associated with the memory of something tremendous—a crisis without equal on earth, the most profound collision of conscience, a decision that was conjured up *against* everything that had been believed, demanded, hallowed so far."[317] One might associate such Nietzschean predictions with Hitler, and many have.[318] Hitler is also associated with

---

316. The Nietzschean work referred to is *The Will to Power*. Metaxas, *Bonhoeffer*, 168.
317. Nietzsche, *Ecce Homo*, 782.
318. Waite, *Psychopathic God*, 319–21. Robert Waite notes that Nietzsche was strongly opposed to anti-Semitism. Ibid., 321.

prophecies by Heinrich Heine who stated, "[W]hen you hear a crashing such as never before has been heard in the world's history, then you know that the German thunderbolt has fallen at last. . . . A play will be performed in Germany which will make the French Revolution look like an innocent idyll."[319]

Summary Assessment—Divinely Sanctioned Human Agency

Of the sixty-two criteria indicative of divinely sanctioned human agency, Hitler satisfies six (four essential and two non-essential), he fails to satisfy fifty-two (forty-one essential and eleven non-essential), and four are indeterminate (two essential and two non-essential). Of the forty-seven essential criteria, only four are met. Of the fifteen non-essential criteria, two are met. Since he fails to satisfy the vast majority of criteria in this category, Hitler cannot be construed as having engaged in divinely sanctioned human agency in accordance with Jehanne's example. A summing up of the three categories with respect to Hitler's case is in order.

Case Study One Results

Having conducted an extensive assessment of Hitler's claim to divinely sanctioned violence, it has been determined that he fails to meet the requirements in each category. Of the one hundred criteria, Hitler satisfies ten (six essential and four non-essential), he fails to satisfy eighty-two (sixty-five essential and seventeen non-essential), and eight are indeterminate (four essential and four non-essential). Of the seventy-five essential criteria, only six are met. Of the twenty-five non-essential criteria, four are met. On the basis of Jehanne's example, Hitler cannot be deemed a practical, prophetic mystic in receipt of divine revelation or divine calling, nor can his war or his behavior be construed as righteous or divinely sanctioned. In fact, one might reasonably classify Hitler as a false prophet and Nazism as an unjust social system against which the prophet rails.

Hitler was exceedingly detailed, organized, thorough, and dedicated in his application of evil, and it is perhaps for this reason that he has become a modern icon of hate, an association that is warranted based upon factual evidence. Given Hitler's reputation for evil, one might argue that an assessment via the model is unnecessary since the result of his

---

319. Heinrich Heine; in Metaxas, *Bonhoeffer*, 164.

case is obvious from the outset, but the fact that millions heeded his call, without whom he could not have accomplished the massive destruction for which he is notorious, suggests otherwise. Moreover, despite the obvious evil perpetrated by the Hitler regime, Nazism remains alive and humanity must remain vigilant. As Weil suggests, regardless of any judgments against Hitler, these "will not stop, in twenty, fifty, a hundred or two hundred years' time, some solitary little dreamer . . . from seeing in Hitler a superb figure, with a superb destiny from beginning to end, and desiring with all his soul to have a similar destiny. In which case, woe betide his contemporaries."[320]

Case Study Two—Dietrich Bonhoeffer

The solitary is one who is called to make one of the most terrible decisions possible to man: the decision to disagree completely with those who imagine that the call to diversion and self-deception is the voice of truth and who can summon the full authority of their own prejudice to prove it. He is therefore bound to sweat blood in anguish, in order to be loyal to God, to the Mystical Christ, and to humanity as a whole, rather than to the idol which is offered to him, for his homage, by a particular group. He must renounce the blessing of every convenient illusion that absolves him from responsibility when he is untrue to his deepest self and to his inmost truth—the image of God in his own soul.
—Thomas Merton, *Disputed Questions*

Karl Barth identifies as a fundamental danger of improper (false) theology that it might serve "the Antichrist instead of . . . Jesus Christ."[321] "Often what masquerades as orthodoxy is highly unorthodox," notes O'Donohue. "When this has the voice of authority, sanction and censure behind it, people do not actually notice that it is unorthodox."[322] Weil confesses:

> What frightens me is the Church as a social structure. Not only on account of its blemishes, but from the very fact that it is something social. It is not that I am of a very individualistic temperament. I am afraid for the opposite reason. I am aware of very

---

320. Weil, *Need for Roots*, 224.
321. Barth, *Evangelical Theology*, 143.
322. O'Donohue, *Four Elements*, 123.

Applying the Model

strong gregarious tendencies in myself. My natural disposition is to be very easily influenced, too much influenced, and above all by anything collective. I know that if at this moment I had before me a group of twenty young Germans singing Nazi songs in chorus, a part of my soul would instantly become Nazi. That is a very great weakness, but that is how I am. I think that it is useless to fight directly against natural weaknesses. One has to force oneself to act as though one did not have them in circumstances where a duty makes it imperative; and in the ordinary course of life one has to know these weaknesses, prudently take them into account, and strive to turn them to good purpose.[323]

Weil's statement recalls Arendt's characterization of Eichmann as one who possessed strong gregarious tendencies.[324] Weil continues:

By social I do not mean everything connected with citizenship, but only collective emotions.

I am well aware that the Church must inevitably be a social structure; otherwise it would not exist. But in so far as it is a social structure, it belongs to the Prince of this World. It is because it is an organ for the preservation and transmission of truth that there is an extreme danger for those who, like me, are excessively open to social influences. For in this way what is purest and what is most defiling look very much the same, and confused under the same words, make an almost undecomposable mixture.[325]

These problems highlight the significance of mysticism, its solitary path of discernment, and the importance of the templates that saints and mystics throughout the ages have provided as illumination to others.

Weil's concerns regarding the Church as social structure are affirmed by the politics of Hitlerite Germany. "At the bottom of our hearts," declared Hitler, "we National Socialists are religious,"[326] while Eichmann dubbed some prominent Nazis "the Popes of the Third Reich."[327] Dietrich Bonhoeffer, a German-born[328] Lutheran pastor and theologian with ecumenical interests, recognized such dangers as they manifested

---

323. Weil, *Waiting for God*, 11–12. Weil died in 1943 and may have been unaware of the full extent of Nazi atrocities committed under Hitler.

324. Arendt, *Eichmann*, 32.

325. Weil, *Waiting for God*, 12–13.

326. Hitler; in Domarus, *Essential Hitler*, 315.

327. Eichmann; in Arendt, *Eichmann*, 114.

328. Bonhoeffer was born in Breslau in 1906.

before him in Nazi Germany. "The prophet knew that religion could distort what the Lord demanded of man, that priests themselves had committed perjury by bearing false witness, condoning violence, tolerating hatred, calling for ceremonies instead of bursting forth with wrath and indignation at cruelty, deceit, idolatry, and violence,"[329] states Heschel. Bonhoeffer maintained that it is the proper purpose of the Church to make "confession to Christ its life."[330] Hence, he became a leading member of the "Confessing Church" that arose in opposition to the Nazi-ruled "German Christian Church" in Hitler's Germany.[331] "The word of the church is the word of the present Christ, it is gospel and commandment," he asserted.[332] Hvidt indicates that "the task of the [Christian] prophet is ... to encourage the church to live the Gospel and to guide it through the rough waters of history; pointing out dangers and admonishing the faithful to keep in union with God and his truth."[333] It is to this task that Bonhoeffer applied himself, defying the German Christians, Nazism, and Hitler himself. Along with several family members, he entered a conspiracy to assassinate the destructive and fanatical Führer and to organize a coup d'état involving several of Germany's military generals. The conspirators also attempted to gain support from England for a coup in Germany. By January of 1938, the vociferous Bonhoeffer was forbidden by the Nazis to maintain residence in Berlin. With war in view, he made a troubled decision to leave Germany in June of 1939 for an academic post in the United States, wishing to avoid fighting in an aggressive, unjust war.[334] "The main reason," he wrote, "is the compulsory military service to which the men of my age will be called up this year. It seems to me conscientiously impossible to join in a war under the present circumstances. . . . Perhaps the worst thing of all is the military oath which I should have to swear [to Hitler]."[335] But Bonhoeffer was not at ease in America as the situation in his country was extremely precarious and he soon returned to Germany where he obtained exemption from conscription by alternative arrangement: through family connections,

329. Heschel, *Prophets: Introduction*, 11.
330. Bonhoeffer, *No Rusty Swords*, 213.
331. Leibholz, "Memoir," xvi.
332. Bonhoeffer, *No Rusty Swords*, 157.
333. Hvidt, *Christian Prophecy*, 111.
334. Leibholz, "Memoir," xvi.
335. Bonhoeffer; in Bethge, *Biography*, 637.

he was employed by the *Abwehr* (German military intelligence office) to work as a secret agent on the pretext that his abundant personal and professional connections in Germany and abroad would serve the National Socialist state, but Bonhoeffer instead utilized his *Abwehr* travels to promote resistance to Hitler.[336]

In 1940, Bonhoeffer was banned from public speaking in Germany, he was forbidden to publish, preach, or teach, and he was required to report regularly to the Gestapo (Nazi secret police) who closed his underground seminary. Nonetheless, Bonhoeffer's involvement in the conspiracy continued. He became engaged to Maria von Wedemeyer in January of 1943 and was arrested and imprisoned shortly thereafter, on April 5 of the same year. The arrest was not due to his participation in the conspiracy, which had not yet become apparent to the Nazis, but Bonhoeffer had publicly railed against the National Socialist state and the collaborating German Christian Church, he had operated illegal seminaries of the Confessing Church, he had avoided conscription, and he had helped to smuggle fourteen Jewish people across the German border into Switzerland.[337] Despite his internal connections, it is surprising that Bonhoeffer was permitted to work for the *Abwehr* given his active opposition to the state. Eventually, evidence concerning the conspiracy came to light leading to the execution of Bonhoeffer, his brother Klaus, two of their brothers-in-law, and several other conspirators. Bonhoeffer was hanged by the Nazis on April 9, 1945 at Flossenbürg concentration camp at age thirty-nine, just days before the camp was liberated and only three weeks before Hitler's death. For his faith, his solidarity with the oppressed, and his active stance against evil, Bonhoeffer paid with his life.

Kierkegaard once observed, "Not just in commerce but in the world of ideas too our age is putting on a veritable clearance sale. Everything can be had so dirt cheap that one begins to wonder whether in the end anyone will want to make a bid."[338] The statement resonates with Bonhoeffer's concept of "cheap grace."

> Cheap grace means grace sold on the market like cheapjack's wares. The sacraments, the forgiveness of sin, and the consolations of religion are thrown away at cut prices. Grace is repre-

---

336. Bethge, *Biography*, 652–53, 793. Bismarck, preface to *Love Letters*, 9. Kabitz; in *Love Letters*, 326.

337. Bethge, *Biography*, 817.

338. Kierkegaard, *Fear and Trembling*, 3.

sented as the Church's inexhaustible treasury, from which she showers blessings with generous hands, without asking questions or fixing limits. Grace without price; grace without cost! The essence of grace, we suppose, is that the account has been paid in advance; and, because it has been paid, everything can be had for nothing. Since the cost was infinite, the possibilities of using and spending it are infinite. What would grace be if it were not cheap?

Cheap grace means grace as doctrine, a principle, a system. It means forgiveness of sins proclaimed as a general truth. . . . An intellectual assent to that idea is held to be of itself sufficient to secure remission of sins. The Church which holds the correct doctrine of grace has, it is supposed, *ipso facto* a part in that grace. In such a Church the world finds a cheap covering for its sins; no contrition is required, still less any real desire to be delivered from sin. . . .

Cheap grace means the justification of sin without the justification of the sinner. Grace does everything, they say, and so everything can remain as it was before. . . . Cheap grace is the grace we bestow on ourselves.

. . . Cheap grace is grace without discipleship, grace without the cross, grace without Jesus Christ, living and incarnate.[339]

In Nazi Germany, Bonhoeffer was confronted with concrete results of "cheap grace" and recognized the necessity of opposing such falsity. Hence, contending with cheap grace is Bonhoeffer's concept of "costly grace," "the only genuine kind of grace" conceivable to him. "Costly grace . . . is the call of Jesus Christ at which the disciple leaves his nets and follows him. . . . Such grace is *costly* because it calls us to follow, and it is *grace* because it calls us to follow *Jesus Christ*. It is costly because it costs a man his life, and it is grace because it gives a man the only true life. . . . Costly grace is the Incarnation of God."[340] This is the concept by which Bonhoeffer lived and died. Let us apply the model in order to ascertain whether or not his example corresponds to that of Jehanne.

---

339. Bonhoeffer, *Discipleship*, 3–4. First published in 1937.
340. Ibid., 4–5, 12.

Applying the Model

Divine, Prophetic Calling Criteria

1. Receipt of divine revelation (e.g., visions, auditions) calling one to a specified task—*indeterminate*

"My calling is quite clear to me," wrote Bonhoeffer at the dawn of 1936. "What God will make of it I do not know.... I must follow the path. Perhaps it will not be such a long one.... But it is a fine thing to have realized my calling.... I believe that the nobility of this calling will become plain to us only in the times and events to come. If only we can hold out!"[341] The prophetic accuracy of the words is stunning; however, they do not reveal the means by which Bonhoeffer discerned his potentially divine calling.

Bonhoeffer interpreted Scripture with a view to revelation. Informing his actions through scriptural passages, being Christian for him required following Christ to the utmost of one's ability in accordance with the gospel texts. It is not necessary to receive "personal revelation" in order to "hear the call of Jesus," he maintained, since Jesus now speaks through Scripture and sacrament.[342] Nevertheless, he approached the Bible meditatively[343] in the belief that it speaks personally to each individual and advised his students to view it as "a love letter from God directed very personally" to each of them.[344] He once inquired of a fellow conspirator, "Is it ... intelligible to you if I say I am not at any point willing to sacrifice the Bible ... , that on the contrary, I ask with all my strength what God is trying to say to us through it? Every other place outside the Bible has become too uncertain for me. I fear that there I will only bump into my own divine *Doppelgänger*."[345] Hence, in seeking divine direction, Bonhoeffer sometimes approached the Bible in oracular fashion, consulting the daily readings in relation to specific events and current concerns.

Hvidt indicates that prophets have often called people to live in accordance with truths revealed through important scriptural passages.[346]

---

341. Bonhoeffer; in Bethge, *Biography*, 205.
342. Bonhoeffer, *Discipleship*, 165.
343. Bethge, *Biography*, 204.
344. Bonhoeffer; quoted by J. Kanitz, in Bethge, *Biography*, 204.
345. Bonhoeffer; in Bethge, *Biography*, 206.
346. Hvidt, *Christian Prophecy*, 249.

Nonetheless, Scripture is potentially dangerous as a source of divine authority since it can be interpreted to almost any end. However, in the absence of specific divine revelation, Scripture might reasonably be consulted as a potential form of divine guidance. While it is indeterminate whether or not Bonhoeffer received specific divine direction through Scripture or other means, the possibility cannot be ruled out.

2. Discernment of spirits (charism)—*indeterminate*

Bonhoeffer wrote that the Holy Spirit shines "in the necessary decision of the moment,"[347] alluding to divine guidance in spirit form. He believed in the numinous and drew comfort from that which he described as "benevolent spirits."[348] "I live in a great, unseen realm of whose real existence I'm in no doubt," he wrote, adding that all are in need of "preservation ... by kindly, unseen powers."[349] His friend, Bethge, noted that Bonhoeffer interacted with "other dimensions ... in a very lively way."[350] "The beyond," wrote Bonhoeffer, "is not what is infinitely remote, but what is nearest at hand."[351] However, one cannot be certain of Bonhoeffer's ability to discern spirits as he has not undergone a process of canonization which rigorously examines such matters.

3. Offers oneself as an instrument of God and willing conduit for divine grace (decision aspect)—*criterion satisfied*

"We are not lords, but instruments in the hand of the Lord of history," Bonhoeffer asserted.[352] He offered himself as an instrument of God and sought to discern God's will for him through Scripture, conscience, and opening to divine grace. When one acts from a position of responsibility, Bonhoeffer explained, "[h]e does not do this in the insolent presumptuousness of his own power, but he does it in the knowledge that this

347. Bonhoeffer; in Bethge, *Biography*, 119.
348. Bonhoeffer, *Love Letters*, 127.
349. Ibid., 269.
350. Bethge; in *Letters*, 330. Bethge was Bonhoeffer's student, close friend, nephew-in-law, co-conspirator, and biographer.
351. Bonhoeffer, *Letters*, 376.
352. Ibid., 14.

liberty is forced upon him and that in this liberty he is dependent on grace. Before other men the man of free responsibility is justified by necessity; before himself he is acquitted by his conscience; but before God he hopes only for mercy."[353]

---

4. Actively engages in divine servantship, operates under willing obedience to divine (vs. human) authority, surrender of personal will to divine will, views him- or herself as being in an absolute relation to the divine—*criterion satisfied*

Bonhoeffer wished "to receive what God bestows … with open, outstretched hands" and, "with a quiet heart," to "sacrifice what God does not yet grant … or takes away."[354] Bonhoeffer engaged in divine servantship as a pastor, theologian, and, above all, a disciple. He held that it is "obedience to the word" of God, "the practical doing of what is commanded," that forms the basis of discipleship, which cannot be derived from religious formulas.[355] "If we inquire the will of God, free from all doubt and all mistrust, we shall discover it," he asserted.[356] "[T]he main thing is that we keep step with God, and do not keep pressing on a few steps ahead—nor keep dawdling a step behind."[357]

Bonhoeffer distinguished between "penultimate" human authority and "ultimate" divine authority.[358] "I must be able to know for certain that I am in God's hands, not in men's," he explained. "Then everything becomes easy."[359] He could bear things in faith so long as he believed they were willed by God. After a year in prison, Bonhoeffer wrote, "Everything seems to have taken its natural course, and to be determined necessarily and straightforwardly by a higher providence."[360] Despite captivity, he did not "for a moment" regret returning to Germany from New York in 1939. "I knew quite well what I was doing, and I acted with

---

353. Bonhoeffer, *Ethics*, 244.
354. Bonhoeffer, *Letters*, 247.
355. Bonhoeffer; in Wüstenberg, *Theology of Life*, 14.
356. Bonhoeffer; quoted by Wedemeyer, in *Love Letters*, 332.
357. Bonhoeffer, *Letters*, 169.
358. Bonhoeffer, *No Rusty Swords*, 199.
359. Bonhoeffer, *Letters*, 174.
360. Ibid., 276.

a clear conscience."³⁶¹ Bonhoeffer viewed himself as being in an absolute relationship with the divine, stating that "the individual knows himself to be completely alone" before the ultimate authority of God.³⁶²

5. Submits to divine judgment and lives in constant awareness of this judgment—*criterion satisfied*

A prayer written by Bonhoeffer reflects awareness of divine judgment. "O holy and merciful God, / my Creator and Redeemer, / my Judge and Saviour, / You know me and all that I do."³⁶³ Bonhoeffer accepted personal guilt in transgressing (via participation in the conspiracy) the commandment, "Thou shalt not kill," and placed himself at the mercy and judgment of God. The deep struggle, the process of discernment, and the weight of responsibility unleashed by the question of whether or not he should return to Germany in 1939 and to his involvement in the conspiracy are evident.

> The decision has been made. . . . It probably means more for me than I can see at the moment. God alone knows what. It is remarkable how I am never quite clear about the motives for any of my decisions. Is that a sign of confusion, of inner dishonesty, or is it a sign that we are guided without our knowing, or is it both? . . . Today's scripture reading speaks dreadfully harshly of God's incorruptible judgement. He certainly sees how much personal feeling, how much anxiety, there is in today's decision [to return to Germany]. . . . The reasons that one gives for an action to others and to one's self are certainly inadequate. One can give a reason for everything. In the last resort one acts from a level which remains hidden from us. . . . I can only ask God to give a merciful judgement on today and all its decisions. It is now in his hands.³⁶⁴

---

361. Ibid., 174.
362. Bonhoeffer, *No Rusty Swords*, 199.
363. Bonhoeffer, *Letters*, 140.
364. Bonhoeffer; in Bethge, *Biography*, 653. Perhaps the hidden level to which Bonhoeffer refers is the level of conscience and promptings by divine grace.

6. Shares in God's happiness, sadness, concern, sympathy, and aspirations for the world, active concern for humanity—*criterion satisfied*

Bonhoeffer maintained that Christians carry "God and the whole world" within themselves.[365] He held that it is "only by living completely in this world that one learns to have faith ... [, by] living unreservedly in life's duties, problems, successes and failures, experiences and perplexities. In so doing we throw ourselves completely into the arms of God, taking seriously, not our own sufferings, but those of God in the world."[366] "Christians stand by God in his hour of grieving," he explained.[367] "Jesus asked in Gethsemane, 'Could you not watch with me one hour?' ... Man is summoned to share in God's sufferings at the hands of a godless world. ... It is not the religious act that makes the Christian, but participation in the sufferings of God in the secular life."[368] "We are not Christ, but if we want to be Christians, we must have some share in Christ's largeheartedness by acting with responsibility and in freedom when the hour of danger comes, and by showing a real sympathy that springs ... from the ... love of Christ for all who suffer. Mere waiting and looking on is not Christian behaviour. The Christian is called to sympathy and action, not in the first place by his own sufferings, but by the sufferings of his brethren."[369] Bonhoeffer lived these words to the fullest in his opposition to Hitler. He displayed great concern for others and was actively committed to improving their circumstances. After a year in Tegel prison, he prepared a report on injustices and inadequacies in the treatment of prisoners with the intention that it might lead to improvements. He also attempted "to have a quiet word with" some abusive guards concerning their treatment "of all the other prisoners," but to no avail.[370] Following an air raid that destroyed part of the prison wall, Bonhoeffer prepared recommendations for improved medical treatment during attacks. He

---

365. Bonhoeffer, *Letters*, 310.
366. Ibid., 369–70.
367. Bonhoeffer, "Christians and Pagans," *Letters*, 349.
368. Bonhoeffer, *Letters*, 361.
369. Ibid., 14.
370. Bonhoeffer, "Report on Prison Life," *Letters*, 248–52. Also, Bethge, *Biography*, 850.

also committed an hour daily to "studying the [prison] manual for medical staff, for any eventuality."[371]

---

7. Destabilizing presence in an unjust social system, exhortation to improve condition of humanity, serves the repair of the world and the common good—*criterion satisfied*

Bonhoeffer was an outspoken, destabilizing presence in the unjust social system of Nazism. Bethge describes a scene following Hitler's rise to power in 1933. "A forest of swastika flags surrounded the altar of Magdeburg Cathedral."[372] "It has simply become the symbol of German hope," explained the cathedral dean. "Whoever reviles this symbol is reviling our Germany. . . . The swastika flags round the altar radiate hope—hope that the day is at last about to dawn."[373] In fact, Hitler's intention in incorporating the swastika in the National Socialist flag was to signify "the mission of the struggle for the victory of the Aryan man, and, by the same token, the victory of the idea of creative work, which," he maintained, "always has been and always will be anti-Semitic."[374] Bonhoeffer spoke out against such outrage, preaching that "[t]he church has only *one* altar, the altar of the Almighty . . . before which all creatures must kneel. . . . Whoever seeks something other than this must keep away; he cannot join us in the house of God. . . . The church has only *one* pulpit, and from that pulpit, faith in God will be preached, and no other faith, and no other will than the will of God. . . ."[375] This is but one example of the many occasions on which Bonhoeffer openly opposed National Socialist aims.

---

8. Lived witnessing of faith in God—*criterion satisfied*

"Only he who cries out for the Jews may sing Gregorian chants," Bonhoeffer announced.[376] He considered divine worship empty unless

---

371. Bonhoeffer, *Letters*, 147, 151–52, 189.
372. Bethge, *Biography*, 257.
373. Ernst Martin; in Bethge, *Biography*, 257.
374. Hitler, *Mein Kampf*, 497.
375. Bonhoeffer; in Bethge, *Biography*, 257.
376. Ibid., 607.

accompanied by lived witnessing of faith in God, faith which he described as "existence for others . . . through participation in the being of Jesus."[377] It is such fullness of commitment to an active life of discipleship that places one in the arena of Bonhoeffer's "costly grace." Bonhoeffer urged Bethge, "Don't worry about me if something worse [than imprisonment] happens."[378] "Lord, whatever this day may bring," he wrote, "Your name be praised."[379] A fellow prisoner wrote of Bonhoeffer, "He was one of the very few men that I have ever met to whom his God was real and ever close."[380] "I'm not religious by nature," Bonhoeffer stated, "but I can't help thinking all the time of God, of Christ."[381]

---

9. Courage (inner strength) in responding to divine directive (accomplishing task)—*criterion satisfied*

"Faint not nor fear, but go out to the storm and the action, / trusting in God whose commandment you faithfully follow," wrote Bonhoeffer.[382] "We are neither of us dare-devils," he told Bethge, "but that has nothing to do with the courage that comes from the grace of God."[383] "What lies behind the . . . dearth of civil courage?" he pondered. "In recent years we have seen a great deal of bravery and self-sacrifice, but civil courage hardly anywhere."[384] He was one of the exceptions. For Bonhoeffer's defiance of the Hitler regime he suffered two years in prison and execution. He demonstrated unshakable faith and courage throughout his tribulations. "I'm sure that it is good for me personally to undergo all this," he wrote.[385]

During interrogation by the Gestapo, Bonhoeffer courageously declared "that he was an enemy of National Socialism. His attitude, so he . . . stated, was rooted in his Christian convictions."[386] Moreover,

377. Bonhoeffer, *Letters*, 381.
378. Ibid., 173.
379. Ibid., 141.
380. Best, *Venlo*, 180.
381. Bonhoeffer; quoted by Kabitz, in *Love Letters*, 327.
382. Bonhoeffer, "Stations on the Road to Freedom," in *Letters*, 371.
383. Bonhoeffer, *Letters*, 156.
384. Ibid., 5–6.
385. Ibid., 29.
386. Schlabrendorff, "In Prison," 229.

Bonhoeffer displayed courage in the following incident relayed by a fellow inmate at Gestapo headquarters:

> When we returned after an air-raid warning from our cement shelter, his brother-in-law lay on a stretcher in his cell, paralysed in both legs. With an alacrity that nobody would have believed him capable of, Dietrich Bonhoeffer suddenly dived into the open cell of his brother-in-law. It seemed a miracle that none of the warders saw it. But Dietrich also succeeded in . . . emerging from [Hans von] Dohnanyi's cell unnoticed and getting into line with the column of prisoners who were filing along the corridor. That same evening he told me that he had agreed with Dohnanyi upon all essential points of their further testimony.[387]

10. General attentiveness—*criterion satisfied*

It is said that Bonhoeffer "listened attentively and attached great value to dealing politely with other people," always directing his gaze fully toward the individual to whom he spoke.[388] "He was as ready to listen as to speak"[389] and "was courteous by nature."[390] Even in prison, Bonhoeffer was attentive to others. "My thoughts go out to . . . the many unknown people in this building who are bearing their fate in silence," he wrote. "I repeatedly find that these and other thoughts keep me from taking my own little hardships too seriously; that would be very wrong and ungrateful."[391] Paul Lehmann describes Bonhoeffer as "a 'man for others,' taken captive by him whom he" celebrated "as '*the* man for others' [i.e., Jesus]."[392]

Memory plays a role in attentiveness and Bonhoeffer viewed "memory, the recalling of lessons . . . learnt," as a component of "responsible living," citing "mental alertness" as conducive to sympathy.[393] He

---

387. Ibid., 228–29.

388. Leibholz, (Bonhoeffer's twin sister, Sabine), "Childhood," 33. Bethge also describes Bonhoeffer as "a good listener." Bethge, *Biography*, 361.

389. Lehmann, "Paradox," 45. Lehmann was an American theologian.

390. E. Bonhoeffer, "Professors' Children," 34. Emmi was Dietrich's childhood friend and sister-in-law.

391. Bonhoeffer, *Letters*, 50.

392. Lehmann, "Paradox," 45.

393. Bonhoeffer, *Letters*, 3, 13.

and his associates were attentive to events transpiring in Nazi Germany and beyond while millions turned a relatively blind eye. "Where is this 'memory' today?" he asked. "Is not the loss of this 'moral memory' (a horrid expression) responsible for the ruin of all obligations, of love, marriage, friendship, and loyalty? Nothing sticks fast, nothing holds firm; everything is here today and gone tomorrow. But the good things of life—truth, justice, and beauty—. . . need time, constancy, and 'memory', or they degenerate. The man who feels neither responsibility towards the past nor desire to shape the future is one who 'forgets.' . . ."[394]

11. Humility—*criterion satisfied*

Bonhoeffer advocated "modesty" over "snobbery"[395] and was characterized as "all humility and sweetness."[396] He was eager to mitigate the burden of others and confided to Bethge that fellow inmates were fabricating excuses to visit him in the sick bay to chat with him, but he instructed Bethge not to "let it get around."[397] When Bethge indicated that his child might be named Dietrich, Bonhoeffer replied, "The name is good, the model less so."[398] "Nothing goes more against prayer than vanity," he maintained.[399]

Bonhoeffer understood that it is "easy to overestimate the importance of our own achievements in comparison with what we owe to others."[400] "The wish to be independent in everything is false pride," he asserted, "and any attempt to calculate what we have 'earned' for ourselves and what we owe to other people is certainly not Christian, and is, moreover, a futile undertaking."[401] "We may have to face events and changes that take no account of our wishes and our rights," he advised,

---

394. Ibid., 203.
395. Ibid., 13.
396. Best, *Venlo*, 180.
397. Bonhoeffer, *Letters*, 172. Bonhoeffer suffered lumbago, rheumatism, stomach problems, and bouts of influenza while incarcerated but also administered to others in the sick bay on the occasion of air attacks. Bethge, *Biography*, 848, 853.
398. Bonhoeffer, *Letters*, 177.
399. Bonhoeffer; in Bethge, *Biography*, 100.
400. Bonhoeffer, *Letters*, 109.
401. Ibid., 150.

"[b]ut if so, we shall not give way to embittered and barren pride, but consciously submit to divine judgment."[402]

12. Production of good fruit—*criterion satisfied*

As a martyr, Bonhoeffer represents faith witnessed to the ultimate degree. He also exemplifies social conscience, civil courage, respect, compassion, generosity, fortitude, and patience. Moreover, Bonhoeffer endowed posterity with insightful and stimulating theological works and helped to save fourteen lives. Additionally, the conspirators proved that not all Germans supported or acquiesced to the Hitler regime but that some were so strongly committed to peace, justice, and decency as to stake their lives for these. This constitutes a great gift of hope to humanity.

13. Initial hesitation, reluctance, resistance, fear, doubt—*criterion satisfied*

Bonhoeffer's decision in 1939 to accept an academic position in New York, thereby suspending his direct involvement in the German resistance movement against Hitler, encompassed elements of hesitation, reluctance, resistance, possibly fear, and certainly doubt with respect to his perceived divine calling. Bethge explains that, apart from his desire to avoid conscription under Hitler, "Bonhoeffer had a growing sense that if he remained in Germany, he would be drawn more deeply into the conspiracy." He was disappointed by failed attempts to overthrow the Führer and needed to consider whether or not it was "right for him as a pastor and theologian to go beyond the role of accessory, to . . . participate [more directly] in such a conspiracy."[403] Bonhoeffer was confused and, perhaps, as Bethge suggests, desirous subconsciously of evading the dilemma. Could he not serve God more effectively abroad?[404] Bonhoeffer struggled with "great conscientious difficulties." He left Germany in early June, 1939 plagued by doubt. "If only the doubts about my own

---

402. Ibid., 299.
403. Bethge, *Biography*, 636.
404. Ibid., 636–38.

course had been overcome," he wrote.[405] Shortly after his arrival in New York, grappling with whether or not to remain there, Bonhoeffer realized that avoidance of conscription had been a secondary consideration in his decision to leave Europe. By July 7, he was on a ship heading back to Germany.[406]

14. Apparent absurdity requiring faith in God—*criterion not satisfied*

It might seem absurd that a Christian minister committed to the Ten Commandments would feel divinely called to violate one of them by participating in a conspiracy to kill another human being; however, this criterion is not primarily concerned with how others view the prophetic task but with whether or not the individual called views it as absurd, perhaps to the point of impossibility in the absence of divine assistance. Since it was Bonhoeffer's conviction that the Church "must share in the secular problems of ordinary human life,"[407] he did not apparently regard his participation in the conspiracy as absurd but as regrettably necessary. "Even the Sermon on the Mount may not become the letter of the law," he maintained. "In its commandments it is the demonstration of what God's commandment can be, not what it is" in the particular, present moment to which God speaks. "The commandment is not there once and for all," he explained, "but it is given afresh, again and again. Only in this way are we free from the law, which interposes itself between us and God; only in this way do we hear God."[408] It was not his involvement in the action against Hitler that Bonhoeffer considered absurd; rather, he viewed attempts to convert Hitler as absurd. "The Oxford Movement has been naïve enough to try to convert Hitler," he wrote, "a ridiculous failure to understand what is going on."[409] He thought it feasible that the conspiracy would succeed and regarded it as a viable solution to a critical problem.

405. Bonhoeffer; in Bethge, *Biography*, 639, 650.
406. Bethge, *Biography*, 636–38, 661.
407. Bonhoeffer, *Letters*, 382.
408. Bonhoeffer, *No Rusty Swords*, 161.

409. Bonhoeffer; in Bethge, *Biography*, 470. Bonhoeffer's frustration with the Oxford Movement parallels Jehanne's frustration with Charles VII in his attempts to negotiate with the Burgundians who were duping him.

15. Prior lack of inclination, skill, or capacity to behave in required manner—*criterion satisfied*

Bethge indicates that Bonhoeffer's "voice grew softer, not louder" whenever he became angry.[410] Participation in an assassination plot requires receptivity to violence, which appears inconsistent with Bonhoeffer's inclination given that, prior to the full emergence of Nazi brutality, he held a strongly pacifist stance. "The weapons [of Christianity] are faith and love, purified by suffering," he wrote. "The pure love, which first seeks God and God's commandments, prefers to see a defenseless brother slain to seeing" him and his soul "stained with blood," he maintained.[411] In his book, *The Cost of Discipleship*, published in 1937, Bonhoeffer wrote that Christians must "renounce all violence" for the sake of peace.[412] In attempting to defeat Hitler, however, Bonhoeffer resorted to restrained violence. From prison he wrote of *Discipleship*, "Today I can see the dangers of that book. . . ."[413]

16. Feelings of inadequacy—*criterion satisfied*

In the early days of struggle between the Confessing Church (still in its seminal form as the Pastors' Emergency League) and Nazi state, when Bonhoeffer found himself standing alone among fellow opponents of Nazism who invariably seemed too soft on the matter of how German pastors ought to respond to Hitler's Reich Church,[414] he began to question his convictions. "All this has frightened me and shaken my confidence so that I began to fear that dogmatism might be leading me astray—since there seemed no particular reason why my own view in these matters should be any better, any more right, than the views of many really capable pastors whom I sincerely respect," he confided to

---

410. Bethge, *Biography*, xviii.

411. Bonhoeffer; quoted by Jürgen Winterhager, in Bethge, *Biography*, 210. Martin Rumscheidt maintains that the statement should be translated as "him and his soul" rather than "us and our souls," as in the Bethge English text. Rumscheidt, email, November 2, 2012.

412. Bonhoeffer, *Discipleship*, 65. The book was originally published in German as *Nachfolge*.

413. Bonhoeffer, *Letters*, 369.

414. Bethge, *Biography*, 325.

Barth.[415] During this period, Bonhoeffer felt inadequate to determine the validity of his position.

---

17. Feelings of unworthiness to carry out the mission, accompanied by assurance of divine assistance and creating a dependency on God—*criterion satisfied*

Bonhoeffer recognized the unworthiness of all humans before God (himself included), taking the apostle Peter as his example.

> Is he [Peter] of such heroic nature that he towers over the others [the other disciples]? He is not. Is he endowed with such unheard-of strength of character? He is not. Is he gifted with unshakable loyalty? He is not. Peter is nothing, nothing but a man confessing his faith, a man who has been confronted by Christ and who has recognised Christ, and who now confesses his faith in him, and this confessing Peter is called the rock on which Christ will build his church. . . .
>
> But Peter's church—this is not something which one could say with untroubled pride. Peter, the confessing, believing disciple, Peter denied his Lord on the same night as Judas betrayed him; in that night he stood at the fire and felt ashamed when Christ stood before the High Priest; he is the man of little faith, the timid man who sinks into the sea; Peter is the disciple whom Jesus threatened: "Get thee behind me Satan"; it is he who later was again and again overcome by weakness, who again and again denied and fell, a weak, vacillating man, given over to the whim of the moment. . . .
>
> But Peter is also the man of whom we read: "He went out and wept bitterly." . . . Peter's church is not only the church which confesses its faith, nor only the church which denies its Lord; it is the church which can still weep. . . .
>
> [W]e are all Peter; . . . all of us, who simply live from our confession of faith in Christ, as the timid, faithless, faint-hearted, and yet who live as men sustained by God.[416]

Bonhoeffer relied on divine assistance and felt dependent on God. "I believe that God will give us all the strength we need to help us to resist

---

415. Bonhoeffer, in Bethge, *Biography*, 325–26.
416. Bonhoeffer, *No Rusty Swords*, 210–12.

in all time of distress," he wrote. "But he never gives it in advance, lest we should rely on ourselves and not on him alone."[417]

18. Severe disruption to or break from previous lifestyle—*criterion satisfied*

Bethge cites the establishment of Hitler's leadership over Germany in January, 1933 as a turning point in Bonhoeffer's life that propelled him from a relatively private existence into public prominence and prompted the severance of several friendships with individuals who abided Nazi policy.[418] His work for the Confessing Church and the conspiracy further turned Bonhoeffer's life upside down. He went from living legally to living illegally (i.e., illegally under the laws of a corrupt state), teaching in underground seminaries, smuggling Jewish people out of Germany, and engaging in other clandestine operations against the regime, not least of all, the conspiracy. He went from living honestly to living dishonestly, feigning to work for the *Abwehr* while actually working for the resistance movement. Moreover, Bonhoeffer's arrest and imprisonment constituted a marked break from his former lifestyle. "A violent mental upheaval such as is produced by a sudden arrest brings with it the need to take one's mental bearings and come to terms with an entirely new situation," he explained.[419]

19. Personal risk, encounters hostility and/or persecution as a result of prophetic ministry—*criterion satisfied*

On the possibility of being transferred to a concentration camp for his opposition to the Nazi state, Bonhoeffer remarked, "I'm really not at all worried about what happens to me personally."[420] "[W]e must think about things much more important to us than life itself."[421] Bethge indicates that, on entering the resistance movement against Hitler, one abandoned "all outer and inner security . . . [and] renounced command,

417. Bonhoeffer, *Letters*, 11.
418. Bethge, *Biography*, 258–59.
419. Bonhoeffer, *Letters*, 21.
420. Ibid., 213.
421. Ibid., 311.

applause, and the backing of general opinion." One accepted condemnation "before everything and everybody." The situation was such that there had been "a diabolical reversal of all values" and "the most conscientious person was the one who had to accept disgrace" and be branded treasonous.[422] When, before a group of clergy, Bonhoeffer proclaimed it a Christian duty to defend persecuted Jews against the Nazi state, several clerics left the room defiantly.[423] Moreover, while Bonhoeffer was under state persecution, the Confessing Church of which he was a leading member declined to place his name on the intercession list. When he was executed, his own church did not recognize Bonhoeffer as a martyr due to his participation in the conspiracy.[424]

20. Experiences intense solitude, stands as the particular against the status quo—*criterion satisfied*

Even within the Confessing Church, Bonhoeffer stood alone in many respects. "I feel that in some way I don't understand, I find myself in radical opposition to all my friends; I became increasingly isolated with my views of things, even though I was and remain personally close to these people," he explained.[425] In defending "decency and order" against the status quo, Bonhoeffer resolved, one must simply "put up with" accusations of self-interest or "anti-social" behavior.[426]

Bonhoeffer's imprisonment brought intense solitude. "I positively hunger for people after so many months of solitude," he wrote,[427] but in some respects, Bonhoeffer grew to appreciate solitary life. "I've got so used to the silence of solitude . . . that after a short time I long for it again. . . . I would certainly like to have a good talk with someone, but aimless gossip gets on my nerves terribly."[428] Nonetheless, the solitude was so intense that visits by family and friends left Bonhoeffer nearly

---

422. Bethge, *Biography*, 675, 794–95.
423. Kabitz, *Love Letters*, 320.
424. Bethge, *Biography*, 794, 931.
425. Bonhoeffer; in Bethge, *Biography*, 325.
426. Bonhoeffer, *Letters*, 12.
427. Bonhoeffer, *Love Letters*, 128.
428. Bonhoeffer, *Letters*, 271.

ecstatic. Following a visit from Bethge, his parents, and his fiancée, he wrote:

> So it really came off! Only for a moment, but that doesn't matter so much; even a few hours would be far too little, and when we are isolated here we can take in so much that even a few minutes gives us something to think about for a long time afterwards. It will be with me for a long time now—the memory of having the four people who are nearest and dearest to me with me for a brief moment. When I got back to my cell afterwards, I paced up and down for a whole hour, while my dinner stood there and got cold, so that at last I couldn't help laughing at myself when I found myself repeating over and over again, "That was really great!" I always hesitate to use the word "indescribable" about anything, ... but at the moment that is just what this morning seems to be.[429]

21. Ability to prophesy (charism)—*criterion satisfied*

"I won't live beyond thirty-seven," Bonhoeffer predicted.[430] He was not far off the mark as he died at thirty-nine. At age fourteen he had stated that he anticipated "an early death."[431] Bonhoeffer demonstrated prophetic vision on many occasions. In 1932, prior to Hitler's installation to power in 1933, Bonhoeffer forecasted that difficult times requiring martyrdom would return, adding that "this blood ... will not be so innocent and dear as that of the first who testified. On our blood a great guilt would lie: that of the useless servant who is cast into the outer darkness."[432] It is prophetic in that Bonhoeffer was later martyred and died guilty of conspiracy to kill, both conditions arising from the darkness into which Germany was plunged under Hitler. Moreover, as early as 1934, Bonhoeffer branded Hitler "guilty of the next war!"[433] In December, 1943, Bonhoeffer asked Bethge, "[D]o you remember that I prophesied to you last March about what the year would bring?"[434]

429. Ibid., 144–45.
430. Bonhoeffer; quoted by Bismarck, in preface to *Love Letters*, 9.
431. Bethge, *Biography*, 661.
432. Bonhoeffer; in Bethge, *Biography*, 795.
433. Ibid., 358.
434. Bonhoeffer, *Letters*, 174.

Although the letter does not disclose the prophecy, the statement implies that it was accurate, perhaps predicting his own arrest. Bonhoeffer also told a fellow Tegel prisoner "that he was not sure that he would see the end [of Hitler], for he feared that he would . . . be taken to a concentration camp where he would be killed along with other political prisoners. In that case he hoped that he would be able to accept death without fear, in the belief that it was in a just cause."[435] That is, in fact, what occurred. Furthermore, while Bethge was serving as a conscripted soldier in Italy, Bonhoeffer wrote, "[S]ince one day you will be called to write my biography, I want to put the most complete material possible at your disposal!"[436] Despite the fact that Bethge was also involved in the conspiracy and was exposed to the additional perils of military service, Bonhoeffer foresaw that Bethge would outlive him and that his own life and work would be viewed posthumously as significant. In April, 1944, Bonhoeffer wrote:

> I have such a strong feeling that great events are moving the world every day and could change all our personal relationships, that I should like to write to you much oftener, partly because I don't know how much longer I shall be able to. . . . I'm firmly convinced that, by the time you get this letter, great decisions will already be setting things moving on all fronts. During the coming weeks we shall have to keep a stout heart. . . . We shall have to keep all our wits about us, so as to let nothing scare us. In view of what is coming, . . . I feel that I "long to look" . . . to see how God is going to solve the apparently insoluble.[437]

In fact, the subsequent twelve months delivered the death of Hitler and the end of the war, but not without first seeing the imprisonment of Bonhoeffer's brother Klaus, his sister Christine, his brother-in-law Rüdiger Schleicher, Bethge, and others involved in the conspiracy.[438] Also within the year, Bonhoeffer, Klaus, Schleicher, and Dohnanyi were murdered by the Nazis along with others of the conspiracy. Bethge survived and wrote Bonhoeffer's biography of approximately one thousand pages.[439]

---

435. Bonhoeffer; quoted by Gaetano Latmiral, in Bethge, *Biography*, 851.

436. Bonhoeffer, *Letters*, 202.

437. Ibid., 278–79.

438. Dohnanyi was arrested the same day Dietrich Bonhoeffer was, but they were held in separate prisons for the most part. Bethge, *Biography*, 785, 800.

439. Criterion 1 of this section contains Bonhoeffer's prophetically accurate de-

22. Ability to perform miracles (charism)—*criterion not satisfied*

There are no indications that Bonhoeffer was a thaumaturge.

SUMMARY ASSESSMENT—DIVINE, PROPHETIC CALLING

Of the twenty-two criteria indicative of divine, prophetic calling, Bonhoeffer satisfies eighteen (ten essential and eight non-essential), he fails to satisfy two (both non-essential), and two are indeterminate (both essential). Of the twelve essential criteria, ten are met and two are indeterminate. Of the ten non-essential criteria, eight are met. Thus, Bonhoeffer satisfies the vast majority of essential and non-essential criteria in this category and does not violate any essential criteria. Hence, his case can be viewed as representative of divine, prophetic calling in accordance with Jehanne's model, but two categories remain to be evaluated before an overall determination can be made.

Divinely Sanctioned Righteous Warfare Criteria

1. Appeal to most sovereign authority (divinity)—*criterion satisfied*

Scripture was the authority to which Bonhoeffer turned for he considered it a source of God's word to him. While attempting to determine the best time for his return to Germany from America, he consulted the Scripture reading for June 26, 1939 and found, "Do your best to come before winter."[440] Bonhoeffer considered this a personal revelation. "[I]t is not a misuse of scripture if I apply that to myself. If God gives me grace to do it," he resolved.[441] On the voyage home to Germany and war, Bonhoeffer wrote, "Since I have been on the ship my inner uncertainty about the future has ceased. I can think of my shortened time in America without reproaches. Reading: 'It is good for me that I was afflicted, that I might learn thy statutes' (Psalm 119:71)."[442] Again, the daily text spoke

---

scription of the nature and unfolding of his perceived calling.

440. 2 Tim 4:21; in Bethge, *Biography*, 655.
441. Bonhoeffer; in Bethge, *Biography*, 656.
442. Ibid., 661.

to Bonhoeffer's immediate situation. God was the sovereign authority to whom Bonhoeffer appealed in this manner.

2. Defensive, not offensive—*criterion satisfied*

Bonhoeffer's stance was defensive, not offensive, since he moved to eliminate one who routinely oppressed, tortured, and murdered innocent people. He also took a defensive stance against Nazi infiltration and control of the Church.

3. Not pre-emptive—*criterion satisfied*

Bonhoeffer had ongoing access through Dohnanyi, a lawyer with the Reich Ministry of Justice and member of the conspiracy, to information detailing atrocities committed by the Nazi state.[443] It was in this knowledge that Bonhoeffer participated in the plot to eliminate Hitler, as a response, not to the mere possibility of evil, but to evil as an ongoing, manifest reality. He did not act pre-emptively but responsively.

4. Last resort, entreats the enemy to leave or desist peacefully, issues ultimatum. Not killing for its own sake (i.e., killing as an end in itself)—*criterion satisfied*

Bonhoeffer did not engage in killing for its own sake but for the preservation of others. Moreover, the Confessing Church repeatedly attempted unsuccessfully to resolve the conflict with the German Christians diplomatically and, in 1936, issued a memorandum to Hitler citing concerns over National Socialist activities within and beyond the Church.[444] Among other things, the memo charged Hitler with propagating anti-Semitism and voiced disapproval of concentration camps and Gestapo activities. The intent was to allow him to respond to the questions and charges raised. Hence, the memo provided an opportunity for the adversary to desist peacefully, but there was no reasoning with Hitler who

---

443. Bethge, *Biography*, 127, 167, 264, 373, 436, 449, 623–25, 672–73.

444. He was not a signatory to the document but Bonhoeffer was involved in its preparation. Ibid., 531–32.

did not trouble himself to respond.[445] If the Führer was to be stopped, it would not be by diplomatic means. "Hitler ought to and cannot hear; he is obdurate," Bonhoeffer observed.[446] Consequently, an ultimatum from the conspirators would have been no more effective than the memorandum was in altering Hitler's position. Moreover, issuance of an outright ultimatum would have defeated the purpose of conspiracy, which was viewed as the only possibly effective means against Hitler.[447] Ultimatum, while applicable to declarations of war, is not compatible with the nature of conspiracy.

5. Aims to establish just peace—*criterion satisfied*

"Today God's commandment for us is the order of *international peace*," Bonhoeffer asserted, adding that "[t]here can only be a community of peace when it does not rest on *lies* and on *injustice*."[448] "[T]here is no peace unless righteousness and truth are preserved," he emphasized. Where this fails to be the case, "the community of peace must be broken and battle joined" as "[t]here can be a peace which is *worse than struggle*."[449] "In this world there is peace only in the struggle for truth and right," he maintained.[450]

Bonhoeffer's goal was to establish just peace by defending the rights of the wrongly oppressed, by seeking to secure the proper role of the Church against a corrupt, state-dominated Church, and by attempting to prevent World War II and then seeking to end it by overthrowing the Nazi state. "The church has an unconditional obligation to the victims of any ordering of society, even if they do not belong to the Christian community," he asserted. Bonhoeffer witnessed a "reality dominated by hate, enmity, and power . . . as though all the powers of the world had conspired together against peace."[451] "[O]ne feels such a tremendous

---

445. Ibid., 533.
446. Bonhoeffer; in Bethge, *Biography*, 358.
447. Bethge, *Biography*, 793.
448. Bonhoeffer, *No Rusty Swords*, 163–64.
449. Ibid., 164, 183.
450. Ibid., 184.
451. Ibid., 182, 221.

longing for real peace, in which all the misery and injustice, the lying and cowardice will come to an end," he wrote.[452]

6. Proportionate cause—*criterion satisfied*

Proportionate cause was not violated by Bonhoeffer as a specific individual (Hitler) was targeted in an attempt to prevent the murder of millions. While small bombs were utilized in several assassination attempts, which endangered members of Hitler's immediate entourage, the potential (and actual) damage was isolated and limited and did not remotely approach the degree of destruction caused by the Hitler regime that the would-be assassins sought to disable.[453]

7. Does not operate from vengeance or hatred—*criterion satisfied*

Bonhoeffer was not hateful or vengeful. He did not seek to subject the Nazis to suffering or to even a score but to stop their destructive activities. The conspirators did not aim to torture or otherwise torment Hitler but to have him speedily assassinated. Moreover, a fellow inmate indicated that he and Bonhoeffer were of like mind in viewing their concentration camp guards as warranting greater pity than themselves.[454]

8. Does not seek to acquire new territory but might protect or recover rightful lands—*criterion satisfied*

Bonhoeffer had no intention of acquiring new territory but sought to protect his country from an internal enemy, the National Socialist state. He traveled extensively and established many friendships and professional contacts abroad. He was genuinely interested in other cultures and sought to learn from them rather than dominate them.[455]

452. Bonhoeffer; in Bethge, *Biography*, 331.
453. Several people died as a result of the July 20, 1944 assassination attempt on Hitler. Domarus, *Essential Hitler*, 778.
454. S. Payne Best; in Bethge, *Biography*, 920.
455. For example, Bonhoeffer was interested in the black community of Harlem, New York, and was particularly moved by their literature and spiritual music. Bethge, *Biography*, 150.

9. Does not seek domination of others (oppression)—*criterion satisfied*

"Bonhoeffer detested binding men to himself," wrote Albrecht Schönherr,[456] and Bonhoeffer also wrote, "I try, and have always tried, to guide people to complete freedom under the Word and not to bind them to myself."[457] He rejected the imposition of "know-it-all dogmatism" on others.[458] While he could not conscientiously perform active duty as a soldier in defense of Hitlerite Germany, he did not condemn those who did so.[459] Bonhoeffer was not oppressive but sacrificed his life in defense of the wrongly oppressed.

10. Does not engage in holy war—*criterion satisfied*

Bonhoeffer did not engage in holy war since it was on the basis of Hitler's deeds, not his religious convictions, that Bonhoeffer acted against him.

11. Formal declaration of intent to engage in war, warning—*criterion not applicable*

It was not warfare in which Bonhoeffer participated but an attempt to assassinate an individual at the head of his own country. In fact, his involvement in the conspiracy began prior to the war. Moreover, the nature of Bonhoeffer's mission differed from that of all-out war in that open disclosure of his intentions would have ensured their failure. As Bethge points out, "Any responsible resistance under the conditions that existed under Hitler had to take the form of a conspiracy. A spontaneous uprising . . . could not be expected to occur. The spontaneous actions of individuals might be brave, but took no responsibility for the future; and there was not the homogeneous group necessary for a revolution with the eruptive force to lead to new social structures."[460]

---

456. Schönherr, former seminarian in Bonhoeffer's Finkenwalde seminary, "Single-heartedness," 126.
457. Bonhoeffer, *Love Letters*, 229.
458. Bonhoeffer; quoted by Kabitz, in *Love Letters*, 315.
459. Bethge, *Biography*, 637.
460. Ibid., 793.

12. Employs minimal appropriate force (proportionality), minimal bloodshed, forbids unnecessary evil or excessive force—*criterion satisfied*

Since Hitler was unshakable in his beliefs and his determination to carry them out, drastic measures were required if he was to be removed from power and National Socialism defeated. The assassination plot against him was specifically targeted and no attempt was made to destroy the entire National Socialist party membership. Hence, while the measure taken was severe, it was also minimal.

13. Does not target noncombatants—*criterion satisfied*

Bonhoeffer disapproved of arbitrary killing, such as in the targeting of noncombatants. "One must speak of arbitrary killing wherever innocent life is deliberately destroyed," he noted. "[I]t would be arbitrary to kill defenceless prisoners or wounded men who can no longer render themselves guilty of an attack on" another's life.[461] Bonhoeffer's sole target was Hitler; if he were to fall, the entire regime might crumble. Hitler can be categorized as a combatant in that he launched World War II and was at the helm of the German military, issuing the directives to attack. He was not an innocent civilian.

14. Does not employ torture—*criterion satisfied*

Bonhoeffer did not employ torture and asserted that no right to "the use of torture may be derived from the necessity of legal procedures in human society."[462] He considered torture "un-Christian."[463]

15. Does not inflict suffering for its own sake—*criterion satisfied*

Bonhoeffer did not inflict suffering for its own sake and participated in the conspiracy, not to cause affliction, but to relieve the suffering of millions.

461. Bonhoeffer, *Ethics*, 158.
462. Bonhoeffer, *No Rusty Swords*, 166, 183.
463. Bonhoeffer, *Ethics*, 94.

16. Forbids looting—*criterion not applicable*

This criterion is not applicable to Bonhoeffer's situation since he was not engaged in combat. Nonetheless, he did not demonstrate a thieving nature but was very generous.[464]

SUMMARY ASSESSMENT—DIVINELY SANCTIONED RIGHTEOUS WARFARE

Of the sixteen criteria—all essential—indicative of divinely sanctioned righteous warfare, two are not applicable to Bonhoeffer's case and the remaining fourteen are satisfied. Hence, Bonhoeffer's involvement in violence accords with divinely sanctioned righteous warfare as exemplified by Jehanne. Let us now apply the final category of criteria to Bonhoeffer's case.

Divinely Sanctioned Human Agency Criteria

1. Undifferentiated compassion, mercy, forgiveness—*criterion satisfied*

In Bonhoeffer's seminary, enemies were prayed for.[465] Bonhoeffer considered "large-heartedness" the most essential element of sympathy.[466] He was quite selfless and described how, during air attacks near the prison, he thought of loved ones and resolved, "better me than one of them."[467] Bonhoeffer did not begrudge his prison guards but conceded that theirs was "a hard job."[468] "He never demanded the impossible of them, since . . . they too were in a nervous state," explains Bethge.[469] He did, however, distinguish between their malevolent and benevolent behaviors. "The tone is set by those warders who behave in the most evil and brutal way towards the prisoners," he reported. "The whole building resounds with vile and insulting abuse, so that the quieter and more fair-

---

464. See criterion 32 below regarding Bonhoeffer's generosity.
465. Bethge, *Biography*, 464.
466. Bonhoeffer, *Letters*, 13.
467. Ibid., 199. Bonhoeffer did not consider himself "completely selfless." Ibid., 312.
468. Ibid., 25.
469. Bethge, *Biography*, 908.

minded warders, too, are nauseated by it, but they can hardly exercise any influence.... I must not omit to say that a number of the warders are even-tempered, matter-of-fact, and as far as possible, friendly towards the prisoners."[470] Bonhoeffer held that "it is only when God's wrath and vengeance are hanging as grim realities over the heads of one's enemies that something of what it means to love and forgive them can touch our hearts."[471] This is consistent with Jehanne's concern for the spiritual welfare of her enemies, particularly with respect to the state of their souls upon death.

With some success, Bonhoeffer made a concerted (though strained) effort to respond mercifully to an enemy. While imprisoned, a Nazi party leader accompanied him for a time on his daily half-hour walk outdoors. "He has completely gone to pieces here," Bonhoeffer reported, "and clings to me just like a child, consulting me about every little thing, telling me whenever he has cried, etc. After being very cool with him for several weeks, I'm now able to ease things for him a little; his gratitude is quite touching, and he tells me again and again how glad he is to have met a man like me here."[472] Later, Bonhoeffer wrote, "The propagandist with whom I walk every day is really getting more and more difficult to put up with. Whereas most people here do try to keep control of themselves, even in the most difficult cases, he has completely gone to pieces, and cuts a really sorry figure. I try to be as nice as I can to him, and talk to him as if he were a child."[473] Eventually, the man triggered Bonhoeffer's righteous anger.

> I've had to take a new line with the companion of my daily walks. Although he has done his best to ingratiate himself with me, he let fall a remark about the Gert [Jewish] problem, etc., lately that has made me more offhanded and cool to him than I have ever been to anyone before; I've also arranged for him to be deprived promptly of all little comforts. Now he feels obliged to go round whimpering for a time, but it leaves me—I am surprised myself, but interested too—absolutely cold. He really is a pitiful figure.[474]

470. Bonhoeffer, *Letters*, 249–50. It was prison guards who smuggled correspondence between Bonhoeffer and Bethge. Bethge, *Biography*, 847–48. Correspondence between Bonhoeffer and his fiancée was also smuggled.

471. Bonhoeffer, *Letters*, 157.

472. Ibid., 157–58.

473. Ibid. 172.

474. Ibid., 194–95. The comforts of which Bonhoeffer had the man deprived had been arranged at Bonhoeffer's request. Bethge, *Biography*, 850.

It seems unlikely that Bonhoeffer intended this as an act of cruelty but more likely as an act of punishment and instruction. The man behaved as a child and was punished as a child in order to convey a lesson—a very critical lesson as anti-Semitism is not child's play. In fact, it was not for Bonhoeffer to forgive the man's offenses against the Jewish people; it is for one to forgive only what is done to oneself. Bonhoeffer perceived an urgent need for humans to develop a "less corruptible" view "of generosity, humanity, justice and mercy,"[475] and his walking companion fell severely short. Bonhoeffer also upbraided the man for extreme cowardice during bombings and for whining as though all the prisoners were not exposed to the same danger.[476] "I don't really think I find it easy to despise anyone in trouble, . . . but I can only regard that as contemptible," he wrote. "It is weakness rather than wickedness that perverts a man and drags him down."[477] "The sins of weakness are the really human sins, whereas the wilful sins are diabolical," he explained.[478] Again, his response to the fellow was instructional, as when Jesus expelled the money changers from the temple.[479]

Jehanne was also stern with those who behaved offensively, and she disliked Burgundians, although this did not remove them from her sphere of compassion when they were wounded or died without confession. It was arguably similar with Bonhoeffer since it was the man's offensive attitude and behavior that repulsed him and did not warrant compassion in his eyes, whereas physical or spiritual crisis would likely have drawn a merciful response. Undifferentiated compassion does not rule out the possibility of a reproachful or sternly disapproving attitude toward others. Bonhoeffer held that "patience and joy and gratitude and serenity and forgiveness must keep fighting and prevailing over all

---

475. Bonhoeffer, *Letters*, 17.

476. Ibid., 204–5. "When the bombs come shrieking down," Bonhoeffer wrote to Bethge, who was on conscripted military duty in Italy, "I always think how trivial it all is compared with what you're going through out there. It often makes me downright angry to see how some people behave in such situations, and how little they think of what is happening to other people. The danger here never lasts more than a few minutes." Ibid., 372.

477. Ibid., 205, 384.

478. Ibid., 392.

479. Matt 21:12–13.

forms of opposition,"⁴⁸⁰ and the offender was not cast beyond his sphere of compassion as Bonhoeffer pitied him.

2. Honors the sanctity of life—*criterion satisfied*

Bonhoeffer believed that "it is only when one loves life and the earth so much that without them everything seems to be over that one may believe in the resurrection and a new world."⁴⁸¹ In honoring the sanctity of the lives of others, he relinquished all personal security.

3. Respects the dignity of the person—*criterion satisfied*

During Bonhoeffer's first trip to America (1930–31), he befriended an Afro-American named Frank Fisher. When the two attempted to dine at a fine restaurant, Fisher was refused customary service on account of his ethnicity and Bonhoeffer responded by "ostentatiously" leaving the establishment.⁴⁸² He considered it the duty of Christianity to "defend passionately human dignity and reserve,"⁴⁸³ and he did this to the death.

4. Fully-engaged conscience—*criterion satisfied*

A colleague described Bonhoeffer as "prepared to accept any sufferings but . . . [unable] in conscience [to] remain in the New [Reich] Church."⁴⁸⁴ Bonhoeffer knew intimately the power of engaged conscience. "[T]he summons of conscience . . . remains irresistible," he wrote.⁴⁸⁵ In 1939, when Bonhoeffer arrived in New York, did an about-face, and headed back to Germany, it was largely conscience that compelled him to do so. "To be here [in New York]," he wrote, "during a catastrophe [in Germany] is simply unthinkable, unless things are so ordained. But to be guilty of it myself, and to have to reproach myself that I left [Germany] unnec-

---

480. Bonhoeffer, *Love Letters*, 69.
481. Bonhoeffer, *Letters*, 157.
482. Bethge, "Friends," 49.
483. Bonhoeffer, *Letters*, 12.
484. H. L. Henriod, a leading ecumenical representative in Switzerland; in Bethge, *Biography*, 356.
485. Bonhoeffer, *Ethics*, 243.

essarily, is certainly devastating."[486] Guilt related to participation in the conspiracy was weighed against the guilt of inaction as Bonhoeffer experienced a conflict of conscience, that is, "the conjunction of conflicting obligations" wherein "conscience can show no possibility of action that does not entail sin."[487] This occurs only when one's conscience is fully engaged.

5. Operates from a driving force of love—*criterion satisfied*

According to one of his associates, "[r]eal faith and love were identical" to Bonhoeffer and comprised the "heart and core" of his existence.[488] Bonhoeffer operated from a driving force of love, distinguishing between emotional, personal love and less personal, spiritual love. "Because spiritual love does not desire but rather serves, it loves an enemy as a brother," he explained. "It originates neither in the brother nor in the enemy but in Christ and his Word. Human love can never understand spiritual love, for spiritual love is from above; it is something completely strange . . . and incomprehensible to all earthly love."[489] "Almost all the people that I find in my present surroundings cling to their own desires," he observed in prison, "and so have no interest in others; they no longer listen, and they're incapable of loving their neighbour. I think that even in this place we ought to live as if we had no wishes and no future, and just be our true selves," he reflected.[490] Bonhoeffer's concern for and efforts to assist others dominated any concern over his physical well-being and demonstrated genuine, spiritual love.

6. Genuine distress concerning all bloodshed, not desensitized to violence or suffering—*criterion satisfied*

The murderous practices of the Nazi regime distressed Bonhoeffer so greatly that he laid his life on the line in opposition. Even the prospect

---

486. Bonhoeffer; in Bethge, *Biography*, 654.
487. Hofmann, "Conscience," 287.
488. Rott, pastor and Bonhoeffer's assistant at the Finkenwalde seminary, "Something Always Occurred," 134.
489. Bonhoeffer, *Life Together*, 35.
490. Bonhoeffer, *Letters*, 233–34.

of shedding the blood of the man at the helm of Nazi brutality troubled him, and he sought pacifist solutions before entering the conspiracy.[491] "The destruction of the life of another may be undertaken only on the basis of an unconditional necessity," he asserted.[492]

After a year in prison, Bonhoeffer pondered the distinction between "the growth of insensitivity" and "the clarification of experience." It is toward unimportant things that one becomes insensitive, he concluded, while important experiences become ingrained and create "convictions, resolutions, and plans, and as such they're important for our lives in the future."[493] "Today I can take a calmer view of other people, their predicaments and needs," he explained, "and so I'm better able to help them. I would speak of clarification rather than of insensitiveness." It is important to "keep a warm heart as well as a cool head," he advised.[494]

7. Sense of duty to God, God served first in all things—*criterion satisfied*

Bishop George K. A. Bell of Chichester stated that when Bonhoeffer visited him "as an emissary from the Opposition [to Hitler], he was . . . completely candid, completely regardless of personal safety, while deeply moved by the shame of the country he loved [i.e., Germany]." He was "undaunted, detached from himself, devoted to his friends, to his home, to his country as God meant it to be, to his Church, to his Master."[495] Bonhoeffer found it extremely difficult to desire Germany's defeat under Hitler but regarded it as necessary since the "Nazis had a fanatically tragic will to involve everyone in the catastrophe"[496] they were creating. Bonhoeffer held that in "light of the great purpose all our privations and disappointments are trivial. . . . However thankful we may be for all

---

491. In 1934 it was "unthinkable to Bonhoeffer to join a conspiracy against Hitler; he sought a prototype for passive resistance that could induce changes without violence" and hoped to visit Gandhi in order to become educated in the practice of nonviolent resistance to despotic rule. Bethge, *Biography*, 409.

492. Bonhoeffer, *Ethics*, 159.

493. Bonhoeffer, *Letters*, 277.

494. Ibid., 276.

495. Bell, foreword to *Discipleship*, xi.

496. Latmiral; in Bethge, *Biography*, 851.

our personal pleasures, we mustn't for a moment lose sight of the great things that we're living for."[497]

8. Love of God, piety—*criterion satisfied*

Lehmann described Bonhoeffer as a man of "quiet piety,"[498] while Reinhold Niebuhr noted his special blend of "sophisticated theology and simple piety."[499] According to Bethge, Bonhoeffer's students sometimes viewed his piety as "too fervent" but simultaneously "impressive . . . because it was accompanied by theological rigor and a broad cultural background."[500]

Bonhoeffer was devoted to God in his ordained ministry and academic pursuits but, above all, in his daily life. In prison, he wrote of reading psalms and hymns as part of his daily routine. "I am reading the Bible straight through from cover to cover. . . . I read the Psalms every day, as I have done for years; I know them and love them more than any other book."[501] "When the bells rang this morning, I longed to go to church," he reported, "but instead I did as John did on the island of Patmos, and had such a splendid service of my own, that I did not feel lonely at all."[502] "It's remarkable what power church bells have over human beings, and how deeply they can affect us," he marveled.[503] Bonhoeffer spoke of the "long months without worship, penitence and eucharist and without the *consolatio fratrum*."[504]

9. Fear of God—*criterion satisfied*

Bonhoeffer's message to his godchild reflects fear and love of God as he explained "that the world lies under the wrath and grace of God" and

---

497. Bonhoeffer, *Letters*, 289–90.
498. Lehmann, "Paradox," 45.
499. Niebuhr, "America and Back," 165.
500. Bethge, *Biography*, 204.
501. Bonhoeffer, *Letters*, 27, 40.
502. Ibid., 53.
503. Ibid., 73. Jehanne was also deeply moved by church bells. "When she was in the fields, she used to go down on her knees every time she heard the bell tolled," a playmate testified. Waterin; in Pernoud, *Retrial*, 87.
504. Bonhoeffer, *Letters*, 128.

the child would be taught "to fear and love God above everything, and to do the will of Jesus Christ."⁵⁰⁵ In 1932, Bonhoeffer warned against false piety and misappropriation of the divine name, declaring that, in such situations, "the more pious we are, the less we let ourselves be told that God is dangerous, that God will not be mocked."⁵⁰⁶

10. Permits nothing to come between self and God, accepts no human deterrent—*criterion satisfied*

When Bonhoeffer discerned that it was God's will that he return to Germany from America in 1939, it was against the wishes of friends who were concerned for his safety in Germany.⁵⁰⁷ "There ... happen to be things that are worth an uncompromising stand. And it seems to me that peace and social justice, or Christ himself, are such things," he maintained.⁵⁰⁸ The prospect of imprisonment—or worse—did not deter him from his mission or faith in God. Bonhoeffer assured Dohnanyi, who was also imprisoned, "[Y]ou must know that there is not even an atom of reproach or bitterness in me about what has befallen the two of us."⁵⁰⁹

11. Mystical relationship transcends institutionalization or religious formulas, mystical defiance—*criterion satisfied*

While Bonhoeffer may not have self-identified as a mystic, he thought, behaved, lived, and died as one in many respects. He longed "to feel divine grace active in his life."⁵¹⁰ Bonhoeffer disapprovingly characterized nineteenth- and twentieth-century religion as "the so-called quiet room to which one gladly withdraws for a couple of hours before returning to the office."⁵¹¹ On the conviction that religion can impede true discipleship, he advocated "religionless Christianity"⁵¹² whereby "[t]he church is

---

505. Ibid., 296–97.
506. Bonhoeffer; in Bethge, *Biography*, 236.
507. Bethge, *Biography*, 651, 656–57.
508. Bonhoeffer; in Bethge, *Biography*, 206.
509. Bonhoeffer, *Letters*, 32.
510. Bethge, "Friends," 48.
511. Bonhoeffer; in Wüstenberg, *Theology of Life*, 3.
512. Wüstenberg, *Theology of Life*, 75.

the incarnate, judged human being in Christ who has been awakened to new life.... [I]t has essentially nothing to do with the so-called religious functions of human beings, but with the whole person in that person's existence in the world," he explained.[513] In suffering with God in faith, Bonhoeffer maintained, "[t]here is nothing of religious method.... The 'religious act' is always something partial; 'faith' is something whole, involving the whole of one's life. Jesus calls men, not to a new religion, but to life." He cautioned, however, that, "[w]hen we speak of God in a 'non-religious' way, we must speak... in such a way that the godlessness of the world is not in some way concealed, but rather revealed."[514]

One who does not conform to the dictates of a particular religious (or moral) system inevitably steps (or is cast) outside of it in some way. This does not mean that such an individual must abandon all aspects of his or her religious practice but that she or he must be willing to transcend ordinary boundaries of religion if necessary. Jehanne maintained her primary commitment to the "Church Triumphant on high,"[515] stepping beyond the earthly Church, and was cast out (excommunicated) by some for her form of discipleship. Bonhoeffer's concept of religionless Christianity and his participation in the conspiracy likewise transcended ordinary religious boundaries and render(ed) his form of discipleship anathema to some.[516]

12. Conviction, determination, persistence, endurance, uncompromised, singular commitment to declared mission— *criterion satisfied*

Bell described Bonhoeffer as "crystal clear in his convictions; and young as he was, and humble-minded as he was, he saw the truth, and spoke it with a complete absence of fear."[517] "I have no wish to live in any other time than our own," Bonhoeffer wrote from prison, "even though it is so inconsiderate of our outward well-being."[518] "[M]y attitude towards my

---

513. Bonhoeffer; in Wüstenberg, *Theology of Life*, 18.
514. Bonhoeffer, *Letters*, 362.
515. Jehanne; in Scott, *Trial*, 122.
516. See criterion 19 above under Divine, Prophetic Calling.
517. Bell, foreword to *Discipleship*, xi.
518. Bonhoeffer, *Letters*, 297.

case is unquestionably one of faith.... I can (I hope) bear all things 'in faith', even my condemnation, and even the other consequences that I fear."[519] Bonhoeffer reminded fellow inmates "that the only fight which is lost is that which we give up."[520] Despite his tribulations and the darkness that permeated Nazi Germany, Bonhoeffer persisted, in faith, to the end.

13. Does not engage in or encourage suicide, does not seek suffering or martyrdom—*criterion satisfied*

Even as a prisoner, Bonhoeffer demonstrated "deep gratitude for the mere fact that he was alive."[521] Bonhoeffer believed "that we ought so to love and trust God in our *lives*, and in all the good things that he sends us, that when the time comes (but not before!) we may go to him with love, trust, and joy."[522] The "not before" qualification suggests disapprobation of suicide confirmed by the following passage:

> The freedom in which man possesses his bodily life requires him to accept this life freely, and at the same time it directs his attention to what lies beyond this bodily life and impels him to regard the life of his body as a gift that is to be preserved and as a sacrifice that is to be offered....
> In his liberty to die, man is given a unique power which can easily lead to abuse. Man can ... by his own free decision seek death in order to avoid defeat....
> A man who takes his own life incurs guilt solely towards God. ... It is because there is a living God that suicide is wrongful as a sin of lack of faith.[523]

Bonhoeffer did not seek suffering but accepted it as a consequence of lived faith. Although he may at times have appeared to carry the burden with ease, he suffered deeply. "Joy is a thing that we want very badly in this solemn building, where one never hears a laugh," he stated, "and we exhaust all our reserves of it from within and without."[524]

---

519. Ibid., 173.
520. Bonhoeffer; quoted by Schlabrendorff, "In Prison," 228.
521. Best, *Venlo*, 180.
522. Bonhoeffer, *Letters*, 168.
523. Bonhoeffer, *Ethics*, 164–66.
524. Bonhoeffer, *Letters*, 49.

> It's possible to get used to physical hardships, and to live for months out of the body, so to speak . . . but one doesn't get used to the psychological strain; on the contrary, I have the feeling that everything that I see and hear is putting years on me, and I'm often finding the world nauseating and burdensome. . . . I often wonder who I really am—the man who goes on squirming under these ghastly experiences in wretchedness that cries to heaven, or the man who scourges himself and pretends to others (and even to himself) that he is placid, cheerful, composed, and in control of himself, and allows people to admire him for it (i.e. for playing the part—or is it not playing a part?). What does one's attitude mean, anyway? In short, I know less than ever about myself, and I'm no longer attaching any importance to it. I've had more than enough psychology, and I'm less and less inclined to analyse the state of my soul. . . . There is something more at stake than self-knowledge.[525]

Bonhoeffer experienced episodes of acedia. He wrote to Bethge, "You are the only person who knows how often *accidie, tristitia*, with all its menacing consequences, has lain in wait for me."[526] "It would probably not be true to say that we welcome death (although we all know that weariness which we ought to avoid like the plague)."[527] "I sometimes feel as if my life were more or less over, and as if all I had to do now were to finish my *Ethics*. But, you know, when I feel like this, there comes over me a longing . . . to have a child and not to vanish without a trace."[528]

During a prison transport in which Bonhoeffer and fifteen fellow captives did not know to where or what they were destined, the driver of the van in which they were travelling was signaled by two police officers to stop and several prisoners were commanded by name to depart with the officers,[529] at which time "Bonhoeffer leaned back so as not to be seen."[530] It was assumed by the remaining prisoners that those who

---

525. Ibid., 162.

526. Ibid., 129.

527. Ibid., 16.

528. Ibid., 163. Bonhoeffer died before finishing his *Ethics*. Bethge retrieved parts of the manuscript which had been hidden from the Nazis; other parts were confiscated. He compiled and organized the work and published it in 1949. Bethge, preface to *Ethics*, 11–14.

529. Best, *Venlo*, 190, 192.

530. Bethge, *Biography*, 922.

Applying the Model

had departed were to be executed,[531] and Bonhoeffer did not wish to offer himself up for martyrdom unnecessarily. Despite his afflictions, he intended to endure.

14. Reluctantly accepts suffering or martyrdom if necessary to mystical witnessing—*criterion satisfied*

"When Christ calls a man," wrote Bonhoeffer, "he bids him come and die."[532] "It is infinitely easier to suffer in obedience to a human command than in the freedom of one's own responsibility," he explained. "It is infinitely easier to suffer with others than to suffer alone. It is infinitely easier to suffer publicly and honourably than apart and ignominiously. It is infinitely easier to suffer through staking one's life than to suffer spiritually. Christ suffered as a free man alone, apart and in ignominy, in body and spirit; and since then many Christians have suffered with him."[533] "It is we ourselves," Bonhoeffer maintained, "and not outward circumstances, who make death what it can be, a death freely and voluntarily accepted."[534]

Bonhoeffer's eldest brother wrote to his children in June of 1945, "Uncle Dietrich spoke to someone at length on 5 April, in the neighbourhood of Passau. From there he is said to have gone to the concentration camp at Flossenbürg. Why isn't he here yet?"[535]

> On the morning of that day [April 9, 1945] between five and six o'clock the prisoners ... were taken from their cells, and the verdicts of the court martial read out to them. Through the half-open door in one room of the huts I saw Pastor Bonhoeffer, before taking off his prison garb, kneeling on the floor praying fervently to his God. I was most deeply moved by the way this lovable man prayed, so devout and so certain that God heard his prayer. At the place of execution, he again said a short prayer and then climbed the steps to the gallows, brave and composed. His

---

531. Best, *Venlo*, 192.
532. Bonhoeffer; quoted by Doberstein, introduction to *Life Together*, 8.
533. Bonhoeffer, *Letters*, 14.
534. Ibid., 16.
535. Karl-Friedrich Bonhoeffer; in Bonhoeffer, *Letters*, 410. On April 5, 1945, a stop was made at the Regensburg prison while Bonhoeffer was being transported. Bonhoeffer's fiancée and family did not learn of his martyrdom for months. Bethge; in Bonhoeffer, *Letters*, 410–11.

death ensued after a few seconds. In the almost fifty years that I worked as a doctor, I have hardly ever seen a man die so entirely submissive to the will of God.[536]

Bonhoeffer knew that to respond affirmatively to what he perceived as his divine calling in the face of Nazi power in Germany was to risk his life.[537] He did not wish to die as a result of this action and maintained hope that he would one day be released from prison,[538] but he accepted the consequences when death arrived to take him. His last known words were, "This is the end. For me the beginning of life...."[539]

15. Steadfast faith in God and divine revelation—*criterion satisfied*

Bonhoeffer advocated "faith that endures *in* the world and loves and remains true to that world in spite of all the hardships it brings."[540] To fellow-prisoner, Dohnanyi, he wrote, "What we cannot do, we must now simply let go of and limit ourselves to what we can and should do, that is, be manly and strong in trust in God in the midst of our suffering." Bonhoeffer firmly believed that Bethge's "ways" were "being directed from above and that this is better than everything that we undertake. Certainly one must try everything, but only to become more certain what God's way is," he advised, adding that, "[i]n suffering, . . . deliverance consists in our being allowed to put the matter out of our own hands into God's hands."[541] Moreover, Bonhoeffer bore witness to God in death by praying at the scene of his execution.[542]

---

536. Fischer-Hüllstrung, doctor at Flossenbürg concentration camp, "Report from Flossenbürg," 232.

537. Bonhoeffer's father wrote of his sons, Dietrich and Klaus, that they were "fully aware of what they could expect if the plot miscarried, and had resolved if necessary to lay down their lives." Karl Bonhoeffer; in Bethge, *Biography*, 933.

538. While in prison, Bonhoeffer anticipated marriage and wrote frequently to his parents of his hope for reunion with them.

539. Bonhoeffer, April 8, 1945, on being summoned for execution; quoted by Best, *Venlo*, 200.

540. Bonhoeffer, *Love Letters*, 64.

541. Bonhoeffer, *Letters*, 32, 320, 375. Bonhoeffer's faith in divine revelation is discussed under criterion 1, Divine, Prophetic Calling category.

542 Fischer-Hüllstrung, "Report from Flossenbürg," 232.

16. Apprehension of the intrinsically evil nature of human violence and war, does not attempt to qualify evil—*criterion satisfied*

Bonhoeffer recognized violence as intrinsically evil. "[Stanley] Baldwin was right," he asserted, "when he said that there was only one greater evil than violence and that this was violence as a principle, as a law and a standard." This does not, however, negate the possibility of an "extraordinary and abnormal necessity of the use of violence" in unusual circumstances, he added.[543]

Bonhoeffer held that "[w]hat is worse than doing evil is being evil."[544] This does not suggest a qualification of evil but a distinction between the good person who commits evil and the evil person who commits evil. The qualification is in the quality of the agent, not of the evil itself; evil remains evil, unqualified. The implication is that it is worse when an evil person commits evil than when a good person commits evil because, when an evil person commits evil, evil intent dominates the situation and compounds the presence of evil whereas, when a good person commits evil (out of necessity), qualities of goodness, such as restraint and compassion, are brought to bear upon the evil action and mitigate the situation in which evil is present. A potential quantitative (but not qualitative) distinction arises between evil committed with evil intent and evil committed with good intent, impacting the quality of the overall situation in which evil occurs.

17. Recognition of personal defilement sustained through the use of violence—*criterion satisfied*

"Evil dwells in the heart of the criminal without being felt there. It is felt in the heart of the man who is afflicted and innocent,"[545] states Weil. Bonhoeffer observed that, when confronted with evil, people sometimes "flee from public altercation into the sanctuary of private *virtuousness*." But a person who behaves in this manner must become silent and blind to the surrounding injustice. "Only at the cost of self-deception," he

---

543. Bonhoeffer, *Ethics*, 235.
544. Ibid., 67.
545. Weil, *Waiting for God*, 70.

maintained, can such an individual "keep himself pure from the contamination arising from responsible action."⁵⁴⁶ Bonhoeffer asserted that one who values one's "personal innocence" over one's responsibility toward others is oblivious to the guilt thereby acquired. "[R]eal innocence," he asserted, arises when one incurs "guilt for the sake of" others. "[I]f . . . I refuse to bear guilt for charity's sake, then my action is in contradiction to my responsibility."⁵⁴⁷ "Civil courage . . . depends on a God who demands responsible action in a bold venture of faith, and who promises forgiveness and consolation to the man who becomes a sinner in that venture."⁵⁴⁸

18. Deep sensitivity to evil vs. indifference—*criterion satisfied*

In the context of Hitler's Germany, Bonhoeffer observed that "the world is controlled by forces against which reason can do nothing."⁵⁴⁹ Contemplating the response of individuals to the evil reign of Nazism, Bonhoeffer asked, "Who stands fast? Only the man . . . who is ready to sacrifice all . . . when he is called to obedient and responsible action in faith and in exclusive allegiance to God—the responsible man, who tries to make his whole life an answer to the question and call of God. Where are these responsible people?"⁵⁵⁰ "I see that composure isn't part of my nature," he conceded, "but that I have to acquire it at the cost of repeated effort. In fact, natural composure is probably in most cases nothing but a euphemism for indifference and indolence, and to that extent it's not very estimable."⁵⁵¹ Bonhoeffer was extremely sensitive to the depth and breadth of evil that surrounded him.

546. Bonhoeffer, *Letters*, 5.
547. Bonhoeffer, *Ethics*, 238, 241.
548. Bonhoeffer, *Letters*, 6.
549. Ibid., 298.
550. Ibid., 5.
551. Ibid., 191.

19. Impatient with injustice, prone to righteous anger—*criterion satisfied*

Bonhoeffer considered "prayer and righteous action" core Christian activities.[552] At age sixteen, Bonhoeffer responded with righteous anger to the assassination of Germany's Foreign Minister, a Jewish man named Walther Rathenau. A classmate recalled "Bonhoeffer's passionate indignation, his deep and spontaneous anger" and the fact that he knew "exactly where he stood" on the matter.[553] Much later, in prison, Bonhoeffer's righteous anger flared in different circumstances.

> Two or three times here I've given people a quite colossal dressing down for indulging in only the slightest rudeness, and they were so disconcerted that they have behaved very correctly since then. I thoroughly enjoy this sort of thing, but I know it's really an impossible over-sensitiveness that I can hardly get rid of.... It makes me furious to see quite defenceless people being unjustly shouted at and insulted. These petty tormentors, who can rage like that and whom one finds everywhere, get me worked up for hours on end.[554]

Observing that several young prisoners in lengthy solitary confinement were unable to cope, Bonhoeffer was again angered. "That's another idiotic thing," he wrote, "locking these people in for months on end with nothing to do; it's absolutely demoralizing in every possible way."[555] Righteousness was an aspect of his character and Bonhoeffer perceived and was angered by an entire spectrum of injustices.

---

20. Righteous character (not self-righteous), ethical code of conduct (e.g., chivalry), moral discernment, holds self and others to high ethical standard of behavior—*criterion satisfied*

There are many examples of Bonhoeffer's righteous character. For instance, he declined appointment to a pastorate in Berlin in 1933 because, "in view of the so-called 'Aryanization' of the clergy under the Nazi laws,

---

552. Ibid., 300.
553. Peter H. Olden; in Bethge, *Biography*, 33.
554. Bonhoeffer, *Letters*, 136.
555. Ibid., 164.

... he could not be in a ministry which had become a racial privilege. I cannot recall or imagine any other man to have taken this line of solidarity with those of us who had to resign their pastorates under the legislation," wrote Franz Hildebrandt.[556]

Bonhoeffer disapproved of "total war," which he described as employing "all conceivable means which may possibly serve the purpose of national self-preservation."[557] "[T]here remain only a few 'last survivors of the age of chivalry,'" he observed.[558] (Bonhoeffer himself reportedly possessed "inborn chivalry."[559]) "[I]n the place of a chivalrous war between Christian peoples ... there comes total war," he explained, "war of destruction, in which everything, even crime, is [considered] justified."[560]

Bonhoeffer practiced moral discernment with intensity. "One may ask whether there have ever before in human history been people with so little ground under their feet—people to whom every available alternative seemed equally intolerable, repugnant, and futile," he wrote against a backdrop of war, genocide, and conspiracy. "The great masquerade of evil has played havoc with all our ethical concepts. For evil to appear disguised as light, charity, historical necessity, or social justice is quite bewildering to anyone brought up on our traditional ethical concepts, while for the Christian who bases his life on the Bible it merely confirms the fundamental wickedness of evil."[561] It is the responsibility of a state to create "law and order," not "lawlessness and disorder," he maintained, and it is within the purview of the individual Christian to proclaim the inhumanity of a corrupt state.[562]

Bonhoeffer held himself and others to a high ethical standard, writing to a colleague, "[I]f we're really honest with ourselves, we do know ... what is right and what is wrong. Someone has got to show the way, fearlessly and unflinchingly—why not you? ... Christ is looking down at us and asking whether there is anyone who still confesses him."[563]

---

556. Hildebrandt, a Jewish friend of Bonhoeffer and fellow theologian, "Oasis," 39.

557. Bonhoeffer, *Ethics*, 93–94.

558. Bonhoeffer, *Letters*, 280.

559. Leibholz, (Gerhard), "Memoir," xiii. Bonhoeffer was described even in childhood as "a very chivalrous boy." Leibholz, (Sabine), "Childhood," 27.

560. Bonhoeffer, *Ethics*, 94.

561. Bonhoeffer, *Letters*, 3, 4.

562. Bonhoeffer, *No Rusty Swords*, 219–20.

563. Bonhoeffer; in Bethge, *Biography*, 368–69. The letter urges Henriod to break

21. Teaches by example over doctrine—*criterion satisfied*

Bonhoeffer taught by example over doctrine. As a theologian, pastor, and director of a seminary, he taught doctrine, but he also questioned it and formulated his own original thought, encouraging others to do likewise.[564] Moreover, he held that doctrine ought to be accompanied by concrete action in the world. Bonhoeffer's concept of cheap grace cites as insufficient the notion of grace as doctrine alone and he advocated costly grace as the true path of Christian discipleship.[565] Bonhoeffer taught ultimately by example, practicing what he preached and preaching only what he was willing to practice.

22. Service-oriented, work ethic, disinclination toward idleness or sloth—*criterion satisfied*

"Bonhoeffer's work habits were especially remarkable," notes Bethge. "He accomplished in two or three hours what to someone else would have seemed a normal day's work."[566] He had a strong, service-oriented work ethic and utilized his time to the utmost, even in prison. "Our day lasts fourteen hours, of which I spend about three walking up and down the cell—several kilometers a day," he explained, "besides half an hour in the yard. I read, learn, and work."[567] He regularly requested books from family members and availed himself of the Tegel prison library. "The stormy happenings in the world . . . go right through one, and I wish I could be doing useful service somewhere or other, but at present that 'somewhere' must be in the prison cell," he resolved. "I've never had a

---

with the German Christian Reich Church.

564. "In the seminary . . . he approved of trial sermons if they were good, though they might be very different from the way he would have composed them." Schönherr, "Single-heartedness," 128.

565. Bonhoeffer, *Discipleship*, 3–5.

566. Bethge, *Biography*, 429.

567. Bonhoeffer, *Letters*, 29. Bonhoeffer repeatedly referred to his academic work conducted in prison. Bethge reproduces Bonhoeffer's extensive reading list pertaining to the period of his captivity. Bethge, *Biography*, 943–46. Bonhoeffer exercised (walked) in prison to maintain health in the interest of holding out under possible torture so as not to betray the conspiracy or its members. Ibid., 811. Bonhoeffer was threatened with torture during interrogation and was warned that his parents, fiancée, and sisters would be arrested if he did not confess. Schlabrendorff, "In Prison," 227–29.

moment's boredom in the five months and more that I've been here. My time is always fully occupied."[568] "I've again been doing a good deal of writing," he later reported, "and for the work that I have set myself to do, the day is often too short, so that sometimes, comically enough, I even feel that I have 'no time' here for this or that less important matter!" After fifteen months in prison, Bonhoeffer wrote, "I'm doing as much writing and composing as much poetry as my strength allows."[569] "You've no idea how liberated I . . . would feel if I were once more able to work for others instead of solely for myself."[570]

23. Seeks to empower the disenfranchised, partisan with the wrongly oppressed—*criterion satisfied*

"[W]here the world oppresses," Bonhoeffer wrote, the Christian "will stoop down and raise up the oppressed."[571] While studying in New York in 1930–31, Bonhoeffer befriended members of the black community in the impoverished Harlem district. "He had a gift for restoring pride and self-confidence to the vulnerable and the sensitive," explains Bethge.[572] Bonhoeffer's involvement in the escape of several Jewish citizens from Nazi Germany[573] also exemplifies his partisanship with the disenfranchised. He spoke out when Jewish citizens were banned from Church and state,[574] from professional posts, and from university education, and also when the Nazis vandalized their property, boycotted their businesses, and murdered them. The state fails "in its function of creating law and order" when it produces an excess or a deficiency of law and order, Bonhoeffer asserted. "There would be too little law if any group of subjects were deprived of their rights, too much where the state intervened in the character of the church and its proclamation, e.g., in the forced

---

568. Bonhoeffer, *Letters*, 22, 27, 109.
569. Ibid., 119, 358.
570. Bonhoeffer, *Love Letters*, 260.
571. Bonhoeffer, *Discipleship*, 194.
572. Bethge, *Biography*, 155.
573. Ibid., 817.
574. Ibid., 335. The "Aryan clause," implemented by the Nazi state in 1933, prohibited Jewish individuals, including those who had received Christian baptism, and their spouses from holding appointments within the Church or state.

exclusion of baptised Jews from our Christian congregations."[575] It was a brave pronouncement in Nazi Germany in support of the outcast.

24. Honors personal responsibility in maintenance of social justice—*criterion satisfied*

Bonhoeffer believed that humans bear strict "responsibility for one another" derived not from an attempt "to escape from the world, but" from hearing "in it the call of Christ in faith and obedience."[576] "Nobility arises from and exists by sacrifice, courage, and a clear sense of duty to oneself and society," he maintained, "and it shows an equally natural regard for others, whether they are of higher or of lower degree."[577] In the face of Nazism, Bonhoeffer announced, "We are called upon to make a decision from which we cannot escape."[578] Bonhoeffer chose his course of action based on a sense of responsibility toward his victimized neighbor, believing that, "as a pastor it was his duty not just to comfort the victims of the man who drove down a busy street like a maniac, but to try to stop him."[579] One must acquire "courage to enter public life," he counseled,[580] apparently aware of an all-too-common tendency to cast personal responsibility onto others. Bonhoeffer condemned such practice and exposed the dynamic publicly. "The authority of the Leader [Führer] means for the individual the free choice of obedience, [and] radical renunciation of his right as an individual. . . . [A]uthority which I accord to another person over me is ultimately only my own authority. . . . [T]he authority of the Leader is . . . in the hands of his followers."[581] We are all responsible in choice, whether we exercise or abdicate personal responsibility.

---

575. Bonhoeffer, *No Rusty Swords*, 221.
576. Ibid., 181, 199.
577. Bonhoeffer, *Letters*, 13.
578. Bonhoeffer, *No Rusty Swords*, 209.
579. Bonhoeffer; paraphrased by Latmiral, in Bethge, *Biography*, 851.
580. Bonhoeffer, *Letters*, 13.
581. Bonhoeffer, *No Rusty Swords*, 196–97.

25. Protects, defends others at potential cost to self—*criterion satisfied*

In response to Nazi persecution of non-Aryans, Bonhoeffer insisted, "This is the time when we must be radical upon all points ... without any fear of the disagreeable consequences for ourselves."[582] For Bonhoeffer, "the substance of God's actions and the substance of man's responsibility for his fellow-men was the idea of deputyship; he therefore staked his life for the liberation of Germany and the world from the curse of murderous tyranny."[583] Protecting and defending others was Bonhoeffer's mandate which cost him his life. "I feel that my own personal future is of quite secondary importance compared with the general situation," he explained. From prison he wrote, "I regard my being kept here ... as being involved in Germany's fate, as I was resolved to be. I don't look back on the past and accept the present reproachfully.... All we can do is to live in assurance and faith."[584] Bonhoeffer suffered imprisonment and death but accepted these as part of his divine mission.

26. Direct participation in mission in a position of vulnerability —*criterion satisfied*

In religion, Bonhoeffer asserted, the "devout want to be among themselves," whereas Christ calls "us to be in the midst of our enemies, just as he was."[585] When Bonhoeffer decided to return to the dangers of Nazi Germany from the relative safety of America, he wrote, "It is as if we were soldiers on leave who then return to action despite everything that awaits them. We cannot get away from it. Not as if we were essential, as if we were needed (by God?!), but simply because that is where our life is, and because we leave our life behind, we destroy it, if we are not back there."[586] He viewed it as his life's mission to fight injustice where it confronted him.

---

582. Bonhoeffer; in Bethge, *Biography*, 337.
583. Schönherr, "Single-heartedness," 129.
584. Bonhoeffer, *Letters*, 174–75, 239.
585. Bonhoeffer; in Wüstenberg, *Theology of Life*, 13.
586. Bonhoeffer; in Bethge, *Biography*, 655.

27. Refuses to love evil, actively opposes evil—*criterion satisfied*

His active opposition to Hitler placed Bonhoeffer in a minority in Nazi Germany, but he refused to bow to evil, unequivocally taking his difficult place against the status quo. Gerhard Leibholz explains that, "to refrain from taking any part in the attempt to overcome the National Socialist regime conflicted . . . deeply with his [Bonhoeffer's] view that Christian principles must . . . be translated into human life and that it is in the sphere of the material, in state and society, that responsible love" must manifest.[587]

28. Prefers peace to war and non-violence to violence—*criterion satisfied*

Bonhoeffer did not desire war but worked to have Hitler deposed before the latter could instigate war.[588] "Today there must be no more war," he urged. "War in its present form annihilates the creation of God." The "next war must be utterly *rejected*." We should "make peace to overcome war."[589] "The church of Christ stands against war for peace among men, between nations, classes and races," he advised.[590] At a 1934 conference, Bonhoeffer strongly advocated peace over war as the ultimate path of Christian discipleship.[591] Amid the reality of war, however, he "did not take the pacifist line, although his aristocratic noble-mindedness and charming gentleness made him, at the bottom of his heart, a pacifist."[592]

29. Does not glorify violence or war—*criterion satisfied*

The fact that Bonhoeffer wished to avoid conscription indicates that he did not glorify war or violence; he was unwilling to participate in war for its own sake.

---

587. Leibholz, "Memoir," xxvii.
588. Bethge, *Biography*, 636.
589. Bonhoeffer, *No Rusty Swords*, 166, 183.
590. Ibid., 183.
591. Bethge, *Biography*, 387–89.
592. Leibholz, "Memoir," xxvii.

30. Concern for spiritual welfare of self and others, apprehends spiritual implications—*criterion satisfied*

"If I were prison chaplain here," Bonhoeffer reflected, "I should spend the whole time from morning till night . . . going through the cells; a good deal would happen."[593] "[A]t the moment I'm trying to write some prayers for prisoners; it's surprising that there are none, and perhaps these may be distributed at Christmas," he wrote. In his report on prison conditions, Bonhoeffer noted the following: "There are no projects for work that would be useful for all the 700 prisoners, such as, for instance, the construction of air-raid shelters. There are no religious services. The prisoners, some of whom are very young . . . are bound to suffer in body and soul from the lack of occupation and of supervision, particularly during a long, solitary confinement."[594] "I think a long imprisonment is extremely dangerous for very young people as far as their spiritual development is concerned," he stated. "The impressions come with such violence that they may well sweep a great deal overboard."[595] Bonhoeffer unofficially "became the pastor of his fellow prisoners, and even, increasingly, of his warders." This activity occurred largely during air raids and during "exercises in the prison yard,"[596] when contact with others occurred. "It will be the task of our generation," he advised, "not to 'seek great things', but to save and preserve our souls out of the chaos."[597]

31. Benevolence, kindness, does not engage in cruelty—*criterion satisfied*

Schönherr wrote of Bonhoeffer, "Never did I discover in him anything low, undisciplined, mean."[598] Bonhoeffer was benevolent, concerned with helping others even when he was similarly afflicted or in an otherwise difficult predicament. In late 1943, when air raids over Berlin

---

593. Bonhoeffer, *Letters*, 53.
594. Ibid., 130, 251.
595. Ibid., 277.
596. Poelchau, prison chaplain, "Freedom," 222.
597. Bonhoeffer, *Letters*, 297.
598. Schönherr, "Single-heartedness," 126.

were frequent and inmates were essentially 'sitting ducks,'[599] Bonhoeffer asserted that the "only really unbearable privation is one's inability to help others in these difficult times."[600] Bonhoeffer routinely encouraged others. "He always cheered me up and comforted me. . . . Many little notes he slipped into my hands on which he had written biblical words of comfort and hope,"[601] wrote a fellow captive, while another reported that Bonhoeffer "did a great deal to keep some of the weaker brethren from depression and anxiety."[602] He did not engage in cruelty, never seeking to inflict harm on others for pleasure's sake.

32. Generosity, charity—*criterion satisfied*

Bonhoeffer shared his food in prison despite scarcity. "My cell is being cleaned out for me," he wrote, "and while it's being done, I can give the cleaner something to eat."[603] "Too many of the inmates here are plain hungry, and it's one of my greatest pleasures to be able to help occasionally."[604] A fellow prisoner recalled Bonhoeffer's generosity: "Each Wednesday he received his laundry parcel [from his parents] which also contained cigars, apples or bread, and he never omitted to share them with me the same evening when we were not watched."[605] Bonhoeffer repeatedly encouraged Bethge to avail himself of his resources. "[I]f you need money, feel free to draw 1000 marks of mine," he wrote. "Please at least help yourself occasionally to some of my bacon."[606] "If there is anything that would help Renate in her present condition [Bethge's wife was pregnant], and you need money for it, please simply take as much as you need without saying any more about it."[607] Bonhoeffer also covered legal expenses for a fellow prisoner and arranged legal representation for

---

599. Dohnanyi's cell was bombed and he suffered cerebral embolism as a result. Bethge, *Biography*, 807.
600. Bonhoeffer, *Love Letters*, 127.
601. Schlabrendorff, "In Prison," 228.
602. Hugh Falconer, British officer; in Bethge, *Biography*, 924.
603. Bonhoeffer, *Letters*, 134.
604. Bonhoeffer, *Love Letters*, 247.
605. Schlabrendorff, "In Prison," 229.
606. Bonhoeffer, *Letters*, 131, 135.
607. Ibid., 136.

several others.[608] He attempted as well to organize a twelve-day retreat for a kindly but sickly prison guard at a property belonging to his future in-laws, but the request was denied."[609]

33. Rejects personal glorification and idolization—*criterion satisfied*

Bethge states that Bonhoeffer neither engaged in self-pity nor sought recognition,[610] and a brother-in-law indicates that he shunned "ambition and vanity."[611] We know that Bonhoeffer did not like to "bind" others to himself.[612] In fact, he "liked to keep his distance, and he did not permit any undue familiarity."[613] Bethge explains that Bonhoeffer "kept a certain distance from others out of respect for their privacy, and he saw to it that he was treated likewise."[614] He was obviously not interested in personal glorification.

34. Is not motivated by self-fulfillment or material gain—*criterion satisfied*

Bonhoeffer advocated "moderation" over "extravagance" and warned that, "[w]hen we tolerate impudence for the sake of material comforts, then we abandon our self-respect, the flood-gates are opened, chaos bursts the dam that we were to defend; and we are responsible for it all."[615] In Hitlerite Germany, Bonhoeffer was branded treasonous. "Throughout the world," explains Bethge, "'treason' is normally viewed as a horrible sentiment, characterized by speculation for personal advantage and the intent to injure one's own country," but the "opposite was true of . . . Bonhoeffer" and his co-conspirators.[616] In England, Winston Churchill

608. Bethge, *Biography*, 849.
609. Bonhoeffer, *Love Letters*, 224, 231.
610. Bethge, *Letters*, 324.
611. Leibholz, "Memoir," xxii.
612. See criterion 9 above, Divinely Sanctioned Righteous Warfare category.
613. Schönherr, "Single-heartedness," 128.
614. Bethge, *Biography*, xviii.
615. Bonhoeffer, *Letters*, 12–13.
616. Bethge, *Biography*, 675.

characterized the German conspirators as "militarists, simply a case of the highest personalities in the German Reich murdering one another."[617] Bonhoeffer's role in the conspiracy promised neither popularity, material gain, nor personal or professional advancement but required that he risk everything.

35. Refuses to benefit from anything unjustly acquired—*criterion satisfied*

Bonhoeffer was initially treated harshly in Tegel prison; however, once prison staff learned that he was related to the prison commandant, he received better treatment,[618] but Bonhoeffer refused any benefit that would disadvantage fellow prisoners. "I was offered larger rations," he reported, "which I always refused, as they would have been at the expense of the other prisoners."[619] Moreover, Bonhoeffer's first cell was on the top floor of the building and, when it became extremely hot during the summer, he wrote to his parents, "I don't want to ask to be moved to another floor, as that would not be fair to the other prisoner who would have to come into my cell."[620]

36. Clarity of purpose—*criterion satisfied*

Bonhoeffer was unequivocal in defending the Jewish people against Nazism, declaring it the responsibility of the Church "not just to bandage the victims under the wheel, but to" halt "the wheel itself."[621] Bonhoeffer's position was clear: the Church is obliged to question the activities of an unjust state, must help the victims of such a state, and must actively op-

---

617. Churchill; in Bethge, *Biography*, 895.

618. Paul von Hase, city commandant of Berlin, was in charge of military prisons. He was a cousin to Bonhoeffer's mother and had inquired at the prison about Bonhoeffer. Hase was executed by the Nazis in August, 1944. Bethge, in *Letters*, 268, n. 184, 366, n. 61. Bethge, *Biography*, 623.

619. Bonhoeffer, *Letters*, 249.

620. Ibid., 87.

621. Bonhoeffer, *No Rusty Swords*, 221.

pose it,[622] while individual Christians might "accuse the state of offenses against morality."[623]

37. Sincerity, authenticity—*indeterminate*

"I'm greatly devoted to sincerity, to life, liberty and mercy—it's just their religious trappings that make me uneasy," wrote Bonhoeffer.[624] He was sincere and authentic with strong moral convictions and a genuine concern for others, yet his false work for the *Abwehr* placed Bonhoeffer in the realm of inauthenticity in the context of counterintelligence wherein he feigned to be doing one thing while actually doing another. His conspiratorial work was case-specific and considered a moral necessity, yet the reasons for Bonhoeffer's dishonesty[625] in feigning to serve the state while actually furthering the conspiratorial cause do not negate the insincerity and inauthenticity in this instance which contended with his generally outspoken and authentic character. While his conspiratorial motives were sincere and authentic, his method was not entirely so. His actions can therefore be classified neither as entirely authentic nor as completely—or even predominantly—inauthentic.

38. Integrity—*criterion satisfied*

Bonhoeffer operated from integrity. In October, 1944, plans were made for his escape from prison but he canceled the arrangement in order not to endanger his fiancée, relatives, or anyone else who might be arrested or otherwise afflicted on account of the action.[626] "To encounter Dietrich was . . . to encounter a person to whom humanity was natural," wrote Lehmann. "Utterly without obsequiousness, he was without a trace of status-seeking or of pretence. . . . Dietrich manifested a contagious free-

---

622. Bethge, *Biography*, 275.
623. Bonhoeffer, *No Rusty Swords*, 219.
624. Bonhoeffer, *Love Letters*, 327.
625. Bonhoeffer discussed the relationship between deception and responsibility in the context of war. Bonhoeffer, *Ethics*, 235, 257.
626. Leibholz, "Memoir," xxiv. Bethge, *Biography*, 827–28. Bonhoeffer did not want to inflict "himself on somebody who had to hide him." Poelchau, "Freedom," 222–23.

dom, openness and integrity in relating to all sorts and conditions of men, to people as *human* beings."[627]

---

39. Treats God as a Subject, not an object to be bent to one's will—*criterion satisfied*

"God is not a general principle," Bonhoeffer asserted, "but the living God who has" bestowed life upon humans and "demands service" of us.[628] "The fact that the Israelites *never* uttered the name of God always makes me think," he declared, "and I can understand it better as I go on."[629] Respect for the unutterability of the divine name represents a refusal to objectify God. "The way of Jesus Christ, and . . . the way of all Christian thinking, leads not from the world to God but from God to the world," he explained.[630] In formulating his religionless Christianity, Bonhoeffer described Christ not as "an object of religion, but something quite different, [as] . . . Lord of the world."[631]

---

40. Does not define or claim elaborate understanding of God, accepts divine mystery—*criterion satisfied*

Bonhoeffer held that "[t]he God who lets us live in the world without the working hypothesis of God is the God before whom we stand continually."[632] "The religious path from human beings to God leads to the idol of our hearts which we have formed after our own image. Neither knowledge, nor morality, nor religion leads to God. . . . If human beings and God are to come together," he maintained, "there can be but one path: God's path to human beings."[633] Bonhoeffer viewed religion as anthropocentric rather than theocentric since humans are at the center of religious reflection on God. "An idea of Christ, a doctrinal system, general religious knowledge of grace or of the forgiveness of sins makes

627. Lehmann, "Paradox," 45.
628. Bonhoeffer, *Ethics*, 359.
629. Bonhoeffer, *Letters*, 135.
630. Bonhoeffer, *Ethics*, 351.
631. Bonhoeffer, *Letters*, 280–81.
632. Ibid., 360.
633. Bonhoeffer; in Wüstenberg, *Theology of Life*, 3.

discipleship unnecessary, ... excludes it, and is hostile to discipleship," he explained. "Christianity without discipleship is always Christianity without Jesus Christ; it is idea, myth."[634] True discipleship must therefore transcend religion.

Bonhoeffer believed that, before God, "there can only be subjection, perseverance, patience—and gratitude. So every question 'Why?' falls silent."[635] "I do not understand your ways, / But you know the way for me," he wrote.[636] Pondering future events, Bonhoeffer resolved, "[W]e mustn't anticipate God's ways, but we do at least know that he never abandons us, even in hard times."[637]

41. Does not hold God responsible for human evil—*criterion satisfied*

Bonhoeffer maintained that "God lets himself be pushed out of the world on the cross. He is weak and powerless in the world...." Humans are not assisted by divine "omnipotence," he asserted, but by divine "weakness and suffering.... Man's religiosity makes him look in his distress to the power of God in the world [but] ... [t]he Bible directs man to God's powerlessness and suffering."[638] "The church is a bit of the world," he noted, "a lost, godless world, ... a complacent, evil world. And the church is the evil world to the highest degree because in it the name of God is misused, because in it God is made a plaything, man's idol."[639] Bonhoeffer well understood the dangers of attributing human aspirations and deeds to God.

---

634. Ibid., 15, 168, n. 63.
635. Bonhoeffer, *Letters*, 32.
636. Bonhoeffer, prayer for prisoners, *Letters*, 139.
637. Bonhoeffer, *Love Letters*, 112.
638. Bonhoeffer, *Letters*, 360–61.
639. Bonhoeffer, *No Rusty Swords*, 149.

42. Does not claim divine sanction with respect to all of one's actions but only those founded on divine revelation—*criterion satisfied*

Bonhoeffer did not claim divine support in all that he did. When he recognized his error in leaving Germany in 1939, he bore full responsibility. "The whole burden of self-reproach because of a wrong decision comes back again and almost overwhelms me," he wrote.[640]

43. Exercises personal responsibility and accountability before God and others—*criterion satisfied*

Bonhoeffer deemed individuals "responsible before God" and held that "the true concept of community . . . rests on responsibility, on the recognition that individuals belong responsibly one to another."[641] The "structure of responsible action," he asserted, "includes both readiness to accept guilt and freedom."[642] "When a man takes guilt upon himself in responsibility, and no responsible man can avoid this, he imputes this guilt to himself and to no one else; he answers for it; he accepts responsibility for it."[643] "Alone before God, man becomes what he is, free and committed in responsibility at the same time." Bonhoeffer acknowledged "that anyone who lays violent hands on" another human being "is infringing eternal laws"[644] and accepted responsibility before God for his actions—most notably his participation in a conspiracy to kill.[645]

44. Accepts unknown consequences, uncertainty—*criterion satisfied*

"Christians in Germany will face the terrible alternative of either willing the defeat of their nation in order that Christian civilization may survive, or willing the victory of their nation and thereby destroying our

640. Bonhoeffer; in Bethge, *Biography*, 652.
641. Bonhoeffer, *No Rusty Swords*, 195, 199.
642. Bonhoeffer, *Ethics*, 236.
643. Ibid., 244.
644. Bonhoeffer, *No Rusty Swords*, 199.
645. This is evident in criterion 5 of the Divine, Prophetic Calling category above.

civilization. I know which of these alternatives I must choose; but I cannot make that choice in security," stated Bonhoeffer.[646]

From prison he wrote, "I believe that nothing that happens to me is meaningless, and that it is good for us all that it should be so, even if it runs counter to our own wishes. As I see it, I'm here for some purpose, and I only hope I may fulfil it."[647] Thus prisoner Bonhoeffer maintained a tranquil composure, "quite calm and normal, seemingly perfectly at his ease."[648]

45. Exercises independent thought—*criterion satisfied*

Bethge indicates that Bonhoeffer "did not want (nor would he have allowed) anyone else to tell him how or when he should act,"[649] while Schönherr stated that he "thought sharply, logically," and "willed what he thought,"[650] and a fellow student described Bonhoeffer as an exceptionally "free, critical and independent" thinker who challenged his professors' ideas when they conflicted with his own.[651] Moreover, Bonhoeffer recognized the relationship between independent thought and human responsibility, referring to "the responsible thinking people."[652] "It is the nature, and the advantage, of strong people that they can bring out the crucial questions and form a clear opinion about them," noted Bonhoeffer,[653] whose independent thought isolated him from others.[654] "The weak always have to decide between alternatives that are not their own."[655]

---

646. Bonhoeffer; in Bethge, *Biography*, 655.
647. Bonhoeffer, *Letters*, 289.
648. Best; in Bethge, *Biography*, 920.
649. Bethge, *Biography*, 326.
650. Schönherr, "Single-heartedness," 128.
651. Helmut Goes; in Bethge, *Biography*, 67.
652. Bonhoeffer, *Letters*, 4.
653. Ibid., 375.
654. Bethge, *Biography*, 325.
655. Bonhoeffer, *Letters*, 375.

46. Offers a merciful gift, promise of a better future—*criterion satisfied*

Bonhoeffer was committed to creating a better future for his country and the world. "The ultimate question for a responsible man to ask is . . . how the coming generation is to live," he wrote. "Thinking and acting for the sake of the coming generation, but being ready to go [i.e., to die] any day without fear or anxiety—that, in practice, is the spirit in which we are forced to live. It is not easy to be brave and keep that spirit alive," he acknowledged, "but it is imperative."[656] "The fact that the horrors of war are now coming home to us with such force will no doubt, if we survive, provide us with the necessary basis for making it possible to reconstruct the life of the nations, both spiritually and materially, on Christian principles."[657] To his godchild and great-nephew, Bonhoeffer pledged, "[W]e do want to preserve for you, the rising generation, what will make it possible for you to plan, build up, and shape a new and better life."[658]

His experience as a prisoner also inspired Bonhoeffer to work toward the establishment of an improved penal system. "I think a lengthy confinement is demoralizing in *every* way for most people," he wrote. "I've been thinking out an alternative penal system on the principle of making the punishment fit the crime. . . . Why does the Old Testament law never punish anyone by depriving him of his freedom?"[659]

47. Normally upholds customary moral laws—*criterion satisfied*

It is important to distinguish between Bonhoeffer's willingness to violate, in a specific instance, a law forbidding killing and transgression that arbitrarily disposes of the law. His participation in the conspiracy did not constitute arbitrary disposal of the law; rather, he recognized the law as valid but considered it necessary to break it in the extreme and particular circumstances that confronted him. He did not assume that the action would be forgiven but accepted God's impending judgment.

656. Ibid., 7, 15.
657. Ibid., 146.
658. Ibid., 297.
659. Ibid., 134.

He did not advocate utter disregard for this law, which he regarded as generally legitimate and otherwise upheld.

> It is true that all historically important action is constantly overstepping the limits set by these laws [i.e., "the permanent laws of human social life"]. But it makes all the difference whether such overstepping ... is regarded in principle as the superseding of them, and is therefore given out to be a law of a special kind, or whether the overstepping is deliberately regarded as a fault which is perhaps unavoidable, justified only if the law and the limit are re-established and respected as soon as possible. It is not necessarily hypocrisy if the declared aim of political action is the restoration of the law, and not mere self-preservation.[660]

48. Does not proclaim divine condemnation of others—*criterion not satisfied*

In the heated struggle between the Confessing Church and the Reich Church, Bonhoeffer once declared, "He who deliberately separates himself from the Confessing Church in Germany, separates himself from salvation."[661] The statement was apparently directed toward the Nazified German Christians and, in discussing the controversial remark with seminary students, Bonhoeffer maintained, "Once the gunpowder smoke has dissolved, everybody who thinks objectively and dispassionately must agree with me."[662] Bonhoeffer was a prominent figure in the ecumenical movement and not inclined to demonize those of differing faiths;[663] however, he did condemn that which he perceived as godless. The statement at issue seems to imply divine condemnation of an adversary, contrary to his assertion that "[i]t is always for God to judge."[664] It is possible that Bonhoeffer viewed salvation in terms of union with God

---

660. Ibid., 10–11.

661. Bonhoeffer; in Schönherr, "Single-heartedness," 128. Also, in Bethge, *Biography*, 494.

662. Bonhoeffer; in Rott, "Something Always Occurred," 134.

663. The day before his death, Bonhoeffer conveyed a message to Best for Bell confirming his belief "in the principle of our Universal Christian brotherhood which rises above all national interests...." Bonhoeffer; quoted by Bell, in Bethge, *Biography*, 1022, n. 54.

664. Bonhoeffer, *Ethics*, 236.

resulting from full participation in right-loving relationship with God, as discussed in chapter 2 above, in which case separation from salvation suggests not divine condemnation but a soul's own failure to honor the divine-human union; nonetheless, it is not for humans to assess the state of others' souls.

---

49. Possible temporary suspension of universal ethic in some regard in relation to a divinely sanctioned higher *telos*— criterion satisfied

"*Any order*—however ancient and sacred it may be—*can be dissolved*, and must be dissolved when it closes itself up in itself, grows rigid and no longer permits the proclamation of revelation," Bonhoeffer asserted.[665] "For the sake of God and of men Jesus became a breaker of the law. ... Thus it is Jesus Christ who sets conscience free for the service of God and of our neighbour."[666] "The dogmatically correct delivery of the Christian proclamation is not enough," he explained, "nor are general ethical principles; what is needed is concrete instruction in the concrete situation. The spiritual forces which sustain the Church are not yet exhausted."[667] He warned that "religion and morality can become the most dangerous enemy of God's advent among human beings."[668] Religion enables humans to construct false gods suited to any purpose or humanly-defined code of morality in order to satisfy fluctuating human desires or alleviate ever-changing fears. Bonhoeffer witnessed this in the supportive stance taken by the German Christian Church toward Hitler. Of course, while religion and morality *can* facilitate destructive attitudes and behaviors, they do not necessarily produce these in every individual or in all instances. Nevertheless, Bonhoeffer recognized that extraordinary circumstances might arise in which no human law can govern adequately.

> In the course of historical life there comes a point where the exact observance of the formal law of a state ... finds itself in violent conflict with the ineluctable necessities of the lives of men; at

---

665. Bonhoeffer, *No Rusty Swords*, 163.
666. Bonhoeffer, *Ethics*, 240.
667. Ibid., 349.
668. Bonhoeffer; in Wüstenberg, *Theology of Life*, 3.

this point responsible and pertinent action leaves behind it the domain of principle and convention, the domain of the normal and regular, and is confronted by the extraordinary situation of ultimate necessities, a situation which no law can control. . . . But it is equally certain that these necessities . . . cannot . . . constitute a law. . . . [T]hey are by nature peripheral and abnormal events.[669]

Accordingly, the situation in Nazi Germany prompted Bonhoeffer temporarily to suspend a universal ethic in favor of a perceived higher divine *telos*, that is, to participate in a conspiracy to assassinate an individual in order to end a reign of terror and destruction wrought by that individual. Bonhoeffer stressed, however, that, "[p]recisely in this breaking of the law the validity of the law [e.g., 'Thou shalt not kill'] is acknowledged. . . . There can be no theoretical answer to the question whether in historical action the ultimate goal is the eternal law or free responsibility in the face of all law but before God," he explained. "[I]n either case man becomes guilty and in either case he can live only by the grace of God and by forgiveness."[670]

---

50. Charism, spiritual gifts, uncanny abilities (including but not limited to those cited under the category of Divine, Prophetic Calling), mediates grace—*criterion satisfied*

A prison chaplain noted Bonhoeffer's "gift for meeting every kind of person in the right spirit."[671] Bonhoeffer had an uncanny ability to soften even harsh SS prison guards. Bethge explains that prisoners were often forced "to humble themselves before some brute in order to avoid" harsh treatment;[672] however, to the astonishment of inmate Fabian von Schlabrendorff, Bonhoeffer was "always good-tempered, always of the same kindliness and politeness towards everybody," quickly winning over hostile guards.[673] One warder apologized to Bonhoeffer for locking his cell door.[674] Moreover, it is noted under criterion 21 of the Divine,

---

669. Bonhoeffer, *Ethics*, 234–35.
670. Ibid., 236.
671. Poelchau, "Freedom," 224.
672. Bethge, *Biography*, 908.
673. Schlabrendorff, "In Prison," 228.
674. Bethge, *Biography*, 848.

Prophetic Calling category that Bonhoeffer demonstrated prophetic ability.

---

51. Honest disposition, transparency—*criterion satisfied*

This criterion refers to an individual's disposition, not to exceptional circumstances wherein dishonesty or the withholding of information is more just or sensible than truthfulness, such as when Jehanne refused to tell the truth in all matters before the Rouen court, particularly those concerning her king. Certainly, there are circumstances in which lying might be considered ethically necessary and the criterion must be judged apart from such exceptional circumstances.[675]

Bonhoeffer advocated "*ultimate* honesty"[676] and considered "decency, honesty, simplicity and a lack of pomposity" to be "admirable character traits."[677] He operated from an honest disposition, being outspoken and presenting his views clearly and straightforwardly, devoid of deceptive, manipulative language.[678] He also considered it the duty of individuals to be honest with ourselves[679] and engaged in serious self-reflection as evidenced in his extant diary entries and letters. He accorded theological significance to the lie, viewing it as "the denial of God" manifest in the world. "[T]he lie is the denial, the negation and the conscious and deliberate destruction of the reality which is created by God and which consists in God, no matter whether this purpose is achieved by speech or by silence," he maintained.[680]

---

675. If a terrorist intends to harm someone and asks another individual where the intended victim is, many would consider it ethically necessary for the person queried to indicate that he or she does not know the whereabouts of the potential victim, even if this is untrue.

676. Bonhoeffer, *Letters*, 360.

677. Bonhoeffer; in Bethge, *Biography*, 107.

678. See next criterion.

679. Bonhoeffer, *Letters*, 382.

680. Bonhoeffer, *Ethics*, 364.

52. Straightforward, honest language, forthrightness—*criterion satisfied*

A student recalled that Bonhoeffer "hated" to produce "a psychological effect" on others and avoided rhetorical speech.[681] Bonhoeffer recognized a need for straightforward, honest, forthright communication and employed it in his publications, lectures, and sermons, often inciting controversy as a result. Consider the following:

> We have been silent witnesses of evil deeds; we have been drenched by many storms; we have learnt the arts of equivocation and pretence; experience has made us suspicious of others and kept us from being truthful and open; intolerable conflicts have worn us down and even made us cynical. Are we still of any use? What we shall need is not geniuses, or cynics, or misanthropes, or clever tacticians, but plain, honest, straightforward men. Will our inward power of resistance be strong enough, and our honesty with ourselves remorseless enough, for us to find our way back to simplicity and straightforwardness?[682]

Bethge describes some of Bonhoeffer's sermons as "startling in their directness" and notes that "[h]is first application for a pastorate . . . failed" because "[h]e was too young, his preaching too severe, and the demands he made on his congregation too" unusual.[683]

53. Unambiguous public statement of purpose and method—*indeterminate*

Bonhoeffer publicly stated his opposition to the Hitler regime, preaching, lecturing, and writing against the Nazi agenda. For example, two days after Hitler came to power in Germany, Bonhoeffer spoke on public radio, intending to finish his talk with a declaration that, if a Führer "does not continually tell his followers quite clearly of the limited nature of his task and of their own responsibility, if he allows himself to surrender to the wishes of his followers, who would always make him their idol—then the image of the Leader [Führer] will pass over into

---

681. Schönherr, "Single-heartedness," 128.
682. Bonhoeffer, *Letters*, 16–17.
683. Bethge, *Biography*, 232, 444.

the image of the misleader, and he will be acting in a criminal way. . . . Leaders or offices which set themselves up as gods mock God and the individual who stands alone before him. . . ."[684] The broadcast was terminated before Bonhoeffer could voice these final, critical points and, in order not to be misconstrued, he subsequently published the entire content of his talk in a German newspaper and delivered an expanded version at the local College of Political Science and at a technical university.[685] While Bonhoeffer openly declared his position and purpose on many occasions, the fact that he concealed his method by participating in a conspiracy must be acknowledged, even though it might have been morally necessary for him to do so. It seems inappropriate to disqualify Bonhoeffer on the basis of circumstantial moral necessity and to ignore the fact that he satisfies the rest of the criterion, yet it is also inappropriate to ignore the fact that he did not declare his method openly; therefore, this criterion is rendered indeterminate. In the unusual context of morally necessary conspiracy, the latter aspect of the criterion might best be viewed as inapplicable.

54. Reliability, consistency, constancy—*indeterminate*

Bonhoeffer was consistent in the matter of the struggle between Church and state. Hildebrandt wrote that "[t]he course for the church was clear to him [Bonhoeffer] from the beginning and remained clear to the end; there could be no compromise with . . . Nazism."[686] Of his character, a fellow prisoner wrote, "He was always cheerful, always consistently friendly and obliging."[687] Another wrote, "He was cheerful, ready to respond to a joke."[688] After encountering him in prison, Dohnanyi wrote, "I have seen Dietrich; he looks cheerful."[689] To be regularly cheerful, providing a reliable and uplifting presence to others throughout two years of Nazi incarceration is a remarkable feat.

---

684. Bonhoeffer, *No Rusty Swords*, 198, 200.
685. Bethge, *Biography*, 259–60, 968, n. 12.
686. Hildebrandt, "Oasis," 38.
687. Schlabrendorff; quoted by Bismarck and Kabitz in *Love Letters*, 267.
688. Best; in Bethge, *Biography*, 919.
689. Dohnanyi; ibid., 908.

Bonhoeffer's theology remained a work in progress when he died. One can locate some inconsistency between his early theological convictions and his practical, experiential application of theology during later years. For example, although his ultimate goal of peace was constant, the degree of pacifism that he advocated varied. Compare, for example, his 1934 declaration that Christians "may not use weapons against one another"[690] with the following from 1942: "He [Bonhoeffer] said it was a tradition with us [Germans] that young men should volunteer for military service and lay down their lives for a cause of which they mightn't approve at all. But there must also be people able to fight from conviction alone. If they approved of the grounds for war, well and good. If not, they could best serve the Fatherland by operating on the internal front, perhaps even by working against the regime."[691] In 1934, Bonhoeffer was attempting to prevent a second world war and declared his position in strong and certain terms but, in 1942, war was manifest and a general condemnation of the use of arms would have been unrealistic and ineffective.

It is arguably to his credit that Bonhoeffer allowed his theology to be informed and shaped by his life experience. The extraordinarily evil events perpetrated by the Hitler regime have wreaked havoc on theology since their occurrence—as they should. Nonetheless, there is substantial consistency throughout Bonhoeffer's theology with respect to many basic tenets. Bethge maintains that "Bonhoeffer's theological development showed an intrinsic consistency and continuity" and he demonstrates how the theology produced by Bonhoeffer in 1944 can be linked "to particular ideas from his early period that he in part had retained and in part given new accents." Bethge attributes differences between Bonhoeffer's early and late theologies to the fact that the former was informed primarily by "a young, critical intellect" while the latter also drew on "experience full to the brim."[692] Theory serves as a substitute for knowledge in the absence of experience and Bonhoeffer's theoretical theology was transformed into experiential theology through its application to concrete reality. Nevertheless, the inconsistency must be acknowledged; however, in terms of his character, his core values, his ultimate goals, and his outward conduct, Bonhoeffer was reliable,

690. Bonhoeffer; ibid., 388.
691. Bonhoeffer; paraphrased by Wedemeyer, in *Love Letters*, 331–32.
692. Bethge, *Biography*, 460, 856, 890.

consistent and constant. Since it seems inappropriate to disqualify him based on a degree of justifiable theological inconsistency, the criterion is best declared indeterminate.

55. Strives with the world, with self, and with God—*criterion satisfied*

Bonhoeffer strove with the world in his opposition to the Hitler regime and in his imprisonment. From prison, he wrote, "[T]here are some lines that say '. . . that we remember what we would forget, that this poor earth is not our home.'"[693] Bonhoeffer also strove with himself. During his first Christmas season in prison, he wrote of homesickness and longing. "The first result of such longing is always a wish to neglect the ordinary daily routine in some way or other, and that means that our lives become disordered. I used to be tempted sometimes to stay in bed after six in the morning. . . . Up to now I've always been able to force myself not to do this; I realized that it would have been the first stage of capitulation, and that worse would probably have followed. . . . Above all, we must never give way to self-pity."[694] Bonhoeffer strove with God as well. Of his long imprisonment following on the heels of his engagement, he wrote, "When a man enters on a supremely happy marriage and has thanked God for it, it is a terrible blow to discover that the same God who established the marriage now demands of us a period of such great deprivation. In my experience nothing tortures us more than longing." Nonetheless, he maintained, "We ought to find and love God in what he actually gives us." Bonhoeffer conceded, however, that "not everything that happens is simply 'God's will.'"[695]

56. Expression of the sublime absolutely in the pedestrian—*criterion satisfied*

As a prisoner, "Bonhoeffer . . . always seemed to diffuse an atmosphere of happiness, of joy in every smallest event in life, and of deep gratitude for

---

693. Bonhoeffer, *Letters*, 168.
694. Ibid.
695. Ibid., 167–68.

the mere fact that he was alive."[696] He desired to be a blessing unto others. "A blessing," he wrote, "is the visible, perceptible, effective proximity of God. A blessing demands to be passed on—it communicates itself to other people.... That someone should be a blessing to others is the greatest thing of all."[697] Bonhoeffer carried God within. After nearly two years in prison, he did "not look in the least like a man who had spent months in prison and who went in fear of his life."[698] During the worst air raid on Berlin, Bonhoeffer stood in a shelter with other prisoners while the whole structure reverberated from a direct hit and threatened to crash in on them, but he "remained quite calm ... [and] did not move a muscle, but stood motionless and relaxed as if nothing had happened."[699] While a bomb blast can hardly be described as 'pedestrian,' the incident demonstrates the consistency with which Bonhoeffer displayed sublime qualities, regardless of circumstance.

57. Wisdom, sound judgment—*criterion satisfied*

Bonhoeffer possessed wisdom in the midst of widespread naïveté. "While we ... thought that all was more or less well with Church and State ... ," wrote Hildebrandt, "he had no illusions about the impending doom."[700] "He was one of the very few people who, as early as January 1933 [when Hitler came to power], saw with absolute clarity what was happening."[701] Bonhoeffer possessed considerable insight concerning stupidity (which contradicts sound judgment). Stupidity, he maintained, "is a more dangerous enemy to the good than evil. One can protest against evil; it can be unmasked and, if need be, prevented by force. Evil always carries the seeds of its own destruction, as it makes people, at the least, uncomfortable. Against" stupidity "we have no defence. Neither protests nor force can touch it; reasoning is no use; facts that contradict personal prejudices can simply be disbelieved—indeed, the" stupid person "can

696. Best; in Bethge, *Biography*, 920.
697. Bonhoeffer, *Love Letters*, 240–41.
698. Best; in Bethge, *Biography*, 907.
699. Schlabrendorff, "In Prison," 229–30. It was in order to keep prisoners alive until information was extracted that they benefited from bomb shelters at Gestapo headquarters, not out of concern for the prisoners. Ibid., 226–27.
700. Hildebrandt, "Oasis," 38.
701. Schönherr, "Single-heartedness," 129.

counter by criticizing them, and if they are undeniable, they can just be pushed aside as trivial exceptions. So the" stupid person "is completely self-satisfied ... [and] can easily become dangerous."[702] One can appreciate the vast extent to which Hitler apparently relied on widespread "stupidity" in support of his reign of evil—"the power of some needs the" stupidity of "others," Bonhoeffer explained. He viewed stupidity as "a moral rather than an intellectual defect. There are people who are mentally agile but" stupid, "and people who are mentally slow but very far from" stupid. One gets "the impression," he observed, that stupidity "is likely to be ... acquired in certain circumstances where people *make*" themselves stupid "or allow others to make" them stupid.[703] Stupidity is thus linked with thoughtlessness. "It is not that certain human capacities, intellectual capacities for instance, become stunted or destroyed," Bonhoeffer asserted, but "that the upsurge of power makes such an overwhelming impression that men ... give up trying to assess the new state of affairs for themselves." When speaking with a stupid individual, he maintained, it seems as though "one is dealing, not with the man himself, but with slogans, catchwords, and the like, which have taken hold of him. He is under a spell."[704] Bonhoeffer's description corresponds to Arendt's assessment of Eichmann, who relied heavily on clichés and slogans.[705] "Having thus become a passive instrument, the" stupid person "will be capable of any evil and at the same time incapable of [or averse to] seeing that it is evil. Here lies the danger of a diabolical exploitation that can do irreparable damage to human beings," warned Bonhoeffer,[706] whose wisdom in the matter proved true. Stupidity "can be overcome" only by living "a responsible life before God," he insisted, adding that stupidity and wisdom "are not ethically indifferent."[707]

702. Bonhoeffer, *Letters*, 8. Rumscheidt indicates that the word "*dummheit*" in Bonhoeffer's text literally translates as "stupidity" rather than "folly" as it is rendered in the cited text. Rumscheidt, email, November 2, 2012. I have adjusted the translation accordingly.

703. Bonhoeffer, *Letters*, 8.

704. Ibid., 8–9.

705. Arendt, *Eichmann*, 48–49, 55, 252.

706. Bonhoeffer, *Letters*, 9.

707. Ibid., 10.

58. Undergoes mystical "dark night," struggle with pain and suffering—*criterion satisfied*

"I wonder why it is that we find some days so much more oppressive than others, for no apparent reason," Bonhoeffer pondered. "Is it growing pains—or spiritual trial? Once they're over, the world looks quite a different place again."[708] Imprisonment brought mystical darkness, pain, and suffering to Bonhoeffer's door. "[T]hings here are revolting, . . . my grim experiences often pursue me into the night and . . . I can shake them off only by reciting one hymn after another, and . . . I'm apt to wake up with a sigh rather than with a hymn of praise to God," he wrote.[709] "I'm sure I never realized as clearly as I do here what the Bible and Luther mean by 'temptation'. Quite suddenly, and for no apparent physical or psychological reason, the peace and composure that were supporting one are jarred, and the heart becomes, in Jeremiah's expressive phrase, 'deceitful above all things, and desperately corrupt; who can understand it?' It feels like an invasion from outside, as if by evil powers trying to rob one of what is most vital."[710] The following passage from his poetry is equally revealing:

> Am I then really all that which other men tell of?
> Or am I only what I know of myself,
> restless and longing and sick, like a bird in a cage,
> struggling for breath, as though hands were compressing my throat,
> yearning for colours, for flowers, for the voices of birds,
> thirsting for words of kindness, for neighbourliness,
> trembling with anger at despotisms and petty humiliation,
> tossing in expectation of great events,
> powerlessly trembling for friends at an infinite distance,
> weary and empty at praying, at thinking, at making,
> faint, and ready to say farewell to it all?
> —Dietrich Bonhoeffer, "Who Am I?"[711]

The inner conflict and confusion described by Bonhoeffer and his struggle to overcome debilitating darkness point to the mystical dark

---

708. Ibid., 276.
709. Ibid., 161–62.
710. Ibid., 39.
711. Ibid., 348.

night of the soul, particularly the night of spirit, whereas his physical deprivations relate more directly to the night of sense. "While he was in the body, the fight between flesh and spirit, Adam and Christ, was going on in him," notes Leibholz. "Sometimes he seemed to have become a riddle to himself."[712]

---

59. Demonstrates grace in extreme suffering—*criterion satisfied*

"He was, without exception, the finest and most lovable man I have ever met. . . . [H]is soul really shone in the dark desperation of our prison,"[713] wrote a fellow Buchenwald inmate. Another fellow prisoner suggested that Bonhoeffer's "noble and pure soul must have suffered deeply" under Gestapo interrogation but that "he betrayed no sign of it."[714] Bonhoeffer wrote to Bethge, "People here keep on telling me . . . that I'm 'radiating so much peace around me,' and that I'm 'always so cheerful,'—so that the feelings that I sometimes have to the contrary must, I suppose, rest on an illusion (not that I really believe that at all!)."[715]

---

60. Embodies paradox—*criterion satisfied*

Bonhoeffer embodied paradox in that he was an ordained minister but advocated a religionless Christianity transcending ecclesiology while attempting to reclaim and conserve the original gospel message. The term, "religionless Christianity," is itself paradoxical. "The church is the presence of God in the world," he explained. "Really in the world, really the presence of God. The church is not a consecrated sanctuary, but the world, called by God to God; therefore there is only *one* church in all the world."[716] He also paradoxically asserted that, "Before God and with God we live without God,"[717] referring to a God who is present but largely incapacitated to act in the world. Bonhoeffer's notion of a permissible

---

712. Leibholz, "Memoir," xviii.
713. Best; in Bethge, *Biography*, 920.
714. Schlabrendorff, "In Prison," 228.
715. Bonhoeffer, *Letters*, 279.
716. Bonhoeffer, *No Rusty Swords*, 150.
717. Bonhoeffer, *Letters*, 360.

violation of a law in order to restore it and his assertion that, in violating an ethical law, its validity might be acknowledged are also paradoxical.[718]

61. Canonization, holiness, posthumous miracles—*criterion satisfied*

Some view Bonhoeffer as a saint despite the Reformation's repudiation of the veneration of saints.[719] "He was a good and saintly man," wrote S. Payne Best,[720] while the Bishop of Chichester considered him "holy and humble and brave."[721] "[A]mong and before" their fellow human beings, the saints are witnesses to the love of God. Martyrdom is considered the "first and supreme form of this testimony," being the most complete and unequivocal, asserts Splett. The "history of the veneration of saints began with the cult of the martyrs." Moreover, the "great saints point out . . . new ways of answering the demands of the world, new ways of answering God's call for the total dedication of man as he finds himself in this or that place and time." Splett cites Jehanne as such a figure.[722] Likewise, Bonhoeffer confessed Christ (God in the world) in an unprecedented situation and was consequently martyred. Since "the special call of God for a given historical period can find expression in . . . representatives of Christian holiness" beyond the Catholic Church, "one can speak of saints in Protestantism," Splett maintains.[723] Hence, Bonhoeffer might be categorized as a saint, or at least as holy. We have no evidence of posthumous miracles attributed to him, but these often become evident during the canonization process which does not generally occur in Protestantism.

62. Identification with a particular, well-established prophecy—*criterion not satisfied*

Bonhoeffer was not evidently associated with any well-established prophecy.

718. See criteria 47 and 49 above.
719. Splett, "Saints," 1498.
720. Best, *Venlo*, 191.
721. Bell; in Bethge, *Biography*, 931.
722. Splett, "Saints," 1496–98.
723. Ibid., 1498.

Summary Assessment—Divinely Sanctioned Human Agency

Of the sixty-two criteria indicative of divinely sanctioned human agency, Bonhoeffer satisfies fifty-seven (forty-six essential and eleven non-essential), he fails to satisfy two (both non-essential), and three are indeterminate (one essential and two non-essential). Of the forty-seven essential criteria, forty-six are met and one is indeterminate. Of the fifteen non-essential criteria, eleven are met. Disregarding the three indeterminate criteria and the two unmet, non-essential criteria, it can be concluded that Bonhoeffer's human agency corresponds to divinely sanctioned human agency as stipulated in Jehanne's model. It is time to draw an overall conclusion with respect to his case.

Case Study Two Results

We have thoroughly assessed Bonhoeffer's implicit claim to divinely sanctioned violence and determined that he meets the requirements of each category. Of the one hundred criteria, Bonhoeffer satisfies eighty-nine (seventy essential and nineteen non-essential), he fails to satisfy four (all non-essential), and seven are indeterminate or inapplicable (five essential and two non-essential). Of the seventy-five essential criteria, seventy are met and five are indeterminate or inapplicable; he does not violate any of these. Of the twenty-five non-essential criteria, nineteen are met. Disregarding the seven indeterminate or inapplicable criteria and the four unmet, non-essential criteria, eighty-nine remain, all of which Bonhoeffer satisfies. The results indicate that, on the basis of the model, Bonhoeffer can be deemed a practical, prophetic mystic who acted in accordance with divine calling. His participation in violence and his manner of behavior can be viewed as righteous and divinely sanctioned in accordance with Jehanne's example.

At a memorial service held shortly after Bonhoeffer's death, it was noted that "he represents both the resistance of the believing soul, in the name of God, to the assault of evil, and also the moral and political revolt of the human conscience against injustice and cruelty. He and his fellows [co-conspirators] are indeed built upon the foundation of the Apostles and the Prophets."[724] Like Jehanne, Bonhoeffer heeded the call to live an extraordinary, mystical life of divine servantship.

---

724. Bell; in Bethge, *Biography*, 931.

This case study demonstrates compatibility between the theologies of Jehanne and Bonhoeffer, exposing common ground in the concrete expression of Catholic and Protestant experiential, practical, prophetic mysticism. This constitutes an ecumenical aspect of the model which lends it strength. The similarities, consisting in the criteria derived from Jehanne that Bonhoeffer satisfies, reflect various aspects of divine servantship which are potentially constant, transcending barriers of time, gender, social class, and denomination. They might be considered some of the most fundamental and enduring features and requirements of active, concrete, faithful engagement in the world.

Reflection on the Case Studies and Model

We have examined and applied the model to two cases revolving around the same event and found that one claimant (Bonhoeffer) emerges as a prophet and the other (Hitler) emerges as a false prophet. These case studies demonstrate the thoroughness with which claims to divine sanction ought to be evaluated, and they also suggest accuracy in the evaluations conducted since the results concur with general reasoned opinion insofar as Hitler is more commonly associated with evil than goodness and Bonhoeffer is more widely viewed as benevolent than malevolent. This indicates that the criteria constitute a potentially effective measuring device with respect to claims of divinely sanctioned violence given that the model was constructed external to the case studies and, to that extent, provides an objective means of evaluation. Objectivity is also afforded by the model in that, under it, all claims are subject to the same scrutiny (i.e., the same criteria). Hence, the model provides a systematic, standardized method of assessing claims to divinely sanctioned violence. While emotional responses are likely to arise with respect to a given case—and these are not necessarily irrelevant[725]—the model serves to focus the evaluative process on facts pertaining to the stipulated criteria and thereby prevents the process from being overwhelmed entirely by emotional considerations.

The case studies demonstrate that, with respect to their involvement in the events of World War II, Bonhoeffer and Hitler viewed (or represented) themselves as acting in accordance with some form of di-

---

725. Emotions can serve a useful purpose when triggered by sympathy, conscience, or righteous considerations. Recall that the suppression of emotions facilitated the perpetration of Nazi atrocities.

vine sanction (as they understood or employed it), but with extremely different intentions and consequences. These studies should trigger an alarm in view of the fact that Hitler, whose claim to divine sanction is clearly repudiated by the assessment, acquired a following of millions complicit in his evil while Bonhoeffer, whose claim to divine sanction is confirmed by the assessment, was supported by a small minority. Weil recognizes the critical dynamic of such situations, pointing to the facility with which the social can be mistaken for the religious, "as a false diamond is like a real one, so that those who have no spiritual discernment are effectively taken in."[726]

> The trap of traps, the almost inevitable trap, is the social one. Everywhere, always, in everything, the social feeling produces a perfect imitation of faith, that is to say perfectly deceptive. This imitation has the great advantage of satisfying every part of the soul. That which longs for goodness believes it is fed....
>
> It is almost impossible to distinguish faith from its social imitation. All the more so because the soul can contain one part of true faith and one of imitation faith. It is almost but not quite impossible.[727]

Jehanne's model, when carefully and correctly employed, can facilitate this nearly impossible yet critical task, serving to distinguish faith from its social imitation as the case studies demonstrate.

In addition to evaluating claims to divine sanction in general, the model can also serve in assessing claims invoking Jehanne specifically in support of a given agenda. Cunningham points out that "both the Nazi-backed Vichy government and the Gaullist government in exile" invoked Jehanne in support of their opposing causes during World War II,[728] and Hitler himself vowed that the National Socialist state would "wage a hundred years' war, if necessary, to stamp out and destroy every last trace within its boundaries of" internal resistance[729]—a possible allusion to Jehanne's mission to rid France of every single one of the occupying enemy and to break Burgundian (internal) opposition to the French king.[730] It is strongly recommended that no such invocation of

726. Weil, *Waiting for God*, 5.
727. Ibid., 129.
728. Cunningham, *Catholic Heritage*, 77.
729. Hitler; in Domarus, *Essential Hitler*, 260.
730. Jehanne, letter to the English; in Pernoud and Clin, *Her Story*, 34.

Jehanne be considered apart from the model of righteous warfare and human agency by which it can be appropriately assessed.

Moreover, the case studies and the model highlight the personal nature of war, engaged conscience, and responsibility, even amid a profoundly impersonal, industrial, mechanistic process of human evil. They call individuals to recognize that these things are fundamentally and essentially personal, no matter what face is put on them, and to respond appropriately.

It should be noted that the case studies represent individuals who either satisfy or fail to satisfy all three categories. It might happen, however, that an individual will satisfy one category but not the other two, or two categories but not the other one. This is also instructive as it might indicate an individual in receipt of divine, prophetic calling who fails to respond righteously to some extent, or it could indicate one who behaves righteously in the absence of divine prophetic calling as represented by the criteria. In any case, the model (when applied properly) serves to contextualize the activities of a claimant in a useful format for understanding them and helps to provide insight and clarity with respect to those activities.

It should also be noted that, although a relatively detailed, written analysis has been performed in the context of each case study in order to demonstrate the process of applying the model appropriately, it is not necessary that one compose such lengthy, written analyses in implementing the model, although one might find it useful to do so. One might instead utilize the appendix as a concise checklist for evaluating claims to divine sanction by placing an "X" through those criteria which are violated and a diagonal line through those that are indeterminate or inapplicable in a given case, allowing one to evaluate degree of conformity quite simply. It cannot be overemphasized, however, that considerable thought and care must be exercised in performing all assessments via the model, whether written or not, if one is to evaluate such critical issues comprehensively, seriously, and effectively.

As a tool for assessing claims to divinely sanctioned violence, the model's effectiveness has been tentatively substantiated via two test-runs. It is now time to consider the implications not only of the model but of the entire undertaking to comprehend Jehanne's claim to divine sanction and its ongoing significance with respect to human violence.

Conclusion

We set out to determine what insights and wisdom Jehanne's example offers regarding evaluation of claims to divinely sanctioned violence and found that she aligns with the Jewish and Christian prophetic traditions as a mystic who claimed to perceive and heed a divine call to participate actively in the establishment of just peace at a particular time and place in history at great cost to herself. We also found that the compelling claim to divine sanction takes shape in the life of a prophet and affects the prophet's life in some specific and significant ways. The fact that there is a general pattern to the unfolding of prophetic life that renders it identifiable must not be overlooked in discerning the sincerity or insincerity of prophetic claims. While Jehanne's behavior was found to resonate with many traditional just war criteria, it was established that her example encompasses a greater number of critical aspects than those stipulated within the just war model, not least of which are the characteristic righteousness and uncompromising appeal to divinity that dominated her activities. Moreover, just war theory was found to rely upon utilitarian calculation, which serves a human purpose and is inherently flawed and susceptible to abuse, whereas Jehanne relied upon guidance in the form of divine revelation and trusted in incalculable outcomes on the basis of faith in a divine purpose.

As a saint, Jehanne is considered an exemplar, and a comprehensive model constructed from her example has proven tenable in evaluating claims to divinely sanctioned violence presented by Hitler and Bonhoeffer. The model thus provides a potentially effective basis for discernment with respect to other such claims as well. Bonhoeffer, presumably inadvertently, mirrored Jehanne's behavior closely with respect to the stipulated criteria while Hitler failed to accord with 90 percent of them. In essence, Hitler and Bonhoeffer constitute a double-edged sword representing opposite sides of the same event. In addition to being evaluative, the model is prescriptive in suggesting that one who engages in necessary acts of violence ought to do so in accordance with Jehanne's example insofar as possible. This model does not constitute a moral aberration but incorporates many traditionally recognized ethical obligations and prohibitions, such as the obligation to respect human dignity and prohibition against torture, into a unified and powerful whole. Given that the model substantially represents shared moral values and internationally established human rights and calls individuals to account in the preservation of these values and rights, one might be considered remiss in ignoring it.

It is irrelevant whether an individual assessing another's claim to divinely sanctioned violence believes in God or not; the fact that the claimant must believe in God for such a claim to have any merit is essential, and the assessor must know how to recognize and identify such belief and the depth of such belief. The model facilitates discernment in this regard by delineating the practical, prophetic mystic's manner of divine servantship.

I did not set out to identify a particular number of criteria but to examine Jehanne's story thoroughly and to extract aspects of her experience, thought, character, and behavior indicative of her faith as manifested in concrete relationship with God and its expression in her relationship with fellow humans, granting particular attention to her military activities. That one hundred criteria were identified is a serendipitous outcome in that it renders the model comprehensive and facilitates calculation of percentage of conformity to the model.[1]

The model is based entirely upon Jehanne's example and was not influenced by the case studies which were necessarily conducted after the model was created. In selecting the case studies for examination, it was anticipated that Bonhoeffer would fare better than Hitler in the assessment and this was considered beneficial in demonstrating application of the model to diverse cases. However, it was not known to what extent either individual would conform or fail to conform to the model until the detailed evaluations were completed. Regardless of any anticipated outcomes, the facts speak for themselves in applying the model and it is a function of the model to confirm or deny anticipated outcomes.

With respect to how it was determined which criteria should be considered essential and which ones non-essential but potentially in-

---

1. This is not a predictive calculation of the utilitarian type but a factual calculation.

dicative of divine sanction, the matter was approached from a logical perspective. While the majority of the criteria are recognized as essential, allowance was made for divine autonomy, for recognition of the fact that God is not predictable, that human knowledge cannot be complete or entirely accurate in such matters, and that different circumstances might warrant different attitudes and behaviors. It was necessary that I proceed on my own discretion in selecting which criteria ought to be designated non-essential. The decision was made individually in each of the twenty-five instances wherein a criterion was deemed non-essential and, therefore, each has a potentially different rationale behind it. For instance, it does not seem essential that an individual demonstrate initial hesitation, reluctance, resistance, fear, or doubt with respect to divine calling since lack of such response would not likely have any negative bearing on fulfillment of the prophetic task; although these constitute characteristics of prophetic response in the Jewish and Christian prophetic traditions and are also exemplified by Jehanne, it is conceivable that a prophet might not respond in like manner to divine calling and this would not necessarily render the calling or the response invalid, less effective, or less appropriate. On the other hand, lack of humility might interfere significantly with a prophet's ability to fulfill a divine calling effectively since humility is required in surrendering personal will to divine will; hence, humility is deemed an essential criterion.

The case studies demonstrate the ongoing relevance of Jehanne's example; this is consistent with the notion that divine revelation offers perpetually relevant and applicable wisdom and that Truth is unchanging and eternal. In other words, if something is True—in the divine sense of ultimate truth—then it not only is, but presumably always has been and always will be so. Heschel maintains that "the manner in which the prophets dealt with the issues of their own time and . . . the solutions they propounded seem to be relevant for all times,"[2] and Watts holds that "[t]he predisposition and action of God towards humanity is ever the same, for his nature does not change, and an event in time and space does not alter his attitude to us; it simply reveals his attitude."[3] Likewise, human behavior has arguably remained essentially unchanged throughout history, although we are capable of changing it. "While we may learn from the past," Ronald Wright observes, "we don't seem to learn much,"

2. Heschel, *Prophets: II*, 184.
3. Watts, *Behold the Spirit*, 78.

and every time that "history repeats itself, the price goes up." He notes that the death toll from the wars of the twentieth century surpasses one hundred million, twice the population of the former Roman Empire at its peak. Humanity's "best chance for avoiding the fate of past societies," Wright asserts, "is that we know about those past societies. We can see how and why they went wrong." If we fail to learn from the past, he predicts, "this new century will not grow very old before we enter an age of chaos and collapse that will dwarf all the dark ages in our past."[4] History repeats itself and is therefore circular as well as linear, unless humanity chooses to learn from past experience and alter our course.

Indeed, in many respects, looking at history is like gazing into a mirror and, in addition to demonstrating how past societies erred, history offers us an opportunity to observe what past societies or individuals did well, how wars and other destructive behaviors were prevented or stopped. It is this possibility of learning from the past, combined with awareness of the power of individuals in shaping human experience and history, that constitutes perhaps the greatest ongoing relevance of history and of Jehanne in particular. Examination of Jehanne's role in the achievement of just peace during her era and demonstration of the applicability of her example to Bonhoeffer's active opposition to the evil that raged throughout Europe under Hitler some five centuries later suggests that, should her example be emulated, not in isolated aspects but quite thoroughly, it might be employed constructively to the benefit of humanity in the promotion of justice and peace currently and in the future. The model derived from Jehanne constituting one hundred security checks against false prophecy is more than a proposition capable of promoting goodness; it is a call to critical reflection and responsibility in responding to claims of divinely sanctioned violence.

There is minimal potential for abuse of such an extensive model which contains seventy-five essential criteria and effectively places claims under a microscope. Though not exhaustive, since an exhaustive model is a practical impossibility, it is highly sufficient and, if applied properly (i.e., with thoroughness, integrity, and thoughtfulness), it poses little to no danger. In fact, the Bible seems more susceptible to abuse than the model, ambiguous and internally contradictory as it is. We have seen that ethical norms are also potentially dangerous and susceptible to abuse; that something is normative does not render it necessarily

---

4. Wright, *History of Progress*, 82, 107, 120–21, 131–32.

good or sufficient, yet the fact that it is normative might imbue it with a false sense of correctness or goodness. Take, for example, the fact that slavery was once normative and considered appropriate. Furthermore, we have observed that utilitarian-based ethical systems, which rely on impossible calculation and lack security against self-serving application, are also insufficient and susceptible to abuse. Hence, the model is not more dangerous than what is commonplace in human society; all human systems are fallible. In fact, Jehanne's model could safeguard against many insufficiencies and abuses of current "ethical" practice and, in that regard, it might pose an inconvenience and a hindrance to those who do not wish their activities to be closely scrutinized.

Validating the usefulness of the model through its application does not validate Jehanne's claim to divinely sanctioned violence and, as informative as the Hitler and Bonhoeffer assessments are, the model must be applied properly and thoroughly to more than two cases in order for its merits (i.e., its internal integrity, value, and usefulness) to be adequately established and any possible shortcomings exposed. The case studies do, however, provide foundational evidence of the model's viability and usefulness in distinguishing between more and less compelling claims to divine sanction. As the model might be employed by numerous individuals with respect to a given case, it can open critical dialogue around a claim such that any discrepancies between various assessments might be resolved, or at least challenged, where misapplication of the criteria appears to have taken place. The model calls for thoroughness in the evaluation of claims to divinely sanctioned violence by steering assessments in the direction of the numerous criteria, and it assists in recognizing and unpacking the language of those claiming divine sanction, revealing critical differences between prophet and false prophet, between one who is willing to sacrifice all that belongs to him/herself personally in the call to violence and one who is willing to sacrifice primarily others (little or nothing personally), between one who respects the sanctity of life and one who tramples it, one who desires to liberate and one who desires to oppress, one who promotes justice and one who thrives on injustice, one who ultimately seeks peace and an end to war and one who initiates war as a first resort.

In addition to its evaluative and prescriptive elements, Jehanne's model is potentially remedial, which is to say that, if humanity were to act in accordance with it, there would be less warfare and a reduction of evil in war. "Her holiness is a beautiful example for lay people engaged in politics," writes Benedict XVI, "especially in the most difficult situations. ... St Joan of Arc invites us to a high standard of Christian living: to make prayer the guiding motive of our days; to have full trust in doing God's will, ... to live charity without favouritism, without limits and drawing" from divine love.[5] The model offers a method for measuring conformity to Jehanne's exemplary standard of living. In light of nuclear technology and the fact that many have called upon and continue to utter the name of God in support of violence, it is imperative, if humans are to have reasonable hope of avoiding unnecessary destruction and possible annihilation at our own hands, that we do not ignore but identify and consider very thoughtfully and systematically all claims to divinely sanctioned violence.

---

5. Benedict XVI, "Saint Joan," online.

Appendix

Model of Righteous Warfare and Human Agency

	Divine, Prophetic Calling Criteria		Divinely Sanctioned Human Agency Criteria		
1	receipt of divine revelation (e.g., visions, auditions) calling one to a specified task	1	undifferentiated compassion/mercy/forgiveness	40	does not define or claim elaborate understanding of God/accepts divine mystery
2	discernment of spirits (charism)	2	honors the sanctity of life	41	does not hold God responsible for human evil
3	offers oneself as an instrument of God and willing conduit for divine grace (decision aspect)	3	respects the dignity of the person	42	does not claim divine sanction with respect to all of one's actions but only those founded on divine revelation
4	actively engages in divine servantship/operates under willing obedience to divine (vs. human) authority/surrender of personal will to divine will/views oneself as being in an absolute relation to the divine	4	fully-engaged conscience	43	exercises personal responsibility and accountability before God and others
5	submits to divine judgment and lives in constant awareness of this judgment	5	operates from a driving force of love§	44	accepts unknown consequences/uncertainty

Divine, Prophetic Calling Criteria		Divinely Sanctioned Human Agency Criteria			
6	shares in God's happiness, sadness, concern, sympathy, and aspirations for the world/ active concern for humanity	6	genuine distress concerning all bloodshed/ not desensitized to violence or suffering	45	exercises independent thought
7	destabilizing presence in an unjust social system/exhortation to improve condition of humanity/serves the repair of the world and the common good	7	sense of duty to God/ God served first in all things	46	offers a merciful gift/ promise of a better future§§
8	lived witnessing of faith in God	8	love of God/piety	47	normally upholds customary moral laws
9	courage (inner strength) in responding to divine directive/ accomplishing task	9	fear of God	48	does not proclaim divine condemnation of others
10	general attentiveness	10	permits nothing to come between self and God/accepts no human deterrent	49	possible temporary suspension of universal ethic in some regard in relation to a divinely sanctioned higher *telos*
11	humility	11	mystical relationship transcends institutionalization or religious formulas/ mystical defiance	50	charism/spiritual gifts/uncanny abilities (including but not limited to those cited under Divine, Prophetic Calling column)/ mediates grace
12	production of good fruit	12	conviction/ determination/ persistence/endurance/uncompromised, singular commitment to declared mission	51	honest disposition/ transparency

Model of Righteous Warfare and Human Agency

	Divine, Prophetic Calling Criteria		Divinely Sanctioned Human Agency Criteria		
13	initial hesitation/reluctance/resistance/fear/doubt	13	does not engage in or encourage suicide/does not seek suffering or martyrdom	52	straightforward, honest language/forthrightness
14	apparent absurdity requiring faith in God	14	reluctantly accepts suffering or martyrdom if necessary to mystical witnessing	53	unambiguous public statement of purpose and method
15	prior lack of inclination, skill, or capacity to behave in required manner	15	steadfast faith in God and divine revelation	54	reliability/consistency/constancy
16	feelings of inadequacy	16	apprehension of the intrinsically evil nature of human violence and war/does not attempt to qualify evil	55	strives with the world, with self, and with God
17	feelings of unworthiness to carry out the mission, accompanied by assurance of divine assistance and creating a dependency on God	17	recognition of personal defilement sustained through the use of violence	56	expression of the sublime absolutely in the pedestrian‡
18	severe disruption to or break from previous lifestyle	18	deep sensitivity to evil vs. indifference	57	wisdom/sound judgment
19	personal risk/encounters hostility/persecution as a result of prophetic ministry	19	impatient with injustice/prone to righteous anger	58	undergoes mystical "dark night"/struggle with pain and suffering
20	experiences intense solitude/stands as the particular against the status quo	20	righteous character (not self-righteous)/ethical code of conduct (e.g., chivalry)/moral discernment/holds self and others to high ethical standard of behavior	59	demonstrates grace in extreme suffering

Divine, Prophetic Calling Criteria		Divinely Sanctioned Human Agency Criteria			
21	ability to prophesy (charism)	21	teaches by example over doctrine	60	embodies paradox
22	ability to perform miracles (charism)	22	service-oriented/ work ethic/ disinclination toward idleness or sloth	61	canonization/holiness/ posthumous miracles
Divinely Sanctioned Righteous Warfare Criteria		23	seeks to empower the disenfranchised/ partisan with the wrongly oppressed	62	identification with a particular, well-established prophecy‡‡
1	appeal to most sovereign authority (divinity)	24	honors personal responsibility in maintenance of social justice	§ Jehanne demonstrated love of human dignity, of peace, of justice, of compassion, of integrity, of conscience, of charity, of freedom, of service, of humility, of courage, of sanctity, of faith and, above all, love of God. Love was the animating force that operated through her with respect to all else; it coursed through her veins. §§ Jehanne's gift was multifold: peace, justice, freedom, courage, charity, compassion, forgiveness, faith, hope, love, and grace.	
2	defensive, not offensive	25	protects/defends others at potential cost to self		
3	not pre-emptive	26	direct participation in mission in a position of vulnerability		
4	last resort/entreats the enemy to leave or desist peacefully/ ultimatum	27	refuses to love evil/ actively opposes evil		
5	aims to establish just peace	28	prefers peace to war and non-violence to violence		
6	proportionate cause	29	does not glorify violence or war		
7	does not operate from vengeance or hatred	30	concern for spiritual welfare of self and others/apprehends spiritual implications		
8	does not seek to acquire new territory but might protect or recover rightful lands	31	benevolence/kindness/does not engage in cruelty		

Model of Righteous Warfare and Human Agency

	Divinely Sanctioned Righteous Warfare Criteria		Divinely Sanctioned Human Agency Criteria	
9	does not seek domination of others (oppression)	32	generosity/charity	‡ Jehanne brought the sublime qualities of compassion, humility, gratitude, charity, respect, dignity, nobility, justice, conscience, sanctity, and love to all manner of activity in which she engaged.
10	does not engage in holy war	33	rejects personal glorification and idolization	
11	formal declaration of intent to engage in war/warning	34	is not motivated by self-fulfillment or material gain	
12	employs minimal appropriate force (proportionality)/ minimal bloodshed/ forbids unnecessary evil/excessive force	35	refuses to benefit from anything unjustly acquired	‡‡ This refers to association with long-existent prophecy, demonstrating a lack of arbitrariness.
13	does not target noncombatants	36	clarity of purpose	
14	does not employ torture	37	sincerity/authenticity	
15	does not inflict suffering for its own sake	38	integrity	
16	forbids looting	39	treats God as a Subject, not an object to be bent to one's will	▢ Essential criteria ▢ Non-essential criteria

Bibliography

Adams, Guy B., and Danny L. Balfour. *Unmasking Administrative Evil.* Advances in Public Administration. Thousand Oaks, CA: Sage, 1998.
Adams, Jeremy duQuesnay. Preface and Prelude to *Joan of Arc: Her Story*, by Régine Pernoud and Marie-Véronique Clin. Edited by Bonnie Wheeler. Translated and revised by Jeremy duQuesnay Adams. New York: St. Martin's Griffin, 1999.
Aquinas, Thomas, Saint. *Summa Theologica.* 1st complete American ed. in 3 vols. Translated by Fathers of the English Dominican Province. Vol. 2. New York: Benziger Brothers, 1947.
Arendt, Hannah. *Eichmann in Jerusalem: A Report on the Banality of Evil.* Rev. ed. Penguin Twentieth-Century Classics. New York: Penguin, 1965.
———. *The Life of the Mind.* One-volume ed. San Diego: Harcourt, 1978.
———. *On Violence.* Orlando: Harcourt, 1969.
Astell, Ann W., and Bonnie Wheeler, eds. *Joan of Arc and Spirituality.* The New Middle Ages. New York: Palgrave Macmillan, 2003.
———. "Joan of Arc and Spirituality." In *Joan of Arc and Spirituality*, edited by Ann W. Astell and Bonnie Wheeler, 1–5. The New Middle Ages. New York: Palgrave Macmillan, 2003.
Augustine, Saint. *The City of God against the Pagans.* Translated by William Chase Greene. Vol. 6. Books 18.36–20. Loeb Classical Library 416. Cambridge: Harvard University Press, 1960.
Backman, Clifford R. *The Worlds of Medieval Europe.* New York: Oxford University Press, 2003.
Ballade contre les Anglais. ca. 1429. In "Ballade contre les Anglais, 1429," by P. Meyer. *Romania* 21 (1892) 50–52.
Barstow, Anne Llewellyn. *Joan of Arc: Heretic, Mystic, Shaman.* Studies in Women and Religion 17. Lewiston, NY: Mellen, 1986.
Barth, Karl. *Evangelical Theology: An Introduction.* Translated by Grover Foley. Grand Rapids: Eerdmans, 1963.
———. *Theological Existence Today: A Plea for Theological Freedom.* Translated by R. Birch Hoyle. London: Hodder and Stoughton, 1933.
Baum, Rainer C. "Holocaust: Moral Indifference as the Form of Modern Evil." In *Echoes from the Holocaust: Philosophical Reflections on a Dark Time*, edited by Alan Rosenberg and Gerald E. Myers, 53–90. Philadelphia: Temple University Press, 1988.
Bell, George K. A. Foreword to *The Cost of Discipleship*, by Dietrich Bonhoeffer. Translated by R. H. Fuller and Irmgard Booth. London: SCM, 2001.

Bellamy, Alex J. *Just Wars: From Cicero to Iraq*. Cambridge: Polity, 2006.
Benedict XVI. "Saint Joan of Arc." General Audience. Paul VI Audience Hall. January 26, 2011. Rome: Libreria Editrice Vaticana, 2011. No pages. Online: http://www.vatican.va/holy_father/benedict_xvi/audiences/2011/documents/hf_ben-xvi_aud_20110126_en.html.
Berenbaum, Michael. "In a World Without a Redeemer, Redeem!" In *Contemporary Jewish Religious Responses to the Shoah*, edited by Steven L. Jacobs, 23–32. Studies in the Shoah 5. Lanham, MD: University Press of America, 1993.
Bernanos, Georges. *Sanctity Will Out: An Essay on St. Joan*. London: Sheed & Ward, 1947.
Best, S. Payne. *The Venlo Incident: A True Story of Double-Dealing, Captivity, and a Murderous Nazi Plot*. New York: Skyhorse, 2009.
Bethge, Eberhard. *Dietrich Bonhoeffer: A Biography; Theologian, Christian, Man for His Times*. Rev. ed. Edited by Victoria J. Barnett. Translated by Eric Mosbacher et al. Minneapolis: Fortress, 2000.
———. "Friends." In *I Knew Dietrich Bonhoeffer*, edited by Wolf-Dieter Zimmermann and Ronald Gregor Smith. Translated by Käthe Gregor Smith, 46–51. The Fontana Library of Theology and Philosophy. London: Fontana, 1973.
———. Preface to the First through the Fifth German Editions of *Ethics*, by Dietrich Bonhoeffer. Edited by Eberhard Bethge. Translated by Neville Horton Smith. New York: Simon & Schuster, 1955.
Bismarck, Ruth-Alice von. Preface to *Love Letters From Cell 92: The Correspondence between Dietrich Bonhoeffer and Maria von Wedemeyer 1943–45*, by Dietrich Bonhoeffer and Maria von Wedemeyer. Edited by Ruth-Alice von Bismarck and Ulrich Kabitz. Translated by John Brownjohn. Nashville: Abingdon, 1994.
Blenkinsopp, Joseph. *A History of Prophecy in Israel*. Rev. ed. Louisville: Westminster John Knox, 1996.
Bonhoeffer, Dietrich. *The Cost of Discipleship*. Translated by R. H. Fuller and Irmgard Booth. London: SCM, 2001.
———. *Ethics*. Edited by Eberhard Bethge. Translated by Neville Horton Smith. New York: Simon & Schuster, 1955.
———. *Letters and Papers from Prison*. Enlarged ed. Edited by Eberhard Bethge. Translated by Reginald Fuller et al. New York: Simon & Schuster, 1971.
———. *Life Together*. Translated by John W. Doberstein. San Francisco: Harper & Row, 1954.
———. *No Rusty Swords: Letters, Lectures and Notes 1928–1936 from the Collected Works*. Edited by Edwin H. Robertson. Revised translation by John Bowden and Eberhard Bethge. The Fontana Library of Theology and Philosophy, Vol. 1. London: Fontana, 1970.
Bonhoeffer, Dietrich, and Maria von Wedemeyer. *Love Letters From Cell 92: The Correspondence between Dietrich Bonhoeffer and Maria von Wedemeyer 1943–45*. Edited by Ruth-Alice von Bismarck and Ulrich Kabitz. Translated by John Brownjohn. Nashville: Abingdon, 1994.
Bonhoeffer, Emmi. "Professors' Children as Neighbours." In *I Knew Dietrich Bonhoeffer*, edited by Wolf-Dieter Zimmermann and Ronald Gregor Smith. Translated by Käthe Gregor Smith, 34–37. The Fontana Library of Theology and Philosophy. London: Fontana, 1973.
Brady, Robert A. *The Spirit and Structure of German Fascism*. London: Gollancz, 1937.

Brueggemann, Walter. "The Prophet as a Destabilizing Presence." In *Prophetic Approaches to Israel's Communal Life*, edited by Patrick D. Miller, 221–44. Minneapolis: Fortress, 1994.

Busch, Eberhard. *Karl Barth: His Life from Letters and Autobiographical Texts*. 2nd rev. ed. Translated by John Bowden. London: SCM, 1976.

Casaldáliga, Pedro. "Mystik der Befreiung." In *Mystik der Befreiung: Ein Portrait des Bischofs Pedro Casaldáliga n Brasilien*, by Teófilo Cabastrero, 83–84. Wuppertal: Youth Service, 1981.

Chilton, Bruce. *Abraham's Curse: The Roots of Violence in Judaism, Christianity, and Islam*. New York: Doubleday, 2008.

Cobos, David. Interview by Anna Maria Tremonti. *The Current*. CBC. December 2, 2010.

Cohen, Leonard. *Stranger Music: Selected Poems and Songs*. Toronto: McClelland & Stewart, 1993.

Copleston, Frederick. *Medieval Philosophy. A History of Philosophy* Vol. 2. New York: Image, 1950.

Cunningham, Lawrence S. *The Catholic Heritage: Martyrs, Ascetics, Pilgrims, Warriors, Mystics, Theologians, Artists, Humanists, Activists, Outsiders, and Saints*. New York: Crossroad, 1983.

De bono et malo spiritu. September, 1429. In "Un nouveau temoignage sur Jeanne d'Arc: la réponse d'un clerc parisien à l'apologie de la Pucelle par Jean Gerson (1429)," by N. Valois. *Annuaire-bulletin de la Société de l'Histoire de France* 43 (1906) 175–79.

De mirabili victoria. 1429. In *Procès en Nullité de la Condamnation de Jeanne d'Arc*, edited and translated by Pierre Duparc, 34–39. La Société de l'Histoire de France, Fondation du Département des Vosges, Vol. 2. Paris: la Société de l'Histoire de France, 1979.

DeVries, Kelly. *Joan of Arc: A Military Leader*. Stroud, UK: Sutton, 1999.

———. "A Woman as Leader of Men: Joan of Arc's Military Career." In *Fresh Verdicts on Joan of Arc*, edited by Bonnie Wheeler and Charles T. Wood, 3–18. The New Middle Ages 2. New York: Garland, 1996.

Doberstein, John W. Introduction to *Life Together*, by Dietrich Bonhoeffer. Translated by John W. Doberstein. San Francisco: Harper & Row, 1954.

Domarus, Max. *The Essential Hitler: Speeches and Commentary*. Edited by Patrick Romane. Wauconda, IL: Bolchazy-Carducci, 2007.

Doncoeur, Paul. *La Minute Française des Interrogatoires de Jeanne la Pucelle: d'après le Réquisitoire de Jean d'Estivet et les manuscrits de d'Urfé et d'Orléans*. Melun, France: Librairie d'Argences, 1952.

Downie, R. S. "Evil, Human." In *The Oxford Companion to Philosophy*, 2nd ed., edited by Ted Honderich, 273–74. Oxford: Oxford University Press, 2005.

Duparc, Pierre, translator. *Procès en Nullité de la Condamnation de Jeanne d'Arc*. Edited by la Société de l'Histoire de France, Fondation du Département des Vosges. Vol. 4. Paris: la Société de l'Histoire de France, 1986.

Dupuy, Jean. *Collectarium historiarum*. 1429. In "Le témoignage de Jean Dupuy, O.P., sur Jeanne d'Arc. Note additionnelle à AFP XII (1942) 167–84," by A. Dondaine. *Archivum fratrum praedicatorum* 38 (1968) 34–41.

Elshtain, Jean Bethke. "Epilogue: Continuing Implications of the Just War Tradition." In *Just War Theory*, edited by Jean Bethke Elshtain, 323–33. New York: New York University Press, 1992.

Fauquembergue, Clément de. *Journal de Clément de Fauquembergue, greffier du Parlement du Paris, 1417-1435.* Edited by A. Tuetey and H. Lacaille. 3 vols. Paris: 1903-15.

Feyerabend, Karl. *Langenscheidt's Pocket Greek Dictionary: Greek-English.* Langenscheidt's Pocket Dictionaries. London: Hodder & Stoughton, no date.

Fischer, Heribert. "Mysticism: Nature and History." In *Encyclopedia of Theology: The Concise Sacramentum Mundi*, edited by Karl Rahner, 1004-10. Mumbai: St. Pauls, 1975.

Fischer-Hüllstrung, H. "A Report from Flossenbürg." In *I Knew Dietrich Bonhoeffer*, edited by Wolf-Dieter Zimmermann and Ronald Gregor Smith. Translated by Käthe Gregor Smith, 232. The Fontana Library of Theology and Philosophy. London: Fontana, 1973.

Flannery, Austin, ed. *Vatican Council II: The Conciliar and Post Conciliar Documents.* New rev. ed. Vol. 1. The Vatican Collection. Northport, NY: Costello, 1996.

Fleischner, Eva, editor. *Auschwitz: Beginning of a New Era? Reflections on the Holocaust; Papers given at the International Symposium on the Holocaust held at the Cathedral of Saint John the Divine, New York City, June 3 to 6, 1974.* New York: KTAV, 1977.

Forest, Jim. Foreword to *Peace in the Post-Christian Era*, by Thomas Merton. Edited by Patricia A. Burton. Maryknoll, NY: Orbis, 2004.

Fraioli, Deborah A. *Joan of Arc: The Early Debate.* Woodbridge: Boydell, 2000.

———. *Joan of Arc and the Hundred Years War.* Edited by Jane Chance. Greenwood Guides to Historic Events of the Medieval World. Westport, CT: Greenwood, 2005.

Franc, Martin Le. *Le champion des dames.* Vol. 4. Edited by R. Deschaux. Paris: 1999.

Gellately, Robert. *Lenin, Stalin, and Hitler: The Age of Social Catastrophe.* New York: Vintage, 2007.

Gerson, Jean. *Jean Gerson: Early Works.* Translated by Brian Patrick McGuire. The Classics of Western Spirituality. Mahwah, NJ: Paulist, 1998.

Girard, René. *Things Hidden since the Foundation of the World.* Translated by Stephen Bann and Michael Metteer. Stanford: Stanford University Press, 1987.

Goldensohn, Leon. *The Nuremberg Interviews: An American Psychiatrist's Conversations with the Defendants and Witnesses.* Edited by Robert Gellately. New York: Vintage, 2005.

Gordon, Mary. *Joan of Arc.* Penguin Lives. New York: Penguin, 2000.

Greenberg, Irving. "Cloud of Smoke, Pillar of Fire: Judaism, Christianity, and Modernity after the Holocaust." In *Auschwitz: Beginning of a New Era? Reflections on the Holocaust; Papers given at the International Symposium on the Holocaust held at the Cathedral of Saint John the Divine, New York City, June 3 to 6, 1974*, edited by Eva Fleischner, 7-55. New York: KTAV, 1977.

———. "Voluntary Covenant." In *Contemporary Jewish Religious Responses to the Shoah*, edited by Steven L. Jacobs, 77-105. Studies in the Shoah 5. Lanham, MD: University Press of America, 1993.

Griscom, Acton. *The Historia Regum Britanniae of Geoffrey of Monmouth.* New York: Longmans, Green, and co., 1929.

Guthrie, Charles, and Michael Quinlan. *Just War: The Just War Tradition; Ethics in Modern Warfare.* London: Bloomsbury, 2007.

Haas, Peter J. "Auschwitz: Re-Envisioning the Role of God." In *Contemporary Jewish Religious Responses to the Shoah*, edited by Steven L. Jacobs, 107-33. Studies in the Shoah 5. Lanham, MD: University Press of America, 1993.

Bibliography 321

Haight, Roger. *The Experience and Language of Grace*. Mahwah, NJ: Paulist, 1979.

Halasz, Joachim von, editor. Introduction to *Hitler: Speeches and Quotes; First Published in 1938 as 'Adolf Hitler From Speeches 1933-1938.'* 1938. Reprint. World Propaganda Classics (Series). London: World Propaganda Classics, 2008.

Heiden, Konrad. Introduction to *Mein Kampf*, by Adolf Hitler. Translated by Ralph Manheim. Boston: Houghton Mifflin, 1943.

Heschel, Abraham J. "The Hiding God." In *Wrestling With God: Jewish Theological Responses during and after the Holocaust*, edited by Steven T. Katz et al., 378–80. New York: Oxford University Press, 2007.

———. *The Prophets: An Introduction*. New York: Harper Torchbooks, 1962.

———. *The Prophets: Part II*. New York: Harper Torchbooks, 1962.

Heyking, John von. "Taming Warriors in Classical and Early Medieval Political Theory." In *Ethics, Nationalism, and Just War: Medieval and Contemporary Perspectives*, edited by Henrik Syse and Gregory M. Reichberg, 11–35. Washington, DC: Catholic University of America Press, 2007.

Hildebrandt, Franz. "An Oasis of Freedom." In *I Knew Dietrich Bonhoeffer*, edited by Wolf-Dieter Zimmermann and Ronald Gregor Smith. Translated by Käthe Gregor Smith, 38–40. The Fontana Library of Theology and Philosophy. London: Fontana, 1973.

Hitler, Adolf. *Mein Kampf*. Translated by Ralph Manheim. Boston: Houghton Mifflin, 1943.

Hobbins, Daniel, translator. *The Trial of Joan of Arc*. Cambridge: Harvard University Press, 2005.

Hofmann, Rudolf. "Conscience." In *Encyclopedia of Theology: The Concise Sacramentum Mundi*, edited by Karl Rahner, 283–88. Mumbai: St. Pauls, 1975.

Hogan, Linda. *Confronting the Truth: Conscience in the Catholic Tradition*. Mahwah, NJ: Paulist, 2000.

Holmes, George, ed. *The Oxford History of Medieval Europe*. Oxford: Oxford University Press, 1988.

Honderich, Ted, ed. *The Oxford Companion to Philosophy*. 2nd ed. Oxford: Oxford University Press, 2005.

Hvidt, Niels Christian. *Christian Prophecy: The Post-Biblical Tradition*. New York: Oxford University Press, 2007.

Ignatieff, Michael. *The Lesser Evil: Political Ethics in an Age of Terror*. The Gifford Lectures. Toronto: Penguin, 2004.

Inwagen, Peter van. *The Problem of Evil: The Gifford Lectures Delivered in the University of St Andrews in 2003*. Oxford: Oxford University Press, 2006.

Jacobs, Steven L. "Judaism and Christianity After Auschwitz." In *Contemporary Jewish Religious Responses to the Shoah*, edited by Steven L. Jacobs, 1–21. Studies in the Shoah 5. Lanham, MD: University Press of America, 1993.

John of the Cross, Saint. *The Collected Works of St. John of the Cross*. Translated by Kieran Kavanaugh and Otilio Rodriguez. Washington, DC: ICS, 1979.

Johnson, James Turner. "Thinking Morally about War in the Middle Ages and Today." In *Ethics, Nationalism, and Just War: Medieval and Contemporary Perspectives*, edited by Henrik Syse and Gregory M. Reichberg, 3–10. Washington, DC: Catholic University of America Press, 2007.

Kabitz, Ulrich, and Ruth-Alice von Bismarck, eds. *Love Letters From Cell 92: The Correspondence between Dietrich Bonhoeffer and Maria von Wedemeyer 1943–45*, by Dietrich Bonhoeffer and Maria von Wedemeyer. Translated by John Brownjohn. Nashville: Abingdon, 1994.

Katz, Steven T., et al., eds. *Wrestling with God: Jewish Theological Responses during and after the Holocaust*. New York: Oxford University Press, 2007.

Kierkegaard, Søren. *On Authority and Revelation: The Book on Adler, or a Cycle of Ethico-Religious Essays*. Edited and translated by Walter Lowrie. The Cloister Library. New York: Harper & Row, 1966.

———. *Fear and Trembling*. Translated by Alastair Hannay. Penguin Books—Great Ideas. London: Penguin, 1985.

———. *Stages on Life's Way*. Translated by Walter Lowrie. New York: Schocken, 1967.

Kren, George M. "The Holocaust: Moral Theory and Immoral Acts." In *Echoes from the Holocaust: Philosophical Reflections on a Dark Time*, edited by Alan Rosenberg and Gerald E. Myers, 245–61. Philadelphia: Temple University Press, 1988.

Lang, Berel. "Language and Genocide." In *Echoes from the Holocaust: Philosophical Reflections on a Dark Time*, edited by Alan Rosenberg and Gerald E. Myers, 341–61. Philadelphia: Temple University Press, 1988.

Lash, Nicholas. *Easter in Ordinary: Reflections on Human Experience and the Knowledge of God*. Notre Dame, IN: University of Notre Dame Press, 1988.

Lehmann, Paul. "Paradox of Discipleship." In *I Knew Dietrich Bonhoeffer*, edited by Wolf-Dieter Zimmermann and Ronald Gregor Smith. Translated by Käthe Gregor Smith, 41–45. The Fontana Library of Theology and Philosophy. London: Fontana, 1973.

Leibholz, Gerhard. "Memoir." In *The Cost of Discipleship*, by Dietrich Bonhoeffer. Translated by R. H. Fuller and Irmgard Booth, xiii–xxx. London: SCM, 2001.

Leibholz, Sabine. "Childhood and Home." In *I Knew Dietrich Bonhoeffer*, edited by Wolf-Dieter Zimmermann and Ronald Gregor Smith. Translated by Käthe Gregor Smith, 19–33. The Fontana Library of Theology and Philosophy. London: Fontana, 1973.

Lewis, C. S. *Surprised by Joy*. London: Bles, 1955.

Mackie, John. "Virtue." In *Vice and Virtue in Everyday Life: Introductory Readings in Ethics*, edited by Christina Hoff Sommers, 224–30. San Diego: Harcourt Brace Jovanovich, 1985.

Margolis, Nadia. "The 'Joan Phenomenon' and the French Right." In *Fresh Verdicts on Joan of Arc*, edited by Bonnie Wheeler and Charles T. Wood, 265–87. The New Middle Ages 2. New York: Garland, 1996.

———. "The Mortal Body as Divine Proof: A Spiritual-Physical Blazon of Joan of Arc." In *Joan of Arc and Spirituality*, edited by Ann W. Astell and Bonnie Wheeler, 9–36. The New Middle Ages. New York: Palgrave Macmillan, 2003.

Marot, Pierre. *Joan the Good Lorrainer at Domremy: The Upper Meuse Marches, Joan's Mission, Memory and Worship of the Heroine in Her Country*. Translated by Laure Brissaud. Colmar, France: Editions S.A.E.P. Ingersheim, 1981.

Mattox, John Mark. *St. Augustine and the Theory of Just War*. Continuum Studies in Philosophy. New York: Continuum, 2006.

McFague, Sallie. *Models of God: Theology for an Ecological, Nuclear Age*. Philadelphia: Fortress, 1987.

McGrath, Alister E. *Christian Theology: An Introduction*. 5th ed. Chichester, UK: Wiley-Blackwell, 2010.

McInerney, Maud Burnett. *Eloquent Virgins: From Thecla to Joan of Arc*. The New Middle Ages. New York: Palgrave Macmillan, 2003.

Merton, Thomas. *Disputed Questions*. San Diego: Harcourt Brace, 1953.

———. *An Introduction to Christian Mysticism: Initiation into the Monastic Tradition 3*. Edited by Patrick F. O'Connell. Monastic Wisdom Series 13. Kalamazoo: Cistercian, 2008.

———. *No Man Is an Island*. San Diego: Harcourt, 1955.

———. *Peace in the Post-Christian Era*. Edited by Patricia A. Burton. Maryknoll, NY: Orbis, 2004.

———. *Run to the Mountain: The Story of a Vocation*. Edited by Patrick Hart. The Journals of Thomas Merton 1, 1939–1941. San Francisco: HarperSanFrancisco, 1995.

Metaxas, Eric. *Bonhoeffer: Pastor, Martyr, Prophet, Spy; A Righteous Gentile vs. the Third Reich*. Nashville: Thomas Nelson, 2010.

Molinari, Paul. "Canonization of Saints." In *New Catholic Encyclopedia*, 55–61. Vol. 3. New York: McGraw-Hill, 1967.

Moltmann, Jürgen. *The Crucified God: The Cross of Christ as the Foundation and Criticism of Christian Theology*. Translated by R. A. Wilson and John Bowden. Minneapolis: Augsburg Fortress, 1993.

Monstrelet, Enguerran[d] de. *La chronique d'Enguerran de Monstrelet en deux livres avec pièces justicatives (1400–44)*. Edited by L. Douët d'Arcq. Vol. 4. Paris: Renouard, 1857–62.

Murray, T. Douglas, ed. *Jeanne d'Arc: Maid of Orleans, Deliverer of France; Being the Story of her Life, her Achievements, and her Death, as attested on Oath and Set forth in the Original Documents*. 1902. Reprint. Whitefish, MT: Kessinger, 2010.

Nash-Marshall, Siobhan. *Joan of Arc: A Spiritual Biography*. Lives & Legacies. New York: Crossroad, 1999.

New Lexicon Webster's Encyclopedic Dictionary of the English Language. Canadian ed. New York: Lexicon, 1988.

Niebuhr, Reinhold. "To America and Back." In *I Knew Dietrich Bonhoeffer*, edited by Wolf-Dieter Zimmermann and Ronald Gregor Smith. Translated by Käthe Gregor Smith, 165. The Fontana Library of Theology and Philosophy. London: Fontana, 1973.

Nietzsche, Friedrich. "Ecce Homo." In *Basic Writings of Nietzsche*, edited and translated by Walter Kaufmann, 655–791. The Modern Library Classics. New York: The Modern Library, 2000.

O'Donohue, John. *Beauty: The Invisible Embrace*. CD, W77OD. Boulder, CO: Sounds True, 2004.

———. *To Bless the Space between Us: A Collection of Invocations and Blessings*. CD, W1197D. Boulder, CO: Sounds True, 2008.

———. *The Four Elements: Reflections on Nature*. London: Transworld Ireland, 2010.

Orléans Manuscript 518. ca. 1498–1515. Bibliothèque Municipale d'Orléans, Orléans.

Overy, Richard. *Interrogations: The Nazi Elite in Allied Hands, 1945*. New York: Viking Penguin, 2001.

Payne, Robert. *The Life and Death of Adolf Hitler*. New York: Praeger, 1973.

Pernoud, Régine. "Epilogue: Joan of Arc or the Survival of a People." In *Fresh Verdicts on Joan of Arc*, edited by Bonnie Wheeler and Charles T. Wood, 289–93. The New Middle Ages 2. New York: Garland, 1996.

———. *Joan of Arc: By Herself and Her Witnesses*. Translated by Edward Hyams. Lanham, MD: Scarborough House, 1964.

———. *The Retrial of Joan of Arc: The Evidence for her Vindication*. Translated by J. M. Cohen. San Francisco: Ignatius, 1955.

———. *Those Terrible Middle Ages: Debunking the Myths*. Translated by Anne Englund Nash. San Francisco: Ignatius, 2000.

Pernoud, Régine, and Marie-Véronique Clin. *Joan of Arc: Her Story*. Edited by Bonnie Wheeler. Translated and revised by Jeremy duQuesnay Adams. New York: St. Martin's Griffin, 1999.

Pia, Jack. *Nazi Regalia*. Ballantine's Illustrated History of the Violent Century. New York: Ballantine, 1971.

Pinzino, Jane Marie. "Joan of Arc and *Lex Privata*: A Spirit of Freedom in the Law." In *Joan of Arc and Spirituality*, edited by Ann W. Astell and Bonnie Wheeler, 85–109. The New Middle Ages. New York: Palgrave Macmillan, 2003.

———. "Just War, Joan of Arc, and the Politics of Salvation." In *The Hundred Years War: A Wider Focus*, edited by L. J. Andrew Villalon and Donald J. Kagay, 365–96. History of Warfare 25. Leiden: Koninklijke Brill, 2005.

Pirruccello, Ann. "Force or Fragility? Simone Weil and Two Faces of Joan of Arc." In *Joan of Arc and Spirituality*, edited by Ann W. Astell and Bonnie Wheeler, 267–81. The New Middle Ages. New York: Palgrave Macmillan, 2003.

Pizan, Christine de. *The Book of Deeds of Arms and of Chivalry*. Edited by Charity Cannon Willard. Translated by Sumner Willard. University Park: The Pennsylvania State University Press, 1999.

———. *Le ditié de Jehanne d'Arc*. Edited and translated by A. J. Kennedy and K. Varty. Oxford: 1977.

Poelchau, Harald. "The Freedom of the Prisoner." In *I Knew Dietrich Bonhoeffer*, edited by Wolf-Dieter Zimmermann and Ronald Gregor Smith. Translated by Käthe Gregor Smith, 222–25. The Fontana Library of Theology and Philosophy. London: Fontana, 1973.

Poulain, R. P. Aug. *The Graces of Interior Prayer (Des Grâces d'Oraison): A Treatise on Mystical Theology*. 6th ed. Translated by Leonora L. Yorke Smith. London: Kegan Paul, Trench, Trübner & Co., 1911.

Pringle, Heather. *The Master Plan: Himmler's Scholars and the Holocaust*. London: Harper Perennial, 2006.

Quicherat, Jules, ed. *Procès de Condamnation et de Réhabilitation de Jeanne d'Arc Dite la Pucelle*. Vol. 4. Paris: la Société de l'Histoire de France, 1847.

Rahner, Karl. "Charism." In *Encyclopedia of Theology: The Concise Sacramentum Mundi*, edited by Karl Rahner, 184–86. Mumbai: St. Pauls, 1975.

———, ed. *Encyclopedia of Theology: The Concise Sacramentum Mundi*. Mumbai: St. Pauls, 1975.

———. *Inquiries: Inspiration in the Bible, Visions and Prophecies, The Church and the Sacraments, The Episcopate and the Primacy, On Heresy*. Translated by Charles H. Henkey et al. New York: Herder and Herder, 1964.

———. "Prophetism." In *Encyclopedia of Theology: The Concise Sacramentum Mundi*, edited by Karl Rahner, 1286–89. Mumbai: St. Pauls, 1975.

Ratzinger, Joseph. "Das Problem der Christlichen Prophetie: Niels Christian Hvidt im Gespräch mit Joseph Kardinal Ratzinger." *Communio* 2 (1999) 177–88.

Romane, Patrick. Preface to *The Essential Hitler: Speeches and Commentary*, by Max Domarus. Edited by Patrick Romane. Wauconda, IL: Bolchazy-Carducci, 2007.

Rosenberg, Alan, and Gerald E. Myers, eds. *Echoes from the Holocaust: Philosophical Reflections on a Dark Time*. Philadelphia: Temple University Press, 1988.

Rott, Wilhelm. "Something Always Occurred to Him." In *I Knew Dietrich Bonhoeffer*, edited by Wolf-Dieter Zimmermann and Ronald Gregor Smith. Translated by Käthe Gregor Smith, 130–37. The Fontana Library of Theology and Philosophy. London: Fontana, 1973.

Russell, Preston. *Lights of Madness: In Search of Joan of Arc*. Savannah, GA: Beil, 2005.

Schlabrendorff, Fabian von. "In Prison with Dietrich Bonhoeffer." In *I Knew Dietrich Bonhoeffer*, edited by Wolf-Dieter Zimmermann and Ronald Gregor Smith. Translated by Käthe Gregor Smith, 226–31. The Fontana Library of Theology and Philosophy. London: Fontana, 1973.

Schönherr, Albrecht. "The Single-heartedness of the Provoked." In *I Knew Dietrich Bonhoeffer*, edited by Wolf-Dieter Zimmermann and Ronald Gregor Smith. Translated by Käthe Gregor Smith, 126–29. The Fontana Library of Theology and Philosophy. London: Fontana, 1973.

Scott, W. S. *Jeanne d'Arc: Her Life, Her Death, and the Myth*. London: Harrap, 1974.

———, trans. *The Trial of Joan of Arc: Being the Verbatim Report of the Proceedings from the Orleans Manuscript*. London: The Folio Society, 1956.

Soelle, Dorothee. *The Silent Cry: Mysticism and Resistance*. Translated by Barbara and Martin Rumscheidt. Minneapolis: Fortress, 2001.

———. *Theology for Skeptics: Reflections on God*. Translated by Joyce L. Irwin. Minneapolis: Augsburg Fortress, 1995.

Sommers, Christina Hoff, ed. *Vice and Virtue in Everyday Life: Introductory Readings in Ethics*. San Diego: Harcourt Brace Jovanovich, 1985.

Southern, R. W. *Western Society and the Church in the Middle Ages*. The Penguin History of the Church 2. London: Penguin, 1970.

Speer, Albert. *Inside the Third Reich: Memoirs*. Translated by Richard and Clara Winston. New York: Simon & Schuster, 1970.

Splett, Jörg. "Saints." In *Encyclopedia of Theology: The Concise Sacramentum Mundi*, edited by Karl Rahner, 1495–99. Mumbai: St. Pauls, 1975.

Spoto, Donald. *Joan: The Mysterious Life of the Heretic Who Became a Saint*. New York: HarperOne, 2007.

Syndor, Charles W., Jr. Foreword to *The Essential Hitler: Speeches and Commentary*, by Max Domarus. Edited by Patrick Romane. Wauconda, IL: Bolchazy-Carducci, 2007.

Syse, Henrik, and Gregory M. Reichberg, eds. *Ethics, Nationalism, and Just War: Medieval and Contemporary Perspectives*. Washington, DC: Catholic University of America Press, 2007.

Tavard, George H. *The Spiritual Way of St. Jeanne d'Arc*. Collegeville, MN: Liturgical, 1998.

Taylor, Craig, trans. *Joan of Arc: La Pucelle*. Manchester Medieval Sources Series. Manchester: Manchester University Press, 2006.

Taylor, Larissa Juliet. *The Virgin Warrior: The Life and Death of Joan of Arc*. London: Yale University Press, 2009.

Taylor, Paul W. *Principles of Ethics: An Introduction*. Belmont, CA: Wadsworth, 1975.

Teresa of Avila, Saint. *The Book of Her Foundations, Minor Works: The Constitutions—On Making the Visitation—A Satirical Critique—Response to a Spiritual Challenge—*

Poetry. *The Collected Works of St. Teresa of Avila*, Vol. 3. Translated by Kieran Kavanaugh and Otilio Rodriguez. Washington, DC: ICS, 1985.

———. *The Book of Her Life, Spiritual Testimonies, Soliloquies*. 2nd rev. ed. *The Collected Works of St. Teresa of Avila*, Vol. 1. Translated by Kieran Kavanaugh and Otilio Rodriguez. Washington, DC: ICS, 1976.

———. *The Way of Perfection, Meditations on the Song of Songs, The Interior Castle. The Collected Works of St. Teresa of Avila*, Vol. 2. Translated by Kieran Kavanaugh and Otilio Rodriguez. Washington, DC: ICS, 1980.

Tisset, Pierre, and Yvonne Lanhers, trans. *Procès de Condamnation de Jeanne d'Arc*. Edited by la Société de l'Histoire de France, Fondation du Département des Vosges. Vol. 1. Paris: la Société de l'Histoire de France, 1960.

———, trans. *Procès de Condamnation de Jeanne d'Arc*. Edited by la Société de l'Histoire de France, Fondation du Département des Vosges. Vol. 2. Paris: la Société de l'Histoire de France, 1970.

Toniolo, Alessandro. "Nostalgia delle Origini: Profezia o Anarchia Celebrativa?" *Rivista Liturgica* 84 (1997) 787–812, 806.

Turner, Denys. *The Darkness of God: Negativity in Christian Mysticism*. Cambridge: Cambridge University Press, 1995.

Turner, Victor Witter. *The Ritual Process: Structure and Anti-Structure*. The Lewis Henry Morgan Lectures. New York: de Gruyter, 1995.

United States Holocaust Memorial Museum. "Nazi Medical Experiments." In *Holocaust Encyclopedia*. Washington, DC. No pages. Online: http://www.ushmm.org/wlc/en/article.php?ModuleId=10005168.

Vale, Malcolm. "The Civilization of Courts and Cities in the North: 1200–1500." In *The Oxford History of Medieval Europe*, edited by George Holmes, 276–323. Oxford: Oxford University Press, 1988.

Vetlesen, Arne Johan. "Genocide: A Case for the Responsibility of the Bystander." In *Ethics, Nationalism, and Just War: Medieval and Contemporary Perspectives*, edited by Henrik Syse and Gregory M. Reichberg, 352–71. Washington, DC: The Catholic University of America Press, 2007.

Villalon, L. J. Andrew, and Donald J. Kagay, eds. *The Hundred Years War: A Wider Focus*. History of Warfare 25. Leiden: Koninklijke Brill, 2005.

Vorgrimler, Herbert. *Sacramental Theology*. Translated by Linda M. Maloney. Collegeville, MN: Liturgical, 1992.

Waite, Robert G. L. *The Psychopathic God: Adolf Hitler*. New York: Basic, 1977.

Walzer, Michael. *Just and Unjust Wars: A Moral Argument with Historical Illustrations*. 4th ed. New York: Basic, 2006.

Warner, Marina. *Joan of Arc: The Image of Female Heroism*. London: Vintage, 1981.

Watts, Alan. *Behold the Spirit: A Study in the Necessity of Mystical Religion*. New York: Vintage, 1971.

Webster's Third New International Dictionary of the English Language Unabridged. Springfield, MA: Merriam, 1964.

Weil, Simone. *Gravity and Grace*. Translated by Emma Crawford and Mario von der Ruhr. Routledge Classics (Series). London: Routledge Classics, 2002.

———. *The Need for Roots: Prelude to a Declaration of Duties towards Mankind*. Translated by Arthur Wills. Routledge Classics (Series). London: Routledge Classics, 2002.

---. *Waiting for God*. Translated by Emma Craufurd. Perennial Classics (Series). New York: Perennial Classics, 2001.

Wheeler, Bonnie, and Charles T. Wood, eds. *Fresh Verdicts on Joan of Arc*. The New Middle Ages 2. New York: Garland, 1996.

Wiesenthal, Simon. *The Sunflower: On the Possibilities and Limits of Forgiveness*. Rev. and exp. ed. Edited by Harry James Cargas and Bonny V. Fetterman. New York: Schocken, 1998.

Wood, Charles T. *Joan of Arc and Richard III: Sex, Saints and Government in the Middle Ages*. New York: Oxford University Press, 1988.

Wright, John J. *The Saints Always Belong to the Present: A Selection from the Sermons, Addresses, and Papers of Cardinal John J. Wright*. Edited by R. Stephen Almagno. San Francisco: Ignatius, 1985.

Wright, Ronald. *A Short History of Progress*. CBC Massey Lectures Series. Toronto: House of Anansi, 2004.

Wüstenberg, Ralf K. *A Theology of Life: Dietrich Bonhoeffer's Religionless Christianity*. Translated by Doug Stott. Grand Rapids: Eerdmans, 1998.

Wykes, Alan. "Symbols of Tyranny." Introduction to *Nazi Regalia*, by Jack Pia. Ballantine's Illustrated History of the Violent Century. New York: Ballantine, 1971.

Yahil, Leni. *The Holocaust: The Fate of European Jewry, 1932–1945*. Translated by Ina Friedman and Haya Galai. Studies in Jewish History. New York: Oxford University Press, 1990.

Zimmermann, Wolf-Dieter, and Ronald Gregor Smith, eds. *I Knew Dietrich Bonhoeffer*. Translated by Käthe Gregor Smith. The Fontana Library of Theology and Philosophy. London: Fontana, 1973.

Index

A

Abraham, 56n107, 94–97, 99
Absolute, the, 96, 99, 129, 220. *See also* God
absurd, the, 76, 96–97, 100, 119, 124, 180, 243
Abwehr. *See* Bonhoeffer, Dietrich, *Abwehr*
accountability, 45, 79–80, 85, 118, 119, 123, 131, 149, 161, 215, 217, 221, 285, 306
Adam, 299
Adams, Guy B., 120–21, 218
Adams, Jeremy duQuesnay, 132
affliction, 50, 65, 87, 91, 109, 138, 143, 144, 250, 255, 267, 269, 278, 282. *See also* suffering
Afghanistan, 121
agency
 human, 67, 84n255, 90, 95, 113–14, 119, 123, 129–30, 157, 161–62, 165, 170, 269, 304
  divinely sanctioned, xii, 130, 158, 162, 194, 227, 256, 301
  model of. *See* model, of righteous warfare and human agency
 prophetic, 158
 righteous, 95, 113, 123, 129, 157, 158, 161, 165, 170, 304
Alacoque, Margaret Mary, 74

Albreth, Lord d', 14n56
Alençon, Jean, Duke of, 14, 48, 58, 85, 93, 133n77
Almighty, the, 171, 214, 219, 238. *See also* God
Ambrose, 149, 155n185
angels, 8, 53, 56, 64, 74, 94, 97, 138. *See also* Gabriel, Archangel; Michael, Archangel
anger, 25, 145. *See also* wrath
 righteous, 145, 203, 257, 271, 298. *See also* indignation
Anglo-Burgundians, 5, 12, 22. *See also* Burgundians
anti-Semitism, 169, 180, 196, 226n318, 238, 251, 258
apostle, 54n92, 130, 161, 245, 301. *See also* knight, of faith
Aqedah, 94, 97, 129
Aquinas, Thomas, Saint, 57n117, 149n159
Aquitaine, 6
Arc, Jacques d', 7
Arc, Jean d', 17n68, 32
Arc, Jehanne d', xi–xiii, 3–34, 82, 85, 96, 120, 123, 148, 155, 163, 167, 232, 243n409, 256, 257, 262n503, 300, 304. *See also* Arc, Jehannette d'; daughter of God; Maid, the; *pucelle, la*
 abjuration, 27–31, 43, 51, 70, 92, 103, 104n342
 recantation, 29–30, 51, 92

Arc, Jehanne d' (*cont.*)
   accountability, 45, 79, 119, 161
   angels, 8, 53, 64
   anger, 145
   appeal to pope, 26
   armor, 10, 11, 59, 134
      offered at basilica of Saint-Denis, 15–16
   articles of accusation, 20n80, 23, 63n161
   attentiveness, 43, 53
   auditions, 56, 75. *See also* Arc, Jehanne d', divine counsel
   beatification, 33, 72
   betrayal, 13, 18–19, 66, 101
   birth, 5
   bravery, 18. *See also* Arc, Jehanne d', courage
   calling, 17, 22, 43, 56, 75, 76, 92, 141, 161, 180, 305
   canonization, 24n98, 32, 33, 36, 63n158, 67, 72, 101, 102n331. *See also* Arc, Jehanne d', saint
   capture, 17–20, 21n89, 22, 25, 26n106, 33, 51, 52, 65, 66, 70, 72, 74, 91, 93n292, 134, 144n141, 160, 183, 217
   charism, 23–25, 54
   charity, 8, 51–52, 61, 122, 144–45, 310
   chivalry, 18, 131–34, 150
   Church Militant
      refusal to submit, 21n89, 23, 26–27n111, 35–36, 40, 46, 77, 89, 99–100
   clothing, 10, 21n89, 26n106, 29–30, 35, 50, 51, 75, 99, 134
   Communion, 48, 137. *See also* Arc, Jehanne d', Eucharist
   compassion, xii, xiii, 34, 45, 95, 97, 100, 106, 116, 142, 143, 147, 154, 258
   condemnation, xii, 20, 23, 29, 31, 32, 71, 122
   trial, 4, 5, 11, 15, 19n80, 20–23, 26–32, 33, 35, 41, 46–47, 49, 51, 59, 60, 63, 64, 68, 70, 71–72, 74, 77, 89, 99–100, 103, 104n342, 107–8, 119, 130, 131, 144n139, 154, 291
   confession, 20n80, 30n125, 45–46, 48, 49, 69, 93, 102, 118, 137–38, 143, 258
   conscience, xiii, 21, 45, 98–99, 118, 134, 135, 136, 137–38, 141
   courage, 24, 43, 76, 88, 92, 93, 102, 121, 134. *See also* Arc, Jehanne d', bravery
   daughter of God, 25, 157
   death of, xii, 4, 17n70, 20, 26, 27, 30, 31, 32, 33, 36, 43, 49n66, 63, 68–69, 70–72, 78n232, 92–93, 101–4, 108, 109, 122, 134, 137, 157, 158, 161, 162. *See also* Arc, Jehanne d', martyrdom
   defilement, 118–19, 131
   desensitization, 45
   devotion, 11, 15, 35, 48, 56, 102, 159n199. *See also* Arc, Jehanne d', piety
   discernment of spirits, 21n89, 24, 44, 63–64, 98
   divine counsel, 8, 9, 21n89, 40, 41, 42, 43, 44, 46, 47, 48, 52, 54, 56, 59, 64, 68–69, 70, 71, 75n222, 88n268, 108, 137, 141n121. *See also* Arc, Jehanne d', auditions; Arc, Jehanne d', messengers; Arc, Jehanne d', visions; Arc, Jehanne d', voices

Arc, Jehanne d' (*cont.*)
  divine judgment, 23, 91–92, 100, 104, 130, 156
  divine servantship, xii, 15, 44, 45, 52, 67, 91, 92, 98, 99, 101, 105, 150, 157, 160, 301, 302
  doctrine, 47, 141n121, 162
  doubt, 8–9
  duty, 23, 131, 137
  escape attempts, 19, 19–20n80, 44, 51, 68, 71, 89n275, 92, 93, 106, 183
  Eucharist, 21n89, 30, 48, 49n66. *See also* Arc, Jehanne d', Communion
  evil, xiii, 11, 45, 79, 115–16, 118–19, 121–22, 137, 157, 309–10
  excommunication, 31, 32, 78, 264
  faith, 10, 21–22, 23, 33, 34, 60, 61, 76, 78n232, 91–92, 93, 95, 99, 100, 101, 102, 109, 129, 130, 134, 152, 153, 160, 180, 302, 303, 305, 306, 310
  family, 6, 7, 8, 9, 17, 18, 32, 50, 56, 87, 159n199
  fear, 8, 87, 89n273, 93
    of capture/imprisonment, 33, 52, 160
    of death by fire, 29, 33, 43, 71–72, 106
    of God, 42, 54, 60
    of treason, 19, 144
  fear of, 18, 22, 25, 31
  forgiveness, 4, 20n80, 34, 44, 102, 108, 118, 159n199
  glorification
    of God, 69
    personal, 51
  grace, 41, 48, 58, 59, 63, 77–78, 99, 102, 141n121
  heretic, 21, 22, 29, 30, 31, 36, 100
  honesty, 11, 121

hope, 32, 60, 68, 71–72, 152
humility, 11, 60–61, 102, 150
idolatry, 21n89, 60
imprisonment, 17, 18, 19, 20, 21, 23, 29, 30, 31, 43, 49, 51, 52, 56, 65, 68, 71, 72, 91, 92, 104
intention, 11, 15, 16, 18, 22, 27, 29, 30–31, 99, 108, 121–22, 145, 152, 154
jealousy toward, 19, 25–26
justice, xii, xiii, 34, 72, 106, 118, 121, 131, 141, 151, 154, 308
love, 45, 46, 47, 48, 109, 116, 144n139, 314n§, 314n§§, 315n‡
  divine, 310
  of God, 42, 45, 48, 51, 91–92, 104
martyrdom, xi, 4, 15, 31n134, 32, 33, 43, 51, 52, 68, 69, 71, 77, 87, 91, 101, 102, 104, 107–8, 137. *See also* Arc, Jehanne d', death of
Mass, 30, 35, 40, 49, 133–34
memory, 41n23
mercy, 3, 143, 146
message, xiii, 4, 17, 34, 56, 62, 64, 69, 70, 75, 103, 108–9, 146–47, 159n199
messengers, xii, 8, 60, 64. *See also* Arc, Jehanne d', divine counsel
military skills, 19, 24, 41, 50, 58–59, 70, 76, 92, 100, 157, 221n291
miraculous, the, 11, 12, 24, 32, 33, 58–59, 66, 66–67n176, 153
mission, 8, 9, 11, 12, 13, 16, 17, 18, 22, 23, 33, 51, 54, 56, 62n156, 63, 69, 72, 75, 76, 89, 91, 93, 97, 100, 101, 103, 107, 122, 131, 141, 144, 145, 149, 151, 159n199, 161, 180, 303

Arc, Jehanne d' (*cont.*)
  mysticism, 4, 36, 40, 43, 44, 45, 46, 47, 49, 50–52, 53, 56, 104, 106, 109, 113, 160, 164, 165, 301, 302, 305
  nullification trial, 5, 8n19, 32, 33, 72, 87, 98–99, 130
  oath controversy, 29, 35, 291
  pacifist-warrior, 142
  partisanship, 68, 69
  peace, xii, xiii, 12, 13, 46, 106, 131, 142, 146–47, 151, 154, 159n199, 305, 308
  piety, 8, 68n190, 102, 137, 154. *See also* Arc, Jehanne d', devotion
  Poitiers examination, 4, 10, 11, 26, 33, 59, 63, 64, 78, 92
    conclusion, 4, 11, 63
    record, 4, 26
  prayer, 8, 15, 16, 24, 35, 41, 49, 101, 102, 103, 108, 118, 310
  pride, 26n106, 122, 160
  prophecy, xii, 4, 9–10, 24, 32, 36, 47, 52, 53, 55, 56, 62–64, 67, 68, 73–77, 78, 87, 95, 98, 106, 129, 136, 158, 160–61, 162, 165, 227, 250, 302, 305, 307, 308
  rape of
    attempted, 30, 104n342
  relapse, 29–31
  rescue
    possible attempts, 31–32
  resentment toward, 25–26
  respect, xii, xiii, 34, 35, 47, 68, 72, 137, 150, 154
  responsibility, xiii, 26n106, 34, 45, 72, 79, 87, 101, 108–9, 119, 121, 137, 161, 308
  restraint, xiii, 34, 45, 137
  revelation, xii, 4, 8, 17, 21, 23, 35, 41, 43, 46, 47–48, 51, 53, 56, 62, 64, 65, 67, 70–72, 74, 75, 77, 89, 91, 92, 93n292, 95, 98–99, 103, 107–8, 136, 141, 146, 152, 217, 305, 307
  sacrifice, 17, 98, 101, 104
  saint, 8–9, 15, 17n70, 29, 30, 32, 45, 46, 49, 52, 59, 64, 68, 70, 100, 101, 102, 103, 107, 133, 141n121, 305, 310. *See also* Arc, Jehanne d', canonization; Arc, Jehanne d', warrior-saint
  sale of, 20, 72, 144n141
  salvation, 48, 77–78, 91
  schismatic, 23, 31
  sentencing, 29, 31, 68, 100, 119
  suicide
    accused of attempting, 19–20n80, 21n89
  sword, 6, 10–11, 15, 73, 118, 131, 133n77, 150
  takes leave of King Charles VII of France, 16–17
  torture
    threat of, 23, 30n125, 122, 161
  virginity, 9, 10, 11, 30, 51, 73, 91, 122
  visions, 56, 63, 75, 89, 141n121
  voices, 8, 16n63, 17, 19, 21–22, 24–25, 29, 35n1, 56, 60, 63, 65, 70–71, 73, 75, 79, 87, 88n268, 89n275, 91, 103, 141, 152. *See also* Arc, Jehanne d', divine counsel
  warrior, xi, xii, 8–9, 10–19, 23, 32, 33, 34, 45, 46, 58–59, 69, 75, 76, 77, 95, 97, 99, 100, 108, 118–19, 131, 136, 142, 143, 151, 152, 153, 154, 157, 158, 158–59n199, 160, 161. *See also* Arc, Jehanne d', pacifist-warrior
  warrior-saint, xi, 100, 157
wisdom, 4, 22, 26, 41, 59, 305
work ethic, 8

Arc, Jehanne d' (*cont.*)
    wounds, 15, 73, 87–88, 93, 101, 134
Arc, Jehannette d', 5, 7, 56. *See also* Arc, Jehanne d'
Arc, Pierre d', 17, 18, 32
Arendt, Hannah, 114, 116, 120, 127, 128, 134, 138, 140, 150, 156, 210, 221–22, 229, 297
Armagnacs, xiin1, 13. *See also* French royalists
Arras, Franquet d', 118n15
Aryan, 169, 206, 212, 214, 238
    clause, 271–72, 274n574
    nation, 212
    race, 169, 177, 206, 212, 213–14, 226
Astell, Ann W., 103, 121
atheism, 47, 80
attentiveness, 43, 53, 89, 113, 177, 240–41. *See also* divine attentiveness
auditions, 65, 170, 171, 233
    of Jehanne d'Arc. *See* Arc, Jehanne d', auditions
Augustine, Saint, 114, 149, 150, 151, 155n185
Aulon, Jean d', 5, 17
Auschwitz, 81, 177, 190n128, 204, 216
Austria, 167, 171, 210, 221
authority, 7, 13, 23, 44, 54, 55, 77, 137, 150, 206, 228
    absolute, 173, 175, 186, 206, 216
    divine, 47–48, 66, 72, 75, 105, 130, 149, 150, 160, 172, 186, 194, 234, 235, 236, 250–51
    obedience to, 17, 56, 58, 66, 75, 77, 89, 98, 99, 107, 123, 129, 130, 135, 136, 150, 157, 172, 175, 198, 235, 275
    human, 105, 116, 130, 149, 160, 172, 235, 275
    lawful, 148–49
    royal, 150
    sovereign, 148–49, 173, 186, 250–51
Auxerre, 12
Avignon, Marie d', 10

B

Baldwin, Stanley, 269
Balfour, Danny L., 120–21, 218
Balkans, the, 211
Barbin, Jean, 59
Barstow, Anne Llewellyn, 24
Barth, Karl, 228, 244–45
Bastard of Orléans. *See* Dunois, Jean, Count of
Baudricourt, Robert de, 7, 9, 10, 11
Baum, Rainer C., 139, 179, 188
Baur, Hans, 200
Beaugency, 12, 45
Beaulieu, 19
Beaurevoir, 19, 19–20n80, 68, 89n275
Beauvais, 12
Bedford, Duke of, 65, 147
Belgium, 187, 191, 208, 221
Bell, George K. A., 261, 264, 288n663
Bellamy, Alex J., 148, 153–54, 155n186
Benedict XIII, 7n14
Benedict XVI, 122n34, 310. *See also* Ratzinger, Joseph
benevolence, 79, 80, 81–82, 134, 137, 140, 169, 209, 234, 256, 278–79, 302. *See also* goodness
Bentham, Jeremy, 125n40
Berenbaum, Michael, 81
Berlin, 200, 230, 271, 278–79, 281n618, 296
Best, S. Payne, 288n663, 300
Bethge, Eberhard, 167, 234, 238, 239, 240n388, 241, 242,

Bethge, Eberhard (*cont.*)
   244, 246, 248, 249, 254, 256,
   257n470, 258n476, 262, 266,
   268, 273, 274, 279, 280, 286,
   290, 292, 294, 299
Bethge, Renate, 279
Bible, 64, 308. *See also* Bonhoeffer,
   Dietrich, Bible; Gospels, the;
   Scripture
Birgitta of Vadstena, 74, 75
Blaha, Franz, 192n139
Blenkinsopp, Joseph, 94
Bois Chesnu, 10
Bonaventure, Saint, 104n343
Bonhoeffer, Dietrich, 167, 228–302,
   303, 305, 306, 309
 Abwehr, 230–31, 246, 282
 accountability, 285
 acedia, 266
 anger, 244, 257, 258n476, 271,
   298
 arrest, 231, 246, 249
 attentiveness, 240–41
 Bible, 233, 262, 272, 284, 287,
   298. *See also* Bonhoeffer,
   Dietrich, gospel; Bonhoeffer,
   Dietrich, Old Testament
   law; Bonhoeffer, Dietrich,
   Scripture
 birth, 229
 bravery, 254, 267, 287, 300. *See
   also* Bonhoeffer, Dietrich,
   courage
 calling, 232, 233–34, 237, 242,
   243, 250, 264, 267, 268, 270,
   275, 276, 290, 299, 301
 charism, 234, 248, 250, 290
 charity, 270, 272, 278–80, 290.
   See also Bonhoeffer, Dietrich,
   generosity
 chivalry, 271–72
 commandment, 230, 236, 239,
   243, 244, 252
 compassion, 242, 256, 258–59

Confessing Church, 230, 231,
   244, 246, 247, 251, 288
conscience, 234, 235, 236, 242,
   259–60, 289, 301
 conflict of, 260
conscription, 230–31, 242–43,
   277
conspirator, 166, 230, 231, 233,
   234n350, 236, 242, 243, 244,
   246, 247, 248, 249, 251, 252,
   253, 254, 255, 260–61, 264,
   268n537, 272, 273n567,
   280–81, 282, 285, 287, 290,
   293, 301. *See also* German
   resistance
 courage, 239–40, 242, 270, 275.
   See also Bonhoeffer, Dietrich,
   bravery
 death of, 231, 239, 248, 249, 259,
   266, 267–68, 276, 288n663,
   301. *See also* Bonhoeffer,
   Dietrich, martyrdom
 defilement, 269–70. *See also*
   Bonhoeffer, Dietrich, guilt
 desensitization, 260–61
 devotion, 267, 276. *See also*
   Bonhoeffer, Dietrich, piety
 discernment of spirits, 233, 234
 discipleship, 232, 235, 239, 245,
   263, 264, 273, 277, 283–84
 divine judgment, 236, 242, 287,
   288
 divine servantship, 235–36, 242,
   248, 261–62, 283, 289, 301,
   302
 doctrine, 232, 273, 283–84
 doubt, 235, 242–43, 245
 duty, 237, 247, 254, 259, 261,
   275, 291
 Eucharist, 262
 evil, 231, 251, 255, 256, 269, 270,
   272, 277, 284, 292, 296–97,
   298, 301, 308

Bonhoeffer, Dietrich (*cont.*)
  faith, 231, 235 237–39, 242–45, 260, 263–65, 268, 270, 275, 276, 288, 301, 302
  family, 230, 231, 234n350, 240, 247–48, 249, 267, 268n537, 268n538, 273, 279, 280, 281, 287
  fear, 233, 239, 242, 244, 249, 264, 265, 276, 287, 289, 296
    of God, 262–63
  forgiveness, 231–32, 256–59, 270, 283, 287, 290
  generosity, 232, 242, 256, 258, 279–80. *See also* Bonhoeffer, Dietrich, charity
  glorification
    personal, 280
    of war, 277
  gospel, 230, 233, 299
  grace, 234–35, 236n364, 239, 250, 262, 263, 283–84, 290, 299
    cheap, 231–32, 273
    costly, 232, 239, 273
  gratitude, 240, 257, 258, 261–62, 265, 284, 295–96
  guilt, 236, 248, 255, 259–60, 265, 270, 285, 290. *See also* Bonhoeffer, Dietrich, defilement
  honesty, 236, 246, 272, 282, 291, 292. *See also* Bonhoeffer, Dietrich, integrity
  hope, 235, 242, 249, 261n491, 265, 268, 279, 286
  humility, 241, 264, 290, 300
  idolatry, 283, 284, 292–93
  imprisonment, 231, 235, 237–38, 239, 240, 241n397, 244, 246, 247, 249, 253, 256–58, 260, 261, 262, 263, 264, 265, 266–67, 267–68, 271, 273–74, 276, 278, 279–80, 281, 282, 286, 287, 290, 293, 295, 296, 298, 299
  integrity, 282–83. *See also* Bonhoeffer, Dietrich, honesty
  intention, 237, 251, 253, 254, 258, 267, 280, 302–3
  justice, 241, 242, 258, 263, 272, 275
  love, 241, 244, 257, 259, 260, 261, 268, 277
    divine, 233, 237
    of God/Christ, 262–63, 265, 288–89, 295
  martyrdom, 242, 247, 248, 265, 267, 300. *See also* Bonhoeffer, Dietrich, death of
  memory, 240–41, 248
  mercy, 235, 236, 256–59, 282, 287
  message, 262–63, 288n663, 299
  mission, 245, 254, 263, 264–65, 276
  mysticism, 263, 267–68, 298–99, 301, 302
  non-violence, 261n491, 277. *See also* Bonhoeffer, Dietrich, pacifism
  Old Testament law, 287
  pacifism, 244, 251–52, 260–61, 277, 294. *See also* Bonhoeffer, Dietrich, non-violence
  partisanship, 274
  peace, 242, 244, 252–53, 263, 277, 294, 298, 299
  piety, 262, 263. *See also* Bonhoeffer, Dietrich, devotion
  prayer, 236, 241, 256, 267, 268, 271, 278, 298
  pride, 242, 245, 274
    false, 241
  prophecy, 230, 233, 243, 246–47, 248–49, 250, 290–91, 300, 301, 302

Bonhoeffer, Dietrich (*cont.*)
   religion, 231, 235, 237, 239, 254, 263–64, 276, 278, 282, 283–84, 289
   religionless Christianity, 263–64, 283–84, 299
   respect, 242, 244, 259, 280, 283, 288
   responsibility, 234–35, 236, 237, 240–41, 254, 267, 269–70, 272, 275, 276, 277, 280, 281–82, 284, 285, 286, 287, 289–90, 292, 297
   restraint, 166, 244, 269
   sacrifice, 233, 235, 239, 254, 265, 270, 275
   salvation, 278, 288–89
   Scripture, 233–34, 236, 250–51, 262. *See also* Bonhoeffer, Dietrich, Bible
   seminaries, 231, 246, 256, 273, 288
   stupidity, 296–97. *See also* thoughtlessness
   suicide, 265
   Tegel prison, 237, 273, 281
   torture, 251, 253, 255, 273n567, 295
   weakness, 245, 258, 279, 284, 286
   wisdom, 296–97
   work ethic, 273–74
Bonhoeffer, Emmi, 240n390
Bonhoeffer, Karl, 268n537
Bonhoeffer, Karl-Friedrich, 267n535
Bonhoeffer, Klaus, 231, 249, 268n537
Boucher, Jacques, 137n100
Boucher, Pierre, 102n330
Bourbon, Duke of, 14n56
Boussac, Lord de, 14n56
Bouzy, Olivier, 18n76, 144n139
Braun, Eva, 184, 193n144

Braunau am Inn, 167
Bréhal, Jean, 87
Bresson, Robert, 160
Britain, 224. *See also* England
Brueggemann, Walter, 55, 67, 106, 175
Buchenwald, 299
Burgundians, xii, 6, 13, 18, 20, 24, 25, 26, 32, 66n175, 74, 118, 144, 158, 243n409, 258. *See also* Anglo-Burgundians
Burgundy, 5, 6, 12, 13, 26, 32, 65, 88, 96, 100n324, 132, 159n199
Bush, George W., 121, 122

C

Cagny, Perceval de, 17n67
Calais, 32
calling
   divine, xii, 17, 22, 43, 53, 56, 69, 75, 76, 92, 135–36, 141, 161, 162, 164, 170–71, 180, 185, 227, 228, 232, 233, 237, 242, 243, 250, 264, 267, 268, 270, 275, 276, 299, 300, 301, 304, 305, 307, 310. *See also* election; mission
   human, 171
   mystical, 44, 53, 77
   prophetic, xii, 53, 69–70, 75, 77, 162, 164, 170, 185, 233, 250, 304, 307
canonization, 24n98, 32, 33, 66, 226, 234, 300
   of Jehanne d'Arc. *See* Arc, Jehanne d', canonization
Catherine of Alexandria, Saint, 8, 8–9n25, 29, 30, 49, 59, 70
Catherine of Siena, Saint, 74, 75, 146
Catherine of Valois, Queen of England, 6, 7

Cauchon, Pierre, 12, 20, 21, 22, 29, 31, 71, 72, 131, 161
Caval, Nicolas, 41n23
Châlons, 12
Chambre, Guillaume de la, 21n85, 27, 102n330
charism, 23–25, 54, 171, 184, 185, 220–21, 234, 248, 250, 290
charity, 122, 134, 141, 144–45, 209, 224, 270, 272, 278–80, 310. *See also* generosity
Charles VI, King of France, 6, 7
Charles VII, 6, 7, 9, 10, 11, 12, 13, 14, 16, 17n67, 18, 26, 31, 32, 51, 65, 88, 107, 132n68, 146, 150
  coronation, 11, 12, 13, 22, 24, 41, 51, 73, 88n268, 144, 145, 159n199
  dauphin, 6, 7, 9, 12, 22, 46, 75n222, 144–45, 149, 150
  King of France, 12, 116, 144, 159n199
  negotiated truces with Burgundy, 12, 13, 14, 26, 88, 96, 243n409
Chartres, Regnault de, 19n78, 25–26
Chastellain, Georges, 26
Chinon, 9, 10, 11, 16, 22, 73, 89n273, 133
chivalry, 18, 114, 131–34, 150, 203, 271–72
Christ, 74, 85–86, 105, 143, 228, 230, 232, 233, 237, 239, 245, 260, 263–64, 267, 272, 275, 276, 277, 283, 284, 289, 299, 300. *See also* Jesus
Christianity, 33–34, 36, 39, 40, 85–86, 136, 137, 143, 147, 164, 212, 220, 239, 241, 244, 247, 255, 259, 271, 273, 277, 283, 284, 287, 288n663, 289, 300, 310. *See also* Bonhoeffer, Dietrich, religionless Christianity; Christ; Christians; Christology; prophetic tradition, Christian; tradition, Christian

Christians, 34, 35, 82, 92, 130, 135–36, 136–37, 143, 144n139, 158, 159n199, 230, 233, 237, 243, 244, 252, 267, 272, 274–75, 281–82, 285, 294, 310. *See also* German Christians
Christology, 85, 86. *See also* Jesus, crucifixion
Church, 7, 11, 23, 24, 25, 28, 32, 33, 35, 36, 40, 46, 61, 63, 75, 77, 78n231, 86, 101, 102, 104, 132, 149, 150, 158n196, 199, 228, 229–30, 232, 238, 243, 245 251, 252, 261, 263, 274, 277, 281, 284, 289, 293, 296, 299
  Confessing. *See* Confessing Church.
  earthly, 78, 264. *See also* Church Militant
  German Christian. *See* German Christian Church
  Protestant, 213
  Reich. *See* Reich Church
  Roman Catholic, 32, 74, 300
Church Militant, 25. *See also* Arc, Jehanne d', Church Militant, refusal to submit; Church, earthly
Church Triumphant, 264
Churchill, Winston, 280–81
Cicero, 149, 155n185
civilian, 126, 132, 155, 156, 202, 206, 255. *See also* noncombatant
Clement VIII, 7n14
cliché, 122, 297

Clin, Marie-Véronique, 27n113, 56, 78, 160
Cobos, David, 139–40
Cohen, Leonard, 101
collateral damage, 140
College of Political Science, Berlin, 293
common good, 98, 119, 149, 153, 174–75, 238
Communists, 169n8, 189, 194
compassion, xii, xiii, 34, 39, 45, 95, 97, 100, 102n330, 106, 113, 114, 116, 134, 142–44, 145, 146, 147, 154, 194, 224, 242, 256, 258–59, 269
Compiègne, 13, 17, 18, 19, 26, 66, 68
  siege, 17, 68
compromise, xii, 96, 160, 199, 263, 264, 293, 305
Confessing Church, 230, 231, 244, 246, 247, 251, 288
confession, 116, 120, 176, 230, 245, 272, 300. See also Arc, Jehanne d', confession
Confucianism, 147
conscience, xiii, 21, 45, 63n160, 70, 85, 98–99, 114, 118, 119, 123, 130, 134–41, 149, 157, 175, 195–96, 197, 215, 216, 226, 234, 235, 236, 242, 259–60, 289, 301, 302n725, 304
contempt, 45, 194, 258. See also hatred
Cost of Discipleship (Bonhoeffer), 244
Council of Basel, 27
coup, 230. See also Hitler, Adolf, putsch
courage, 24, 25, 43, 60, 76, 88, 92, 93, 96, 102, 121, 131, 134, 176–77, 182, 222, 239–40, 242, 270, 275

Creator, the, 45, 65, 91, 100, 159n199, 171, 179, 213, 214, 236. See also God
Créil, 13
Crépy-en-Valois, 17
cruelty, 72, 101, 104, 143, 145, 147, 192, 209, 230, 258, 278–79, 301
crusade, 157, 159n199
Cunningham, Lawrence S., 114, 195, 303
Czechoslovakia, 221

D

damnation, 30, 48, 65, 70–71, 103
daughter of God, 25, 157. See also Arc, Jehanne d'
dauphin. See Charles VII, dauphin; Louis XI of France, dauphin
death, 7, 20, 24, 27, 33, 45, 46, 48, 73, 105–6, 107, 108, 116, 119, 120, 121, 140, 146, 157, 168, 176, 178, 195, 196, 205, 206, 209, 218, 219, 221, 257, 265, 267, 308
  of Adolf Hitler. See Hitler, Adolf, death of
  of Dietrich Bonhoeffer. See Bonhoeffer, Dietrich, death of
  of Jehanne d'Arc. See Arc, Jehanne d', death of
  of Jesus, 33, 85–87, 105. See also Jesus, crucifixion
Decalogue, 172, 243, 244. See also divine command
deception, 103, 140, 222, 282n625. See also self-deception
defilement, 118–19, 131, 179, 202, 214, 269–70
dehumanization, 115, 122, 128, 194–95
deity, 79, 80, 86

demonization, 59, 117, 122, 169, 218–19, 288
Denis, Saint, 15
Denmark, 191, 193, 221
dependence, 176
  divine, on humans, 83, 84, 87n265
  human, on God, 75, 83, 182–83, 234–35, 245–46, 270
depersonalization, xiii, 69, 139
desensitization, 45–46, 196, 202–3, 260–61
Désert, Guillaume du, 28n119
detachment, 45, 60, 261
Deutschland, 172, 174. *See also* Germany
DeVries, Kelly, 14n56, 26n106, 76–77
Dignitatis Humanae, 130, 135
dignity, 69, 135, 137, 160, 195, 209, 259, 306
discernment
  ethical. *See* ethical discernment
  moral. *See* moral discernment
  of spirits, 21n89, 24, 48, 61–64, 98, 141, 149, 171, 234
  spiritual, 44, 229, 303
discipleship, 77, 264. *See also* Bonhoeffer, Dietrich, discipleship
discretio spirituum. *See* discernment, of spirits
discrimination, 144, 154
divine, the, 23, 36, 37, 39, 40, 43, 46, 47, 48, 49, 50, 52, 70, 77, 79, 80, 81, 82, 87, 88, 107, 129, 136, 158, 166, 172, 173, 186, 214, 235, 236, 250, 305. *See also* God
divine ambiguity, 70–73, 87
divine agent, xii, 130.
divine anger, 145. *See also* wrath, of God
divine aspiration, 67, 136, 163, 174, 237

divine assistance, 9, 16, 17, 43, 68, 70, 71–72, 75, 78n232, 86, 123, 142, 176, 182–83, 214, 243, 245–46
divine attentiveness, 67
divine authority. *See* authority, divine
divine autonomy, 47, 307
divine calling. *See* calling, divine
divine chosenness, 46, 47n53, 98, 123, 171, 207, 210
divine command, 19, 26n106, 64, 75, 79, 86, 88n268, 89, 91, 93n292, 94, 97, 98, 99, 103, 108, 119, 131, 133, 144n139, 149, 158, 159n199, 172, 197, 230, 235, 236, 239, 252. *See also* Decalogue; divine directive; divine instruction
divine concern, 36, 67, 68, 84, 95, 174, 237
divine condemnation, 97, 174, 218, 288–89
divine dependence. *See* dependence, divine, on humans
divine directive, 55, 57, 69, 94–95, 99, 176–77, 239. *See also* divine command
divine favor, 64–65, 66, 85, 123
divine forgiveness, 20n80, 44, 79–80, 85–86, 108, 231–32, 270, 283–84, 287, 290
divine guidance, 56, 70, 77n230, 93, 141, 186, 233, 234, 305
divine inspiration. *See* inspiration, divine
divine instruction, xii, 56, 70, 74, 87–88, 91, 93n292, 98, 99, 135, 141, 150, 152, 166, 173, 258, 289. *See also* divine command
divine intention, 38, 48, 55, 108, 175

divine judgment, 23, 54, 91–92, 100, 104, 130, 135, 156, 174, 214, 236, 242, 287, 288
divine justice. *See* justice, divine
divine law. *See* law, divine
divine light, 8, 34, 43, 50, 62, 80, 101
divine limitation, 81, 84, 88, 284. *See also* divine Self-limitation
divine love. *See* love, divine
divine mercy. *See* mercy, divine
divine message, 4, 38, 53, 56, 62, 64, 70, 78n233, 87, 90n278, 103, 299
divine messenger, xii, 8, 54, 60, 64, 67–68, 92. *See also* Arc, Jehanne d', divine counsel
divine mystery, 37, 46, 47, 48, 62, 70, 72, 92, 93, 160, 214, 283
divine nature, 8, 36–37, 41, 48, 53–54, 57, 214, 307
divine omnipotence, 79–80, 82–84, 85, 88, 186, 284
divine *pathos*, 54, 145. *See also* divine sympathy
divine protection, 24, 51, 93, 197
divine punishment. *See* punishment, divine
divine revelation. *See* revelation, divine
divine sanction, xii–xiii, 55–56, 63, 64, 65–66, 67, 79, 95, 97, 98, 106, 107, 108, 119, 123, 128, 129, 130, 131, 157, 158, 159n199, 161, 162, 163, 164, 170–71, 172, 198, 215, 217, 219, 220, 285, 289, 302–3, 304, 305, 306–7, 309. *See also* agency, human, divinely sanctioned; warfare, divinely sanctioned
divine Self-limitation, 79, 81, 82–83, 92. *See also* divine limitation

divine servantship, xii, 15, 44, 45, 52, 67, 91, 92, 98, 99, 101, 105, 136, 150, 157, 158n197, 160, 172–73, 197, 235–36, 242, 248, 261–62, 283, 289, 301, 302, 306
divine sympathy. *See* sympathy, divine
divine truth. *See* truth, divine
divine virtue. *See* virtue, divine
divine will. *See* will, divine
divine wisdom, 50, 52
divine word, 38, 40, 54, 55, 62, 75, 92, 230, 235, 250, 254, 260
doctrine, 23, 24, 39, 40, 47, 55, 105, 114, 118, 141n121, 149, 162, 179, 188, 204, 213, 232, 273, 283–84
Dohnanyi, Christine von, 249
Dohnanyi, Hans von, 240, 249, 251, 263, 268, 279n599, 293
Domarus, Max, 191, 194n147, 197, 207n222, 211, 218, 225
Domremy, 5, 6, 7, 8, 9, 50, 52n80, 56, 75, 87, 91, 144, 159n199
Doncoeur, Paul, 30n125
doubt, 8–9, 11, 84, 179, 200, 210, 217, 235, 242–43, 245, 307
Downie, R. S., 115
dual monarchy, 6, 22
Dunkirk, 211
Dunois, Jean, Count of, 31, 143n132, 145
duty, 23, 90, 130–31, 137, 146, 178, 197, 214, 219, 229, 237, 247, 254, 259, 261, 275, 291

E

Eckhart, Meister, 104n343
Egypt, 147
Eichmann, Adolf, 188, 196, 206, 210, 217, 229, 297
election, 47–48, 55, 123, 161. *See also* calling, divine

Elshtain, Jean Bethke, 156–57
emotion, 21, 48–49, 81, 88, 122, 135, 196, 222, 229, 260, 302
England, 5, 6, 7, 12, 32, 65, 73, 102n330, 103, 146, 152, 187, 189, 211, 230, 280
   king of, 12, 22, 32, 65, 146
English, the, xii, 5, 6, 7, 9, 10, 11, 12, 13, 17n70, 18, 20, 22, 23–24, 25, 31, 32, 45–46, 47, 56, 60n140, 62, 65, 70, 72, 74, 93, 102, 122, 131, 132, 142, 143, 144n141, 145, 146, 152, 158, 159n199
Épinal, Gérardin d', 144–45
Érard, Guillaume, 31
Érault, Jean, 10
Erigena, 104n343
Estivet, Jean d', 22
ethic of faith, 129, 130–31. *See also* morality, mystical
ethic, universal, 130–31, 156, 219–20, 289–90. *See also* law, universal
ethical discernment, 148–49, 206. *See also* moral discernment
ethics, 82, 94, 100, 114, 120–21, 124, 128, 131, 132, 156, 202, 203, 206, 222, 271–72, 289, 291, 297, 299–300, 306, 308, 309. *See also* morality
   teleological, 124
   teleological suspension. *See* teleological ethical suspension.
   utilitarian. *See* utilitarianism
Ethics (Bonhoeffer), 266
Europe, 189n118, 206n216, 207, 211, 243, 308
evil, xiii, 43, 86, 114–23, 129, 134, 135, 136, 138, 140, 145, 146, 157, 269
   active, 142
   Arc, Jehanne d', on. *See* Arc, Jehanne d', evil.

Bonhoeffer, Dietrich, on. *See* Bonhoeffer, Dietrich, evil
   of complicity, 141–42, 303
   of fanaticism, 115. *See also* Hitler, Adolf, fanaticism
   "greater," 117–18, 128, 154–55, 269
   Hitler, Adolf. *See* Hitler, Adolf, evil
   human, 45, 79, 80, 81, 83, 87, 114, 115, 116–18, 120, 136, 138, 140, 149, 201, 207, 215, 269, 284, 304
   intrinsic, xiii, 123, 125, 136, 201, 269
   "lesser," 117–18, 128, 164
   moral, 82, 114, 115, 116, 121–22, 123, 136–37, 138, 140, 151, 154–55, 157, 188, 272
   morally necessary, 123
   natural, 123
   ordinary, 115, 123
   passive, 142, 297
   privation doctrine, 114–15, 118
   qualified, 117–18, 119, 128, 201–2, 269
   radical, 115
   of self-interest, 115
   unqualified, 117–18, 119, 269
extermination, 169–70, 174–75, 177, 184, 187–88, 189n118, 191, 193, 194–95, 202, 204, 206n216, 207, 216, 218, 219, 221, 223. *See also* genocide; Hitler, Adolf, "final solution"; killing

F

Fabri, Jean, 68n190
faith, 24, 38, 44, 49–50, 60, 74, 78, 80, 82, 87n265, 90, 92, 94–97, 99, 101, 105, 106, 107, 108, 109, 123, 129, 130,

faith (*cont.*)
132, 135, 155n185, 158, 163–64, 230, 302, 303, 306. *See also* Arc, Jehanne d', faith; Bonhoeffer, Dietrich, faith; Hitler, Adolf, faith
fanaticism. *See* evil, of fanaticism
Fauquembergue, Clément de, 14
fear, 21n86, 43, 46, 49–50, 90, 106, 114, 126, 228–29, 307. *See also* Arc, Jehanne d', fear; Bonhoeffer, Dietrich, fear; Hitler, Adolf, fear; terror
of God, 39, 42, 44, 54, 60, 82n251, 136, 138
Fear and Trembling (Kierkegaard), 94
Ffastolf, John, 70, 145
Fisher, Frank, 259
Flavy, Guillaume de, 18–19, 26
Flossenbürg, 231, 267
force, xiii, 15, 25, 28–29, 46, 63, 69, 80, 81, 82, 90, 102, 117, 129, 135, 136, 142, 148, 156–57, 161, 168, 173, 193, 195, 196, 198, 213, 221, 226, 229, 234–35, 254, 260, 270, 274–75, 287, 289, 290, 295, 296
minimal, xii, 148, 154, 155, 191–92, 255
necessary, 155
Forest, Jim, 121
forgiveness, 4, 34, 102, 108, 118, 159n199, 194, 256–59. *See also* divine forgiveness
Fraioli, Deborah A., 6, 62n156, 63–64, 132n68
Franc, Martin Le, 106
France, xii, 3, 5, 6, 7, 9, 10, 13, 14n56, 15, 16, 22, 23, 24, 25, 32, 41, 42–43, 44, 46, 47, 55, 60, 65, 66, 66–67n176, 68, 70, 72, 74, 75, 76, 78, 87, 91, 96, 122, 131, 132–33, 141n121, 142, 144n139, 146–47, 150, 151, 152, 154, 159n199, 184, 221, 303
Gaullist government, 303
King of, 9, 12, 13–14, 16, 22, 25, 31, 32, 40, 52, 65, 68, 73, 75n222, 107, 116, 119, 144, 159n199, 291, 303. *See also* Charles VI, King of France; Charles VII, King of France
Vichy government, 303
Francis, Saint, 104n343
free will. *See* will, free
freedom, 22, 48, 77, 79, 81, 83, 84, 90–91, 98, 119, 134, 154, 179, 202, 205, 209, 212, 216, 223, 237, 254, 265, 267, 282–83, 285, 287. *See also* liberty; will, free
Freemasons, 186
French, the, xii, 12, 19n77, 47, 62, 65, 68, 73, 74, 100, 143, 189
French royalists, xiin1, 158, 159n199. *See also* Armagnacs
Frick, Wilhelm, 191–92
Fritzsche, Hans, 202–3
Führer, 167, 170–71, 178, 181, 184, 199, 210–11, 219, 230, 242, 252, 275, 292–93. *See also* Hitler, Adolf

G

Gabriel, Archangel, 8, 9n25
Gandhi, 261n491
Gellately, Robert, 180
generosity, 131, 144, 209, 232, 242, 256, 258, 279–80. *See also* charity
genocide, 129, 142, 189, 272. *See also* extermination; killing
German Christian Church, 208–9, 212, 230, 231, 289. *See also* Reich Church

Index

German Christians, 212, 230, 251, 288
German expansion, 169–70, 174, 177, 186–87, 187–88, 190, 201, 209, 211, 214, 225
German nation, 168, 170–71, 176, 178, 186, 197, 201, 204, 208–9, 211, 212, 216, 285. *See also* Volk
German people, 127, 168, 170, 172, 173, 175, 176, 179, 184, 185, 186, 187, 195, 202, 203, 204, 206, 208–9, 210, 213, 214, 216, 220, 294
German race, 168, 169–70, 179, 186–87, 188, 193. *See also* Aryan, race
German resistance, 231, 242, 246–47, 254, 261n491, 303. *See also* Bonhoeffer, Dietrich, conspirator; Hitler, Adolf, conspiracy against
Germany, 168, 169, 171, 173, 174, 176, 178, 180, 186, 187, 189, 193, 202, 206n215, 209, 210, 211, 212, 215, 216, 218, 219, 223, 225, 227, 230, 231, 235, 236, 238, 242, 243, 246, 248, 250, 259, 261, 263, 271, 276, 285, 288. *See also* Deutschland; Nazi Germany
overpopulation, 169–70
Gerson, Jean, 61n143, 67n177
Gertrude the Great of Helfta, 74
Gestapo, 231, 239, 251, 299
Gethsemane, 105, 237
Girard, René, 86, 109
God, xii, 4, 8, 9, 15, 16, 17, 23, 25, 30, 33–109 passim, 114, 117, 119, 122, 123, 129–38 passim, 141n121, 142–51 passim, 155–64 passim, 167, 170–76 passim, 180, 182, 183, 186, 197–201 passim, 213–16 passim, 219, 223, 228–39 passim, 242–45 passim, 249–52 passim, 257, 261–70 passim, 276, 277, 283–301 passim, 306, 307, 310. *See also* Absolute, the; Almighty, the; Creator, the; Divine, the; Heaven; King of Heaven; Lord; Omnipotent, the; Providence
absence, 37, 81, 109. *See also* John of the Cross, Saint, dark night of the soul; mystical experience, apophatic
as object, 47, 69, 213, 283
as Subject, 69, 213, 283
Goebbels, Josef, 188, 204, 207
Goering, Hermann, 195, 205
Goldensohn, Leon, 216n274, 220
Gomorrah, 33
goodness, 11, 43, 81, 97, 114–15, 116, 118, 124–25, 136, 138, 151, 155, 157, 269, 296, 302, 303, 308, 309. *See also* benevolence; common good
intrinsic, 125. *See also* value, intrinsic
Gospels, the, 86, 230. *See also* Bonhoeffer, Dietrich, gospel
grace, 24, 36, 39, 54, 63, 65, 78, 84, 85, 88, 94, 122n34, 135, 153. *See also* Arc, Jehanne d', grace; Bonhoeffer, Dietrich, grace; Hitler, Adolf, grace
infused, 58, 59, 98, 99. *See also* infused contemplation
mediated, 78, 220, 290
Gratian of Bologna, 149
gratitude, 144. *See also* Bonhoeffer, Dietrich, gratitude
Great Schism, 7. *See also* schism, papal
Greece, 147
Greenberg, Irving, 81, 82n251
Greux, 52n80
Grouchet, Richard de, 21n86

guilt, 22, 116, 118, 120, 127, 136, 139. *See also* Bonhoeffer, Dietrich, guilt; Hitler, Adolf, guilt; remorse.
Guthrie, Charles, 142, 151, 153, 156
Gypsies, 189, 192

H

Haas, Peter J., 81–82
Hase, Paul von, 281n618
hatred, 47, 122, 144, 145, 153, 170, 179, 188, 189, 196, 212, 227, 230, 252, 253. *See also* contempt
Heaven, 41, 46, 67, 69, 71, 91–92, 99, 107, 133, 146, 147, 159n199, 171, 178, 266. *See also* God
Heiden, Konrad, 181, 191, 222
Heine, Heinrich, 226–27
Henriod, H. L., 272–73n563
Henry V, King of England, 6, 7
Henry VI, King of England, 7, 12, 22, 32, 65
heresy, 29, 30, 57, 78n231, 122, 157. *See also* Arc, Jehanne d', heretic
Heschel, Abraham J., 36, 41, 43, 47, 48, 52, 53–54, 54–55, 65, 67–68, 69–70, 82, 87n265, 88, 90, 96–97, 116–17, 123, 129, 139, 141, 145, 146, 147, 160, 162, 199, 230, 307
Heyking, John von, 122
Hildebrandt, Franz, 271–72, 293, 296
Himmler, Heinrich, 199, 216
Hinduism, 147
Hiroshima, 126
Hitler, Adolf, 80n244, 165–66, 167–228, 237, 239, 242, 243, 244, 246, 252, 254, 277, 289, 292, 295, 296, 305, 306, 309. *See also* Führer.

accountability, 215, 217
anger, 203
assassination attempts. *See* Hitler, Adolf, conspiracy against
attentiveness, 177
birth, 167
bravery, 172, 178, 214. *See also* Hitler, Adolf, courage
calling, 170–71, 185, 220, 227
charism, 171, 184, 185, 220–21
compassion, 194, 224
conscience, 175, 195–96, 197, 215, 216, 226
conspiracy against, 166, 183, 192n139, 230, 251, 253, 255, 290. *See also* Bonhoeffer, Dietrich, conspirator; German resistance
contempt, 194. *See also* Hitler, Adolf, hatred
courage, 176–77, 182, 222. *See also* Hitler, Adolf, bravery
death of, 184, 201, 217, 231, 249. *See also* Hitler, Adolf, suicide
defilement, 179, 202, 214
demonization, 169, 218–19
desensitization, 196, 202–3
divine judgment, 174, 214
divine servantship, 172–73, 197
doctrine, 179, 188, 204, 213
doubt, 179, 200, 210, 217
duty, 178, 197, 214, 219
evil, 169, 188, 189, 191–92, 194n147, 201–2, 215, 218, 227–28, 270, 294, 297, 302, 303, 308
incarnate, 207
personification of, 207
faith, 168, 171, 172, 173, 176, 180, 190, 197, 200, 201, 213, 214
family, 168, 181
fanaticism, 173, 180, 181, 199–200, 230, 261

Hitler, Adolf (*cont.*)
  fear, 179, 188, 200, 224
    of God, 198
  "final solution," 127, 128, 175n44, 195–96, 206, 221
  forgiveness, 194
  glorification
    personal, 172, 209–10
    of war, 208
  grace, 172, 174, 220, 225–26
  guilt, 178, 189, 195, 202, 206, 248
  hatred, 170, 179, 188, 189, 196, 212, 227. *See also* Hitler, Adolf, contempt
  honesty, 214, 221–22. *See also* Hitler, Adolf, integrity
  humility, 178, 224
  ideology, 82, 168–69, 171, 177, 179, 186–87, 195, 210, 212, 213–14, 222, 226
  imprisonment, 168
    of others, 187, 188–89, 190, 192, 193, 195, 196, 208, 211
  integrity, 213. *See also* Hitler, Adolf, honesty
  intention, 169, 191, 196, 203, 206, 208, 211, 214, 219, 221, 222, 226, 238, 302–3
  Jewish conspiracy, 188
  justice, 172, 188, 189, 205, 220
  love
    of the German *Volk*, 204
    of God, 197
    of peace, 208
  manipulation, 170, 184, 185, 224, 226. *See also* Hitler, Adolf, speeches
  memory, 177n53
  mercy, 194, 199, 218, 221
  mission, 170, 171, 172, 178, 179, 180, 182, 186, 198, 199, 201, 204, 206, 210, 219–20, 238
  mysticism, 173, 198–99, 200, 225, 227
  peace, 188, 208, 218
  Personal Testament, 200, 201
  piety, 197
  Political Testament, 201, 202
  prayer, 178, 186, 212
  pride, 178, 207, 210
  prophecy, 170, 183, 184, 185, 226–27
  putsch, 168
  religion, 170, 172, 190–91, 194, 197, 198–99, 209, 212–13, 229
  respect, 178, 194, 195, 208
  responsibility, 181, 197, 205–6, 215–17, 219–20
  restraint, 166, 179, 191, 199
  salvation, 170
  speeches, 166, 167, 185, 212, 221
  suicide, 176, 184, 199, 200, 201, 217, 225. *See also* Hitler, Adolf, death of
  torture, 192, 193, 207, 253
  weakness, 170, 175, 182–83, 185, 204, 205
  wisdom, 224–25
  work ethic, 204–5, 206–7, 225
Hitler Youth, 201
Hitlerism, 202
Hitlerite Germany, 229, 230, 254, 270, 280. *See also* Nazi Germany
Hobbins, Daniel, 116
Hofmann, Rudolf, 135, 138–39
Hogan, Linda, 216
holiness, 32, 103, 145, 226, 300, 310. *See also* sanctity
Holland, 187, 208
Holocaust, the. *See Shoah*, the.
Holy Roman Empire, 5n4
Holy Spirit, 11, 24, 36, 48, 49, 54, 63, 78, 87n263, 99, 234

holy war, 158, 159n199, 190–91, 254
honesty, 11, 121, 140, 214, 221–22, 236, 246, 272, 282, 291, 292. *See also* integrity
honor, 13, 16, 131, 148, 197, 201–2
hope, 96, 114, 146, 153, 160, 238, 242, 310. *See also* Arc, Jehanne d', hope; Bonhoeffer, Dietrich, hope
Höss, Rudolf, 190n128, 204, 216
Houppeville, Nicolas de, 20, 21n85, 31n130, 68n190
humility, 11, 57–58, 60–61, 66, 102, 122n34, 150, 178, 224, 241, 264, 290, 300, 307
Hundred Years' War, xii, 5–7, 64, 76
Hussites, 158–59n199
Hvidt, Niels Christian, 49, 58, 61, 66, 74, 75, 78, 87n265, 95, 162, 230, 233

I

idolatry, 21n89, 47, 55, 60, 88, 230, 283, 284, 292–93
Ignatieff, Michael, 117, 122
immorality, 82n251, 133, 158. *See also* vice
indifference, 82, 96–97, 116–17, 118, 128, 136–37, 139, 140, 147, 170, 202–3, 270, 297
indignation, 117, 141, 145, 230, 271. *See also* anger, righteous.
infused contemplation, 57. *See also* grace, infused
injustice, 16, 20, 26, 72, 117, 123, 141, 145, 159, 203, 206, 237, 252, 253, 269, 271, 276, 301, 309
Inquisition, 21n89, 32, 33, 35
insanity, 96–97, 113
inspiration, divine, 54, 57–58n117, 59, 88, 90, 108, 166, 184, 198, 220

integrity, xiii, 121, 213, 282–83, 308, 309. *See also* honesty.
intention, 41–42, 153. *See also* Arc, Jehanne d', intention; Bonhoeffer, Dietrich, intention; divine intention; Hitler, Adolf, intention
  evil, 114, 116, 148–49, 269
  right/good, 151, 153, 269
  wrong, 153, 291n675
Inwagen, Peter van, 115
Iraq, 121
Isaac, 94, 97
Isabeau of Bavaria, Queen of France, 6, 10n31
Iscariot, Judas. *See* Judas Iscariot
Islam, 147
Israelites, 47n53, 283
Italy, 249, 258n476

J

Jacobs, Steven L., 81, 85
Japan, 126
Jargeau, 12, 93, 133
Jean IV, Count of Armagnac, 7n14
Jehovah's Witnesses, 190
Jeremiah, 298
Jesus, 101, 102, 106, 109, 159n199, 163n210, 228, 232, 233, 237, 238–39, 240, 245, 258, 262–63, 264, 283, 289. *See also* Christ
  crucifixion, 85–87, 105, 143, 284. See also death, of Jesus
Jews, 80n244, 85, 127, 169, 171, 177, 179, 181, 184, 186, 187, 188, 189, 190–91, 192, 193, 194, 195, 202, 203, 204, 206n216, 207, 215, 216, 218–19, 223, 231, 238, 246, 247, 258, 271, 272n556, 274–75, 281. *See also* Israelites
John of the Cross, Saint, 38, 61, 62, 63, 66, 67, 87n265

John of the Cross (*cont.*)
  dark night of the soul, 49–52, 198, 225, 298–99
  purgation
    sensory, 50, 51–52, 299
    spiritual, 50, 52, 299
John of Patmos, 262
John the Fearless, Duke of Burgundy, 6, 132
Judaism, 33, 85, 147
Judas Iscariot, 245
Julian of Norwich, 74
jus ad bellum, 148–49, 150, 151–54, 155
jus in bello, 148, 154–55
jus post bellum, 148
just cause, 141n121, 149, 150, 151 153, 249
just war, 142, 148, 149, 150, 151, 158, 159
  model, 148, 305
  theory, 142, 147–57, 158, 164, 305
  tradition, xii, xiii, 149, 305
justice, xii, xiii, 34, 72, 106, 118, 121, 122, 123, 131, 132, 141, 149, 150, 151, 153, 154, 159, 172, 188, 189, 220, 241, 242, 258, 263, 272, 275, 308, 309
  divine, 159–60, 220
  objective, 149–50
  social, 85, 121, 122, 141, 205–6, 263, 272, 275
  subjective, 150

K

Kierkegaard, Søren, 39, 42, 43, 44, 47, 54, 60, 61, 65, 92, 94, 95, 96, 97–98, 99, 100, 101, 104, 105, 106, 107, 119–20, 128, 129, 130–31, 160, 161, 220, 231
killing, 97, 118–19, 123, 127, 131, 143, 187–88, 192, 201, 221, 236, 243, 248, 251–52, 255, 285, 287, 290. *See also* extermination; genocide; murder
King of Heaven, 91–92, 132–33, 146–47, 159n199. *See also* God
knight, 11, 12, 17n70, 28, 50, 58, 131–32
  of faith, 95, 97, 129, 130. *See also* apostle
Kren, George M., 120, 206
Kristallnacht, 215

L

La Charité, 16, 93n292
Ladvenu, Martin, 31n134, 103
Lagny-sur-Marne, 16, 24
La Hire, 14n56, 31–32
Lang, Berel, 222
language, 121–22, 157, 158–59n199, 229, 292, 297, 309
  deceptive, 121–22, 140, 170, 212, 221–22, 291. *See also* propaganda
  limited, 38, 47
  mathematical, 127–28
  mystical, 38, 48, 113
la Pierre, Isambart de, 27, 30n127, 31n130, 31n135, 59, 102n330
Lash, Nicholas, 38
last resort, 46, 142, 151, 152, 153, 187–88, 251–52
Laval, Count of, 14n56
law, 59, 120, 122, 151n169, 175, 178, 190, 219–20, 243, 246, 269, 271–72, 274, 287, 289–90, 299–300
  canon, 21n89, 22, 23, 32, 98, 100
  divine, 98, 99, 130, 135, 178, 198, 243, 285, 290. *See also lex divina*
  human, 130, 243, 288, 289–90
  international, 213

law (*cont.*)
  moral, 128, 218, 287–88, 299–300
  of nature, 57n117, 185
  public, 98, 219. See also *lex publica*
  universal, 57, 95n301. See also universal, the; ethic, universal
Laxart, Durand, 9, 10
Lehmann, Paul, 240, 262, 282
Leibholz, Gerhard, 277, 299
Lemaître, Jean, 20, 22
Lewis, C. S., 79, 89–91
lex divina, 130, 219. See also law, divine
lex privata, 98–99, 130
lex publica, 99, 130, 219. See also law, public
liberty, 107, 208, 234–35, 265, 282. See also freedom
liminality, 53, 95, 136
Lohier, Jean, 20, 21n85
Loire, the, 9, 16, 88
Lord, 7, 20n80, 52, 60, 71–72, 89n273, 91n282, 92, 99, 100, 133, 138, 149n160, 150, 169, 171, 213–14, 230, 234, 239, 245, 283. See also God
Lorraine, 5, 10
Louis XI of France, dauphin, 26n109
Louis of Orléans, 132
Louviers, 31–32
love, 44, 45, 48, 69, 86, 87, 101, 109, 116, 118–19, 122, 130, 134–35, 139, 145, 147, 197. See also Arc, Jehanne d', love; Bonhoeffer, Dietrich, love; Hitler, Adolf, love
  divine, 36, 39, 44, 45, 47, 48–49, 50, 54, 80, 81, 82, 87, 109, 145, 310
  of God, 39, 40, 42, 44, 46, 48–49, 50, 81, 82, 89, 103, 104, 107, 109, 135, 138, 300
Luther, Martin, 298
Luxembourg, 187, 191, 221
Luxembourg, Jean de, 19n77, 20

M

Mackie, John, 140
Macy, Haimond de, 17n70, 28, 29
madness. See insanity
Magdeburg Cathedral, 238
Maid, the, 9, 12, 18, 24, 25, 65, 102n331, 133, 159n199. See also Arc, Jehanne d'
Manchon, Guillaume, 20, 24n96, 28n115, 59, 103
Margaret of Antioch, Saint, 8, 8–9n25, 29, 30, 49, 59, 70
Margny, 19
Margolis, Nadia, 3, 59, 78n234, 108
Marguerie, André, 30n127
martyr, 66, 104n340, 105–6, 107, 108, 109, 130, 199, 300
martyrdom, 15, 66, 103–4, 105–6, 107, 108, 137, 160, 300. See also Arc, Jehanne d', martyrdom; Bonhoeffer, Dietrich, martyrdom
Marx, Karl, 219
Marxism, 169n8, 181, 219
Mary, Virgin. See Virgin Mary
Massieu, Jean, 20, 25, 27, 28n118, 29, 30, 59
Mattox, John Mark, 150n167
McFague, Sallie, 79–80
Mein Kampf (Hitler), 168, 179, 181, 210, 211, 222
Melun, 17
memory, 37, 41n23, 77, 177n53, 226, 240–41, 248
mercy, 3, 65, 69, 107, 139, 146, 194, 218, 221, 256–59, 282, 287

mercy (*cont.*)
  divine, 70, 96, 106, 109, 145, 199, 235, 236
Merlin prophecy, 10
Merton, Thomas, 41, 54, 60, 106, 119, 121, 128, 134–35, 136–37, 138, 139, 142, 146, 148, 153, 156
Metz, Jean de (or de Nouillonpont), 52
Meung-sur-Loire, 12
Michael, Archangel, 8, 9, 68, 141n121
Midland, Texas, 139–40
Miget, Pierre, 27, 68n190
Mill, John Stuart, 125n40
Minier, Pierre, 21n86
miraculous, the, 9, 11, 12, 24, 32, 33, 57, 57–58n117, 58–59, 64, 66, 66–67n176, 81, 88, 153, 169, 170, 175, 183, 185, 226, 240, 250, 300
mission, 56, 69, 70, 75, 90, 90–91n279, 98, 141. *See also* Arc, Jehanne d', mission; Bonhoeffer, Dietrich, mission; calling; Hitler, Adolf, mission; vocation
model
  just war. *See* just war, model
  of righteous warfare and human agency, xii, 67, 95, 113, 123, 129, 157, 158, 165, 170, 304, 311–15
  saint as. *See* saint, as exemplar/model
Moltmann, Jürgen, 86, 92, 96, 139, 143
Monstrelet, Enguerrand de, 18, 66n175
Montmorency, Count of, 14n56
Moore, G. E., 125n40
moral collapse, 139–40, 202, 203, 217, 218, 222, 241
moral discernment, 57, 70, 98, 135, 136, 140, 141, 158, 203, 271–72. *See also* ethical discernment
moral vacuity, 129, 218
morality, 8, 57, 58, 67, 79, 82, 97, 99, 105, 115, 116, 119, 123–31, 132–38, 141, 142, 145, 147–48, 149, 155, 156–57, 158, 159–60, 187, 218, 264, 281–82, 283, 287–88, 289, 293, 297, 301, 306. *See also* ethics
  mystical, 123, 158. *See also* ethic of faith
Munich, 181
murder, 86, 94, 97, 106, 107, 118, 119, 127, 129, 132, 177, 179, 189, 191, 192, 196, 202, 210, 218, 222, 249, 251, 253, 260, 274, 276, 280–81. *See also* killing
Murray, T. Douglas, 133n79
mystical experience, 36–38, 39, 40, 43–44, 45, 46, 49–50, 57–58n117, 61–63, 98, 113, 164
  apophatic, 37, 41, 70. *See also* God, absence
  cataphatic, 37, 41, 70
  ineffability, 37, 38
  objective, 38
  subjective, 38
mystical knowledge, 38–39, 40, 46–48, 57
mystical morality. *See* morality, mystical
mysticism, 35–109, 113, 128, 136, 164, 229. *See also* Arc, Jehanne d', mysticism; Bonhoeffer, Dietrich, mysticism; Hitler, Adolf, mysticism
  false, 199

mysticism (*cont.*)
   practical, 36, 39, 43–45, 53
   practical, prophetic, 4, 35, 36, 53–56, 101, 106, 160, 165, 227, 301, 302, 306
   operative elements, 77, 78–94

N

Nagasaki, 126
Nash-Marshall, Siobhan, 15, 19n80, 30, 31n134, 131n60, 134
National Socialism, 169, 170, 171, 173, 175, 177, 184, 186, 190, 198, 199, 201, 204, 211, 212, 213, 217, 221, 224, 229, 231, 238, 239, 251, 253, 255, 277, 303. *See also* Nazism
National Socialist Party, 173, 176, 178, 186, 188, 195, 197, 198, 200, 204, 210, 218, 219, 255. *See also* Nazi Party
National Socialist Revolution, 177, 196
Nazi death camps, 177, 187, 188, 193, 202, 204, 207, 216, 221, 222
Nazi Germany, 190, 202, 229–30, 232, 240–41, 265, 268, 274, 275, 276, 277, 290, 292. *See also* Hitlerite Germany
Nazi medical experiments, 192
Nazi paramilitary. *See* SS
Nazi Party, 168, 169, 181–82, 217, 257. *See also* Gestapo; National Socialist Party; Nazi regime; Nazis; SA; SS
Nazi regime, 80n244, 165, 167, 201, 224, 252, 260. *See also* Nazi Party
Nazi secret police. *See* Gestapo
Nazi storm troopers. *See* SA

Nazis, 177, 192–93, 195, 199, 209, 215, 217, 218, 222, 229, 230, 231, 249, 253, 257, 261, 266n528, 274, 281n618. *See also* Nazi Party
Nazism, 82, 188, 199, 201–2, 212, 221, 227, 228, 229, 230, 238, 244, 246, 247, 251, 268, 270, 271–72, 274n574, 275, 276, 281, 292, 293, 302n725. *See also* National Socialism
Netherlands, the, 191, 221
Neufchâteau, 6
New York, 235, 242, 243, 253n455, 259, 274
Niebuhr, Reinhold, 262
Nietzsche, Friedrich, 226
"Night of the Long Knives." *See* Röhm Purge
non-Aryan, 169–70, 195, 276
noncombatant, 121, 143, 148, 153–54, 155, 192, 255. *See also* civilian
non-violence, 142, 208, 261n491, 277. *See also* pacifism
Normandy, 14–15n57, 25
Norway, 191, 221
Nostradamus, 226
Nostredame, Michel de. *See* Nostradamus
NSDAP, 168, 169, 181–82. *See also* National Socialist Party
Nuremberg trials, 177, 213, 216, 220–21

O

O'Donohue, John, 37, 142, 143, 228
Omnipotent, the, 186. *See also* God
Origen, 114
Orléans, 11–12, 15, 17n70, 24, 25, 56, 64, 70, 73, 74, 76, 100n324, 132, 133, 137, 143, 146, 147, 158

Orléans (cont.)
  Duke of, 16n63, 73, 132
  siege, 8, 9, 11, 12, 22, 59, 73, 91,
    145, 146–47
Orléans Manuscript, 4, 15n61,
  18n76, 29, 144n139
Overy, Richard, 177, 202
Oxford Movement, 243

P

pacifism, 33–34, 136, 141–42, 188,
  244, 251–52, 260–61, 277,
  294. *See also* non-violence
pacifist-warrior. *See* Arc, Jehanne d',
  pacifist-warrior
paradox, 83, 93, 94, 96, 97, 98,
  100, 101, 106, 130–31, 226,
  299–300
Paris, 6, 9, 13, 14, 32, 59, 73, 74, 146
  battle for, 14, 15–16, 87–88,
    93n292
  University of, 11, 22, 23,
    144n139
Pasquerel, Jean, 134n82, 137,
  158–59n199
Pastors' Emergency League, 244
Patay, 12, 25, 41, 73
patience, 145, 242, 258–59, 284
Payne, Robert, 193n144
peace, xiii, 6, 18, 32, 123, 142,
  148–49, 150–51, 153, 309.
  See also Arc, Jehanne d',
  peace; Bonhoeffer, Dietrich,
  peace; Hitler, Adolf, peace
  false, 138, 139
  just, 151, 153, 154, 188, 252, 305,
    308
Pernoud, Régine, 11, 13, 22,
  26n111, 27n113, 28, 56,
  73n213, 78, 119, 132, 160
Peter, apostle, 56n107, 245
Philippe the Good, Duke of
  Burgundy, 6, 12, 13, 32, 65,
  159n199

piety, 8, 58, 68n190, 102, 131, 137,
  154, 197, 262, 263
Pigache, Jean, 21n86
Pinzino, Jane Marie, 47n53, 98, 99
Pirruccello, Ann, 3
pity, 132, 139, 143, 147, 253, 259,
  280, 295. *See also* sympathy.
Pizan, Christine de, 60–61n140,
  132n67
Plotinus, 114
Pohl, Oswald, 193, 222
Poitiers, 4, 10, 11, 26, 33, 59, 63, 64,
  78, 92
  inquiry. *See* Arc, Jehanne d',
    Poitiers examination
Poland, 174, 205, 221
Poles, 169n8, 174, 189, 191, 192,
  205
Pont Saint-Maxence, 13
pope, 7, 21, 26, 35, 100, 149,
  158n196, 229
Poulain, R. P. Aug., 57n117
prayer, 89, 91, 139. *See also*
  Arc, Jehanne d', prayer;
  Bonhoeffer, Dietrich, prayer;
  Hitler, Adolf, prayer
pre-emption, 187, 251
pride, 26n106, 46, 60–61n140, 122,
  160, 178, 207, 210, 241, 242,
  245, 274
  national, 60
Pringle, Heather, 169n8
propaganda, 170, 188, 197, 202–3,
  257. *See also* language,
  deceptive
prophecy, xii, 9–10, 24, 47, 49, 53–
  56, 57, 58, 61, 62–63, 64, 65,
  66, 69–70, 72, 74–76, 77, 78,
  84, 85, 90–91, 94, 95, 96–97,
  98, 113, 123, 129, 136, 141,
  145, 146, 149, 160, 162–65,
  199, 230, 233, 304, 305–7,
  309. *See also* Arc, Jehanne d',
  prophecy;

prophecy (*cont.*)
    Bonhoeffer, Dietrich, prophecy; Hitler, Adolf, prophecy; Merlin prophecy
  false, 129, 161, 164, 165, 184, 227, 302, 308, 309
prophetic accuracy, 55, 88
prophetic ambiguity, 74, 87
prophetic consciousness, 52, 67
prophetic destabilization, 55, 96–97, 106, 117, 141, 174, 227, 238
prophetic inaccuracy, 74, 87–88
prophetic message, 10, 41, 47, 53–55, 62, 67–68, 74, 75, 78n233, 90n278, 94, 146, 160
prophetic persecution, 65–66, 106, 141, 183, 246–47
prophetic revelation. *See* revelation, prophetic
prophetic sympathy. *See* sympathy, prophetic
prophetic tradition
  Christian, 36, 55, 56, 64, 67, 74, 161, 165, 230, 301, 302, 305, 307
  Hebrew. *See* prophetic tradition, Jewish
  Jewish, 36, 55, 56, 64, 67, 75–76, 117, 149, 161, 165, 301, 305, 307
proportionality, 152, 154–55, 163, 191–92, 255
proportionate cause, 150, 151–52, 154, 155, 188–89, 253
Protestantism, 300, 302
Providence, 171, 172, 175, 182, 183, 197, 198, 205, 207, 210, 220, 235. *See also* God
pucelle, la, 9, 18, 56, 100, 120, 146–47. *See also* Arc, Jehanne d'
punishment, 100, 147, 150, 178, 187, 258, 287. *See also* vengeance
  divine, 70–71, 131

Q

Quinlan, Michael, 142, 151, 153, 156

R

Rahner, Karl, 55, 56–57, 64, 68, 95n301
Rais, Gilles de, 14n56
Rathenau, Walther, 271
Ratzinger, Joseph, 77n230. *See also* Benedict XVI
Reformation, the, 300
Reich Bishop, 212
Reich Chancellery, 200
Reich Church, 212, 244, 259, 273n563, 288. *See also* German Christian Church
Reichberg, Gregory M., 148
Reichsbank, 193
Reichstag, 189
religion, 8, 24, 34, 36, 39–40, 43, 44, 46, 55, 69, 74, 82, 86, 94–98, 104, 115, 158, 164, 230, 264, 303. *See also* Bonhoeffer, Dietrich, religion; Hitler, Adolf, religion
religious experience. *See* mystical experience
remorse, 138, 207. *See also* guilt
respect, xii, xiii, 34, 35, 47, 68, 72, 131–32, 137, 150, 154, 178, 194, 195, 208, 242, 244, 259, 280, 283, 288, 306, 309
responsibility, xiii, 33, 44, 55, 79, 82, 85, 86, 95, 98, 117–18, 119–21, 126, 136, 139, 140, 141, 149, 161, 163, 304, 308. *See also* Arc, Jehanne d', responsibility; Bonhoeffer, Dietrich, responsibility; Hitler, Adolf, responsibility

restraint, xiii, 34, 45, 82n251, 83, 132, 137, 145, 166, 179, 191, 199, 244, 269
retaliation, 175–76, 225–26. *See also* vengeance
revelation, 108, 109, 199, 222. *See also* Arc, Jehanne d', revelation; vision
  authenticity, 55–56, 57–58, 61–62, 65, 66–67, 141
  divine, xii, 21n89, 23, 33, 35, 36–37, 38, 39, 43, 47, 48, 53–58, 61–63, 64, 65, 66–67, 69–70, 72–73, 75, 78n233, 84–85, 87n265, 88, 89, 92, 95, 97, 99, 103, 123, 128–30, 135–36, 141, 150, 152, 158, 166, 170–71, 178, 201, 213, 215, 227, 233–34, 268, 285, 289, 307
  inadvertent, 108
  personal/private, 38, 56–57, 77n230, 98, 130, 172, 233, 250–51. *See also lex privata*
  prophetic, 53–56, 57, 62, 69–70, 78n233, 85, 88–89, 95, 98, 123, 136
Revelation, book of, 33
revenge, 18n76, 153. *See also* vengeance
Rheims, 9, 11, 12, 13, 19, 22, 24, 25, 41, 73, 88, 144
Ribbentrop, Joachim von, 223
Rieux, Marchal, 18n76
righteousness, xii, 69, 158, 159, 252, 271–72, 305. *See also* agency, righteous; anger, righteous; model, of righteous warfare and human agency; warfare, righteous
rights, 122, 132n67, 148, 154, 206n215, 217, 241, 252, 274, 306
Riom, 16
Röhm Purge, 175

Roman Empire, 308
Romane, Patrick, 177, 178–79, 188, 197
Rome, 26, 86, 147, 149. *See also* Roman Empire
Romée, Isabeau, 7
Rosenberg, Alfred, 199
Rouen, 20, 21, 23–24, 26, 30n127, 31–32, 49n66, 103
  trial of Jehanne d'Arc. *See* Arc, Jehanne d', condemnation, trial
Ruhr, 208
Rumscheidt, Martin, 244n411, 297n702
Russell, Preston, 36n2, 64
Russia, 187, 209, 211, 221, 224
Russians, 189, 200, 224
Rwanda, 142

S

SA, 175, 178, 215
sacrament, 24, 35, 40, 48, 49, 69, 77–78, 118, 137, 231, 233. *See also* Arc, Jehanne d', Communion; Bonhoeffer, Dietrich, Eucharist; confession
sacrifice, 17, 79, 80n244, 86, 98, 101, 103–4, 105, 233, 235, 239, 254, 265, 270, 275, 309
  human, 86, 94, 97
  self-, 17, 98, 103–4, 107, 134–35, 143, 239, 254
saint, 33n139, 42, 69, 78n231, 92, 108, 163n210, 199, 229, 300. *See also* Arc, Jehanne d', saint
  as exemplar/model, 32–33, 67, 229, 305, 310
Saint-Avit, Jean de, 21
Saint-Denis, 14, 15, 87, 88n268
Saint Gabriel. *See* Gabriel, Archangel
Saint-Loup, 143

Saint Michael. *See* Michael,
    Archangel
Saint-Ouen, 27, 28, 30, 31, 71
Saint-Pierre-le-Moûtier, 16
Sainte-Catherine-de-Fierbois, 73,
    133
salvation, 48–49, 55, 77–78, 79–80,
    85–87, 91, 170, 278, 288–89
sanctity, 34, 41, 67, 69, 94, 102n331,
    123, 137, 160, 194, 202, 224,
    259, 309. *See also* holiness
Saracens, 159n199
scapegoat, 82, 207
Schacht, Hjalmar, 223
schism, 23
    papal, 5. *See also* Great Schism
Schlabrendorff, Fabian von, 290
Schleicher, Rüdiger, 249
Schmundt, Rudolf, 207n220
Schönherr, Albrecht, 254, 278, 286
Scott, W. S., 9, 19n78, 19n80, 22
Scripture, 56, 233–34, 236, 250–51,
    262. *See also* Bible
self-deception, 216, 228, 269–70.
    See also deception
self-defense, 123, 131, 137, 142,
    150, 151, 206
self-interest, 61, 115–16, 134, 135,
    168, 247
self-righteousness, 158, 203
self-sacrifice. *See* sacrifice, self-
Senlis, 13
Serbs, 189
Servatius, Robert, 222
Shoah, the, 80–82, 85–86, 179, 206,
    207, 216
sin, 20n80, 54, 60, 79–80, 131n60,
    134, 139, 145, 174, 178,
    214, 231, 232, 258, 260, 265,
    283–84
    mortal, 137
    original, 169, 213
Sodom, 33

Soelle, Dorothee, 39, 42, 44, 46, 47,
    50, 61, 69, 80, 86, 89, 103,
    109, 138, 145–46, 199
solitude, 8, 40–42, 44, 49, 54, 95–
    96, 103, 119, 121, 160, 183,
    184, 229, 236, 244, 247–48,
    267, 271, 278, 285, 293
Speer, Albert, 177n53, 182, 194,
    207n220, 207n222, 216, 217,
    225
Splett, Jörg, 108, 300
SS, 178, 191, 193, 199, 201, 290
Stangl, Franz, 216
success, 12, 22, 66, 122, 152,
    171–73, 203, 204, 214, 216,
    217, 224, 237, 257. *See also*
    victory
    probability of, 152–53
suffering, xii, 6, 15–16, 17, 19, 22,
    43, 45, 48–49, 51, 52, 54,
    68–69, 71, 72, 73, 77, 80,
    86, 87, 91, 92, 93, 96, 101–3,
    105–9 passim, 115, 116, 131,
    132, 138, 142–44, 146, 147,
    161, 186–87, 192–93, 196,
    200, 202, 207, 218, 225–26,
    232, 237, 239, 241n397, 244,
    245–46, 253, 255, 259, 260,
    264, 265, 267, 268, 276, 278,
    279n599, 284, 298–99. *See
    also* affliction; torment
Suffolk, Earl of, 10
suicide, 19–20n80, 21n89, 105–6,
    195, 225, 265
    of Hitler. *See* Hitler, Adolf,
    suicide
swastika, 238
Switzerland, 231
sympathy. *See also* pity
    divine, 145, 174, 237. *See also*
    divine *pathos*
    human, 142–43, 147, 237, 240,
    256, 302n725

sympathy (*cont.*)
  prophetic, 67–68, 88–89, 145, 174, 237
Syndor, Charles W., Jr., 178, 196, 212
Syse, Henrik, 148

T

Taquel, Nicolas, 27
Tauler, Johannes, 104n343
Tavard, George H., 122
Taylor, Craig, 7n14, 58n123, 159n199
Taylor, Paul W., 125n40
technology, 69, 81, 139, 155, 169, 310
teleological ethical suspension, 95, 98, 128–29, 156, 219–20, 289–90
telos, 95, 97, 219, 220, 289, 290
Teresa of Avila, Saint, 38, 45, 53, 60–61, 61–62, 63n160, 65, 66, 67, 95–96, 117, 138, 139
terror, 21n86, 67, 121, 186, 191, 222, 224, 290. *See also* fear; terrorism
terrorism, 5–6, 121, 189, 291n675. *See also* terror
Therage, Geoffroy, 103
Thibault, Gobert, 11n39, 27n114, 75n222
Third Reich, 167, 170–71, 172–75 passim, 178, 180, 184, 186, 201, 203, 216, 219, 221, 223, 225, 229, 251, 280–81
thought, xii, 37, 42, 43–44, 47, 82, 85–86, 92, 121, 135, 139, 140, 141, 162, 168, 171, 173, 179, 204, 205–6, 210, 216, 217, 239, 240, 246, 248, 256, 258n476, 263, 273, 283, 286–88, 298, 304, 306, 308, 310

thoughtlessness, 92. *See also* Bonhoeffer, Dietrich, stupidity
  moral, 116, 121, 140, 217, 297
Tiphaine, Jean, 24n96
torment, 17, 43, 50, 72, 196, 253, 271. *See also* suffering
torture, 23, 30n125, 116, 122, 143, 155, 161, 192, 193, 207, 251, 253, 255, 273n567, 295, 306
Tournai, 141n121
Touroulde, Marguerite La, 58, 61
Tours, 17n68
tradition, 39, 164, 199, 213, 218, 272, 294, 306
  Catholic, 33, 74
  Christian, 33, 56n107, 85–86, 213, 220. *See also* prophetic tradition, Christian
  Hebrew, 56n107. *See also* prophetic tradition, Hebrew
  just war. *See* just war, tradition
  prophetic. *See* prophetic tradition
treason, 18–19, 118, 144, 189, 247, 280
Treaty of Arras, 32, 74
Treaty of Troyes, 6, 10n31, 22
Treblinka, 216
Trémoïlle, Georges de La, 16–17n67, 19n78, 25–26
Trinity, the, 62, 102, 109
Troyes, 12, 46, 58, 142
  treaty. *See* Treaty of Troyes
truce, 5, 12–13, 14, 26, 88
truth, 35n137, 38, 40, 63, 64, 66, 77, 146, 168, 195, 219, 221, 229, 232, 233, 241, 252, 264, 291
  divine, 36, 54, 82, 103, 109, 230, 307
Turner, Denys, 37

U

Übermensch, 226

ultimatum, 152, 187, 251–52
union, spiritual, 39, 40, 46, 48, 49–50, 57n117, 61, 105, 129, 230, 288–89
United States of America, 121, 126, 187, 191, 230, 250, 259, 263, 276
universal, the, 95, 96, 97, 98. *See also* law, universal
universal ethic. *See* ethic, universal
Urfé Manuscript, d', 4, 15n61
USSR, 213
utilitarianism, 124–28, 129, 152–53, 155, 162–63, 164, 305, 306n1, 309
  act, 124n38
  agathistic, 125n40
  eudaimonistic, 125n40
  hedonistic, 125n40
  rule, 124n38

V

Vale, Malcolm, 78n231
value, xii, xiii, 48, 68, 84, 124, 125, 127, 129, 131, 135–36, 140, 157, 240, 247, 270, 294–95, 306, 309
  instrumental, 124, 127
  intrinsic, 124, 125, 127. *See also* goodness, intrinsic
Vaucouleurs, 7, 9, 10–11, 75, 87, 144, 152
Vendôme, Count of, 14n56
vengeance, 154, 187–88, 189, 253, 257. *See also* punishment; retaliation; revenge
Vetlesen, Arne Johan, 119
vice, 140. *See also* immorality
Victorines, the, 104n343
victory, 12, 15, 26n109, 32, 41, 47, 51, 64, 71, 76, 78, 92, 107, 122, 143, 150, 152, 153, 168, 173, 182–83, 208, 209, 210, 215–16, 225, 238, 285–86. *See also* success
Vienna, 168, 181, 189, 193
  Academy, 168
Vignolles, Étienne de. *See* La Hire
violence, xi, xii, xiii, 30, 33–34, 45, 79, 86, 94, 97, 99, 109, 114, 118, 119, 121, 131, 136–37, 141–42, 145–46, 147, 151, 156, 165, 166, 186, 187, 191, 196, 201, 202, 208, 230, 244, 256, 260, 261n491, 269, 277, 278, 285, 289, 301, 304, 306, 309, 310
  divinely sanctioned, xi, xiii, 33–34, 97, 113, 118, 119, 147, 162. *See also* warfare, divinely sanctioned
  claim to, xi, xii, xiii, 4, 17, 21n89, 22, 33, 36, 94, 164, 165, 227, 301, 302, 304–10 passim
  sacrificial. *See* sacrifice
  state-sanctioned, 120, 121–22, 166, 179, 194, 251
  unnecessary, 69, 87, 115
Virgin Mary, 74, 102, 146
virginity
  of Jehanne d'Arc. *See* Arc, Jehanne d', virginity
  of soul, 122
virtue, 68, 122–23, 148, 157, 220, 269
  divine, 130
vision, 36, 65, 80, 96, 139. *See also* revelation
  prophetic, 54–56, 74, 248
  revelatory, 47, 57–58, 61–62, 63, 64, 75, 89, 141n121, 170, 171, 233
vocation, 69, 77, 130, 137, 139, 221n291. *See also* mission
Volk, 171–74 passim, 176, 178, 184, 186, 189, 190, 198, 203, 204,

Volk (cont.)
    205, 208, 211, 216, 218, 223.
    See also German nation
Vorgrimler, Herbert, 53

W

Waite, Robert G. L., 226n318
Walzer, Michael, 126
war, xi, xii–xiii, 4, 12, 15–16, 32–34,
    36, 45, 58, 66, 69, 95, 99, 100,
    108, 118, 119, 121, 126–28,
    131, 136, 138, 142, 143,
    150–51, 155–56, 157–61
    passim, 163, 172, 177, 181,
    184, 186, 187, 194, 196, 198,
    201, 202, 206–8, 211, 225,
    227, 230, 248–50, 254, 269,
    272, 277, 282n625, 287, 294,
    303, 304, 308–10. *See also*
    World War I; World War II
    aggressive, 166, 169, 176, 177,
        187, 202, 206, 213, 221, 223,
        230
    biological, 153, 155, 156
    chemical, 153, 155, 156
    declaration, 149, 152, 191, 194,
        252, 254
    defensive, xiii, 15–16, 46, 143,
        148, 150, 151, 186, 251
    holy. *See* holy war
    just. *See* just war
    nuclear, 126, 153, 155, 156
    offensive, 16, 186, 189, 224
    total, 272
warfare, xi, xii, 8, 21n89, 44, 95, 97,
    114, 123, 132, 136, 149, 155,
    156, 158, 161, 164, 166, 254,
    309
    divinely sanctioned, xi, xii–xiii,
        33, 36, 65, 118, 136, 149–50,
        157, 158, 159n199, 160–61,
        162, 164, 186, 194, 250, 256.

    See also violence, divinely
    sanctioned
    indiscriminate, 161
    righteous, xii, xiii, 95, 113, 123,
        129, 157–60, 161–62, 164,
        165, 170, 186, 194, 250,
        256, 304. *See also* model, of
        righteous warfare and human
        agency
Warner, Marina, 77n230
Watts, Alan, 38n8, 39, 40, 42,
    46–48, 49–50, 61, 69, 83, 100,
    104n343, 105, 106, 129, 307
weakness, 50, 52, 96, 126, 131,
    138–39, 141, 152, 164, 170,
    175, 182–83, 185, 204, 205,
    229, 245, 258, 279, 284, 286
Wedemeyer, Maria von, 231
Weil, Simone, 40, 43, 45, 61, 67,
    83, 89, 91, 104, 109, 118–19,
    122–23, 142, 143–44,
    145–46, 155, 157, 228–29,
    269, 303
weltanschauung, 173
Wiesenthal, Simon, 195
will
    divine, 41, 47, 48, 52, 53, 56–57,
        64, 65–66, 70, 82–92, 93,
        116, 122, 130, 134, 135, 149,
        158n197, 170–71, 172, 173,
        183, 186, 198, 205, 213–16
        passim, 223, 234, 235, 238,
        262–63, 268, 295, 307, 310
    free, 54, 57, 77, 78–79, 80, 81,
        82–92, 116, 121, 205, 237,
        265, 275
    human, 36, 50, 57, 78–79, 81,
        82–92, 115, 116, 168, 171,
        173, 186, 195, 198, 216, 261
    personal, 65–66, 90, 92, 109,
        114, 116, 158n197, 168, 172,
        173, 181, 184, 195, 198, 199,
        210, 213, 216, 217, 235, 283,
        307

Will to Power (Nietzsche), 226n316
William of Ockham, 79
witness, 4, 32, 45–46, 53, 54, 68n190, 103, 104, 108, 117, 133n77, 146, 160, 163–64, 174, 176, 178, 200, 201, 230, 238–39, 242, 252, 267–68, 289, 292, 300
World War I, 168, 170, 174, 180, 225
World War II, 126, 128, 165–66, 169, 174, 252, 255, 302, 303

worship, 21n89, 42, 84–85n255, 88, 105, 197, 238–39, 262
wrath, 230. *See also* anger
of God 107, 145, 257, 262. *See also* divine anger
Wright, John, J., 32–33, 69, 130, 137, 139
Wright, Ronald, 307–8

X

Xantrailles, Ponton de, 14n56

www.ingramcontent.com/pod-product-compliance
Lightning Source LLC
Chambersburg PA
CBHW071148300426
44113CB00009B/1123